The Decisionist Imagination

THE DECISIONIST IMAGINATION

Sovereignty, Social Science, and Democracy in the 20th Century

Edited by
Daniel Bessner and Nicolas Guilhot

berghahn
NEW YORK • OXFORD
www.berghahnbooks.com

First published in 2019 by
Berghahn Books
www.berghahnbooks.com

© 2019, 2023 Daniel Bessner and Nicolas Guilhot
First paperback edition published in 2023

All rights reserved. Except for the quotation of short passages for the purposes of criticism and review, no part of this book may be reproduced in any form or by any means, electronic or mechanical, including photocopying, recording, or any information storage and retrieval system now known or to be invented, without written permission of the publisher.

Library of Congress Cataloging-in-Publication Data

Names: Bessner, Daniel, 1984- editor. | Guilhot, Nicolas, 1970- editor.
Title: The decisionist imagination : sovereignty, social science, and democracy in the 20th century / edited by Daniel Bessner and Nicolas Guilhot.
Description: New York : Berghahn Books, 2019. | Includes bibliographical references and index.
Identifiers: LCCN 2018018022 (print) | LCCN 2018041090 (ebook) | ISBN 9781785339165 (ebook) | ISBN 9781785339158 (hardback : alk. paper)
Subjects: LCSH: Political science--Methodology. | Political science--Decision making.
Classification: LCC JA71 (ebook) | LCC JA71 .D448 2019 (print) | DDC 320.01/9--dc23
LC record available at https://lccn.loc.gov/2018018022

British Library Cataloguing in Publication Data

A catalogue record for this book is available from the British Library

ISBN 978-1-78533-915-8 hardback
ISBN 978-1-80073-925-3 paperback
ISBN 978-1-78533-916-5 ebook

https://doi.org/10.3167/9781785339158

Contents

List of Figures and Tables		vii
Acknowledgments		viii
Introduction	Who Decides? *Daniel Bessner and Nicolas Guilhot*	1
Chapter 1	Reading the International Mind: International Public Opinion in Early Twentieth Century Anglo-American Thought *Stephen Wertheim*	27
Chapter 2	Militant Democracy as Decisionist Liberalism: Reason and Power in the Work of Karl Loewenstein *Carlo Invernizzi-Accetti and Ian Zuckerman*	64
Chapter 3	Parliamentary and Electoral Decisions as Political Acts *Kari Palonen*	85
Chapter 4	Decision and Decisionism *Nomi Claire Lazar*	109
Chapter 5	How Having Reasons Became Making a Decision: The Cold War Rise of Decision Theory and the Invention of Rational Choice *Philip Mirowski*	135
Chapter 6	Computable Rationality, NUTS, and the Nuclear Leviathan *S. M. Amadae*	173
Chapter 7	The Unlikely Revolutionaries: Decision Sciences in the Soviet Government *Eglė Rindzevičiūtė*	217

Chapter 8	Prediction and Social Choice: Daniel Bell and Future Research *Jenny Andersson*	250
Chapter 9	Predictive Algorithms and Criminal Sentencing *Angèle Christin*	272
Conclusion	The Myth of the Decision *Daniel Bessner and Nicolas Guilhot*	295
Index		303

Figures and Tables

Figure

Figure 0.1: "Decision making" in US political science journals, 1900–2000 — 2

Tables

Table 6.1: Standard Prisoner's Dilemma — 184
Table 6.2: Reciprocal Fear of Surprise Attack — 185
Table 6.3: Nuclear Arms Race — 185

Acknowledgments

The editors want to thank all the contributors for their input during the workshops that led to this volume. We are also indebted to Hunter Heyck, Anna Kronlund, and Daniel Steinmetz-Jenkins for their suggestions and comments at different stages of the discussion.

The research leading to these results has received funding from the European Research Council under the European Community's Seventh Framework Programme (FP7/2007–2013) Grant Agreement no. [284231].

 Introduction

WHO DECIDES?
Daniel Bessner and Nicolas Guilhot

> All masters of decision are dangerous.
> —Kenneth Waltz, *Foreign Policy and Democratic Politics*

In 1940, a reader of the *American Political Science Review* would have been hard-pressed to find a single article in the journal that discussed decision-making. A decade later, the same reader may have come across a couple of pieces on the subject, though these were most likely reviews of Herbert Simon's *Administrative Behavior*. By 1960, however, a political scientist could expect to discover a treatment of decision-making in every single issue of the discipline's flagship journal, including reviews of Richard Snyder, H. W. Bruck, and Burton Sapin's *Decision-Making as an Approach to the Study of International Politics*; papers on the decision process at national conventions; articles on judicial decision-making; and explorations of the relationship between decision-making and mass communication. Eventually, our aging reader would have been introduced to the formalism of various types of "rational choice" theory. Between 1940 and 1960, decision-making had migrated from the margins to the center of political science. This trend, moreover, was not merely statistical; on the contrary, it shaped the discipline's self-image. In 1962, rational choice theorist William Riker asserted, in no uncertain terms, that "the subject studied by political scientists is decision-making."[1] A few years later, Simon himself argued that decision-making was not just one topic among others, but was rather the "central core" of the discipline.[2]

The turn to decision-making in political science was just one instance of a broader trend evident throughout the midcentury social sciences. "To a historian," Judith Shklar noted in 1964, "the most interesting

2 • *Daniel Bessner and Nicolas Guilhot*

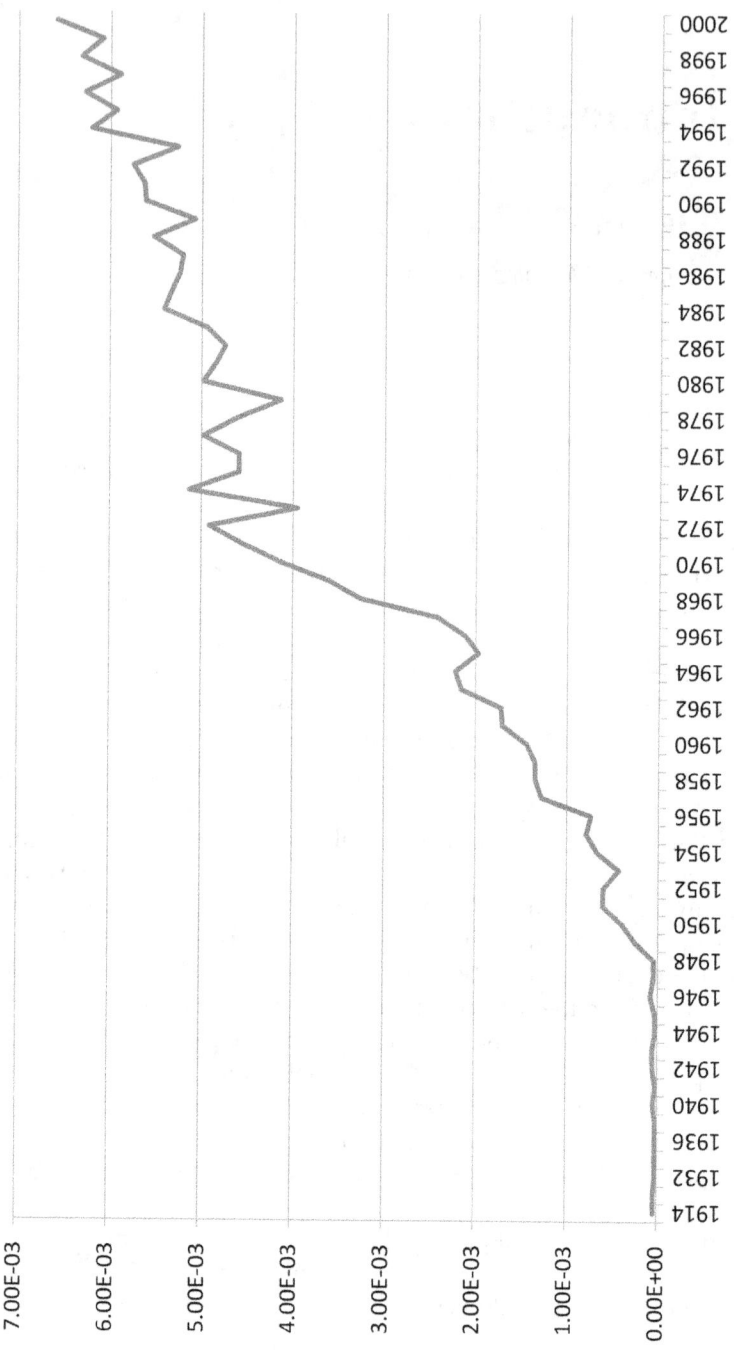

Figure 0.1: "Decision making" in US political science journals, 1900–2000. Source: JStor data for research. Figure created by the authors.

thing about decisions is the fact that everyone is talking about them."[3] Decision-making became a central focus of the social sciences because the subject appeared to contribute to scholars' longing for their disciplines to become "true" sciences. Social scientists insisted that only by shedding their concrete determinations and by designating a formal mechanism that could arbitrate between different possible states of the world independently of social or historical context could they make their disciplines objective. The study of decisions appeared as a perfect means for social scientists to demonstrate that there were fundamental human behaviors that could be abstracted, analyzed, and, potentially, predicted. The result of this intellectual shift, as Paul Lazarsfeld once suggested, was that social scientists began to understand all choices, whether they centered upon choosing politicians or bars of soap, as essentially identical rational and content-independent determinations arrived at by working through coherent sets of preferences.[4] Over the course of the 1950s and 1960s, the analysis of political decisions contributed to the emergence of "rational choice," one of the most influential methodological innovations of the postwar social sciences.

Despite the enormity of this transformation, neither social scientists nor historians have analyzed it as a consistent phenomenon. As yet, there has been no attempt to connect the prewar history of decisionism as an important paradigm in political and legal theory with decision theory in the postwar social sciences; there has likewise been no attempt to explore the rise of "rational choice" in its various guises as a form of political theory.[5] Instead, the study of decision-making remains siloed in different disciplinary specialties: at first glance, after all, nothing seems more different than interwar constitutional doctrine, in which decisionism emerged as an important issue, and the notion of rational choice, which defined the postwar social sciences.[6] Bridging this divide is the primary goal of this volume.

In the last decades, legal and political theorists have devoted an enormous amount of energy to examining the thought of Carl Schmitt, with whom the notion of "decisionism" is associated. For Schmitt, decisionism was only one aspect of the analysis of law that placed the emphasis not on legal norms or on the underlying social order from which they stemmed, but on the decision that created law in the first place.[7] Decisionism, in other words, was a theory of sovereignty that pointed to an authority that is not itself established by, or justified on the basis of, law, but is rather established on a pre-legal, pre-rational, and absolute basis. It considers political decisions, as Kari Palonen puts it in this volume, "a fait accompli that forever alters the conditions of political action."[8] In this perspective, law could not be understood without bringing into focus the concrete decision upon which it is fundamentally premised. According to Schmitt, only with political modernity—indeed, with Hobbes—was the decision properly recognized as a *terminus ab quo* that put an end to chaos and conflict, instead of as an entitlement embedded in a preexisting order. As Schmitt affirmed, "pure decisionism presupposes a disorder than can only be brought into order by actually making a decision (*not* by how a decision is to be made)."[9] Initially an extension of a Weberian intuition about the effective reality of the law, decisionism became in Schmitt an organizing concept highlighting the primordial political choice upon which existing institutional orders are premised.[10]

While the resurgence of interest in Schmitt has resulted in significant intellectual gains, it has also come at a steep price. Namely, decisionism has become conflated with its most famous proponent, which obscures the fact that thinking about politics in terms of decision was historically a concern of scholars across the political and disciplinary spectrums. In addition to Schmitt, a number of contemporaneous German political theorists like Carl Friedrich, jurists like Karl Loewenstein, and sociologists like Karl Mannheim adopted decisionistic perspectives on politics. By this, we mean that they saw politics as essentially grounded in sovereign, decisive authority, and not in the regularity and rationality of law or in the deliberative mechanisms of parliaments. For these thinkers, decisionism underlined a foundational dimension of politics that could not be countenanced by positive legal science: politics started where reason, or rationality, lost its grip. To take one example, for Mannheim politics did not refer to the routine affairs of state, which he called "administration," but to a sphere of unique events that was "irrational" because it was not organized or codified according to rules. In the "rationalized sphere ... of routinized procedures," Mannheim affirmed, everything is a matter of applying preexisting rules or following predetermined courses of action. The modes of behavior executed within this rational framework are "merely 'reproductive,'" and they "entail no personal decision whatsoever." "Conduct," he continued, "does not begin until we reach the area where rationalization has not yet penetrated, and where we are forced to make decisions in situations which have as yet not been subjected to regulation."[11]

A number of thinkers who came of age during the Weimar Republic (1918–33), where political decisions first became a self-contained notion detached from the traditional mechanisms of collective will-formation, analyzed their development. For instance, in his masterful *Behemoth* (1942), Franz Neumann examined the ways in which the

Reichstag was increasingly dispossessed of its decision-making powers in favor of the governmental cabinet, which led political decisions to emanate mysteriously from the depths of an impenetrable ministerial bureaucracy.[12] Neumann's colleague Otto Kirchheimer, who had himself been a student of Schmitt, developed a similar critique of Weimar's *Rechtsstaat*, offering as a counter-example the concrete political decision behind the Marxist notion of a dictatorship of the proletariat in what was probably the first version of Left-Wing Schmittianism.[13]

A sociological or realistic approach to law thus developed out of Weimar-era legal philosophy and influenced an entire generation of scholars, not least those who later played a crucial role in the development of a realist theory of international relations.[14] But decisionist perspectives were also influential in philosophy. Heidegger, for example, made decisionism a central element of his thought. It also influenced postwar existentialism, as well as the work of the theologian and philosopher Jacob Taubes.[15] The current obsession with Schmitt therefore obscures the much wider conceptual and political space in which the question of sovereign decision-making was raised.

Analyzing decisionism as a phenomenon that straddles the inter- and post-war periods suggests that, against much of the literature on the history of the social sciences, 1945 *was not* a *terminus ab quo* for the disciplines. The official story of the social sciences asserts that after World War II, scholars sought to break with the more speculative approach that characterized prewar social science by developing more "scientific" or systematic theories of politics. The persuasiveness of this tale relies upon the supposed overlap between the behavioral social science movement and the Cold War, with the latter having become the unquestioned background of the former to the point that the expression "Cold War social science" is almost a pleonasm.[16] In spite of this story's neatness, however, recent research has questioned its chronological boundaries and begun to explore the interwar origins of Cold War social science generally, and political thought in particular.[17] Nonetheless, the pushback against the Cold-War periodization of social science research developments has often deepened the extant fragmentation of the various intellectual projects examined.

The essays collected in this volume contribute to the "new history of the social sciences" by examining decision-making as an intellectual problem that cut across temporal, disciplinary, political, and national boundaries. By piecing together "the decisionist imagination" running through the twentieth century, from Weimar-era *Staatslehre* to postwar American social science, the essays reveal the linkages between apparently disconnected approaches to the question of political decision-making and integrate the history of the postwar social sciences into a coherent historical narrative.

Science and Democracy in Twentieth-Century Decisionism

The rise of decision-making as an object of scientific analysis was the most visible aspect of a tectonic reorganization of the relationship between science and politics that emerged as one of the most distinctive features of post-World War II modernity. While interwar political thinkers equated politics with the "irrational" area of human conduct characterized by conflict, uncertainty, and existential threats, in a puzzling reversal, postwar theorists associated politics with rationality, a concept that referred to nothing more than formal consistency in the ordering of subjective preferences. For postwar thinkers, rationality did not exist independently from decision-making—each structured the other. As the economist Thomas Schelling declared, "defining 'rational,' 'consistent' or 'noncontradictory' for interdependent decisions is itself part of the business of game theory," the most influential decision theory after 1945.[18] Unlike prewar decisionism, in which political conduct was understood as strategic behavior in the face of doubt, postwar decision theory redefined politics as a manageable activity.

The *prima facie* contrast between anti-rational decisionism and rationalist decision theory, though, risks obfuscating the continuities that connected these two intellectual programs. For example, as the political scientist Karl Deutsch noted, the assumption of transitivity in game theory was similar to absolutistic models of politics that posited that "the political decision system of each country must be transitive."[19] Game theory, Deutsch argued, implied "the notion that in every political system there ought to be one sharply defined place of ultimate decision." This claim resonated uncannily with Carl Schmitt's understanding of sovereignty as a specific, crucial, yet often invisible feature of constitutional orders.[20] Such observations highlight the overlooked family resemblances between prewar decisionism and postwar rational choice theory. Indeed, the post-conflict contexts in which both programs emerged were strikingly similar, and were likely the reason decisionists across time and space were obsessed with existential threats and uncertainties.

Postwar rational choice methodologies in particular developed around what Schmitt termed "decisions upon the exception," which involved absolute enemies or existential threats. In the Cold War, the primary decision upon the exception that occupied social scientists was the decision to fight or avoid a nuclear war. Social scientists, in short, called upon rational choice theories in order to manage the highly uncertain, "non-rational," and concrete dimensions of politics that prewar decisionism declared unmanageable. Despite social scientists' best efforts, however, the concrete and nonformal dimensions of the decision were never fully expelled from postwar decision theory. As Schelling admitted, game theory was defined by mathematized formalism as well as unforeseeable contingencies and concrete contents that thwarted formalization.[21] Similarly, in *Essence of Decision*, the most influential study of the 1962 Cuban missile crisis, Graham T. Allison suggested that decision-making could be understood only through incommensurable analytical frameworks and, for this reason, was ultimately unfathomable.[22] Simply put, postwar attempts to rationalize politics, and hence decision-making, never fully succeeded.

Prewar decisionism and postwar decision theory were both concerned with defining the decisive political authority. The question of "Who decides?" was initially formulated in the context of the interwar crisis of democracy, and decisionism bears the antidemocratic burdens of this moment. Beginning in the 1920s, manifold thinkers on both sides of the Atlantic began to doubt the capacity of democratic publics to make wise political decisions. Specifically, World War I, the Great Depression, and the collapse of the Weimar Republic compelled the gradual unraveling of the mystique of a judicious public—previously considered the fount of democratic decisions—and propelled decision-making onto the center stage of the modern social sciences. In other words, political decision-making became thematized as an object of social–scientific inquiry at the very moment that intellectuals started to question whether liberal democracy as traditionally imagined was a viable political form. The various traumas of the twentieth century's first decades led many political theorists to argue that, no matter what, the public could not be the sole, or even the most important, decision-maker in a democracy. As we chart below, this legacy decisively shaped the postwar decision sciences.

A Decisionist History of the Twentieth Century

Recovering the history of decisionist thought makes it possible to explore how intellectuals' understandings of governance, democracy, and collective choice changed over the course of the twentieth century. Until World War II, American social scientists largely ignored the problem of decision-making. Throughout US academia, intellectuals insisted that political decisions emerged naturally from the democratic process. In terms of domestic policy, American scholars believed that an enlightened and informed public could generate an opinion that provided the basis for legitimate decision-making, either through representation or consultation. Similarly, in the field of foreign affairs a vaguely defined, and likewise enlightened and informed, global public opinion was supposed to be the ultimate sanction behind international law. As Stephen Wertheim shows in his contribution to this volume, "public opinion" was a master concept of *fin de siècle* internationalism, one that assumed a "collective rationality" and a harmony of interests running through an ill-defined world public that transcended national boundaries.

American scholars thus offered the public as the answer to the question of "Who decides?" Of course, intellectuals did not naively adopt a sanguine view of public opinion's wisdom. Many, most prominently the pragmatist philosopher John Dewey, admitted that the public was not yet as informed and sophisticated as it needed to be. Nonetheless, before World War II, Dewey and the majority of social scientists trusted that the public *could* be enlightened, and considered it their duty to serve as the educators, interpreters, and executors of the public will.[23] What Wertheim reveals in Chapter 1, however, is that even this Dewey-style invocation of public opinion was tied to a form of decisionism that "elevated the ineffable discernment of leaders," who bestowed upon themselves the role of authorized guides and translators of the public.

The prewar dominance of the Deweyan perspective must not obfuscate the fact that many on both sides of the Atlantic doubted its veracity. In the United States, the Progressive journalist Walter Lippmann wrote *Public Opinion* (1922) and *The Phantom Public* (1925) to rail against what he considered the simple-minded belief that the contemporary public retained the capacity for enlightenment.[24] Lippmann argued that modern industrial society was simply too complex for an ordinary person to understand. It was therefore impossible, he insisted, for the public will to guide decision-making—even in a democracy like the United States. Instead, Lippmann desired for intellectual and political elites to accept that they must work together to make the best decisions *for* the ignorant masses. Meanwhile, in Weimar Germany, Carl Schmitt published *Die geistesgeschichtliche Lage des heutigen Parliamentarismus* (1926), which attacked liberal parliamentarian democracy as a utopian project that transformed the state into an economic organization unable to make existential decisions. Through minority positions in the 1920s, such critiques of democracy began to enter the mainstream of US social science in the 1930s and beyond.

Between 1929 and 1933, US scholars witnessed several events that seemed to prove Lippmann—most were not yet familiar with Schmitt—correct. Most crucially, the Great Depression and the collapse of democracy in Germany began to shatter US intellectuals' faith in the righteousness and efficacy of public opinion. To contemporary observers, the Depression, with its panic movements and bank runs, illustrated the irrational nature of the public. Similarly, the success of Nazism, which enjoyed widespread popular support, indicated that "the people" could not be trusted to defend democracy. Informed by these dramatic episodes, the nascent social sciences increasingly painted a portrait of a modern public whose rational capacities were easily swayed by demagoguery, propaganda, and other forms of political manipulation. From the influential post-Weberian sociology practiced at Heidelberg University (which was transmitted to the United States by the cohort of intellectual exiles forced to flee Nazi Germany) to the behaviorist and Freudian psychology that permeated the North Atlantic, modern social scientific research seemed to confirm the suppositions of earlier theorists of mass society that ordinary people were prisoners of economic status, genetic inheritance, unconscious psychological drives, and collective moods.[25] For this reason, the long-standing faith in traditional democratic theory, at the center of which stood an informed public, was slowly replaced with the conviction that too much freedom could impel democracy's dissolution. This belief eventually became the basis for studies of decision-making. As Philip Mirowski argues in Chapter 5, the "'scientific' distrust of the ability of the masses to reason [was] the prime motivation for the rise of 'decision theory' from the mid-twentieth century" onward.

As suggested above, Americans' steady embrace of Lippmann was bolstered by the arrival of a remarkable generation of German intellectuals who fled Europe for the United States between 1933–41.[26] Many of the most influential intellectuals of the twentieth century, including Theodor Adorno, Hannah Arendt, Hans Morgenthau, Hans Speier, and Leo Strauss, arrived in the United States during this short period. In their first years of exile, manifold émigré intellectuals argued that Weimar fell because ordinary Germans turned *en masse* toward a National Socialist regime that capitalized on the nonrational drives of the multitude. Several émigrés, including Morgenthau and Speier, embraced aspects of Schmitt's critique of liberal democracy and sought to establish an intellectual and political elite disconnected from politics and able to make wise decisions for the people.[27] Likewise, Carl Friedrich, a self-avowed former decisionist who had immigrated to the

United States before the Nazi takeover, defended a restricted conception of democracy in which authority was ultimately vested in enlightened administrators.[28] Even Marxists like Adorno and his colleague Max Horkheimer doubted workers' willingness to take on Nazism. As physical reminders of democracy's weakness, bearers of a political theory skeptical of parliamentarianism, and inheritors of German academic traditions esteemed by Americans, the exiles lent intellectual credence to the Lippmannite position.

Trends in the funding sources of US social science further encouraged American intellectuals to embrace Lippmann's skepticism of democracy. In the 1920s, officials working for the Rockefeller Foundation and Carnegie Corporation—two of the largest private foundations in the United States—insisted that the methods of rational organization that had allowed for the management of large organizations such as industrial conglomerates should be applied to a variety of social institutions, from universities to government bodies. They thus supported social scientists who promoted rationalistic visions of governance and associated forms of technocratic expertise. Throughout the interwar period, foundation officials and their chosen intellectuals worked to establish an expert elite capable of solving the manifold management problems posed by industrial society. Embedded in this philanthropy-funded technocracy was a subtle disregard for the democratic process and a belief that the liberal consensus could be maintained absent public political engagement.

The discussion between Deweyan social scientists who desired to educate the public and Lippmannite social scientists who desired to manage it was largely suspended once the United States entered World War II in December 1941. For the duration of the war, social scientists, many of whom joined the wartime government, focused on the immediate exigency of helping the United States defeat the Axis powers. Between 1945 and 1953, however, five atomic detonations quickly refocused intellectuals' attentions on the problem of decision. In August 1945, the United States dropped two atomic bombs on Hiroshima and Nagasaki; four years later to the month, the Soviet Union detonated its own bomb, ending the US nuclear monopoly; then, in 1952, the United States detonated a hydrogen bomb, with the Soviets following one year later. If any potential historical event ever approximated the Schmittian notion of a pure "decision upon the exception," it was the decision to fight a nuclear war and potentially eradicate humanity.[29] In a very real way, nuclear strategy placed decision-making at the center of political debate and academic research. The question of "Who decides?" again became as important as it was in the interwar years, when the United States confronted the existential threats of depression and fascism. Unlike in the 1920s and 1930s, though, a younger generation of American social scientists, whose foundational political experiences had been the Great Depression, the crisis of democracy, and World War II, rejected Dewey's vision in favor of Lippmann's.

Atomic arsenals influenced the study of decision-making in three distinct ways. First, they engendered attempts to tame uncertainty. Nuclear weapons were wholly unprecedented. Not only were there no historical examples or legal frameworks for informing or regulating their deployment, but also the extent of the devastation they could wreak remained unknown down to the very day of use. Moreover, in the hypothetical case of a nuclear confrontation, the reaction of the opponent remained unpredictable. The decision to use nuclear weapons, if it was ever to be taken, had to be confronted without the comfort of historical precedent, past wisdom, battlefield experience, accurate intelligence, or reliable scientific data. Nuclear strategists such as Thomas Schelling and Herman Kahn, to name just two prominent thinkers, struggled with the need to codify the decisional process, reduce the vertiginous uncertainty any nuclear decision-maker would face, and bring the decision to deploy a nuclear weapon under some semipredictable logic. Unsurpringly, nuclear strategy was the original breeding ground for several technologies—including Monte Carlo experiments, political gaming, system theory, and game theory—meant to facilitate or even enable decision-making in highly complex and uncertain situations. In unique ways, each of these approaches was developed to address the problem of decision-making in a nuclearized international environment.

Second, the existence of nuclear arsenals encouraged scholars to examine structures of command-and-control. The geographic distribution of atomic weapons, the interservice rivalries between the Army, Navy, and Air Force for custody of the bomb, and the contingency plans designed to be implemented following a surprise nuclear attack all necessitated a high level of coordination in the United States' decision process. Yet almost immediately after atomic weapons were developed, social scientists recognized that the chain of decision surrounding their deployment would be subject to flaws and potentially uncoordinated or unauthorized decisions. Thinkers therefore began to argue that the capacity for human error and duplicity necessitated that the decision to use nuclear weapons be made via processes that removed discretion from the decisional equation. The entanglement of nuclear strategy and decision theory provides the focus of S. M. Amadae's chapter (Chapter 6), which points to the key role military planning played in establishing the legitimacy of game theory, the most influential decision technology of the postwar period.

Last but not least, nuclear weapons compelled social scientists to return to the problem of authoritative decision-making in a democracy. While the atomic bomb forced strategists to "think … the unthinkable," as Herman Kahn famously declared, it also led some social scientists to think about the "constitutionally" unthinkable. Namely, anxieties about nuclear war encouraged intellectuals to devise and promote alternative modes of governance capable of ensuring swift and efficient decisions before, during, and after a nuclear conflict. For example, the political scientist Clinton Rossiter avowed that were a bomb to be detonated on US soil, "some form of executive-military dictatorship" must emerge to manage the nation's defense.[30] Similarly, when the exile sociologist Hans Speier learned that the Soviets had gained atomic capabilities, he affirmed that "a point has been reached in world history where some American leaders should consider themselves to be called upon to sacrifice secretly their own cherished values [i.e., they should ignore public opinion] in order to enable their counterparts to live with these values in the future."[31] Nuclear wizardry summoned back into relevance antidemocratic theories of decision from the interwar era. Specifically, the notion that it was crucial during a period of existential crisis to secure an authoritative decision-making capacity unconstrained by democratic niceties became popular amongst midcentury social scientists. Rossiter, Speier, and many of their colleagues were convinced that elites needed to "sacrifice" democratic norms to ensure western civilization survived its potentially world-ending conflict with the Soviet Union.

These antidemocratic perspectives fed on immediate and concrete historical experiences. American military government in Germany was an especially formative experience for a number of postwar intellectuals that seemed to demonstrate the positive relationship that could exist between democracy and dictatorship. Carl Friedrich, for instance, insisted that military dictatorship was a constitutionally legitimate form of governance to the extent that it protected constitutionalism.[32] Even less enthusiastic supporters of centralized authority like Franz Neumann admitted that the relationship between dictatorship and democracy was not one of symmetrical opposition, but could rather accommodate many nuances.[33] Over the course of midcentury, "military government," "constitutional dictatorship," and "emergency government" became almost interchangeable notions that highlighted the perceived need to take exceptional measures exempt from democratic strictures in order to save democracy.

Yet what distinguished these musings about prodemocratic dictatorship from earlier historical or legal thinking was a sustained concern for its "rationality." Schmitt had already foreshadowed a distinctly modern understanding of dictatorship when he wrote in 1921 that it was premised on "rationalism, technicality and the executive."[34] In the 1960s, Friedrich, an erstwhile disciple of Schmitt's, built upon this intuition in order to justify making authoritative political decisions absent democratic participation.[35] Simply put, Friedrich claimed that the authoritative decision, taken in the face of emergencies, time constraints, and high uncertainties, represented a concentrated form of rationality and was hence legitimate. As Carlo Invernizzi Accetti and Ian Zuckerman show in Chapter 2, which examines the liberal intellectual exile Karl Loewenstein, the framing of authoritarian decision-making as rational had a rich history dating back to the Weimar period. In particular, Loewenstein's concept of "militant democracy" was an effort to "neutralize—or at least tame—the presumptively 'irrational' element of politics associated with decisionism through the appeal to a countervailing conception of 'legal rationalism.'" Nevertheless, as the authors highlight, the impossibility of elucidating an incontrovertible criterion distinguishing between democrats and antidemocrats ended up requiring a capacity for arbitrary decision-making that did not operate according to strict rules. Despite what Friedrich and Loewenstein desired, the tensions between democracy and authoritarianism could not be easily overcome with appeals to rationality.

The emergence of "rational choice" in the postwar social sciences must be situated in the broader context of discussions about rationality and authority, not least because these provided a new form of legitimacy for decisions that circumvented or delegitimized any kind of democratic process. Understanding this political function of "rationality" requires stepping back from the traditional disciplinary histories that confine rationality to economics and obfuscate the connections between rational choice and decisionism. Normally, the political history of rational choice is organized around a *de rigueur* reference to neoclassical economics as the putative birthplace of decision theory. But, as Philip Mirowski shows in Chapter 5, neoclassical economics was premised on a model that was lifted from physics and in which there was no room for anything resembling a psychological "choice." While the exact pathways through which a self-standing and authoritative "decision" was detached from its social context and reintroduced at the heart of economic rationality still have to be fully explored—Mirowski suggests that the exile economist Oskar Morgenstern was the main conduit for this translation—there is no doubt that rational choice rested upon a form of decisionism. As Mirowski notes, "early game theory bore the marks of the German decisionist temperament in that it still reified the decision as relatively free of context and prior reason." Indeed, rational choice shared a number of formal attributes with Schmittian decisionism, beginning with its complete break with any prior sequence of causes, reasons, and norms. To quote Mirowski again, "in America, 'The decision' was ... extracted from the dire state of exception to become the essence of mechanical choice."

American social scientists' embrace of the notion that choice was a mechanical phenomenon was encouraged by the fact that a significant number of them refused to accept Speier's claim that ignoring the public was a "sacrifice" that indicated the reluctant approval of some form of authoritarian elitism. Instead, US social scientists attempted to resolve their distrust of the public with their hatred of authoritarianism by, in Judith Shklar's apt phrase, "de-ideologiz[ing] politics entirely."[36] As Mirowski puts it in his chapter, "the rise of decision theory was first and foremost an expression of a conscious rejection of a charismatic construction of leadership and rationality" in favor of algorithmic—and thus potentially liberal and democratic, or at least not explicitly antidemocratic—versions of them.

Generations of postwar social scientists endorsed a form of technocratic politics in which decisions were made by systems or equations, not people. Because social scientists assumed that what made Nazism and communism "totalitarian" was their inherently ideological character, a de-ideologized politics was, if not exactly democratic, certainly not authoritarian. In the 1950s and beyond, systems theory, cybernetics, game theory, and rational choice methodologies appealed to intellectuals partly because they seemed to offer nonideological languages of sovereign decision that eschewed the need for democratic decision-making at the same time that they promised to make decision processes as efficient as they could possibly be. In his chapter, Mirowski highlights the various intellectual and disciplinary pathways through which the decision of the postwar decision sciences was gradually hypostasized and elevated to the status of a supra-individual entity. By the 1970s, "rationality" was reified in the general operation of The Market, which was understood as an information processor superior to democratic forms of governance that could attain rationality on its own or through the corrective intervention of enlightened and authoritative elites.

Mirowski wonders why rational choice, which always lacked empirical validation, permeated the postwar social sciences. One possible reason for its popularity may be that rational choice appeared well suited to an age that was widely described as post-ideological, in the sense that the decisions Western society required were supposedly technical rather than political. In particular, the sociologist Daniel Bell's famous 1960 declaration of an "end of ideology," which was echoed by a number of intellectuals, underlines an important cultural context for the evolution of decision theory in the 1960s and 1970s. As Jenny Andersson discusses in Chapter 8, by assuming that "the fundamental political problems of the industrial revolution have been solved," the end of ideology discourse accelerated decision theory's displacement of politics by transforming social problems into purely technical ones. Once social scientists concluded that all basic political questions had been answered, they sought to refine a technical rationality about "*where* one wants to go, *how* to get there, the costs of the enterprise, and some realization of, and justification for, the determination of *who* is to pay."

The end of ideology discourse shored up the old Lippmannite notion that the simplistic and chaotic processes of representative democracy could not manage the complexities of (post-) industrial society. For example, *The Crisis of Democracy*, the 1975 report of the Trilateral Commission, averred that the decision-making systems of western governments were overloaded, undermined by the operation of democracy itself, and needed to be replaced with technical rationality.[37] But intellectuals struggled to differentiate this technocratic program from an authoritarian, undemocratic one. All these issues come to the fore in Andersson's chapter, which explores Daniel Bell's efforts to bring "algorithmic judgment" to bear upon decision-making through new technologies of forecasting. The kind of rationality Bell wanted to integrate into politics aimed at displacing "interest politics" with a higher form of rationality in which an elite of experts would play a decisive role in shaping social futures. At the same time, however, Bell sought to accommodate the liberal bedrock of American politics by emphasizing the ability of forecasting technologies to preserve and even enhance freedom of choice. Eschewing Marxist models of centralized planning, Bell intended his forecasting technologies to operate as "facilitators" rather than prescribers of social change. Through her analysis of Bell's work on forecasting, Andersson illuminates the dilemmas that plagued attempts to develop specifically liberal planning efforts that charted a middle path between centralized planning and the formidable obstacle raised by Kenneth Arrow's "impossibility theorem," which posited the impossibility of achieving collective rationality on the basis of free choice. Bell, Andersson notes, believed that "future research could solve Kenneth Arrow's problem of social choice" by preemptively rationalizing individual preferences through an analysis of their future consequences. "Rationally prioritiz[ing] different social programs," he insisted, would overcome the conflict of values that Arrow identified. Nonetheless, Angèle Christin demonstrates in Chapter 9 that forecasting technologies similar to those championed by Bell did not solve the problems he hoped they would and could often have quite illiberal effects. Specifically, Christin shows that predictive algorithms intended to rationalize judicial sentencing regularly lead to harsh and unjustified criminal sentences, increasing human misery rather than alleviating it.

The 1960s and 1970s were defined in large part by the paradoxical search for forms of governance that would ignore or manipulate the public without being authoritarian. In essence, intellectuals hoped that technocratic rationality would compensate for the insufficiencies of democracy. The dilemma, as the political scientist John Steinbruner noted in 1974, was how to "achiev[e] effective performance without stumbling into some new form of tyranny."[38] This framing of the problem largely explains the remarkable intellectual success of cybernetics, the "science of command and control," during this period. Social scientists embraced cybernetics because its impersonal and mechanistic patterns, feedback loops, and rejection of anything resembling intentionality made it possible for them to think about governance in a way that did not rely upon either the public or a centralized and authoritative decision-maker. By embracing cybernetics, intellectuals believed they had transcended the antidemocratic elitism of Lippmann and his supporters while answering the latter's criticisms of democracy's deficiencies. Systemic representations of political processes tended to disaggregate decision-making into articulated, nonlinear circuitries replete with embranchments and feedback loops. In these elaborate political schematics, "decisions" did not exist as such. Instead, a cybernetic "decision" was in actuality the outcome of multiple, interdependent inputs and complex sociotechnical networks naturally endowed, it was maintained, with superior rationality. Cybernetics engendered a transformation of the decisionist imagination away from top-down and centralized models toward horizontal mechanisms in which the very notions of hierarchy and power were erased.

These deconcentrated visions of power tended to be associated with neoliberalizing projects. This was true even in the Soviet Union, where, as Eglė Rindzevičiūtė shows in Chapter 7, the decision sciences of the 1960s and 1970s helped legitimate new representations of Soviet society and governance that moved away from linear, centralized planning models. Meanwhile, in the United States, the sciences of complex systems encouraged the transition from classical models of government to depersonalized, system-centered notions of governance. In these latter frameworks, neither the public nor some unaccountable elite made decisions. Rather, it was the disembodied system itself, *ultimately controlled by no one*, which generated the important choices. Cybernetics and other systems methodologies made it possible for social scientists to analyze political processes while eliding the central question of twentieth century political theory: "Who decides?" Scholars could thus reconcile their skepticism of democracy with their commitment to liberalism. Kenneth Waltz's neorealism, the international relations theory that swept through political science departments in the late-1970s and 1980s, provides a case in point. In neorealist theory, state behavior was not explained with reference to individual decision-makers or domestic political structures, but rather through an international "system" in which there was ultimately no sovereign power.[39]

Despite their claims of neutrality, cybernetics and systems theory were often used to promote politically conservative goals. The 1960s and 1970s witnessed the rise of new social movements, such as the Black Power, Chicana/o rights, women's rights, gay liberation, antinuclear, and environmental movements, which expressed novel interests and identities and asserted unique forms of autonomy and self-governance. To some degree, social scientists employed the new decision sciences to delegitimize these movements as irrational, unrealistic, and damaging. Waltz's neorealism, the sociology of Niklas Luhmann, and the emerging consensus surrounding The Market's ability to rationalize the preferences of diverse populations were all intellectual trends that dismissed identity-based claims for democratic participation in decision-making by obfuscating the locus of decisional power and diluting it in the supra-human netherworld of complex and autonomous systems. Furthermore, social scientists regularly claimed that for these systems to work, they could broker no resistance of the type expressed by the new social movements. Whether or not their advocates intended them to, cybernetics and systems theory often functioned as reactionary methodologies that bolstered the claims of political conservatives.

Continuing a trend initiated by Lippmann in the 1920s, the embrace of systems thinking shifted power away from the sphere of traditional politics toward a new intellectual technostructure whose members were allegedly more rational than policy-makers and the demos precisely because they were insulated from the pressures of the democratic process.[40] Just like Lippmann, who called for expert advice to replace the public will, the policy intellectuals of the 1970s called for the establishment of a new cadre of technocrats endowed with the ability to exercise decisional power above and beyond politics. Ironically, a cybernetic turn intended to transcend elitism wound up bolstering it.

Nevertheless, two contributions to this volume make clear that there are ways to think about the relationship between political decision and democracy that expand beyond the "authoritarian neoliberalism" described above. In their chapters, both Nomi Claire Lazar (Chapter 4) and Kari Palonen (Chapter 3) delineate alternative genealogies and intellectual traditions in which the concept of decision is democratically articulated. Lazar's chapter explores the question of whether all authoritative, sovereign decisions taken in a liberal constitutional context fall under the category of "decisionism." Decisionism, she argues, may be considered a coherent doctrine only as long as it artificially isolates the concrete moment of decision from the thicket of norms, events, and causes that surround it. In fact, Lazar suggests that the blending of decisionistic elements with liberalism, which characterized much of postwar political theory, may ironically conceal liberalism's longstanding capacity to govern during moments of exception without invoking sovereign power. Derogations to rights and "police power," Lazar argues, are part of the normative and administrative arsenal that liberal states may legitimately deploy to deal with emergencies. As she puts it, the power "to make exceptions to quotidian rights protections to serve the public good is part of the organic fabric of every liberal democracy." In his piece, Kari Palonen similarly underlines the limitations of decisionism as a means to understand actual liberal democratic politics. The contingency and uncertainty that are associated with decisionism, he declares, also define freedom of choice. For this reason, Palonen maintains that the limitation of rationality that accompanies decisionism should not be understood as antithetical to democratic deliberation and will formation. He further asserts that the same is true of the time constraints under which sovereign decisions are made. "All politics," Palonen emphasizes, "operate with limited times." Surveying the Westminster parliamentary tradition, he shows how parliamentary procedure and rhetoric addressed time constraints and the need to make authoritative decisions. Far from being defined by the endless chatter denounced by authoritarian decisionists and democratic skeptics, Palonen demonstrates that parliaments are spaces in which forms of truly "political" thinking—in the sense of thought having a concrete relationship to contingency and time—occur.

From the 1920s until today, the decisionist imagination was shaped by a pessimistic sensibility in which liberal democracy was considered an ineffective form of governance whose representatives were incapable of making existential decisions. Before World War II, decisionism sought to contain politics within a sphere insulated from the processes of rationalization and democratization characteristic of modernity. The postwar social sciences, however, recast decisionism along scientistic lines. After 1945, the social sciences provided the testing ground for new versions of decisionism that sought to salvage liberalism while legitimizing robust forms of unaccountable, and hence more "rational," decision-making. "Rational choice" emerged within this context as a scientific and "liberal" form of decisionism. Indeed, over the course of the twentieth century, decisionists of all stripes were remarkably successful in convincing people that they had a monopoly on the true understanding of political decisions. As Lazar and Palonen remind us, however, decisionists were wrong to assume that modern democrats had lost—or never had—the capacity to think and act politically. Moreover, the essays contained in this volume suggest that decisionists naively ignored the ways in which their doctrine deracinated political decisions from the ethical, economic, normative, social, and cultural contexts in which they were actually made, which severely restricted the utility of their perspective. Perhaps most tragically, decisionists presented the decision as an isolated moment in the life of political communities, which excised from democracy one of its most fundamental purposes: the making of *collective* decisions. In an era when Western democracies have increasingly inflated executive power while simultaneously depriving their publics of the capacity to make truly political choices, it might be time to move beyond the decisionist imagination.

Daniel Bessner is the Anne H. H. and Kenneth B. Pyle Assistant Professor in American Foreign Policy in the Henry M. Jackson School of International Studies at the University of Washington. He is the author of *Democracy in Exile: Hans Speier and the Rise of the Defense Intellectual* (Cornell University Press, 2018).

Nicolas Guilhot is research professor at the CNRS (Centre National de la Recherche Scientifique). His work sits at the intersection of political theory, the history of political thought, and international relations. His publications include *After the Enlightenment: Political Realism and International Relations in the Mid-Twentieth Century* (Cambridge University Press, 2017); *The Democracy Makers: Human Rights and* the Politics of Global Order (Columbia University Press, 2005); and The Invention of International Relations Theory: Realism, the Rockefeller Foundation, and the 1954 Conference on Theory (Columbia University Press, 2011).

Notes

1. William H. Riker, *The Theory of Political Coalitions* (New Haven, CT: Yale University Press, 1962), 11.
2. Herbert A. Simon, "Political Research: The Decision-Making Framework," in *Varieties of Political Theory*, ed. David Easton (Englewood Cliffs, NJ: Prentice-Hall, 1966), 15.
3. Judith N. Shklar, "Decisionism," in *Rational Decision*, ed. Carl J. Friedrich (New York: Atherton Press, 1964), 3.
4. Paul F. Lazarsfeld, "An Episode in the History of Social Research: A Memoir," *Perspectives in American History* 2 (1968): 279.
5. See, however, S. M. Amadae, *Rationalizing Capitalist Democracy: The Cold War Origins of Rational Choice Liberalism* (Chicago, IL: University of Chicago Press, 2003); and S. M. Amadae, *Prisoners of Reason: Game Theory and Neoliberal Political Economy* (Cambridge, UK: Cambridge University Press, 2016).
6. The term "rational choice" refers loosely to a set of methods, including but not limited to game theory, statistical decision theory, and systems analysis, which permeated the postwar social sciences. Simply put, rational choice theory is postwar decision theory.
7. Carl Schmitt, *On the Three Types of Juristic Thought*, trans. Joseph W. Bendersky (Westport, CT: Praeger, 2004).
8. Palonen, "Parliamentary and Electoral Decisions as Political Acts."
9. Schmitt, *On the Three Types of Juristic Thought*, 62.
10. On this "generalized decisionism," see the excellent analysis by Augustin Simard, *La Loi Désarmée. Carl Schmitt Et La Controverse Légalité/Légitimité Sous Weimar* (Québec: Presses de l'Université de Laval, 2009).
11. Karl Mannheim, *Ideology and Utopia: An Introduction to the Sociology of Knowledge*, trans. Louis Wirth and Edward Shils (London: Routledge and Kegan Paul, 1936), 101–2.
12. Franz L. Neumann, *Behemoth: The Structure and Practice of National Socialism, 1933–1944* (Chicago, IL: Ivan R. Dee, 2009), 23–29.
13. Otto Kirchheimer, *Politics, Law, and Social Change: Selected Essays of Otto Kirchheimer*, ed. Frederic S. Burin and Kurt L. Shell (New York: Columbia University Press, 1969).
14. Martti Koskenniemi, *The Gentle Civilizer of Nations: The Rise and Fall of International Law, 1870–1960* (Cambridge, UK: Cambridge University Press, 2002). See also Bernhard Schlink and Arthur J. Jacobson, eds., *Weimar: A Jurisprudence of Crisis* (Berkeley and Los Angeles: University of California Press, 2000); and Nicolas Guilhot, *After the Enlightenment: Political Realism*

and *International Relations in the Mid-Twentieth Century* (Cambridge, UK: Cambridge University Press, 2017).
15. Jacob Taubes, *To Carl Schmitt: Letters and Reflections*, trans. Keith Tribe (New York: Columbia University Press, 2013).
16. See, for instance, Nils Gilman, *Mandarins of the Future: Modernization Theory in Cold War America* (Baltimore, MD: Johns Hopkins University Press, 2003); Mark Solovey and Hamilton Cravens, eds., *Cold War Social Science: Knowledge Production, Liberal Democracy, and Human Nature* (New York: Palgrave Macmillan, 2012); Paul Erickson et al., *How Reason Almost Lost Its Mind: The Strange Career of Cold War Rationality* (Chicago, IL: The University of Chicago Press, 2013); and Mark Solovey, *Shaky Foundations: The Politics-Patronage-Social Science Nexus in Cold War America* (New Brunswick, NJ: Rutgers University Press, 2013). For a discussion of the Cold War paradigm in the history of the social sciences, see David C. Engerman, *Know Your Enemy: The Rise and Fall of America's Soviet Experts* (New York: Oxford University Press, 2009); Joel Isaac and Duncan Bell, eds., *Uncertain Empire: American History and the Idea of the Cold War* (Oxford: Oxford University Press, 2012); and, in particular, Philip Mirowski, "A History Best Served Cold," in *Uncertain Empire: American History and the Idea of the Cold War*, ed. Duncan Bell and Joel Isaac (Oxford: Oxford University Press, 2012), 61–74.
17. Udi Greenberg, *The Weimar Century: German Émigrés and the Ideological Foundations of the Cold War* (Princeton, NJ: Princeton University Press, 2014); Daniel Bessner, *Democracy in Exile: Hans Speier and the Rise of the Defense Intellectual* (Ithaca, NY: Cornell University Press, 2018).
18. Thomas C. Schelling, *Choice and Consequence: Perspectives of an Economist* (Cambridge, MA: Harvard University Press, 1984), 215.
19. "Transitivity" refers to logical coherence in the ordering of preferences. Simply put, it means that if one prefers A to B and B to C, then one also prefers A to C.
20. Karl Deutsch, *The Nerves of Government: Models of Political Communication and Control* (New York: The Free Press, 1963), 54–55. See also page 209: "If all important decisions are concentrated at one point, and if decisions made at that point tend to override all decisions made elsewhere in the system, the performance of the system may resemble the situation of concentrated sovereignty, familiar from the absolute monarchies of seventeenth- and eighteenth-century Europe." For a discussion of Schmitt's decisionistic understanding of sovereignty, see Simard, *La Loi Désarmée*: 93–103.
21. Thomas C. Schelling, "The Strategy of Conflict: Prospectus for a Reorientation of Game Theory," *The Journal of Conflict Resolution* 2, no. 3 (September 1958): 203–64.
22. Graham T. Allison, *Essence of Decision: Explaining the Cuban Missile Crisis* (Boston, MA: Little, Brown and Company, 1971).
23. John Dewey, "Public Opinion: Review of *Public Opinion* by Walter Lippman," *The New Republic* 30, no. 387 (3 May 1922): 286–88; John Dewey, "Practical Democracy: Review of *The Phantom Public* by Walter Lippman," *The New Republic* 45, no. 374 (2 December 1925): 52–54; John Dewey, *The Public and Its Problems* (Athens, GA: Swallow Press / Oxford University

Press, 1954); Andrew Jewett, *Science, Democracy, and the American University: From the Civil War to the Cold War* (New York: Cambridge University Press, 2012), 10–11.
24. Walter Lippmann, *The Phantom Public* (New Brunswick, NJ: Transaction Books, 1993); Walter Lippmann, *Public Opinion* (Blacksburg, VA: Wilder Publications, 2010).
25. Edward A. Purcell, *The Crisis of Democratic Theory: Scientific Naturalism and the Problem of Value* (Lexington: University of Kentucky Press, 1973); Mark C. Smith, *Social Science in the Crucible: The American Debate Over Objectivity and Purpose, 1918–1941* (Durham, NC: Duke University Press, 1994); Bessner, *Democracy in Exile*, chapter 3.
26. Jewett, *Science*, chapter 11.
27. Daniel Bessner and Nicolas Guilhot, "How Realism Waltzed Off: Liberalism and Decisionmaking in Kenneth Waltz's Neorealism," *International Security* 40, no. 2 (Fall 2015): 87–118.
28. Greenberg, *Weimar Century*, chapter 1.
29. Gar Alperovitz, *The Decision to Use the Atomic Bomb* (New York: Vintage Books, 1995).
30. Clinton Rossiter, "Constitutional Dictatorship in the Atomic Age," *The Review of Politics* 11, no. 4 (October 1949): 395–418.
31. Hans Speier, "Comments on Current Policy Requirements," November 21, 1949, 6, Folder 32, Box 9, Hans Speier Papers, German and Jewish Intellectual Émigré Collection, M. E. Grenander Department of Special Collections and Archives, University Libraries, University at Albany, State University of New York, Albany, NY.
32. Carl J. Friedrich, *Constitutional Government and Democracy: Theory and Practice in Europe and America* (Boston, MA: Ginn and Company, 1950), 588–96.
33. Franz L. Neumann, "Notes on the Theory of Dictatorship," in *The Democratic and the Authoritarian State*, ed. Herbert Marcuse (New York: The Free Press, 1957), 233–56.
34. Carl Schmitt, *Dictatorship* (Cambridge, MA: Polity, 2014), 9.
35. Carl J. Friedrich, "On Rereading Machiavelli and Althusius: Reason, Rationality, and Religion," in *Rational Decision*, ed. Carl J. Friedrich, *Nomos* (New York: Prentice-Hall, 1964), 180.
36. Shklar, "Decisionism," 15.
37. Michel Crozier et al., *The Crisis of Democracy: Report on the Governability of Democracies to the Trilateral Commission*, The Triangle Papers (New York: New York University Press, 1975), 12–16.
38. John D. Steinbruner, *The Cybernetic Theory of Decision: New Dimensions of Political Analysis* (Princeton, NJ: Princeton University Press, 1974), 7.
39. Bessner and Guilhot, "How Realism Waltzed Off."
40. Sidney Verba, "Assumptions of Rationality and Non-Rationality in Models of the International System," *World Politics* 14, no. 1 (October 1961): 93–117.

Bibliography

Allison, Graham T. *Essence of Decision: Explaining the Cuban Missile Crisis*. Boston, MA: Little, Brown and Company, 1971.
Alperovitz, Gar. *The Decision to Use the Atomic Bomb*. New York: Vintage Books, 1995.
Amadae, S. M. *Rationalizing Capitalist Democracy: The Cold War Origins of Rational Choice Liberalism*. Chicago, IL: University of Chicago Press, 2003.
———. *Prisoners of Reason: Game Theory and Neoliberal Political Economy*. Cambridge, UK: Cambridge University Press, 2016.
Bessner, Daniel. *Democracy in Exile: Hans Speier and the Rise of the Defense Intellectual*. Ithaca, NY: Cornell University Press, 2018.
Bessner, Daniel, and Nicolas Guilhot. "How Realism Waltzed Off: Liberalism and Decisionmaking in Kenneth Waltz's Neorealism." *International Security* 40, no. 2 (Fall 2015): 87–118.
Crozier, Michel, Samuel P. Huntington, Jåoji Watanuki, and Trilateral Commission. *The Crisis of Democracy: Report on the Governability of Democracies to the Trilateral Commission*. The Triangle Papers. New York: New York University Press, 1975.
Deutsch, Karl. *The Nerves of Government: Models of Political Communication and Control*. New York: The Free Press, 1963.
Dewey, John. "Public Opinion: Review of *Public Opinion* by Walter Lippman." *The New Republic* 30, no. 387 (3 May 1922): 286–88.
———. "Practical Democracy: Review of *The Phantom Public* by Walter Lippman." *The New Republic* 45, no. 374 (2 December 1925): 52–54.
———. *The Public and Its Problems*. Athens, GA: Swallow Press / Oxford University Press, 1954.
Engerman, David C. *Know Your Enemy: The Rise and Fall of America's Soviet Experts*. New York: Oxford University Press, 2009.
Erickson, Paul, Judy L. Klein, Lorraine Daston, Rebecca M. Lemov, Thomas Sturm, and Michael D. Gordin. *How Reason Almost Lost Its Mind: The Strange Career of Cold War Rationality*. Chicago, IL: The University of Chicago Press, 2013.
Friedrich, Carl J. *Constitutional Government and Democracy: Theory and Practice in Europe and America*. Boston, MA: Ginn and Company, 1950.
———. "On Rereading Machiavelli and Althusius: Reason, Rationality, and Religion." In *Rational Decision*, edited by Carl J. Friedrich. Nomos, 177–96. New York: Prentice-Hall, 1964.
Gilman, Nils. *Mandarins of the Future: Modernization Theory in Cold War America*. Baltimore, MD: Johns Hopkins University Press, 2003.
Greenberg, Udi. *The Weimar Century: German Émigrés and the Ideological Foundations of the Cold War*. Princeton, NJ: Princeton University Press, 2014.
Guilhot, Nicolas. *After the Enlightenment: Political Realism and International Relations in the Mid-Twentieth Century*. Cambridge, UK: Cambridge University Press, 2017.
Isaac, Joel, and Duncan Bell, eds. *Uncertain Empire: American History and the Idea of the Cold War*. Oxford: Oxford University Press, 2012.

Jewett, Andrew. *Science, Democracy, and the American University: From the Civil War to the Cold War*. New York: Cambridge University Press, 2012.

Kirchheimer, Otto. *Politics, Law, and Social Change: Selected Essays of Otto Kirchheimer*, edited by Frederic S. Burin and Kurt L. Shell. New York: Columbia University Press, 1969.

Koskenniemi, Martti. *The Gentle Civilizer of Nations: The Rise and Fall of International Law, 1870–1960*. Cambridge, UK: Cambridge University Press, 2002.

Lazarsfeld, Paul F. "An Episode in the History of Social Research: A Memoir." *Perspectives in American History* 2 (1968): 270–337.

Lippmann, Walter. *The Phantom Public*. New Brunswick, NJ: Transaction Books, 1993.

———. *Public Opinion*. Blacksburg, VA: Wilder Publications, 2010.

Mannheim, Karl. *Ideology and Utopia: An Introduction to the Sociology of Knowledge*. Translated by Louis Wirth and Edward Shils. London: Routledge and Kegan Paul, 1936.

Mirowski, Philip. "A History Best Served Cold." In *Uncertain Empire: American History and the Idea of the Cold War*, edited by Duncan Bell and Joel Isaac, 61–74. Oxford: Oxford University Press, 2012.

Neumann, Franz L. "Notes on the Theory of Dictatorship." In *The Democratic and the Authoritarian State*, edited by Herbert Marcuse, 233–56. New York: The Free Press, 1957.

———. *Behemoth: The Structure and Practice of National Socialism, 1933–1944*. Chicago, IL: Ivan R. Dee, 2009.

Purcell, Edward A. *The Crisis of Democratic Theory: Scientific Naturalism and the Problem of Value*. Lexington: University of Kentucky Press, 1973.

Riker, William H. *The Theory of Political Coalitions*. New Haven, CT: Yale University Press, 1962.

Rossiter, Clinton. "Constitutional Dictatorship in the Atomic Age." *The Review of Politics* 11, no. 4 (October 1949): 395–418.

Schelling, Thomas C. "The Strategy of Conflict: Prospectus for a Reorientation of Game Theory." *The Journal of Conflict Resolution* 2, no. 3 (September 1958): 203–64.

———. *Choice and Consequence: Perspectives of an Economist*. Cambridge, MA: Harvard University Press, 1984.

Schlink, Bernhard, and Arthur J. Jacobson, eds. *Weimar: A Jurisprudence of Crisis*. Berkeley and Los Angeles: University of California Press, 2000.

Schmitt, Carl. *On the Three Types of Juristic Thought*. Translated by Joseph W. Bendersky. Westport, CT: Praeger, 2004.

———. *Dictatorship*. Cambridge, MA: Polity, 2014.

Shklar, Judith N. "Decisionism." In *Rational Decision*, edited by Carl J. Friedrich, 3–17. New York: Atherton Press, 1964.

Simard, Augustin. *La Loi Désarmée. Carl Schmitt Et La Controverse Légalité/Légitimité Sous Weimar*. Québec: Presses de l'Université de Laval, 2009.

Simon, Herbert A. "Political Research: The Decision-Making Framework." In *Varieties of Political Theory*, edited by David Easton, 15–24. Englewood Cliffs, NJ: Prentice-Hall, 1966.

Smith, Mark C. *Social Science in the Crucible: The American Debate over Objectivity and Purpose, 1918–1941*. Durham, NC: Duke University Press, 1994.

Solovey, Mark. *Shaky Foundations: The Politics-Patronage-Social Science Nexus in Cold War America*. New Brunswick, NJ: Rutgers University Press, 2013.

Solovey, Mark, and Hamilton Cravens, eds. *Cold War Social Science: Knowledge Production, Liberal Democracy, and Human Nature*. New York: Palgrave Macmillan, 2012.

Speier, Hans. "Comments on Current Policy Requirements." Hans Speier Papers, German and Jewish Intellectual Émigré Collection, M. E. Grenander Department of Special Collections and Archives, University Libraries, University at Albany, Albany, NY, State University of New York, Box 9, Folder 32.

Steinbruner, John D. *The Cybernetic Theory of Decision: New Dimensions of Political Analysis*. Princeton, NJ: Princeton University Press, 1974.

Taubes, Jacob. *To Carl Schmitt: Letters and Reflections*. Translated by Keith Tribe. New York: Columbia University Press, 2013.

Verba, Sidney. "Assumptions of Rationality and Non-Rationality in Models of the International System." *World Politics* 14, no. 1 (October 1961): 93–117.

Waltz, Kenneth. *Foreign Policy and Democratic Politics: The American and British Experience*. Boston, MA: Little, Brown and Company, 1967.

 **1**

READING THE INTERNATIONAL MIND

International Public Opinion in Early Twentieth Century Anglo-American Thought

Stephen Wertheim

In 1939, E. H. Carr assailed those naive utopians who supposed that something called public opinion could usher in world peace. A generation of internationalists, he charged, had placed their faith in a "double fallacy": first, that public opinion would ultimately prevail, and second, that public opinion was always right.[1] After twenty years of crisis, and a failed League of Nations, such nostrums looked absurd. Carr hardly needed to argue against them, only to state them plainly. But had League supporters really been so naive? Carr had evidence. He rattled off quotation after quotation from US President Woodrow Wilson, British diplomat Robert Cecil, and others, all seeming to affirm what Cecil told the House of Commons about the League in 1919: "The great weapon we rely upon is public opinion ... and if we are wrong about it then the whole thing is wrong."[2]

The whole thing did rely on public opinion, on a belief that public opinion could surmount international conflict. Yet that belief was not as straightforward as Carr suggested or as conventional usage ever since would imply. "Public opinion" today evokes the momentary preferences of individuals aggregated together, as expressed in scientific opinion polls. Such polls, however, came into being in the latter half of the 1930s, just when Carr was writing. Outside the United States, they became widely used only after World War II.[3] Until then, the internationalists Carr criticized possessed no reliable method for quantifying momentary mass preferences within their own nations, let alone across nations. And they knew it. When they invoked international public opinion—staking the peace of the world on it in 1919—what did they mean, and what were they doing?

Carr at least recognized the importance of the discourse of public opinion, despite neglecting to theorize it. By contrast, subsequent scholars of liberal internationalism have sidelined the subject altogether, centering their accounts on world organization instead. Yet in the long-range history of internationalism, public opinion is as fundamental a category as world organization. Public opinion served as a discursive and conceptual frame for internationalist's projects well before constructing a permanent organization of states became part of their agenda during World War I. It signified, in part, the harmony of interest they assumed to be immanent in the world, beneath the violent clashes constantly on display. Through "public opinion," through its expression and enlightenment, international society would transcend power politics. On that much, liberal internationalists, ranging from diplomatic officials to legal and business professionals to peace activists, could agree. But what the public was, and how to discern its opinion, was another matter.

This chapter charts a genealogy of the concept of international public opinion in Anglo-American political discourse. It follows the lead of scholars who have reconstructed the diverse meanings of "public opinion" within national and transnational contexts since the eighteenth century.[4] These scholars have generally emphasized that, given its historical origins, "'public opinion' in its common usage is a positively Orwellian expression," as John Durham Peters writes.[5] Although public opinion is today manifested by solitary individuals answering surveys, the concept was formerly imagined as a form of collective rationality, often forged from deliberative debate (despite, or because of, the many categories of persons excluded from the public sphere). Notions of corporate will and cultivated reason also attached to the compound concept of *international* public opinion, although the latter presents a special case given the relative paucity of associational life at the international level.[6] The real conditions of international society before the twentieth century, then, make all the more important the illocutionary force of public opinion talk—who deployed it and to what end.

In anointing "public opinion" as the watchword of their new diplomacy, the founders of the League scarcely intended to anoint popular preferences as the guide of diplomatic practice. While trading on the term's democratic connotations, they valorized something closer to Kantian will or Hegelian spirit. Most important, they empowered national politicians to interpret public opinion through decision processes they declined to specify. In so doing, they elaborated on the usage of "public opinion" by prewar internationalists, particularly liberal legalists, who for decades held up themselves as public opinion's arbiters. As invoked by these successive groups of internationalists, in short, the concept of international public opinion differed in several ways from that of momentary mass preferences. The "public" in an international context designated anything from states vis-à-vis each other to literate civil society to broad populations. Its "opinion" tended to be enduringly rooted, more akin to customs, norms, will, or spirit than to mere preferences obtaining at a point in time. Because these various meanings were seldom parsed, internationalist elites assigned to themselves the authority to articulate public opinion, regardless of actual public sentiment. In the name of public opinion, they exercised their own discretion, practicing a kind of Schmittian decisionism *avant la lettre*. Before Walter Lippmann launched his attack on "public opinion" in 1922, and Carr and others developed the critique into International Relations (IR) realism, opinions about public opinion were hardly egalitarian.[7]

This interpretation implies that mid-twentieth-century realists misunderstood, or misrepresented, the idealists they named and criticized. They charged that idealists, in thrall to popular judgment and legalist–moralist rules, evaded the policymaker's responsibility to decide.[8] But the so-called idealists were elitists, too. Both idealism and realism, not just the latter, elevated the ineffable discernment of leaders—except that if idealists dared not speak the name of their decisionism, realists were only too glad to do so. In this regard, the real break occurred not in the 1930s and 1940s but rather in the 1950s and beyond, when the decision, having been exalted as the locus of international relations, was claimed by "decision sciences" like rational choice and systems analysis, which jettisoned the Schmittian mystique of unconditioned judgment. By the same token, neither realism nor the decision sciences were responsible for removing the public from International Relations (or international relations). The public was barely there to begin with, a discursive entity above all. Before faulting the postwar social sciences for evacuating the public and its opinion from political life, one must begin by asking which prior version of "public opinion" one means.[9]

The Judgment of History: Public Opinion and International Law, 1870–1914

"Public opinion" featured in internationalist debates no less than a century before World War I began. Its rise accompanied the gradual spread of popular sovereignty within European states. Contrary to

Carr, however, public opinion as an international concept was not simply transposed from domestic doctrines of *laissez faire* liberalism, as though individuals within the civil state were easily analogized to states within the anarchic international arena.[10] Public opinion had a distinct career in the realm of international thought. It addressed concerns specific to international relations, and those who invoked it intended to shape the global power structure as well as advance transnational interests and solidarities that took form in an increasingly interconnected world, particularly across the North Atlantic.[11]

Following the Napoleonic wars, diplomats, newspaper writers, salon-lobbyists, and festivalgoers gathered at the Congress of Vienna and made claims in the name of public opinion.[12] In his chronicle of the Congress, Abbé de Pradt, Napoleon's former secretary, dramatized how statesmen had begun to take account of the wider public, to heed "a new power, called opinion, from the empire of which nothing can be taken, at the tribunal of which governments themselves incessantly appeal."[13] In accounts like de Pradt's, public opinion began its long career as an evaluative–descriptive term linked to reason and civilization and opposed to military force and power politics. Many emergent internationalists employed the term in a similar manner but, unlike de Pradt, believed that the great powers trampled "public opinion" rather than respecting it. In particular, Quaker peace societies, Cobdenite free traders, and Mazzinian nationalists defended what they called public opinion against its armed suppression by the Concert of Europe and Holy Alliance.[14]

By the mid-nineteenth century, these internationalists formulated manifold programs to transform international society. Through the "people-diplomacy" of free trade, open congresses, and national autonomy, states would express their true, harmonious interests and prevent disputes from arising.[15] Through disarmament and arbitration, states would resolve whatever disputes arose by discussion rather than war. Such formulae glorified a "public opinion" irreconcilable with the existing order of monarchical and aristocratic states. To many internationalists, therefore, the ideal of public opinion precluded rather than required international organization. Any practicable international organization would necessarily have great powers at its core and "public opinion" at its mercy.[16]

In the latter half of the nineteenth century, "public opinion" claim-making ascended to the centers of power in international politics—but not because pacifists or revolutionaries ascended as well. To the contrary, public opinion entered the vocabulary of reformist liberals who organized transnationally to construct international society as a legalistic project. In the 1870s, the first international law society, the Institut de Droit International, formed in Europe, and British and American peace movements promoted the codification of law and the arbitral and judicial settlement of disputes.[17] Seeking to square their aspiration to transcend power politics with their confidence in the rising middle and professional class, liberal legalists articulated public opinion in a nonliteral, historico-cultural way. Although not necessarily contradicting the vague position of Benthamite advocates of publicity in the first half of the nineteenth century, they distanced themselves more explicitly from any support for popular decision-making.[18]

"Public opinion!" wrote Gustave Rolin-Jaequemyns, the Belgian founder of the Institut, in 1869. Rolin, echoing Blaise Pascal, hailed public opinion as "really and rightly the queen and legislator of the world," the "very voice of reason." But he was quick to clarify what he was not endorsing—namely mass preferences. "It goes without saying," Rolin wrote, "that by this word we do not mean to speak of wavering and ephemeral assessments, which introduce every day the passion, interest, and prejudice of the moment and an incomplete knowledge of facts." In fact, Rolin defined public opinion *against* momentary whims. As he continued, "we mean a public opinion that is serious and calm ... that is gradually confirmed and generalized, becoming the judgment of history." Accordingly, the content of public opinion was to be adduced not from popular sentiment but, Rolin wrote, from "the collective opinion of enlightened men," like international lawyers themselves.[19] In this way, lawyers positioned themselves as the arbiters of public opinion, the bearers of the "conscience of the civilized world."[20]

That Rolin hastened to clarify his meaning of public opinion betrayed the existence of a more egalitarian version that stood in contrast to his own. Perhaps for this reason, not all likeminded international lawyers on the European continent deployed the terminology of public opinion. Some chose to ground international law in public "conscience" or "consciousness," or Hegelian "Geist," or "will" in the Kantian sense of rational self-legislation by the state. For instance, the Swiss lawyer Johann Bluntschli followed the Herderian teachings of jurist Friedrich Carl von Savigny that held that law, like language, emerged spontaneously from the historical process of a people's organic communal life.[21] Such historicism banished actual public preferences to irrelevance. It barely mattered, in a sense, whether international lawyers used the language of public opinion or conscience, consciousness, spirit, or will. Whatever formulation was said to ground international law, the whims of the masses were scorned, the public's preferences given no direct role in international governance.

In the Anglo-American world, the language of public opinion was rife. By the mid-Victorian era, the possession of a sensible and powerful "public opinion" constituted an important part of the national identities of Great Britain and the United States. Although gesturing beyond the opinions of ruling elites, "public opinion" connoted a cultivated public and a settled opinion. This remained the case whether the term referred to concrete social activity, including associational life and press discourse, or a more homogenous national will. In *The English Constitution*, Walter Bagehot lionized what he called "formed public opinion" and "corporate public opinion." He famously personified public opinion as "the opinion of the bald-headed man at the back of the omnibus," conceiving the public as male, mature, urban, mobile, and, Bagehot emphasized, educated.[22] Intellectuals like Bagehot, the editor of *The Economist*, could safely champion public opinion in part because of their own position in the British public sphere. They enjoyed influence in the pages of reputable periodicals, whose editorial lines were clearly identifiable and mutually legitimated politics and policy.[23]

In the United States, public opinion was theorized similarly, notwithstanding the judgments of European visitors Alexis de Tocqueville and James Bryce that public opinion was uniquely salient in American government.[24] In the nineteenth and early twentieth century, US commentators tended to conceive public opinion in sociological more than psychological terms and embedded their analyses of public opinion into analyses of the political process.[25] An influential treatment of public opinion was provided by Francis Lieber, a founder of US political science and Abraham Lincoln's jurist of the laws of war. While Lieber associated public opinion with the press and admitted the public could make poor judgments, true public opinion was for Lieber the will of the whole community, "influenced either by the modifying correction of time, or the talent or knowledge of those who are peculiarly able to judge upon the subject in question." Lieber directly distinguished this normative–descriptive version of public opinion from the "aggregate opinion of many individuals singly taken." The latter he dubbed "general" as opposed to "public" opinion. Insofar as it did not involve men influencing each other in the organs of the body politic, it was not public.[26]

Through the concept of public opinion, then, Anglo-American thinkers theorized not only democracy but nationalism as well. Unsurprisingly, they theorized internationalism through the same concept. In fact, the concept of public opinion performed special work in the context of international society by allowing late nineteenth century legal theorists to meet the Austinian challenge of the English analytical school.²⁷ In the 1830s, jurist John Austin maintained that international law was not actually law because it was not commanded by a superior authority wielding force. Because no supranational polity existed to create legal code and coerce violators, so-called positive international law represented mere "positive international morality."²⁸ By the *fin de siècle*, most lawyers thought Austin wrong. Not armed force but "public opinion," they repeated, was the ultimate sanction of law, whether national or international. Because of public opinion, international law was law, and, for that matter, international society a society.

Given the legitimacy it conferred on international law and society, public opinion was a subject explicitly addressed by the most prominent lawyers and legalists of the turn of the twentieth century: Henry Maine, Lassa Oppenheim, and John Westlake in Britain, and Nicholas Murray Butler, John Bassett Moore, Elihu Root, James Brown Scott, and William H. Taft in America. Although often described as positivists, they are better understood as representing a school of historicist jurisprudence in line with the evolutionary social thought of the era.²⁹ They tended to idealize customary law because it emerged organically from the facts of social life, not from the imposition of abstract rules. Whereas Austin had recognized only statutory law to be real law, customs too inspired routine compliance. Sir Henry Maine, the pioneer of legal historicism, set forth an anthropological sequence in which customary law governed "primitive" societies and codification had to come at the right stage of social progress lest it impose excessive rigidity.³⁰ By concluding that the basis of law could be deference to custom, not physical compulsion, Maine placed international law on a footing as sure as domestic law.

Historically conceived, customary international law became no different from customary domestic law, and the international treaty became akin to a domestic contract. The key task of the jurist was to ascertain when mere habit congealed into settled custom. It was "public opinion" that distinguished habit from custom. According to liberal legalists, a genuine rule of law existed when "the general *consensus* of opinion within the limits of European civilisation" favored it, as John Westlake, Maine's successor as Whewell Professor of International Law at Cambridge, wrote in 1894. What constituted a consensus of opinion? The practice of states furnished the best evidence, Westlake wrote, though such evidence did not interpret itself. Westlake elevated scholarly jurists as interpreters of state practice, as well as articulators of the "general consent of men, especially when the writer's reputation proves that he represents many persons besides himself."³¹ Similarly, despite associating public opinion with the "man in the street" who found himself "at the mercy of the press and the agitator," Lassa Oppenheim held that an international legal rule existed when "public opinion of the world at large approved of and expected this attitude"—that is, when, among other things, "all authoritative writers considered this attitude necessary."[32]

Strikingly, some lawyers welcomed the indeterminacy of international public opinion because it freed international society to develop organically and enabled international lawyers to guide that development. Westlake made a virtue of the common lament that international law lacked a legislature to enact law and a judiciary to interpret law. "Legislatures and judicatures, by the very fact of their fixing the law, are sometimes a hindrance to its improvement," he contended. If these institutions stifled historical development, "the living tissue of the law may become ossified." By contrast, international law benefitted from public opinion being its source and sanction. Uninhibited by political institutions, international law also gave lawyers a pivotal function that exceeded their domestic role. As Westlake put it: "If a branch of law is still free to develop itself under the influence of public opinion, the student has the power, and with it the responsibility and the privilege, of assisting in its evolution."[33] Institutions that actually registered public preferences were a hindrance. "Public opinion" worked best when the public remained vague, allowing learned lawyers to pronounce the public's opinion.

Whereas public opinion in a national context sometimes signified the communal formation of views through discussion and intercourse, this connotation became less operative and more metaphorical in an international context. International lawyers inferred common consent from the passage of time; when a practice became customary, they considered it approved by international opinion and a matter of international law. In fact, according to James Brown Scott, editor of the *American Journal of International Law*, custom need not be conscious in the mind of anyone and public opinion could be inferred from custom.[34] Therefore public opinion could exist without being consciously believed, let alone openly communicated.

A telling synonym for "international public opinion" was the "international mind," coined by Nicholas Murray Butler, the president of Columbia University and the Carnegie Endowment for International Peace. Although Butler usually used the terms interchangeably and favorably, he once clarified that the international mind operated when the world's "strong, brave, enlightened men" could "stand with patience and self-control in a post of high responsibility when a strong current of *public opinion* goes sweeping by, careless of consequences and unrestrained in its expression of feeling." For Butler, the international mind was a normative "habit of thinking" that might as well resist the public will as follow it. His theory of internationalism regarded national opinion with the same suspicion with which theorists of nationalism regarded popular opinion: both were portrayed as selfish, emotional, and manipulable. Butler's antidote was an international elite—"soberminded leaders of opinion"—positioned to swim against national and popular currents when they pulled in the wrong direction.[35]

In addition to being paternalistically interpreted by enlightened men, the public in liberals' "international public opinion" sometimes comprised states as opposed to individuals or groups of people. After all, the constituents of international society were in the first instance states. Even after one applied the domestic analogy, the international public contained fictive legal persons rather than, or along with, corporal persons. The lawyer and politician Elihu Root, a respected US senator and secretary of state, drew the domestic analogy explicitly. Within states, he argued, citizens ordinarily obeyed the law not for fear of imprisonment but rather "because they are unwilling to incur in the community in which they live the public condemnation and obloquy" that law breaking would provoke.[36] When Root transposed this logic to the international realm, it was states that feared condemnation and obloquy from other states. Transgressing law would leave a nation "without respect or honor in the world and deprived of the confidence and good-will necessary to the maintenance of intercourse."[37] Yet in the process of moving from the national to the international, Root shifted from moral-phenomenological to instrumental language, suggesting a diminished sociability. Whereas domestic public opinion caused individuals to suffer a "disgrace ... more terrible than the actual physical effect," international public incentivized states to preserve their interest in intercourse.[38] In any case, in Root's international public opinion, the public was first and foremost the club of civilized states, in which the opinion of national publics (to say nothing of peoples not deemed civilized) might figure secondarily or not at all.

In sum, at the turn of the century, "international public opinion" signified nothing like the aggregated momentary preferences of individuals within a global public or across several national publics. Indeed, Anglo-American international lawyers had mixed feelings about the expansion of suffrage at home and the extension of democracy abroad, trends that empowered people ignorant of the rules of international law.[39] On the one hand, US President William H. Taft ardently promoted treaties for the compulsory arbitration of disputes, professing the utmost confidence in "international public opinion" to enforce the judgments of the court. Carr highlighted this objective of Taft in *The Twenty Years' Crisis*.[40] But Carr passed over Taft's statement, in the same source Carr cited, that democratic states were more warlike than nondemocracies because publics demanded retribution for small slights to national honor. As Taft declared, "Nice distinctions based on precedents in international law have more weight with learned statesmen representing a dynasty than with an angered people."[41] In Taft's conceptual universe, international public opinion could profit from less democracy, not more.

For all their enthusiasm for public opinion, Anglo-American liberal internationalists undertheorized the public and how it might form an opinion. The concept as they used it was not only vague but indeterminate, containing several incompatible meanings at once. The international public might consist of aggregated individuals, organic groups, or states in the diplomatic arena, and its opinion spanned from momentary preferences to unconscious customs. This indeterminacy had the virtue of allowing internationalists to bring rules of law into being through their own decisions, which they shrouded in the guise of interpretation.

By the same stroke, however, internationalists grounded their project in some notion of popular consent, which was not supposed to be reducible to the rule of elites. While rejecting the mass public's judgment in the present, they held out hope of enlightening the broad public in the future. Moreover, as the basis of legal and social norms, "international public opinion" had to be imagined as a discernable entity, and highly efficacious at that. Internationalists *did* repose faith in "public opinion" in contradistinction to armed sanctions. Because they believed elite men could discern a harmony immanent in the world, they evinced little interest before World War I in putting physical sanctions behind international law or erecting an international political organization. Instead, they promoted the voluntary arbitral or judicial settlement of international disputes. Before the war, liberal internationalists continued to assume that public opinion, or the enlightened men who pronounced it, sufficed to discipline national egoism and overcome power politics.

What No Man Else Knows: Public Opinion and International Organization, 1914–1920

In February 1919, Woodrow Wilson unveiled the Covenant of the League of Nations and explained to the world why the League would succeed. The linchpin was international public opinion. "We are depending primarily and chiefly upon one great force," the American president proclaimed, "and this is the moral force of the public opinion of the world—the pleasing and clarifying and compelling influences of publicity." In the dawning age of public opinion, he continued, sinister schemes "may be promptly destroyed by the overwhelming light of the universal expression of the condemnation of the world."[42] To observers then as now, Wilson's words might evoke an image of mass publics rising up to register their views through the new machinery of the League. At the end of World War I, such rhetoric helped Western liberalism to compete with Bolshevism for popular allegiances in Europe and the global South.[43]

But the context in which Wilson spoke his words complicates their meaning. He was unveiling the Covenant because it had previously been veiled, drawn up largely by the heads of the four wartime victors. For months the leaders met privately in Paris, shut off from journalists and shutting out delegates from small states and colonial peoples. Furthermore, the Covenant described new machinery that answered first and foremost to states, not their publics. The main bodies of the League, the big-power Council and the universal Assembly, comprised appointees of state executives, not representatives elected by publics. How, then, did international organization come to look—both to contemporaries and to subsequent interpreters—like the obvious ally of public opinion, when it might have appeared the contrary?

To answer this question, one must not accept the self-presentation of the League as an unprecedented leap from secret diplomacy to a New Diplomacy guided by public opinion.[44] Wilson was less an innovator than an elaborator of the concept of public opinion developed by the previous generation of liberal internationalist jurists. Nor was he alone. The other drafters of the League Covenant, including Jan Smuts and Alfred Zimmern, invoked international public opinion in a similar, nonliteral manner. As we will see, even when they referred to the nonelite populace, they expected the public not so much to influence the League as the League would educate the public. To be precise, the politicians in the League's councils would interpret and mold public opinion. The New Diplomacy was new primarily insofar as it replaced the decisions of lawyers with the decisions of politicians.

Consider, first, South African General and Prime Minister Jan Christiaan Smuts. In the pamphlet *The League of Nations: A Practical Suggestion*, published in December 1918, he garnered support from the Imperial War Cabinet, Woodrow Wilson, and internationalist activists alike, aligning popular demands for international organization with British interests in maintaining the empire and bringing the United States into the European balance of power.[45] Smuts did more than anyone to devise the Mandates system, through which the wartime victors divvied up former German and Ottoman colonies, with South Africa effectively annexing German South West Africa (postcolonial Namibia).[46] When Smuts addressed "public opinion" more than a dozen times in *A Practical Suggestion*, he did so as an unflinching imperialist steeped in Victorian paternalism.

Like Wilson, Smuts hung the fortunes of the League on what he called public opinion. "The league will never be a great success," he wrote, "until there is formed as its main support a powerful international public opinion." At one point, Smuts imagined that public opinion might rise up against the "clandestine ambitions of statesmen," who would have to cast votes publicly in the League. At the Paris Peace Conference, he mooted a proposal for the League Assembly to convene special meetings, at least once every four years, that included "representatives of national parliaments and other bodies representative of public opinion."[47] In the main, however, public opinion figured in Smuts's writing as something for the League to tutor, not to register. Under his plan for the League, only the great powers of the Council could make binding decisions. The Council would do the "real work" and set the agenda for the general Assembly, which would be a "powerful and influential factor in moulding international public opinion."[48] Public opinion required molding because the people, according to Smuts, were fickle. He lamented how the jingoistic press "whip up public opinion on every imaginable occasion" and insisted that because "national passions are easily inflamed," the Assembly must discuss only those subjects dictated by the Council.[49] Smuts sought the uplift of public opinion far more than he did its expression.

Smuts modeled the League on the British Empire, and he may have regarded international public opinion as a ward of the civilized statesmen who would occupy the councils of the new international organization. In emphasizing the League's "educative influence on public opinion," Smuts articulated an idealist philosophy of history in which the sphere of moral concern would gradually enlarge.[50] In his words, "The enlightened public all over the world will have to be taught to think internationally, to look at public affairs, not merely from the sectional national point of view, but also from a broad human international point of view." Aspiring to international enlightenment, Smuts denigrated British Parliament for exhibiting a "narrow national influence," a move that rebutted radicals who advocated the parliamentary control of foreign policy.[51] Here internationalism served to minimize the authority of elected officials and the expression of public opinion. Smuts hoped that rather than weigh popular preferences and arbitrate among conflicting views, the League would cultivate a "fundamental unity of aims, methods, and spirit," a "singleness of mind."[52]

Conceiving public opinion so vaguely allowed Smuts to put the concept to special use in his international thought. His philosophical tome, *Holism and Evolution*, fashioned biological, social, and political history into a single trajectory wherein human units achieved ever-greater synthesis without sacrificing their particularity.[53] Smuts adored the white British Commonwealth of Nations for uniting the dominions while preserving the independence and nationality of each.[54] It was this formula, "co-operation on the basis of freedom," that Smuts wanted the League to follow.[55] "Public opinion" was one way of phrasing that invisible glue that would somehow bind the nations together without coercion. For Smuts, as for antebellum prewar legalists, public opinion contrasted with armed force more than it denoted positive content. This made public opinion a critical concept, but also a replaceable term. Thus Smuts could describe the "ever-increasing wholeness of our human relationships" in a 1934 lecture and not mention "public opinion" once.[56]

Alfred Zimmern, an adviser in the Political Intelligence Division of the British Foreign Office, was no more inclined than Smuts to see the League take its cues from mass preferences. During the war, Zimmern penned the Foreign Office memorandum that formed the basis of the Covenant draft of Robert Cecil, the British delegate at the Paris Peace Conference.[57] Afterward, as the first Woodrow Wilson chair in international politics at Aberystwyth, and then the first Montague Burton professor of international relations at Oxford, he became a foundational figure in academic International Relations.[58] Zimmern also led interwar efforts to educate public opinion, serving as deputy director of the interwar International Institute of Intellectual Cooperation.[59]

While reflecting optimism about the public's capacity to be educated, Zimmern's work also reflected his suspicion of the public as it actually existed. Early in World War I, he ruled out schemes for world government on the grounds that they presupposed "an educated public opinion incomparably less selfish, less ignorant, less unsteady, less materialistic, and less narrowly national than has been prevalent hitherto."[60] It was because he distrusted the past and present condition of public opinion that Zimmern designed the League to be an "impalpable Something," impotent by itself and effective only when the peoples of its member states acquired a unified will.[61]

In advancing cautious notions of both public opinion and international machinery, Zimmern drew on his education at late-nineteenth-century Oxford. There neo-Hegelian reformists surrounding the moral philosopher T. H. Green critiqued classical liberalism for conceiving of man atomistically. Zimmern imbibed this Oxford communitarianism, melding the historicist and organicist thought of Hegelianism, the ethical bent of classicism, and a liberal fear of state power. Zimmern's eclectic intellectual fusion took historical progress to come from the natural evolution of civil society, guided by feelings of ethical responsibility toward the whole.[62] What Zimmern valorized might be termed "public opinion," but it better resembled spirit.

Zimmern himself lectured on the "international mind," not public opinion, in 1926. He defined the international mind as "the habit of intellectual integrity," the application of reason and open-mindedness to all matters.[63] In theory, anyone could access the international mind, though depressingly few succeeded because of the innate reluctance of the human mind to confront disagreeable thoughts. The international mind was decidedly not an aggregation of multivalent preferences; it was a single moral truth and spiritual feeling, nurtured through the practical experience of life.[64] Bringing it about was no job for the common man (much less woman), at least at his present level of enlightenment. Zimmern continually called for international education, to which his Lamarckian leanings lent further significance.[65] When he expressed confidence in public opinion, it was in the belief that "public opinion at the present time does not function in foreign affairs," as Zimmern said even in the heady atmosphere of Geneva 1928.[66] National publics had only just begun a long journey toward the formation of an international opinion. For the foreseeable future, the peace of the world would depend on the judgment of statesmen with moral authority.

If any founder of the League placed confidence in momentary mass preferences, it might seem to have been Woodrow Wilson. Historians have highlighted the idealism and distinctiveness of the American president's international ideas, known as Wilsonianism. Alas, historians have seldom connected Wilson's international vision, articulated during his presidency, to the body of thought he produced as a political scientist.[67] One must square the Wilson who championed international public opinion with the Wilson who wrote, in 1895, "The people should not govern; they should elect the governors: and these governors should be elected for periods long enough to give time for policies not too heedful of transient breezes of public opinion."[68]

An admirer of Edmund Burke and Walter Bagehot, Wilson, in his formative years, developed an organicist understanding of social and political evolution.⁶⁹ To this he added a loose neo-Hegelian teleology, which made Burkean organicism not conservative but progressive because the future direction of society could be discerned and its realization hastened. As a graduate student at Johns Hopkins University, Wilson was influenced by economist Richard Ely and historian Herbert Baxter Adams, both of whom had studied under Bluntschli in Heidelberg.⁷⁰ In his own extensive theorizing, Wilson echoed Bluntschli's view that the will of the state is "the one national will, which is different from the average will of the multitude"—in other words, emphatically not summed mass preferences.⁷¹ Despite dubbing his object of study "modern democracy," Wilson was fundamentally a theorist of nationalism. In his telling, all nations passed through four stages before becoming mature democracies, in which the people were self-conscious and self-directive, able to think and act as a "whole."⁷²

Wilson considered it "ridiculous" to think the people could formulate an opinion on each political issue. For one, they lacked the time. More importantly, the masses were too fickle and thoughtless simply to be followed. History proved "that the will of majorities is *not* the same as the general will: that a nation is an *organic* thing, and that its will dwells with those who do the *practical* thinking and organize *the best concert of action*: those who hit upon opinions *fit to be made prevalent*, and have *the capacity to make them so*."⁷³ As Wilson implied, the general will could be discerned through the introspection of enlightened men more directly than through an analysis of public preferences. Though Wilson shied from such openly elitist phrasings, his view amounted just to this. Leaders, as he wrote, had to "distinguish the firm and progressive popular *thought* from the momentary and whimsical popular *mood*, the transitory or mistaken popular passion."⁷⁴

What separated thought from mood, firmness from whimsy? Wilson offered no answer, except that it was up to the leader to determine, by his special intuition, the general will. The leader "must have such sympathetic and penetrative insight as shall enable him to discern quite unerringly the motives which move other men *in the mass*." Wilson clarified that this ideal leader "need not pierce the particular secrets of *individual* men: [he] need only know what it is that lies waiting to be stirred in the minds and purposes of groups and masses of men."⁷⁵ Had scientific polls been available to Wilson, he would have found them valuable but not decisive. Reading true public opinion required "sympathetic and penetrative insight" rather than knowledge of individual preferences. The leader tapped the latent, potentially unexpressed or inexpressible desires of the nation. These were desires of the whole community, construed as more than the sum of individual minds. In the end, the leader, by virtue of his position, could rest assured that he discerned public opinion, however intangible, "quite unerringly."

Wilson's vaunted "public opinion" was therefore shot through with paternalism. In his view, leaders had wide latitude to shape the public's desires and ignore its stated preferences. "Men are as clay in the hands of the consummate leader," Wilson wrote.[76] "How we *cheat* ourselves by living in subjection to public opinion when we *might make it!*"[77] As a matter of fact, Wilson, like many progressive intellectuals, entertained the suspicion that the people wanted to be told what to think. The public sought "a President whom it trusts can not only lead it but form it to his own views."[78] To devise the public's views, the leader did two things. He "interpreted" the general will and foresaw glimpses of the future ("across the mind of the statesman flash ever and anon brilliant, though partial, intimations of future events," wrote a young Wilson). Then he educated the people, in effect to inform them of their own collective will.[79] Framing leadership as an act of interpretation, Wilson cleared space within democratic theory for unconditioned decisions.

As a political scientist, Wilson clearly minimized the normative significance of the momentary preferences of the public, the main exception coming in the election of leaders. Nor did his valuation of "public opinion" change when he entered elective politics. In 1909, before running for the New Jersey governorship, Wilson contended that leaders do not simply repeat "the talk of the street-corners or the opinions of the newspapers." To the contrary:

> A nation is led by a man who hears more than those things; or who, rather, hearing those things, understands them better, unites them, puts them into a common meaning ... a man in whose ears the voices of the nation do not sound like the accidental and discordant notes that come from the voice of a mob, but concurrent and concordant like the united voices of a chorus, whose many meanings, spoken by melodious tongues, unite in his understanding in a single meaning and reveal to him a single vision, so that he can speak what no man else knows, the common meaning of the common voice.[80]

For Wilson, the people may disagree, but in fact they possess a single common will, which the politician alone is able to interpret.

Appreciating the multiple valences, but profound paternalism, of Wilsonian "public opinion" makes sense of seeming contradictions in Wilson's conduct as a peacemaker. Wilson did, after all, undertake extraordinary measures to publicize treaties and canvass public sentiment. In his Fourteen Points address, he vowed to settle the war by making "open covenants of peace, openly arrived at," that would permit "no secret understandings of any kind."[81] Most remarkably, in May 1919, Wilson sent a commission to the Middle East for the purpose of determining the "real wishes and true interests" of formerly Ottoman populations regarding their political future.[82] The resulting King-Crane Commission toured the greater Syrian region for forty-two days, meeting hundreds of delegations and collecting more than a thousand petitions. One scholar infers from this incident that American politicians, epitomized by Wilson, "conceived of 'public opinion' as the gross aggregate of individual opinions freely expressed rather than a consentient position articulated by an elite."[83]

Yet Wilson ignored the commission's detailed report after he received it in August 1919.[84] The King-Crane report became public only three years later, when it was published under the headline: "A Suppressed Official Document of the United States Government."[85] Whatever purpose Wilson originally intended for the commission—he dispatched it late in the peace conference, when Britain, France, and Italy pressed claims to ex-Ottoman territory—he evidently did not regard popular opinion to be dispositive of true "public opinion," nor did he send equivalent commissions elsewhere. More broadly, Wilson and the other big powers negotiated the major issues of the peace in the secret Council of Four. Wilson even tried unsuccessfully to designate minutes of these negotiations as "private conversations" not to be deposited in official state files.[86]

Such conduct does not so much make Wilson hypocritical as it reveals tensions within the concept of public opinion that he upheld. "Public opinion" signified expressed mass preferences *and* latent moral spirit, the latter divined by elected officials. But despite appealing to both meanings, Wilson consistently prized spirit over preferences. While believing that actual mass preferences could inform him, he nonetheless reserved the right to override public judgment—in the name of public opinion. When Wilson claimed that the Paris Peace Conference was "the first conference in which decisions depended upon the opinion of mankind," one suspects the opinion of mankind mostly meant Wilson's own.[87]

Reflecting the neo-Hegelianism of his teachers, Wilson's guiding light was "the spirit of the age," as he termed it.[88] In actuality, the zeitgeist provided slight guidance. What did the spirit demand? For what measures were the people organically ready? Expressions of public preferences could help fill in these abstractions, but the ultimate criterion of judgment was the decision of Wilson himself. In 1889, Wilson recorded reflection in his diary on how and why he analyzed politics. It is a task, he wrote, "not of origination, but of interpretation. Interpret the age: i.e., interpret myself. Account for the creed I hold in politics." Wilson envisaged himself the embodiment of his age: "Why may not the present age write, through me, its political *autobiography*?"[89]

In espousing public opinion, the founders of the League followed in the footsteps of legalist internationalists who valued elite interpretation above mass expression. If anything, they proffered an even more pronounced decisionism than their forebears because they wanted politicians to interpret ineffable spirit where jurists preferred to formulate legal rules. Considered in this light, wartime references to international public opinion did not centrally engage with questions of political representation; the subject fits only tangentially into the theme of "democratizing foreign policy," where scholars have placed it.[90] Rather, the discourse of public opinion served to sustain a traditional mystique of the leader who embodies the sovereign authority and will of the nation. It deserves to be located in the genealogies of (inter)nationalism, sovereignty, and elitism more than that of democratic theory.

Still, even though the decisionist invocation of public opinion had roots in nineteenth-century liberal internationalism, that tradition contained other possibilities that Wilson and his cohort largely bypassed. "Public opinion" *could* refer to the preferences of a voting public. And as a synonym for peaceful intercourse and immanent harmony, "public opinion" could be arrayed *against* the free play of politicians to conduct diplomacy and wield force. Indeed, when World War I broke out, liberal internationalists on both sides of the Atlantic offered peace plans along precisely these lines. But the League's founders rejected these alternatives. Their unspoken decisionism best explains their location within the spectrum of liberal internationalist thought.

In contrast to Smuts, Zimmern, and Wilson, one set of wartime internationalists took "public opinion" relatively literally, making their central demand the popular control and parliamentary oversight of foreign policy. The most prominent such group was the Union of Democratic Control (UDC) in Britain, led by radicals and Labourites including Ramsay MacDonald, E. D. Morel, Arthur Ponsonby, and Charles Trevelyan.[91] To the UDC, the growth of democracy within nations contradicted how "the people remain helpless and inarticulate" in international affairs. Although the government pledged to be "guided by public opinion," Ponsonby wrote, "no steps whatever are taken to ascertain what the people think."[92] Under the UDC platform of 1915, Parliament would approve every "Treaty, Arrangement, or Undertaking" in foreign policy; any transfer of territory would require the "consent, by plebiscite or otherwise," of the population concerned; and states would join an international organization that would deliberate and make decisions in public.[93] UDC members also proposed that states send members of parliament, rather than appointees of the executive, to represent them in a new international organization. In February 1919, at the initiative of MacDonald, the Labour and Socialist International called for national parliamentarians from every political party to sit on the councils of the League; then the League would become "not an alliance of Cabinets or Governments but a union of peoples."[94] UDC members were not uncritical of the present state of public opinion, but they blamed governments and the press for keeping the people in the dark.[95] They believed the people, when given responsibility and information in a systematic fashion, to be as capable of making decisions as their leaders, and more likely to choose peace.

After the war ended in November 1918, however, the leaders of the victorious Allied powers declined to invest greater formal authority in the voting public or directly elected representatives, whether within or across nations. The most they did to conform with the UDC's view was to advance the principle of publicity by mandating the publication of treaties in Article 18 of the Covenant.[96] But as Zimmern explained, he and the League's founders rejected the democratic control of foreign policy not merely because they thought the public as yet was unready to assume the role of decision-maker. Rather, so-called democratic control struck Zimmern as *un*democratic. In a tortured talk on "public opinion," he claimed that democratic control harked back to the "rigid constitutions" of the eighteenth century, when rulers sought checks and balances against their publics. Zimmern argued such constitutions were outmoded now that the electorate had expanded and education had diffused. There was nothing to gain, Zimmern declared, by "introduc[ing] an element of delay and of further complexity which interferes with the power of Governments to keep up with the rapid movement of events." The League of Nations was "better adapted to modern conditions" without a rigid constitution than it would be with one.[97] Here Zimmern laid bare the monism of his nationalism and thus his internationalism. In his view, state representatives fully embodied their public's opinion, such that direct public expressions added nothing to (or somehow detracted from) the calculation of public opinion. Furthermore, Zimmern's concern with preserving timely decision-making betrayed the absence of public judgment in his notion of public opinion; instead, he was defending the independent judgment of politicians in situations not yet fathomed by the public.

A second challenge to the political discretion of leaders came from legalists, who wished to replace politics with law, and decisions with rules. Whereas advocates of the democratic control of foreign policy blamed the diplomatic system for being unrepresentative, legalists faulted it for being expedient. Building on the prewar promotion of voluntary arbitration, they proposed to codify international legal code and, in a dramatic innovation, to obligate and militarily enforce the judicial settlement of disputes. By 1917, this model of world organization, espoused by ex-President Taft's League to Enforce Peace (LEP), ranked as the preeminent plan for the postwar world in the United States and commanded significant popularity in Britain and France.[98] But when the official League covenant came out, it co-opted and occluded the legalists' blueprints. Although many LEP members favored US membership in the League, the arch-legalist Elihu Root recognized the eclipse of his cause. The new League of Nations, he lamented, "rests the hope of the whole world for future peace in a government of men, and not of laws, following the dictates of expediency, and not of right."[99]

Despite assuming too stark a polarity between politics and law, Root was correct to detect an antilegalistic ethos behind the Covenant. "I don't want lawyers drafting this treaty," Wilson snapped when his secretary of state directed two lawyers to develop an outline.[100] The drafters of the Covenant believed only politicians could discern true "public opinion" and shepherd its development. Law was too rigid and confining; it shackled those who would interpret and guide the growth of common spirit, although it could play a subordinate role. As Zimmern wrote, "law courts and arbitration machinery are neither designed nor expected to breed sympathy and understanding between rival litigants. They can but follow and consolidate the swifter advance of the international spirit in more fruitful and less contentious spheres of activity."[101] Again, the desire to preserve the power of national political leaders to make decisions distinguished the League from the popular and elite-legalist alternatives promoted by contemporaneous liberal internationalists. The Covenant created, in Wilson's words, "not a strait-jacket, but a vehicle of life"—for politicians most of all.[102]

During World War I, liberal internationalists yoked the longstanding ideal of public opinion to the new objective of international organization. Opposed in the nineteenth century, public opinion and international organization now would go together. Yet the League failed to confront the contradictions between the two, producing attenuated versions of each. On the one hand, international organization seemed necessary because public opinion appeared insufficient to prevent war. Understood as mass preferences, public opinion was not to be trusted, and understood as immanent spirit, public opinion required material sanctions to strengthen it. On the other hand, international organization could be only so strong if it were imagined as a vehicle for a fictive public opinion. The League's founders worried that new international machinery constantly risked stifling the growth of common consciousness. Thus they both introduced forcible sanctions into the Covenant and denied force would have to be used, with Wilson baffling the US Senate by declaring the League's enforcement provisions to be "binding in conscience only, not in law."[103] The amalgam of public opinion and international organization, unstable from the start, would not survive long.

The Interwar Apotheosis: Untried and Found Wanting?

Never mind original intent, one might argue: the interwar experiment in international government ended up mobilizing a public opinion far more participatory and egalitarian than what the drafters of the Covenant envisioned. Having put "public opinion" front and center, they could not control the semantic indeterminacy they harnessed. As historians have recently shown, nongovernmental international organizations proliferated in the twenties, partly because they could participate in the official organizations of Geneva.[104] By the early 1930s, an American political scientist counted hundreds of groups "dealing with practically every subject of interest to human beings."[105] The largest, the British League of Nations Union, boasted a mass membership exceeding four hundred thousand people.[106] Through the Secretariat's Information Section, the League invited popular scrutiny of international politics, publicizing all manner of materials in addition to the treaties required by the Covenant.[107] Not least, the League devised procedures for receiving thousands of petitions from individuals subject to the minorities and mandates regimes. Although these were screened and ventriloquized, petitions provided individuals with direct contact to international society for the first time. They fired jurists' hopes of establishing a "right of petition" under international law.[108] The panoply of actors that converged on interwar Geneva took seriously the power of a public opinion that went beyond governmental representatives. How "public opinion" was manifested and contested in particular contexts deserves further scholarly exploration.[109]

On the whole, however, popular involvement in international governance remained circumscribed. Mass electorates gained little formal authority under the League.¹¹⁰ And if legitimating the League as a fount of public opinion opened up unforeseen possibilities, it also came at a price. When the League experiment did not prevent World War II, public opinion appeared to be implicated. Already in the 1920s, social scientists used psychology to demonstrate the irrationality of the masses. Intellectuals like Walter Lippmann doubted the capacity of publics to rule themselves—a newly overt rejection of "public opinion," albeit a less substantial break with previous orthodoxies than Lippmann portrayed at the time and scholars thereafter have assumed.¹¹¹

It was the catastrophe of the 1930s that sullied international public opinion even among the faithful. The breakdown of collective security, first over the Manchuria crisis and fatally over the Italian invasion of Abyssinia, discredited international public opinion conceived as a peaceful sanction opposed to armed force.¹¹² The rise of totalitarian powers, coupled with the hobbling of liberal democracies in the Depression, discredited international public opinion understood as an immanent harmony or civilized conscience. By indicating the susceptibility of publics to state propaganda, the same conditions discredited international public opinion interpreted as mass preferences.¹¹³ The world crisis besieged all three meanings of public opinion. By 1938, Nicholas Murray Butler despaired that "international law, like international morality, has disappeared in a fog."¹¹⁴ Butler had lost his international mind.

What Butler ruefully gave up, the next generation aggressively dismissed. Around World War II, realists constituted themselves in opposition less to international organization—which they could support, if expectations were kept modest—than to international public opinion in all its guises. Faith in public opinion seemed to embody the perils of transplanting the tenets of liberal democracy in the alien soil of international affairs, where no amount of rational discussion or neutral adjudication could transcend politics and war. In this respect, realists, from across the left–right political spectrum, truly and profoundly diverged from their predecessors: they considered and rejected "public opinion" as an alternative to forcible sanctions and an immanent harmony of interest. In the process, moreover, they developed a critique of the discourse of public opinion. In 1948, Hans Morgenthau unmasked "world public opinion" as representing little more than the opinion of whoever claimed its warrant. He wrote:

> when a nation invokes "world public opinion" or "the conscience of mankind" in order to assure itself, as well as other nations, that its

international policies meet the test of standards shared by men everywhere, it appeals to nothing real ... world public opinion becomes the mythical arbiter who can be counted upon to support one's own, as well as everybody else's, aspirations and actions.[115]

Realists like Morgenthau might well have stopped there. If public opinion had functioned merely as Morgenthau claimed—as a device for universalizing parochial interests, without consulting actual publics—realists would have possessed little reason to deprecate publics or their opinion. Untried, public opinion could hardly be found wanting.

In the event, realists did not stop there. They also disparaged "public opinion" literally conceived, as though all liberal internationalists had wished to delegate decision-making to the masses. Morgenthau himself lumped together Woodrow Wilson, "the perfect interpreter of liberal thought," with the Union for Democratic Control: all liberal internationalists, in Morgenthau's telling, had favored the disastrous "democratization of foreign affairs."[116] Ironically, Morgenthau echoed Wilson in conflating elite-defined public opinion with actual mass decisions. His realism inherited the conceptual indeterminacy of Wilsonian "public opinion" with the normative signs reversed. Because the *discourse* of public opinion had failed to prevent war, realists concluded that popular rule had failed too.

Thus they prescribed more elitism, not less, for the future. Realists deemed the public incapable of uplift, discarding liberal internationalists' chary optimism that mass publics could be educated eventually. Now the rulers would rule, the deciders decide, shorn of pretense. Yet in discarding international public opinion, even as discourse, realists laid bare the chasm between the concentrated control of political decisions and the normative expectation of popular control. Thinking they had rescued elite judgment from oblivion, they would expose it to fresh challenge, both from social movements in search of democracy and from social scientists who tamed the decision as a rational choice or a cybernetic process. "Little do they know," as Morgenthau wrote of nations, "that they meet under an empty sky from which the gods have departed."[117]

Stephen Wertheim is Visiting Assistant Professor in History at Columbia University and Visiting Scholar at the Saltzman Institute of War and Peace Studies. He is a historian of US foreign relations and international order from the nineteenth century to the present, with a focus on concepts of politics and law. His articles have appeared in *Diplomatic History, Journal of Global History, Journal of Genocide Research,* and *Presidential Studies Quarterly,* and his book on the origins of US global supremacy is forthcoming from Harvard University Press. Stephen received his PhD in History from Columbia University in 2015, after which he held research fellowships at Princeton University and King's College, University of Cambridge.

Notes

I thank Emily Baughan, Daniel Bessner, Nicholas Guilhot, Kristen Loveland, Mark Mazower, Jeanne Morefield, Glenda Sluga, and Natasha Wheatley for their valuable comments. Special thanks to Susan Pedersen: the results are unlikely to justify her generous feedback. Thanks also to panelists and attendees of "Towards a New History of the League of Nations," Graduate Institute of International and Development Studies, Geneva, August 2011; the Annual Conference of the American Society for Legal History, Atlanta, November 2011; "Decision, Decisionism, Decision-making," Center for International Research in the Humanities and Social Sciences, New York University, October 2015; and "Communicating International Organisations in the 19th and 20th Centuries," European University Institute, Florence, March 2016.

1. E. H. Carr, *The Twenty Years' Crisis, 1919–1939* (New York: Harper & Row, 1964), 31.
2. British Parliament, Parliamentary Debates, House of Commons, Fifth Series, vol. 118, 21 July 1919, col. 992.
3. Laura Beers, "Whose Opinion?: Changing Attitudes Towards Opinion Polling in British Politics, 1937-1964," *Twentieth Century British History* 17, no. 2 (2006): 177-205; Michael X. Delli Carpini, "Constructing Public Opinion: A Brief History of Survey Research," in *The Oxford Handbook of American Public Opinion and the Media*, ed. George Edwards III, Lawrence Jacobs, and Robert Shapiro (Oxford: Oxford University Press, 2011), 284-301; Michael Korzi, "Lapsed Memory? The Roots of American Public Opinion Research," *Polity* 33, no. 1 (Fall 2000): 49-73; Sarah Igo, *The Averaged American: Surveys, Citizens, and the Making of a Mass Public* (Cambridge, MA: Harvard University Press, 2007), 103-49.
4. Among an extensive literature in history, media studies, and political science, see John Gunnell, "Democracy and the Concept of Public Opinion," in *The Oxford Handbook of American Public Opinion*, 269–83; Igo, *The Averaged American*; Theodore Lewis Glasser and Charles Salmon, eds, *Public Opinion and the Communication of Consent* (New York: Guilford Press, 1995); Mark Schmeller, *Invisible Sovereign: Imagining Public Opinion from the Revolution to Reconstruction* (Baltimore, MD: Johns Hopkins University Press, 2016); James Thompson, *British Political Culture and the Idea of 'Public Opinion', 1867–1914* (Cambridge, UK: Cambridge University Press, 2013).
5. John Durham Peters, "Historical Tensions in the Concept of Public Opinion," in *Public Opinion and the Communication of Consent*, 21.
6. Existing treatments of the concept of public opinion in international society include Hans-Martin Jaeger, "'World Opinion' and the Founding

of the UN: Governmentalizing International Politics," *European Journal of International Relations* 14, no. 4 (2008): 589–618, whose Luhmannian account picks up chronologically where this one leaves off; and the classic Hans Speier, "Historical Development of Public Opinion," *American Journal of Sociology* 55, no. 4 (January 1950): 376–88.

7. Walter Lippmann, *Public Opinion* (New York: Harcourt Brace, 1922); Lippmann, *The Phantom Public* (New York: Macmillan, 1927).
8. Judith Shklar, "Decisionism," in *Rational Decision*, ed. Carl J. Friedrich (New York: Atherton Press, 1964), 3–17.
9. Contra Daniel Bessner and Nicholas Guilhot, "How Realism Waltzed Off: Liberalism and Decisionmaking in Kenneth Waltz's Neorealism," *International Security* 40, no. 2 (Fall 2015): 87–118; Andrew Jewett, *Science, Democracy, and the American University: From the Civil War to the Cold War* (New York: Cambridge University Press, 2012).
10. For the varieties of the domestic analogy, see Hidemi Suganami, *The Domestic Analogy and World Order Proposals* (Cambridge, UK: Cambridge University Press, 1989).
11. See, generally, Jürgen Osterhammel, *The Transformation of the World: A Global History of the Nineteenth Century* (Princeton, NJ: Princeton University Press, 2014); Emily Rosenberg, ed., *A World Connecting, 1870–1945* (Cambridge, MA: Harvard University Press, 2012).
12. Brian Vick, *The Congress of Vienna: Power and Politics after Napoleon* (Cambridge, MA: Harvard University Press, 2014); Glenda Sluga, "Women, Diplomacy and International Politics, Before and After the Congress of Vienna," in *Women, Diplomacy and International Politics since 1500*, ed. Glenda Sluga and Carolyn James (London: Routledge, 2016), 120–36.
13. M. de Pradt, *The Congress of Vienna* (London: Samuel Leigh, 1816), 25.
14. C. A. Bayly and Eugenio Biagini, eds., *Giuseppe Mazzini and the Globalisation of Democratic Nationalism 1830–1920* (Oxford: Oxford University Press, 2008); Martin Ceadel, *The Origins of War Prevention: The British Peace Movement and International Relations, 1730–1854* (Oxford: Oxford University Press, 1996), chs. 6–7; Mark Mazower, *Governing the World: The History of an Idea* (New York: Penguin, 2012), chs. 1–2.
15. The phrase is from "learned blacksmith" Elihu Burritt, founder of the League of Universal Brotherhood: *People-Diplomacy, or The Mission of Friendly International Addresses Between England and France* (London: W. and F. G. Cash, 1852). See also Martin Ceadel, *Semi-Detached Idealists: The British Peace Movement and International Relations, 1854–1945* (Oxford: Oxford University Press, 2000).
16. On international organizations as vehicles for hegemonic power, see the classic F. H. Hinsley, *Power and the Pursuit of Peace: Theory and Practice in the History of Relations Between States* (Cambridge, UK: Cambridge University Press, 1963).
17. On the professionalization of international law in Europe and the United States, see Benjamin Coates, *Legalist Empire: International Law and American Foreign Relations in the Early Twentieth Century* (New York: Oxford

University Press, 2016); Mark Janis, *America and the Law of Nations, 1776–1939* (New York: Oxford University Press, 2010); Martti Koskenniemi, *The Gentle Civilizer of Nations: The Rise and Fall of International Law, 1870–1960* (Cambridge, UK: Cambridge University Press, 2001); Casper Sylvest, "International Law in Nineteenth-Century Britain," *British Year Book of International Law* 75, no. 1 (2005): 9–69.

18. Compare with Jeremy Bentham, James Mill, and their follower William Ladd, the first president of the American Peace Society: Jeremy Bentham, "A Plan for an Universal and Perpetual Peace," in *The Works of Jeremy Bentham*, ed. John Bowring, 11 vols. (Edinburgh: William Tait, 1843), vol. 2, 546–60; James Mill, "Law of Nations," in *Essays on Government, Jurisprudence, Liberty of the Press, and Law of Nations* (London: J. Innes, 1825), 3–33; William Ladd, *An Essay on a Congress of Nations for the Adjustment of International Disputes without Resort to Arms* (Boston, MA: Whipple and Damrell, 1840).

19. Gustave Rolin-Jaequemyns, "De L'étude du Droit International et de la Législation Comparée," *Reveue de Droit International et de Législation Comparée* 1 (1869): 225.

20. Koskenniemi, *Gentle Civilizer*, 41.

21. Ibid., 43–47; Betsy Baker Röben, "The Method behind Bluntschli's 'Modern' International Law," *Journal of the History of International Law* 4 (2002): 249–92.

22. Walter Bagehot, *The English Constitution* (London: Oxford University Press, 1867), 31, 50, 203, 286; see Thompson, *British Political Culture and the Idea of 'Public Opinion'*, 35–41.

23. For example, William T. Stead, "Government by Journalism," *The Contemporary Review* 49 (May 1886): 653–74.

24. Gunnell, "Democracy and the Concept of Public Opinion," 271–76.

25. Korzi, "Lapsed Memory," 51–56.

26. Francis Lieber, *Manual of Political Ethics* (Boston, MA: C. C. Little and J. Brown, 1839), pt 2, 370, 438–39.

27. Michael Lobban, "Was there a Nineteenth Century 'English School of Jurisprudence?'" *Journal of Legal History* 16, no. 1 (1995): 34–62.

28. John Austin, *The Province of Jurisprudence Determined*, ed. Wilfrid Rumble (Cambridge, UK: Cambridge University Press, 1995 [1832]), 112.

29. See J. W. Burrow, *Evolution and Society: A Study in Victorian Social Theory* (London: Cambridge University Press, 1966); Peter Stein, *Legal Evolution: The Story of an Idea* (Cambridge, UK: Cambridge University Press, 1980); Casper Sylvest, "The Foundations of Victorian International Law," in *Victorian Visions of Global Order: Empire and International Relations in Nineteenth-Century Political Thought*, ed. Duncan Bell (Cambridge, UK: Cambridge University Press, 2007), 47–66.

30. Karuna Mantena, *Alibis of Empire: Henry Maine and the Ends of Liberal Imperialism* (Princeton, NJ: Princeton University Press, 2010), 98–107.

31. John Westlake, *Chapters on the Principles of International Law* (Cambridge, UK: Cambridge University Press, 1894), 78, 84.

32. Lassa Oppenheim, "The Science of International Law: Its Task and Method," *American Journal of International Law* 2, no. 2 (April 1908): 324, 338. On Oppenheim, see Mónica García-Salmones Rovira, *The Project of Positivism in International Law* (Oxford: Oxford University Press, 2013), 43–119.
33. Westlake, *Chapters on the Principles of International Law*, 274.
34. James Brown Scott, "The Legal Nature of International Law," *American Journal of International Law* 1, no. 4 (October 1907): 847–48.
35. Emphasis added. Nicholas Murray Butler, *The International Mind: An Argument for the Judicial Settlement of International Disputes* (New York: Scribner, 1912), 98–99, 102, 105.
36. Elihu Root, "The Sanction of International Law," *American Journal of International Law* 2, no. 3 (July 1908): 452.
37. Elihu Root, "The Outlook for International Law," *American Journal of International Law* 10, no. 1 (January 1916): 6.
38. Root, "The Sanction of International Law," 452.
39. For instance, Henry Maine, *Popular Government: Four Essays* (London: J. Murray, 1886); Elihu Root, *Miscellaneous Addresses*, ed. Robert Bacon and James Brown Scott (Cambridge, MA: Harvard University Press, 1917), 275–94.
40. Carr, *The Twenty Years' Crisis*, 31.
41. William H. Taft, *The United States and Peace* (New York: Scribner, 1914), 41, 180.
42. Woodrow Wilson, Address on Unveiling the League Covenant, Paris, 14 February 1919, in Woodrow Wilson, *America and the League of Nations: Addresses in Europe* (Chicago, IL: Rand, McNally, 1919), 164.
43. Erez Manela, *The Wilsonian Moment: Self-Determination and the International Origins of Anticolonial Nationalism* (Oxford: Oxford University Press, 2007); Arno Mayer, *Political Origins of the New Diplomacy, 1917–1918* (New Haven, CT: Yale University Press, 1959).
44. David Kennedy, "The Move to Institutions," *Cardozo Law Review* 8, no. 5 (1987): 841–988.
45. George Curry, "Woodrow Wilson, Jan Smuts, and the Versailles Settlement," *The American Historical Review* 66, no. 4 (July 1961): 968–86; George Egerton, *Great Britain and the Creation of the League of Nations: Strategy, Politics, and International Organization, 1914–1919* (Chapel Hill: University of North Carolina Press, 1978), 101–5; Mark Mazower, *No Enchanted Palace: The End of Empire and the Ideological Origins of the United Nations* (Princeton, NJ: Princeton University Press, 2009), chapter 1.
46. Susan Pedersen, *The Guardians: The League of Nations and the Crisis of Empire* (New York: Oxford University Press, 2015), 27–35; I. C. Smith, "J. C. Smuts' Role in the Establishment of the League of Nations and the Mandate for S.W.A.," *South African Historical Journal* 5, no. 1 (November 1973): 94–104.
47. Minutes (English) of the Commission on the League of Nations, Ninth Meeting, 13 February 1919, in David Hunter Miller, *The Drafting of the Covenant* (New York: Putnam's Sons, 1928), vol. 2, 299–301.
48. Jan Smuts, *The League of Nations: A Practical Suggestion* (New York: The Nation Press, 1919), 31.

49. Ibid., 32, 49.
50. Ibid., 32.
51. Ibid., 31.
52. Ibid., 15.
53. Jan Smuts, *Holism and Evolution* (New York: Macmillan, 1926).
54. W. K. Hancock, *Smuts: The Sanguine Years, 1870–1919* (Cambridge, UK: Cambridge University Press, 1962), 198; Mazower, *No Enchanted Palace*, 31–39.
55. Jan Smuts, *War-Time Speeches: A Compilation of Public Utterances in Great Britain* (London: George H. Doran, 1917), vi.
56. Jan Smuts, "The Present International Outlook," *International Affairs* 14, no. 1 (January–February 1935): 17.
57. Egerton, *Great Britain and the Creation*, 95–100; Peter Yearwood, *Guarantee of Peace: The League of Nations in British Policy, 1914–1925* (Oxford: Oxford University Press, 2009), 65–73, 84–86.
58. On Zimmern's career and thought, see D. J. Markwell, "Sir Alfred Zimmern Revisited: Fifty Years On," *Review of International Studies* 12, no. 4 (October 1986): 279–92; Mazower, *No Enchanted Palace*, chapter 2; Jeanne Morefield, *Covenants Without Swords: Idealist Liberalism and the Spirit of Empire* (Princeton, NJ: Princeton University Press, 2005); Paul Rich, "Alfred Zimmern's Cautious Idealism: The League of Nations, International Education, and the Commonwealth," in *Thinkers of the Twenty Years' Crisis: Inter-War Idealism Reassessed*, ed. David Long and Peter Wilson (Oxford: Oxford University Press, 1995), 77–99.
59. Daniel Laqua, "Transnational Intellectual Cooperation, the League of Nations, and the Problem of Order," *Journal of Global History* 6, no. 2 (July 2011): 223–47.
60. Alfred Zimmern, "German Culture and the British Commonwealth," in *The War and Democracy*, ed. R. W. Seton-Watson, et al. (London: Macmillan, 1915), 374, 379.
61. Alfred Zimmern, *The League of Nations and the Rule of Law, 1918–1935* (London: Macmillan, 1935), 284.
62. Morefield, *Covenants Without Swords*, chapter 1.
63. Alfred Zimmern, "The Development of the International Mind," in *Problems of Peace: Lectures Delivered at the Geneva Institute of International Relations* (London: Oxford University Press, 1927), 4.
64. Zimmern, "The Influence of Public Opinion on Foreign Policy," in *Problems of Peace: Lectures Delivered at the Geneva Institute of International Relations* (London: Oxford University Press, 1929), 299–320.
65. Rich, "Alfred Zimmern's Cautious Idealism," 86.
66. Zimmern, "The Influence of Public Opinion on Foreign Policy," 299.
67. Notable exceptions are Lloyd Ambrosius, *Wilsonianism: Woodrow Wilson and His Legacy in American Foreign Relations* (New York: Palgrave Macmillan, 2002); John A. Thompson, *Woodrow Wilson* (London: Longman, 2002); Henry A. Turner, "Woodrow Wilson and Public Opinion," *The Public Opinion Quarterly* 21, no. 4 (Winter 1957-8): 505–20.

68. Woodrow Wilson, "Random Notes for 'The Philosophy of Politics,'" 26 January 1895, *The Papers of Woodrow Wilson*, ed. Arthur Link, 69 vols. (Princeton, NJ: Princeton University Press, 1966–1993), vol. 9, 132 (hereafter cited as *Wilson Papers*).
69. Henry Bragdon, *Wilson: The Academic Years* (Cambridge, MA: Harvard University Press, 1967), 443.
70. Bragdon, *Woodrow Wilson: The Academic Years*, 103; John Mulder, *Woodrow Wilson: The Years of Preparation* (Princeton, NJ: Princeton University Press, 1978), 75; Ronald Pestritto, *Woodrow Wilson and the Roots of Modern Liberalism* (Lanham, MD: Rowman & Littlefield, 2005), 8, 34–40, 67–94; Niels Aage Thorsen, *The Political Thought of Woodrow Wilson, 1875–1910* (Princeton, NJ: Princeton University Press, 1988), 69–70, 94.
71. Johann Bluntschli, *The Theory of the State*, 2nd ed. (Oxford: Oxford University Press, 1885), 19–20; compare with Wilson, "Lecture on Democracy," 5 December 1891, *Wilson Papers*, vol. 7, 354–55.
72. Wilson, "The Modern Democratic State," *Wilson Papers*, vol. 5, 58–92; Woodrow Wilson, *Constitutional Government in the United States* (New York: Columbia University Press, 1908), 28, 40; Woodrow Wilson, *The State* (Boston, MA: D.C. Heath, 1889), 607–9.
73. Wilson, "Lecture on Democracy," 355. Emphasis in original.
74. Wilson, "Leaders of Men," 17 June 1890, *Wilson Papers*, vol. 6, 659. Emphasis in original.
75. Ibid., 649.
76. Ibid., 650.
77. Wilson, "Lecture on Democracy," 359.
78. Wilson, *Constitutional Government*, 68.
79. Wilson, "Leaders of Men," 660; Wilson, "The Ideal Statesman," 30 January 1877, *Wilson Papers*, vol. 1, 244. See Jeffrey Tulis, *The Rhetorical Presidency* (Princeton, NJ: Princeton University Press, 1987), 129; Scot Zentner, "President and Party in the Thought of Woodrow Wilson," *Presidential Studies Quarterly* 26, no. 3 (Summer 1996): 667–68.
80. Woodrow Wilson, "Abraham Lincoln: A Man of the People," 12 February 1909, *Wilson Papers*, vol. 19, 42.
81. Woodrow Wilson, "Address to a Joint Session of Congress," 8 January 1918, *Wilson Papers*, vol. 45, 536.
82. Richard Drake, *The Education of an Anti-Imperialist: Robert La Follette and U.S. Expansion* (Madison: University of Wisconsin Press, 2013), 302. On the King-Crane Commission, see also Harry Howard, *The King-Crane Commission: An American Inquiry in the Middle East* (Beirut: Khayat, 1963); Andrew Patrick, *America's Forgotten Middle East Initiative: The King-Crane Commission of 1919* (London: I. B. Tauris, 2015).
83. Michael Reimer, "The King-Crane Commission at the Juncture of Politics and Historiography," *Middle East Critique* 15, no. 2 (Summer 2006): 134–35.
84. Drake, *The Education of an Anti-Imperialist*, 304.
85. "King-Crane Report on the Near East," *Editor & Publisher* 55, no. 27, 2nd section (2 December 1922): 1–28.

86. Megan Donaldson, "From Secret Diplomacy to Diplomatic Secrecy: Secrecy and Publicity in the International Legal Order c 1919–1950" (JSD diss., New York University School of Law, 2016), 128.
87. Isaiah Bowman, "Memorandum on Remarks by the President, 10 December 1918," *Wilson Papers*, vol. 53, 353.
88. Wilson, "Leaders of Men," 664.
89. Wilson, "Confidential Journal, December 28, 1889," *Wilson Papers*, vol. 6, 463.
90. Recent histories of the League framed around the democratization of international affairs are Thomas Davies, "A 'Great Experiment' of the League of Nations Era: International Nongovernmental Organizations, Global Governance, and Democracy Beyond the State," *Global Governance* 18, no. 4 (October–December 2012): 405–23; McCarthy, *The British People and the League of Nations*, esp. 15–78, 243–48.
91. See Sally Harris, *Out of Control: British Foreign Policy and the Union of Democratic Control, 1914–1918* (Hull: University of Hull Press, 1996); Marvin Swartz, *The Union of Democratic Control in British Politics during the First World War* (Oxford: Clarendon Press, 1971). For likeminded groups in the United States, see David Patterson, *The Search for Negotiated Peace: Women's Activism and Citizen Diplomacy in World War I* (New York: Routledge, 2008).
92. Arthur Ponsonby, *Parliament and Foreign Policy* (London: Union of Democratic Control, 1915), 1–2.
93. Union of Democratic Control, *The Morrow of the War* (London: Union of Democratic Control, 1915).
94. John de Kay, *The Spirit of the International at Berne* (Berne: John Welsey de Kay, 1919), 34–35, 83.
95. Arthur Ponsonby, *Democracy and Diplomacy: A Plea for Popular Control of Foreign Policy* (London: Meuthen, 1915), 22–33.
96. On the publicity and secrecy of treaties in the League, see Donaldson, "From Secret Diplomacy to Diplomatic Secrecy," chs. 4–5.
97. Zimmern, "The Influence of Public Opinion on Foreign Policy," 306–7.
98. Stephen Wertheim, "The League of Nations: A Retreat for International Law?" *Journal of Global History* 7, no. 2 (2012): 210–32.
99. Root to Henry Cabot Lodge, 19 June 1919, Box 161, *Elihu Root Papers*, Library of Congress, Manuscript Division, Washington, DC.
100. Quoted in David Patterson, in "The United States and the Origins of the World Court," *Political Science Quarterly* 91, no. 2 (Summer 1976): 293.
101. Alfred Zimmern, "Some Principles and Problems of the Settlement," *Round Table* 9, no. 33 (December 1918): 100–1.
102. Woodrow Wilson, "Address on Unveiling the League Covenant Draft, 14 February 1919," *America and the League of Nations: Addresses in Europe*, 165.
103. *Congressional Record*, 66th Cong., 1st Sess., 20 August 1919, 4014.
104. Thomas Davies, *NGOs: A New History of Transnational Civil Society* (New York: Oxford University Press, 2014), 77–122; Daniel Gorman, *The Emergence of International Society in the 1920s* (Cambridge, UK: Cambridge University Press, 2012).

105. Lyman Cromwell White, *The Structure of Private International Organizations* (Philadelphia, PA: George S. Ferguson, 1933), 11.
106. Helen McCarthy, *The British People and the League of Nations: Democracy, Citizenship and Internationalism, c. 1918–45* (Manchester: Manchester University Press, 2011), 4.
107. Donaldson, "From Secret Diplomacy to Diplomatic Secrecy," chapter 4; Ken Millen-Penn, "Democratic Control, Public Opinion, and League Diplomacy," *World Politics* 157, no. 4 (Spring 1995): 207–18.
108. Nathan Feinberg, "La Pétition en Droit International," *Recueil des Cours* 40 (1932): 525–644; see Natasha Wheatley, "Mandatory Interpretation: Legal Hermeneutics and the New International Order in Arab and Jewish Petitions to the League of Nations," *Past and Present* 227 (May 2015): 205–48.
109. Stellar examples include Donaldson, "From Secret Diplomacy to Diplomatic Secrecy"; Pedersen, *The Guardians*.
110. On unsuccessful attempts to supplement the League with a popular chamber, composed of representatives elected by national publics or drawn from national parliaments, see Martin Albers, "Between the Crisis of Democracy and World Parliament: The Development of the Inter-Parliamentary Union in the 1920s," *Journal of Global History* 7, no. 2 (2012): 198–203.
111. Edward Purcell, *The Crisis of Democratic Theory* (Lexington: University Press of Kentucky, 1973), 95–114; Lippmann, *Public Opinion*.
112. See Hans Morgenthau, "Théorie des Sanctions Internationales," *Revue de Droit International et de Législation Comparée* 16, nos. 3–4 (1935): 474–503, 809–36.
113. See John Herz, "The National Socialist Doctrine of International Law and the Problems of International Organization," *Political Science Quarterly* 54, no. 4 (December 1939): 536–54; Quincy Wright, ed., *Public Opinion and World-Politics* (Chicago, IL: University of Chicago Press, 1933).
114. Carnegie Endowment for International Peace, *Year Book, 1938* (Washington, DC: Carnegie Endowment for International Peace, 1938), 44.
115. Hans Morgenthau, *Politics Among Nations: The Struggle for Power and Peace* (New York: Knopf, 1948), 206.
116. Hans Morgenthau, *Scientific Man Vs. Power Politics* (Chicago, IL: University of Chicago Press, 1947), 61.
117. Morgenthau, *Politics Among Nations*, 196.

Bibliography

Primary Sources

Austin, John. *The Province of Jurisprudence Determined*. ed. Wilfrid Rumble. Cambridge, UK: Cambridge University Press, 1995 [1832].
Bagehot, Walter. *The English Constitution*. London: Oxford University Press, 1867.

Bentham, Jeremy. "A Plan for an Universal and Perpetual Peace." In *The Works of Jeremy Bentham*, edited by John Bowring, vol. 2, 546–60. Edinburgh: William Tait, 1843.

Bluntschli, Johann. *The Theory of the State*. 2nd ed. Oxford: Clarendon, 1885.

Burritt, Elihu. *People-Diplomacy, or The Mission of Friendly International Addresses Between England and France*. London: W. and F. G. Cash, 1852.

Butler, Nicholas Murray. *The International Mind: An Argument for the Judicial Settlement of International Disputes*. New York: Scribner, 1912.

Carr, E. H. *The Twenty Years' Crisis, 1919–1939*. New York: Harper & Row, 1964 [1939].

Elihu Root Papers, Library of Congress, Manuscript Division, Washington, DC.

Feinberg, Nathan. "La Pétition en Droit International." *Recueil des Cours* 40 (1932): 525–644.

Herz, John. "The National Socialist Doctrine of International Law and the Problems of International Organization." *Political Science Quarterly* 54, no. 4 (December 1939): 536–54.

de Kay, John Welsey. *The Spirit of the International at Berne*. Berne: John Welsey de Kay, 1919.

"King-Crane Report on the Near East." *Editor & Publisher* 55, no. 27, 2nd section (2 December 1922): 1–28.

Ladd, William. *An Essay on a Congress of Nations for the Adjustment of International Disputes without Resort to Arms*. Boston, MA: Whipple and Damrell, 1840.

Lieber, Francis. *Manual of Political Ethics*. Boston, MA: C. C. Little and J. Brown, 1839.

Link, Arthur, ed. *The Papers of Woodrow Wilson*. 69 vols. Princeton, NJ: Princeton University Press, 1966–1993.

Lippmann, Walter. *The Phantom Public*. New York: Macmillan, 1927.

———. *Public Opinion*. New York: Harcourt Brace, 1922.

Maine, Henry. *Popular Government: Four Essays*. London: J. Murray, 1886.

Mill, James. *Essays on Government, Jurisprudence, Liberty of the Press, and Law of Nations*. London: J. Innes, 1825.

Miller, David Hunter. *The Drafting of the Covenant*. New York: Putnam's Sons, 1928.

Morgenthau, Hans. *Politics Among Nations: The Struggle for Power and Peace*. New York: Knopf, 1948.

———. *Scientific Man Vs. Power Politics*. Chicago, IL: University of Chicago Press, 1947.

———. "Théorie des Sanctions Internationales." *Revue de Droit International et de Législation Comparée* 16, nos. 3–4 (1935): 474–503, 809–36.

Oppenheim, Lassa. "The Science of International Law: Its Task and Method." *American Journal of International Law* 2, no. 2 (April 1908): 313–56.

Ponsonby, Arthur. *Democracy and Diplomacy: A Plea for Popular Control of Foreign Policy*. London: Meuthen, 1915.

———. *Parliament and Foreign Policy*. London: Union of Democratic Control, 1915.

de Pradt, M. *The Congress of Vienna*. London: Samuel Leigh, 1816.

Rolin-Jaequemyns, Gustave. "De L'étude du Droit International et de la Législation Comparée." *Reveue de Droit International et de Législation Comparée* 1 (1869): 225–43.
Root, Elihu. *Miscellaneous Addresses.* Edited by Robert Bacon and James Brown Scott. Cambridge, MA: Harvard University Press, 1917.
———. "The Outlook for International Law." *American Journal of International Law* 10, no. 1 (January 1916): 1–11.
———. "The Sanction of International Law." *American Journal of International Law* 2, no. 3 (July 1908): 451–57.
Scott, James Brown. "The Legal Nature of International Law." *American Journal of International Law* 1, no. 4 (October 1907): 831–66.
Smuts, Jan. *Holism and Evolution.* New York: Macmillan, 1926.
———. *The League of Nations: A Practical Suggestion.* New York: The Nation Press, 1919.
———. "The Present International Outlook." *International Affairs* 14, no. 1 (January–February 1935): 3–19.
———. *War-Time Speeches: A Compilation of Public Utterances in Great Britain.* London: George H. Doran, 1917.
Speier, Hans. "Historical Development of Public Opinion." *American Journal of Sociology* 55, no. 4 (January 1950): 376–88.
Stead, William T. "Government by Journalism." *The Contemporary Review* 49 (May 1886): 653–74.
Taft, William H. *The United States and Peace.* New York: Scribner, 1914.
Union of Democratic Control. *The Morrow of the War.* London: Union of Democratic Control, 1915.
Westlake, John. *Chapters on the Principles of International Law.* Cambridge, UK: Cambridge University Press, 1894.
White, Lyman Cromwell. *The Structure of Private International Organizations.* Philadelphia, PA: George S. Ferguson, 1933.
Wilson, Woodrow. *America and the League of Nations: Addresses in Europe.* Chicago, IL: Rand, McNally, 1919.
———. *Constitutional Government in the United States.* New York: Columbia University Press, 1908.
———. *The State.* Boston, MA: D.C. Heath, 1889.
Wright, Quincy, ed. *Public Opinion and World-Politics.* Chicago, IL: University of Chicago Press, 1933.
Year Book, 1938. Washington, DC: Carnegie Endowment for International Peace, 1938. Oxford: Oxford University Press, 2009.
Zimmern, Alfred. "German Culture and the British Commonwealth." In *The War and Democracy*, edited by R. W. Seton-Watson, et al. London: Macmillan, 1915.
———. *The League of Nations and the Rule of Law, 1918–1935.* London: Macmillan, 1935.
———. *Problems of Peace: Lectures Delivered at the Geneva Institute of International Relations.* London: Oxford University Press, 1927–29.
———. "Some Principles and Problems of the Settlement." *Round Table* 9, no. 33 (December 1918): 88–113.

Secondary Sources

Albers, Martin. "Between the Crisis of Democracy and World Parliament: The Development of the Inter-Parliamentary Union in the 1920s." *Journal of Global History* 7, no. 2 (2012): 198–203.

Ambrosius, Lloyd. *Wilsonianism: Woodrow Wilson and His Legacy in American Foreign Relations*. New York: Palgrave Macmillan, 2002.

Bayly, C. A. and Eugenio Biagini, eds. *Giuseppe Mazzini and the Globalisation of Democratic Nationalism 1830–1920*. Oxford: Oxford University Press, 2008.

Beers, Laura. "Whose Opinion?: Changing Attitudes Towards Opinion Polling in British Politics, 1937–1964." *Twentieth Century British History* 17, no. 2 (2006): 177–205.

Bessner, Daniel and Nicholas Guilhot. "How Realism Waltzed Off: Liberalism and Decisionmaking in Kenneth Waltz's Neorealism." *International Security* 40, no. 2 (Fall 2015): 87–118.

Bragdon, Henry. *Wilson: The Academic Years*. Cambridge, MA: Harvard University Press, 1967.

Burrow, J. W. *Evolution and Society: A Study in Victorian Social Theory*. London: Cambridge University Press, 1966.

Ceadel, Martin. *The Origins of War Prevention: The British Peace Movement and International Relations, 1730–1854*. Oxford: Oxford University Press, 1996.

———. *Semi-Detached Idealists: The British Peace Movement and International Relations, 1854–1945*. Oxford: Oxford University Press, 2000.

Coates, Benjamin. *Legalist Empire: International Law and American Foreign Relations in the Early Twentieth Century*. New York: Oxford University Press, 2016.

Curry, George. "Woodrow Wilson, Jan Smuts, and the Versailles Settlement." *The American Historical Review* 66, no. 4 (July 1961): 968–86.

Davies, Thomas. "A 'Great Experiment' of the League of Nations Era: International Nongovernmental Organizations, Global Governance, and Democracy Beyond the State." *Global Governance* 18, no. 4 (October–December 2012): 405–23.

———. *NGOs: A New History of Transnational Civil Society*. New York: Oxford University Press, 2014.

Donaldson, Megan. "From Secret Diplomacy to Diplomatic Secrecy: Secrecy and Publicity in the International Legal Order c 1919–1950." JSD diss., New York University School of Law, 2016.

Drake, Richard. *The Education of an Anti-Imperialist: Robert La Follette and U.S. Expansion*. Madison: University of Wisconsin Press, 2013.

Edwards III, George, Lawrence Jacobs, and Robert Shapiro, eds. *The Oxford Handbook of American Public Opinion and the Media*. Oxford: Oxford University Press, 2011.

Egerton, George. *Great Britain and the Creation of the League of Nations: Strategy, Politics, and International Organization, 1914–1919*. Chapel Hill: University of North Carolina Press, 1978.

Glasser, Theodore Lewis, and Charles Salmon, eds. *Public Opinion and the Communication of Consent*. New York: Guilford Press, 1995.

Gorman, Daniel. *The Emergence of International Society in the 1920s*. Cambridge, UK: Cambridge University Press, 2012.
Hancock, W. K. *Smuts: The Sanguine Years, 1870–1919*. Cambridge, UK: Cambridge University Press, 1962.
Harris, Sally. *Out of Control: British Foreign Policy and the Union of Democratic Control, 1914–1918*. Hull: University of Hull Press, 1996.
Hinsley, F. H. *Power and the Pursuit of Peace: Theory and Practice in the History of Relations Between States*. Cambridge, UK: Cambridge University Press, 1963.
Howard, Harry. *The King-Crane Commission: An American Inquiry in the Middle East*. Beirut: Khayat, 1963.
Igo, Sarah. *The Averaged American: Surveys, Citizens, and the Making of a Mass Public*. Cambridge, MA: Harvard University Press, 2007.
Jaeger, Hans-Martin. "'World Opinion' and the Founding of the UN: Governmentalizing International Politics." *European Journal of International Relations* 14, no. 4 (2008): 589–618.
Janis, Mark. *America and the Law of Nations, 1776–1939*. New York: Oxford University Press, 2010.
Jewett, Andrew. *Science, Democracy, and the American University: From the Civil War to the Cold War*. New York: Cambridge University Press, 2012.
Kennedy, David. "The Move to Institutions." *Cardozo Law Review* 8, no. 5 (1987): 841–988.
Korzi, Michael. "Lapsed Memory? The Roots of American Public Opinion Research." *Polity* 33, no. 1 (Fall 2000): 49–73.
Koskenniemi, Martti. *The Gentle Civilizer of Nations: The Rise and Fall of International Law, 1870–1960*. Cambridge, UK: Cambridge University Press, 2001.
Laqua, Daniel. "Transnational Intellectual Cooperation, the League of Nations, and the Problem of Order." *Journal of Global History* 6, no. 2 (July 2011): 223–47.
Lobban, Michael. "Was there a Nineteenth Century 'English School of Jurisprudence?'" *Journal of Legal History* 16, no. 1 (1995): 34–62.
Manela, Erez. *The Wilsonian Moment: Self-Determination and the International Origins of Anticolonial Nationalism*. Oxford: Oxford University Press, 2007.
Mantena, Karuna. *Alibis of Empire: Henry Maine and the Ends of Liberal Imperialism*. Princeton, NJ: Princeton University Press, 2010.
Markwell, D. J. "Sir Alfred Zimmern Revisited: Fifty Years On." *Review of International Studies* 12, no. 4 (October 1986): 279–92.
Mayer, Arno. *Political Origins of the New Diplomacy, 1917–1918*. New Haven, CT: Yale University Press, 1959.
Mazower, Mark. *Governing the World: The History of an Idea*. New York: Penguin, 2012.
———. *No Enchanted Palace: The End of Empire and the Ideological Origins of the United Nations*. Princeton, NJ: Princeton University Press, 2009.
McCarthy, Helen. *The British People and the League of Nations: Democracy, Citizenship and Internationalism, c. 1918–45*. Manchester: Manchester University Press, 2011.

Millen-Penn, Ken. "Democratic Control, Public Opinion, and League Diplomacy." *World Politics* 157, no. 4 (Spring 1995): 207–18.
Morefield, Jeanne. *Covenants Without Swords: Idealist Liberalism and the Spirit of Empire.* Princeton, NJ: Princeton University Press, 2005.
Mulder, John. *Woodrow Wilson: The Years of Preparation.* Princeton, NJ: Princeton University Press, 1978.
Osterhammel, Jürgen. *The Transformation of the World: A Global History of the Nineteenth Century.* Princeton, NJ: Princeton University Press, 2014.
Patrick, Andrew. *America's Forgotten Middle East Initiative: The King-Crane Commission of 1919.* London: I. B. Tauris, 2015.
Patterson, David. *The Search for Negotiated Peace: Women's Activism and Citizen Diplomacy in World War I.* New York: Routledge, 2008.
———. "The United States and the Origins of the World Court." *Political Science Quarterly* 91, no. 2 (Summer 1976): 279–95.
Pedersen, Susan. *The Guardians: The League of Nations and the Crisis of Empire.* New York: Oxford University Press, 2015.
Pestritto, Ronald. *Woodrow Wilson and the Roots of Modern Liberalism.* Lanham, MD: Rowman & Littlefield, 2005.
Purcell, Edward. *The Crisis of Democratic Theory.* Lexington: University Press of Kentucky, 1973.
Reimer, Michael. "The King-Crane Commission at the Juncture of Politics and Historiography." *Middle East Critique* 15, no. 2 (Summer 2006): 129–50.
Rich, Paul. "Alfred Zimmern's Cautious Idealism: The League of Nations, International Education, and the Commonwealth." In *Thinkers of the Twenty Years' Crisis: Inter-War Idealism Reassessed,* edited by David Long and Peter Wilson, 77–99. Oxford: Oxford University Press, 1995.
Röben, Betsy Baker. "The Method behind Bluntschli's 'Modern' International Law." *Journal of the History of International Law* 4 (2002): 249–92.
Rosenberg, Emily, ed. *A World Connecting, 1870–1945.* Cambridge, MA: Harvard University Press, 2012.
Rovira, Mónica García-Salmones. *The Project of Positivism in International Law.* Oxford: Oxford University Press, 2013.
Schmeller, Mark. *Invisible Sovereign: Imagining Public Opinion from the Revolution to Reconstruction.* Baltimore, MD: Johns Hopkins University Press, 2016.
Shklar, Judith. "Decisionism." In *Rational Decision,* edited by Carl J. Friedrich, 3–17. New York: Atherton Press, 1964.
Sluga, Glenda. "Women, Diplomacy and International Politics, Before and After the Congress of Vienna." In *Women, Diplomacy and International Politics since 1500,* edited by Glenda Sluga and Carolyn James, 120–36. London: Routledge, 2015.
Smith, I. C. "J. C. Smuts' Role in the Establishment of the League of Nations and the Mandate for S.W.A." *South African Historical Journal* 5, no. 1 (November 1973): 94–104.
Stein, Peter. *Legal Evolution: The Story of an Idea.* Cambridge, UK: Cambridge University Press, 1980.
Suganami, Hidemi. *The Domestic Analogy and World Order Proposals.* Cambridge, UK: Cambridge University Press, 1989.

Swartz, Marvin. *The Union of Democratic Control in British Politics during the First World War*. Oxford: Clarendon Press, 1971.
Sylvest, Casper. "The Foundations of Victorian International Law." In *Victorian Visions of Global Order: Empire and International Relations in Nineteenth-Century Political Thought*, edited by Duncan Bell, 47–67. Cambridge, UK: Cambridge University Press, 2007.
———. "International Law in Nineteenth-Century Britain." *British Year Book of International Law* 75, no. 1 (2005): 9–69.
Thompson, James. *British Political Culture and the Idea of 'Public Opinion,' 1867–1914*. Cambridge, UK: Cambridge University Press, 2013.
Thompson, John A. *Woodrow Wilson*. London: Longman, 2002.
Thorsen, Niels Aage. *The Political Thought of Woodrow Wilson, 1875–1910*. Princeton, NJ: Princeton University Press, 1988.
Tulis, Jeffrey. *The Rhetorical Presidency*. Princeton, NJ: Princeton University Press, 1987.
Turner, Henry A. "Woodrow Wilson and Public Opinion." *The Public Opinion Quarterly* 21, no. 4 (Winter 1957–58): 505–20.
Vick, Brian. *The Congress of Vienna: Power and Politics after Napoleon*. Cambridge, MA: Harvard University Press, 2014.
Wertheim, Stephen. "The League of Nations: A Retreat for International Law?" *Journal of Global History* 7, no. 2 (2012): 210–32.
Wheatley, Natasha. "Mandatory Interpretation: Legal Hermeneutics and the New International Order in Arab and Jewish Petitions to the League of Nations." *Past and Present* 227 (May 2015): 205–48.
Yearwood, Peter. *Guarantee of Peace: The League of Nations in British Policy, 1914–1925*. Oxford: Oxford University Press, 2009.
Zentner, Scot. "President and Party in the Thought of Woodrow Wilson." *Presidential Studies Quarterly* 26, no. 3 (Summer 1996): 666–77.

 2

Militant Democracy as Decisionist Liberalism
Reason and Power in the Work of Karl Loewenstein
Carlo Invernizzi-Accetti and Ian Zuckerman

This chapter examines one of the ways in which the relationship between legal rationalism and political decisionism was thematized during the twentieth century by exploring the theory of "militant democracy" developed by the German émigré scholar Karl Loewenstein. Loewenstein first introduced this notion in two articles published in 1937 in the American Political Science Review in which he responded to Hitler's consolidation of power in Germany.[1] It gained much wider prominence, however, in the context of the Cold War as a justification for banning communism and other presumptively subversive organizations, both in Europe and the United States.[2] More recently, a number of European courts have employed the concept of militant democracy to justify restrictions on several forms of religious practice perceived as threatening for the stability and viability of democratic regimes.[3]

At the most abstract level, militant democracy can be defined as the legal restriction of democratic rights for the purpose of protecting democratic regimes from the threat of being overthrown legally by democratic means.[4] In other words, it is the idea that presumptive "enemies" of democracy should not be granted the legal right to participate in the democratic process if doing so runs the risk of endangering the stability of the democratic regime itself. What we show in this paper is that Loewenstein developed this concept in the context of a broader intellectual and political project whose overarching goal was to neutralize—or at least tame—the presumptively irrational element of politics associated with decisionism through an appeal to a countervailing conception of "legal rationalism." Exploring the intellectual context in which the concept of militant democracy was forged is therefore a way to examine a specific reconfiguration of the complex relation between legal rationalism and political decisionism that proved particularly influential in the course of the twentieth century.

This chapter is divided into three parts. In the first part, we provide a reconstruction of Loewenstein's overall intellectual project, drawing in particular from his magnum opus, *Political Power and the Governmental Process*.[5] This text codifies and systematizes the main ideas Loewenstein had been developing since the 1920s. These are shown to revolve around the polarity between a fundamentally "irrational" element of politics, successively associated with the notions of "radical democracy," "fascism," and "totalitarianism," and the attempt to neutralize or tame these through the "rational" means of what Loewenstein consistently referred to as "constitutionalism" or "constitutional democracy." Thus, Loewenstein's overall intellectual project can be understood as an exploration of the multiple ways in which legal rationality may keep the irrational forces, which for him constitute the substance of politics, at bay.

In the second part, we show that, despite Loewenstein's strenuous efforts to evacuate—or at least tame—the "irrational" dimension of politics, an uncanny element of political decisionism reemerges at the heart of his thought, precisely in his theory of militant democracy. The reason is because this theory is incapable of providing a juridically operational criterion to distinguish between presumptive friends and enemies of democracy, and therefore ultimately falls back into an equivocal call for a "supreme arbiter" of politics whose power of decision cannot be controlled by any prior legal norm. The unrestricted exercise of political power, which Loewenstein initially sought to expel through the front door, therefore, ultimately comes back in through the window of militant democracy. On this basis, we contend that Loewenstein's overall intellectual project is best understood as articulating a form of decisionist or authoritarian liberalism, which—although seemingly paradoxical from a purely conceptual point of view—proved to be extremely influential over the course of the ensuing decades.

To demonstrate this, in the third part of the paper, we turn to a discussion of Loewenstein's direct involvement in several US foreign policy endeavors during World War II and its immediate aftermath. In particular, we focus on his participation in the arrest and deportation of several thousand so-called subversive individuals across Latin

America during the war itself, and on his activities working for the United States administration in Germany during the post-war period. Far from being contingently related to his intellectual work, we show that these political activities, which aggressively imposed liberal constitutionalism upon civilian populations, are intimately tied to the logic of Loewenstein's thought. The theory of militant democracy and the practice of a form of authoritarian liberalism, therefore, prove to be closely related to one another.

Taming the Irrational: Loewenstein's Constitutional Theory

As the (few) commentators on Loewenstein's work have pointed out, his whole political and constitutional theory revolves around a basic polarity, which he sought to elaborate and refine throughout his intellectual career.[6] On one hand, Loewenstein construed power as a fundamentally irrational drive that is successively associated in his work with the notions of "decisionism," "emotionalism," and "autocracy." On the other hand, Loewenstein understood the basic function of constitutional design as finding ways to neutralize—or at least tame—this fundamentally irrational element of power through the rationalistic means of law. Politics, for him, was therefore essentially about the interplay between reason and unreason; law and power.

This was an approach Loewenstein shared with many of his contemporaries from Weimar Germany. The same basic polarity is, for instance, at the core of the two main forms of legitimacy that for Max Weber (under whom Loewenstein studied at Heidelberg in 1913–14) were relevant in the modern age: charismatic and legal–rational legitimacy.[7] Similarly, Carl Schmitt's entire constitutional theory revolves around the opposition between a voluntaristic conception of the "constitution-making power" and the rationalism of the liberal conception of the Rechstaat as "rule of law."[8]

Unlike these predecessors (who remained important influences on Loewenstein's thought throughout his career), however, Loewenstein was not primarily worried about the fact that the progressive rationalization of politics drains human experience of meaning and purpose.[9] His overarching concern was rather that the irrational element of political decisionism might undermine the rule of law, and thereby threaten individual rights and social peace. Loewenstein's was therefore a sort of "liberalism of fear" *ante litteram*, where constitutionalism and the rule of law play the role of "safe-guards" against the ever-present threats of political oppression and abuse.[10]

It is tempting to trace this basic theoretico-political orientation to Loewenstein's background as a Jew coming of age in Germany during the first few decades of the twentieth century—and many commentators of his work have done so.[11] It should also be noted, however, that the first articulation of this theme occurs in Loewenstein's reading of the historical experience of the French Revolution. In his doctoral dissertation of 1922, entitled *People and Parliament in the Theory of the State of the French National Assembly of 1789*,[12] Loewenstein distinguished between two rival conceptions of democracy: a "radical" one, which he traced back to Jean-Jacques Rousseau and which he believed was embodied in the modern idea of "popular sovereignty," and a "constitutional" or "representative" conception of democracy, which he traced back to the Anglo-Saxon tradition of parliamentary representation and the separation of powers. The key thesis was that radical democracy represents a threat for modern politics, because it contains within itself the germ of tyranny, whereas constitutional democracy is the only way of bringing the dangerous forces that had been unleashed by the modern revolutions under control.[13]

After Hitler's rise to power in Germany, the historical referent of Loewenstein's theoretical categories became much more immediate—and explicit. The distinction between radical and constitutional democracy was progressively reformulated in terms of a distinction between fascism and liberal, or constitutional, democracy. The core of fascism, for Loewenstein, was emotionalism, which he defined as the appeal to the masses' irrational drives and desires for the purpose of achieving one's political ends. Conversely, constitutional government is defined as "the rule of law, which guarantees rationality and calculability of administration."[14] As Loewenstein himself makes clear, the overarching purpose of most of his writings from the 1930s is to find ways of ensuring that the irrational element of fascism does not prevail over constitutional government by exploiting the inherent vulnerability of the democratic idea of collective self-government to its own detriment.[15]

Finally, in the post-war period, the distinction between fascism and constitutional government is subsumed into an even broader distinction between autocracy and constitutionalism.[16] This chimes with the Cold War preoccupation of forging a set of categories capable of identifying—and ideally establishing a link between—the twin dangers posed for constitutional democracy by fascism on one hand and bolshevism on the other. Loewenstein was in fact among the first to use the term "totalitarianism" to refer to the main political threat confronted by liberal, or constitutional, democracies starting in the early 1940s.[17] The basic underlying polarity that structured his political thought, however, remained essentially the same throughout his political career, and consisted of pitching a fundamentally irrational element of political decisionism—successively associated with radical democracy, fascism, and autocracy or totalitarianism—against the rationality and calculability of liberal constitutionalism.

The means Loewenstein recommended to keep this irrational element of politics at bay can be gleaned from his magnum opus, *Political Power and the Governmental Process*, which, as Loewenstein himself suggests, ought to be read as an extended meditation on the basic insight from Montesquieu's constitutional theory: "If powers are shared amongst the several power holders," Loewenstein writes, "the individual power holder is restrained by checks and balances; le pouvoir arrête le pouvoir, to use Montesquieu's celebrated formula."[18] The core tenet of Loewenstein's constitutional and political theory is, accordingly, the idea that power must be divided and set against itself in order to tame—or more precisely, rationalize—its fundamentally irrational core.

Analogous to other German émigré scholars writing in the United States during the second post-war period, however, Loewenstein hardened this basic insight from Montesquieu into the idea that the constitutional state must, in effect, make use of political power, despite its fundamentally "demonic" aspect, in order to limit it and control it. In his treaties on *Constitutional Reason of State* (which was published in the same year as Loewenstein's *Political Power and the Governmental Process*), for instance, Carl Joachim Friedrich wrote, "From Machiavelli to Hegel, writers on politics who were tough-minded enough to appreciate the problems of survival would readily admit that there is no such thing as absolute security. ... That is to say, security is not the absolute antithesis to risk, but can only be realized through risk-taking."[19]

In Loewenstein's and Friedrich's hands, therefore, Montesquieu's fundamental insight that "le pouvoir arrête le pouvoir" ("power stops power") is therefore transformed into the idea that constitutional regimes must "fight fire with fire," employing authoritarian and potentially even antidemocratic means to protect constitutional democracies from the threat of being undermined from within.[20] This way of understanding Loewenstein's constitutional theory raises a question that Loewenstein himself never addresses squarely in his work, despite its centrality for his argument: who is supposed to "assign the different state functions to different organs" in order to ensure "they are ultimately compelled to cooperate in producing the valid will of the state"?[21] Or, to put it in other terms: how is the rational distribution of powers, which is meant to guarantee that all the individual power holders are "restricted and controlled," to be discovered and enforced?[22]

This was not a problem Montesquieu had to confront, since he assumed that laws are "the necessary relations deriving from the nature of things." From this, it follows that all the most important distinctions between the different "powers" he sought to set against each other were implicit in the nature of law itself.[23] This assumption was in turn sustained by Montesquieu's essentially providential conception of history, which allowed him to take for granted that the spontaneous interplay of the forces at work in human history would naturally tend toward the rational equilibrium he had uncovered in his examination of the spirit of the laws.[24] Thus, for Montesquieu, the question of who was supposed to impose the rational equilibrium among competing powers could not emerge because it was already resolved in advance by the assumption that such a rational order was implicit in the nature of law itself.

Loewenstein could not share Montesquieu's optimism. Living in a very different historical period and having first-hand experience of Hitler's rise to power in Germany, he was acutely aware that the spontaneous interplay between historical forces need not necessarily lead to a rational distribution of powers, but could also have catastrophic outcomes. This is stated very clearly in a troubled—and troubling—passage from the very last page of Loewenstein's *Political Power and the Governmental Process*, in which he writes:

> Unless human ingenuity in politics, which invented the representative technique, the separation of functions and the political party, devises a new approach, the danger threatens that the immensely delicate and complex plural mechanism will get stalled and break down. ... Ultimately—this can be safely predicted—the superbly organized anarchy of the intermediary bodies, political parties as well as socioeconomic interest groups and "oligopolies" will have to be brought under social control.[25]

The reason this is a troubling passage from Loewenstein's own perspective is that the idea of bringing the "superbly organized anarchy," which guarantees the rationality of political outcomes, "under social control" seems to involve the reintroduction of a concentrated and unrestricted layer of political power as the guarantor of the very system that was designed to exclude precisely such a form of power. This becomes explicit when Loewenstein adds:

> It is this writer's considered opinion that one of the crucial issues confronting the state society in the mid-twentieth century is that of overcoming

the untrammeled laissez-faire pluralism of our age by integrating the plural groups, parties as well as interest groups into the social process through effective and socially enforceable legal arrangements. How this fundamental reform of our contemporary social state can be brought about is beyond his knowledge or imagination. But one thing appears certain to him: a supreme arbiter between the competing social forces that dominate the power process and choke the individual must move in, and this can be none other than the state itself.[26]

A text that had begun by asserting that the fundamental task of constitutional theory is to find ways of taming and controlling the untrammelled exercise of political power, therefore, ironically, ends with a call for a "supreme arbiter" of politics as a necessary means to achieve that purpose. It would be hard to think of a starker example of "dialectical self-contradiction" in Hegel's sense: whereas the original goal was for reason to assert itself over power through law, in the final analysis, this proves to be possible only by reinstating the sovereignty of power over reason in the form of a "supreme arbiter" or law. In order to better uncover the logic that drives this dialectic in Loewenstein's thought—and to show that this is not merely an accidental consequence of an error or deficiency on his part, but rather a logically necessary outcome of the way in which he set out the problem from the start—it is useful to turn back to the specific conceptual innovation for which Loewenstein's work has remained most famous and influential: his theory of militant democracy.

In the following section, we turn to a more detailed discussion of this idea in order to demonstrate that the principle of militant democracy is merely a specific application of the more general logic of Loewenstein's constitutional theory, and accordingly, displays the same internal contradictions in an even more acute form.

The Return of the Repressed: Loewenstein's Theory of the Militant Democracy

Loewenstein originally introduced the concept of militant democracy in a series of two articles published in the *American Political Science Review* in 1937 that responded to Hitler's rise to power in Germany. In these texts, Hitler's movement is presented as a particular instantiation of a wider "fascist movement" that is said to have already asserted its dominance in several other European countries, but also threatens constitutional democracy "all over the world."[27] Its core feature is said to consist of the use of "emotional methods," such as "high-pitched nationalist enthusiasm" and "permanent psychic coercion," which amount to "intimidation and terrorization, scientifically applied."[28]

The central thesis is that modern constitutional democracies are particularly vulnerable to the threat posed by this form of "emotionalism" because the alliance between constitutionalism and democracy implies that the people could potentially use their sovereign power to overthrow the constitutional order—and therefore democracy itself. From this, Loewenstein infers what is probably the most famous line from his whole political oeuvre: "Fascism could only be victorious under the extraordinary conditions offered by democratic institutions. Its success is based on its perfect adjustment to democracy. Democracy and democratic tolerance have been used for their own destruction."[29]

In light of this diagnosis, Loewenstein recommends that existing constitutional–democratic regimes become "militant," describing this as a sort of "self-abnegation" of democracy involving the denial of "the full use of free institutions" to those seeking to overturn them. In practice, for him, this meant "restricting the rights of freedom of speech, the press, assembly and political participation" of political actors who used emotional techniques to manipulate the masses to support them. "It is the exaggerated formalism of the rule of law," Loewenstein writes, "which under the enchantment of formal equality does not see fit to exclude from the democratic game the parties that deny the very existence of its rules."[30]

Loewenstein explicitly frames his conception of militant democracy as a species of "emergency powers"—i.e., as a set of temporary, exceptional measures intended to overcome a diagnosed crisis and return to the status quo ante. For instance, he states that, traditionally, "the liberal-democratic order reckons with normal times," whereas in 1937, Western democracy found itself in a "state of war," or a "virtual state of siege," in which it confronted existential threats. Loewenstein considers institutionalized rights part of political normalcy whose "temporary suspension is justified" during an emergency.[31] In this sense, militant democracy suspends basic democratic rights of participation for the sake of the very democratic order established by those rights. And yet, it is clear from Loewenstein's own analysis that militant democracy cannot be a temporary, self-abolishing emergency power that returns to the constitutional status quo ante.

This emerges when we consider that militant democracy effectively involves the authorization of whatever agency is empowered to arbitrarily decide who is to be allowed to participate in the democratic game and who isn't. Thus, the very thing that was to be expelled from the start—the exercise of a form of political power that is not controlled by any prior rational or calculable law—comes back in through the window of militant democracy. To see why this is the case, consider how the relevant decision over who is to be allowed to participate in the democratic game is to be made by whatever authority is entitled to do so.

Clearly, the distinction between "emotionalism" and "constitutional government" is incapable of providing a juridically operational criterion to establish who is to be treated as a legitimate target of militant democracy, since all political actors within a democratic framework must necessarily make use of emotional cues and strategies to compete for power.[32] But the problem is deeper. For, if we start from the assumption that democracy is a regime based on the principle of popular sovereignty, as Loewenstein does, it follows that any decision over who to include or exclude from participation in the democratic game must ultimately be a decision over the boundaries of the "political entity" in Carl Schmitt's sense. And, as Schmitt demonstrates in his *Constitutional Theory*, this decision, by definition, cannot be taken in a rational or calculable way because the very idea of democracy presupposes that the boundaries of the demos are already defined.[33]

Thus, the question of who is entitled to establish who is allowed to participate in democratic governance—in Schmitt's terms, the decision over who is a friend or an enemy of the regime in question—is not merely an accidental detail of Loewenstein's theory of militant democracy, but rather another way of posing what Schmitt would have described as the "unavoidable" question of sovereignty.[34] In this sense, an element of Schmittian decisionism reemerges at the very core of a theory that Loewenstein had initially set out to develop precisely in order to keep such forms of "irrationalism" at bay.[35]

The same point also emerges if we dig deeper into the conceptual status of the notion of "emotionalism." In addition to his worries about the strength and power of fascism's emotional appeal, Loewenstein held even more pessimistic views about democracy's own ideological–emotional hold among the masses. This was not just a contingent feature of Loewenstein's theory of democracy, but rather a consequence of his definition of democracy as the rule of law, characterized above all by "rationality" and "calculability in administration."[36] Like his mentor Max Weber, Loewenstein did not believe in any form of democratic legitimacy apart from the charismatic type that he reframed as emotionalism.[37] Since constitutional democracy eschews emotionalism, the only form of legitimacy available to it is rational–legal, a weaker source of legitimacy than the charismatic one.[38] This weakened form of legitimacy helps explain Loewenstein's emphasis on democracy's extreme fragility: "Democracy is utterly incapable of meeting an emotional attack by an emotional counter-attack. Constitutional government, by its very nature, can appeal only to reason; it never could successfully mobilize emotionalism."[39]

As reason's political valiance collapsed in the age of mass politics, democracy, left with no other source of legitimacy, found itself at a loss:

> The emotional past of early liberalism and democracy cannot be revived. Nowadays, people do not want to die for liberty. ... As a rational system, democracy can prove its superiority only by its achievements, which are obfuscated by economic distress and discredited by social shortcomings. The values of liberty seem secure, with the result that to many they appear worn out by routine, faded, pale, and glamourless.[40]

In other words, because democracy lacks an emotional core, it can only establish its legitimacy through beneficial outcomes, which, due to a variety of historically contingent circumstances, are sometimes lacking. And even where its achievements are obvious and secure, democracy nonetheless can seem boring and routine because of its inability to generate meaning. This deeply pessimistic appraisal of democracy's capacities is an outcome of Loewenstein's adoption of Weber's legitimacy typology. In doing so, Loewenstein assimilated democratic legitimacy to legal–rational legitimacy, and interpreted the latter not as an ideal type but an empirically exhaustive category.

Loewenstein is thus forced to conclude that democracy must somehow be sustained without democrats. In other words, democratic institutions and procedures must be propped up without a reliable mass constituency of democratic citizens who can be counted on to believe in democracy for its own sake. For example, Loewenstein points out that in order to fully secure democracy, "it would be necessary to remove the causes, that is, to change the mental structure of this age of the masses and of rationalized emotion."[41] Such a task, of course, cannot succeed, because "rationalist" democracy means precisely eschewing the capacity to transform the mentalities and emotional commitments of the masses. Loewenstein's conclusion is harsh, but in his opinion, "realistic"—we must open our eyes, he writes, "to the fact that liberal democracy, suitable, in the last analysis, only for the political aristocrats among the nations, is beginning to lose the day to the awakened masses."[42]

Since a properly democratic emotionalism is unavailable to Loewenstein, the only solution to the threat posed by fascism and communism to liberal governance is to take a hard turn to authoritarianism on behalf of democracy itself. This, he insists, will require the new instrumentalities of "disciplined" or even—let us not shy from the word—"authoritarian democracy." The necessity of such authoritarian democracy is set out in Loewenstein's gloomy diagnosis of democracy's predicament. Whether the change from procedural to protected democracy is accomplished through constitutional or statutory means, Loewenstein concludes, "Democracy has to be redefined. It should be—at least for the transitional stage until a better social adjustment to the conditions of the technological age has been accomplished—the application of disciplined authority, by liberal-minded men, for the ultimate ends of liberal government: human dignity and freedom."[43]

It is clear, therefore, that this redefinition of democracy that Loewenstein calls for cannot fit without contradiction into the framework of temporary emergency powers which return to the status quo ante as conventionally understood.[44] This is because the causes of the crisis are themselves not temporary. Rather, they are rooted in Loewenstein's truncated understanding of the nature of democracy itself as limited to legal–rational legitimacy; his understanding of fascism and communism in terms of theories that emphasize the inherent irrationality of the masses and crowd psychology; and his tendency to think of such mass irrationality in terms of world historical developments of the spirit. Together, these core beliefs necessarily mean that the crisis facing democracy is fundamental and will persist for the foreseeable future. Militant democracy, while superficially packaged as a temporary emergency power, clearly must take a more permanent and ongoing form, which Loewenstein offers in his call for a fundamental shift to a "protected" or managed democracy that remains disciplined by liberal minded men over the irrational masses.

Far from being a merely abstract conceptual problem, Loewenstein's conclusions about the necessity of protected democracy have had concrete political consequences, not least because of the significant influence exercised by Loewenstein's theory of militant democracy on European and American politics in the second half of the twentieth century. To illustrate this, in the following section we discuss some of the practical political endeavors Loewenstein himself was involved in during and after World War II.

Militant Democracy in Practice: Toward a Notation of Authoritarian Liberalism?

One reason Loewenstein offers an especially interesting case study for the reconfiguration of decisionist theory is that he was not only an extremely influential author and theorist, he was also, as Rober

Kostal notes, "committed to the ethic of 'praxis,' of ideas in action."[45] At two different junctures—first, as part as the Emergency Advisory Committee for Political Defense (CPD) during World War II, and second, as a member of the Office of Military Government in the occupation of Germany in 1945—Loewenstein was directly involved in political projects at a sufficiently high level, providing him insight into how he could put his ideas into practice.

The CPD had its origins in a pan-American diplomatic mission that began in 1942 to combat the Axis influence throughout Latin America. Led by diplomats and legal scholars, some twenty-one North, Central, and South American countries coordinated their efforts to deport and intern citizens who were suspected of disloyalty and who were of predominantly Japanese, German, and Italian origin. Substantially surpassing its better-known counterpart (the internment of Japanese Americans on the US West Coast), the CPD eventually interned and deported nearly ten thousand Latin American nationals who were housed in camps spread across the states of Texas and Montana. Of these detainees, most were deported back to Europe and Japan regardless of citizenship at the war's end, many never seeing home again.[46]

Loewenstein played a significant role in designing the CPD's program, coordinating legal and political research and guiding US diplomats in the construction of the internment. The results, as Udi Greenberg notes in his history of the episode, was "militant democracy incarnate."[47] In a series of studies originally commissioned by the CPD on Chile, Brazil, and Argentina, Loewenstein praised these governments for banning "totalitarian and anti-government organizations" not only on the far right but on the left as well. His praise was especially high for the autocratic and repressive Vargas regime in Brazil, which banned all foreigners outright from forming associations, conducting rallies, or engaging in political expression.[48]

Loewenstein's views were particularly emphatic on the question of citizenship. While some members of the CPD delegation, such as Mexico, held citizenship to be an inalienable right that could not be revoked, Loewenstein argued that citizenship should be seen as conditional on the individual's loyalty to the democratic order. Not only was the democratic state entitled to strip citizenship from disloyal persons, it was actually sufficient, he argued, to show that a person had "mental reservations or other fraudulent intent at the time of taking the oath of allegiance."[49]

Thus, Loewenstein saw his work for the CPD as a faithful rendering of militant democracy in action. As Udi Greenberg puts it, "Latin America ... became the site where Loewenstein's ideas from Weimar directly informed U.S. diplomacy."⁵⁰ In addition, Greenberg emphasizes another characteristic of the CPD that mirrors Loewenstein's own theoretical rendering of decisionistic democracy. For him, the CPD was not a dictatorial or authoritarian program but an emphatically democratic one. The reason is that Loewenstein considered the liberal democratic project in Latin America as one that stood in need of sturdy guidance, disciplined authority, and a firm hand. He thus regarded extraordinary violations of the basic rights of thousands of Latin Americans not as a decisionistic abrogation of democratic principles, but as an exemplar of them.

Loewenstein enjoyed another opportunity to translate militant democratic theory into practice in August 1945 when he joined the US occupation administration in Germany as a senior advisor to the Legal Division of the Office of Military Government, United States (OMGUS) in Berlin. On questions such as de-Nazification of the German administrative state of even low ranking party functionaries, Loewenstein argued strenuously that, even in the face of total military defeat, Germans were "sick" and wholly unprepared for self-government. As late as 1950, Loewenstein affirmed that "the authoritarian predisposition of the Germans had changed very little during four years of Allied military occupation. ... even the West Germans were merely 'going through the motions of democracy'" and required militant supra-democratic oversight.⁵¹

Although perhaps unsurprising, what is nevertheless interesting about Loewenstein's conviction about the superficiality of West German democracy, and bears emphasis in our context, is that it enacts the same paradox that Loewenstein was to encounter theoretically in *Political Power and the Governmental Process*—namely, the problem of who is to impose the distribution of powers so that they will result in a rational outcome. When Loewenstein confronted this question in practice, his answer was unequivocal: such a distribution can be and must only be imposed externally by the unified sovereign power, in this case the occupying force. Thus, Loewenstein saw no contradiction between his conviction that the Americans should act as political sovereign and impose a democratic order on a German population, and his belief that Germans would remain "sick" and fundamentally undemocratic for the foreseeable future. As with his enthusiasm for internment and deportation in Latin America, the notion of militant democracy allowed Loewenstein to advocate for straightforwardly authoritarian and decisionistic political forms as an instantiation of the logical prerequisites of democracy itself. Both in theory and in practice, Loewenstein's militant democracy shows itself to be more than just a repressive form of emergency powers. Rather, in framing decisionistic repression as a necessary condition for the existence of the democratic order, the theory of militant democracy represents an example of how decisionism came to be reformulated in the post-war period as an intrinsic element of liberal democratic politics itself.

Conclusion

There is a substantial coherence that unites Loewenstein's work from the 1920s to the 1960s. An element of this intellectual continuity is that certain basic paradoxes emerge in all stages of his career, none of which Loewenstein ever acknowledges or openly confronts. One of these paradoxes stems from Loewenstein's tendency to avoid defending authoritarian measures—such as the internment of thousands of suspected "disloyals" on the basis of ancestry alone, or his advocacy of stripping citizenship for imputed disloyalty, or his view that the German public will remain undemocratic for the foreseeable future—as necessary, per se. Rather, the theoretical architecture of militant democracy allows him to advocate for such measures as democratic requirements for the defense of liberal governance. The massive, wholesale violation of the basic rights of thousands was not for Loewenstein an authoritarian measure, but rather evidence of impressive democratic zeal and militancy. In this way, Loewenstein's subsuming of authoritarian practice into the terminology of democracy prefigured an important rhetorical theme in the Cold War and beyond.

A second paradox emerges from Loewenstein's enfeebled definition of democracy and his concomitant assumptions about the irrationality and antidemocratic emotionalism of the masses. These premises led Loewenstein to conclude that democracy in the twentieth century must sustain itself without democrats, a state of affairs that required not only the imposition of temporary emergency powers but also a permanent authoritarian infrastructure within which democracy could be housed and preserved. From this perspective, the consequences of Loewenstein's theory appear to be the very inverse of the project he hoped would preserve democracy in an antidemocratic age. Rather, Loewenstein's militant democracy succeeds at providing a putative democratic legitimacy to fundamentally antidemocratic forms of decisionism. In doing so, he breathed new life into authoritarian decisionism in an era in which explicitly nondemocratic forms of political rule had been discredited.

Carlo Invernizzi-Accetti is Assistant Professor of Political Theory at the City College of the City University of New York and Associate Researcher at the Center for European Studies of Sciences Po, Paris. He is the author of *Relativism and Religion: Why Democratic Societies Do Not Need Moral Absolutes* (Columbia University Press, 2015); *What Is Christian Democracy? The Forgotten Ideology* (Cambridge University Press, forthcoming); and *Between Populism and Technocracy: Politics in the Age of the Crisis of Party Democracy* (coauthored with Christopher Bickerton, Oxford University Press, forthcoming).

Ian Zuckerman (PhD 2012, Columbia University) is a Postdoctoral Fellow in the Thinking Matters program at Stanford University. He has published articles and book chapters on the history of modern political thought, democratic theory, and constitutional thought. He is currently at work on a book entitled *The Politics of Emergencies*, which examines the intersection of emergency powers and the idea of security in modern constitutional theory and practice in the United States.

Notes

1. Karl Loewenstein, "Militant Democracy and Fundamental Rights," *American Political Science Review* 31, nos. 3 and 4 (1937): 417–432.
2. For historical remarks on the successive uses of the concept of "militant democracy" in European and American jurisprudence, see A. Sajò, ed., *Militant Democracy* (Utrecht: Eleven International Publishing, 2004); M. Thiel, ed., *The "Militant Democracy" Principle in Modern Democracies* (London: Ashgate, 2007); M. Klamt, "Militant Democracy and the Democratic Dilemma: Different Ways of Protecting Democratic Constitutions," in *Explorations in Legal Cultures*, ed. F. Bruinsma, D. Nelken (The Hague: Elsevier, 2008); and C. Invernizzi-Accetti and I. Zuckerman, "What's Wrong with Militant Democracy," *Political Studies* 65 no. 1 (2017): 182–199.
3. For discussions of the application of the concept of militant democracy to religious practice in recent European jurisprudence, see P. Harvey, "Militant Democracy and the European Convention on Human Rights," *European Law Review* 29 (2004): 407–420; C. Evans, "Islamic Scarf in the European Court of Human Rights," *Melbourne Journal of International Law* 52 (2006): 52–73; and P. Macklem, "Guarding the Perimeter: Militant Democracy and Religious Freedom in Europe," *Constellations* 19, no. 4 (2012): 575–590.
4. For further discussions of the definition of militant democracy, see also G. Nolte and G. Fox, "Intolerant Democracies," *Harvard International Law Journal* 36, no. 1 (1995): 1–70; P. Niesen, "Anti-Extremism, Negative

Republicanism, Civil Society: Three Paradigms for Banning Political Parties," *German Law Journal* 3, no. 7 (2002): 81–112; S. Issacharoff, "Fragile Democracies," *Harvard Law Review* 120, no. 6 (2007): 1405–1467; J. W. Muller, "A 'Practical Dilemma Which Philosophy Alone Cannot Resolve'? Rethinking Militant Democracy," *Constellations* 19, no. 4 (2012): 536–539; A. Bourne, "The Proscription of Parties and the Problem with Militant Democracy," *The Journal of Comparative Law* 7, no. 1 (2012): 196–213.; G. Capoccia, "Militant Democracy: The Institutional Bases of Democratic Self-Preservation," *Annual Review of Law and Social Sciences* 9 (2013): 207–226; A. Kirshner, *A Theory of Militant Democracy: The Ethics of Combatting Political Extremism* (New Haven, CT: Yale University Press, 2014); as well as Invernizzi-Accetti and Zuckerman, "What's Wrong with Militant Democracy."

5. For a discussion of the editorial vicissitudes of this text, see Karl Loewenstein, "Author's Preface," in *Political Power and the Governmental Process* (Chicago, IL: University of Chicago Press, 1957).

6. For an overview of the existing secondary literature on Loewenstein's work, see M. Lang, "Karl Loewenstein: From Public Law to Political Science" in *German Scholars in Exile*, ed. A. Fair-Schulz and M. Kessler (City: Lexington Books, 2011); R. W. Kostal, "The Alchemy of Occupation: Karl Loewenstein and the Legal Reconstruction of Nazi Germany, 1945–1946," *Law and History Review* 29 (2011): 1–52; U. Greenberg, "Individual Liberties and Militant Democracy: Karl Loewenstein and Aggressive Liberalism," in *The Weimar Century: German Emigrés and the Ideological Foundations of the Cold War*, ed. NAME (Princeton, NJ: Princeton University Press, 2014); Werner Sollors, "Dilemmas of Denazification: Karl Loewenstein, Carl Schmitt, Military Occupation, and Militant Democracy" in *The Temptation of Despair*, ed. NAME (Cambridge, MA: Harvard University Press, 2014); A. Kornhauser, *Debating the American State: Liberal Anxieties and the New Leviathan 1930–1970* (City: University of Pennsylvania Press, 2015).

7. On this point, see, for instance, Max Weber, "Politics as a Vocation," in *From Max Weber: Essays in Sociology* (Oxford: Oxford University Press, 1958).

8. Carl J. Schmitt, *Constitutional Theory* (City: Duke University Press, 2008).

9. For a fuller exposition of this reading of Weber's—and especially Schmitt's—political theory, see, for instance, J. McCormick, *Carl Schmitt's Critique of Liberalism: Against Politics as Technology* (Cambridge, UK: Cambridge University Press, 1995). See also Duncan Kelly, *The State of the Political: Conceptions of Politics and the State in the Thought of Max Weber, Carl Schmitt and Franz Neumann* (Oxford: Oxford University Press, 2003).

10. Judith Shklar, "The Liberalism of Fear," in *Political Thought and Political Thinkers* (Chicago, IL: University of Chicago Press, 1998).

11. See, for instance, Ben Plache, "Soldiers for Democracy: Karl Loewenstein and John H. Herz, Militant Democracy and the Defense of the Democratic State," *Virginia Commonwealth University Scholars Compass* (2013), available at https://scholarscompass.vcu.edu/cgi/viewcontent.cgi?referer=https://

www.google.it/&httpsredir=1&article=3994&context=etd (last accessed 19 July 2018).
12. Karl Loewenstein, *Volk und Parlament nach der Staatstheorie der Französischen Nationalversammlung von 1789*, (Drei Masken Verlag, 1922).
13. Ibid., esp. 89–224.
14. Karl Loewenstein, "Militant Democracy and Fundamental Rights," 418. On the same point, see also Karl Loewenstein, "Dictatorship and the German Constitution," *University of Chicago Law Review* 4, no. 4 (1937): 537–574; and Karl Loewenstein, "Legislative Control of Political Extremism in European Democracies," *Columbia Law Review* 38, no. 4 (1938): 725–774.
15. More on this later. Cf. Section II.
16. Loewenstein, *Political Power and the Governmental Process*, 4.
17. On this point, see in particular Greenberg, "Individual Liberties and Militant Democracy," 176–81.
18. Loewenstein, *Political Power and the Governmental Process*, 49.
19. Carl J. Friedrich, *Constitutional Reason of State* (Brown University Press, 1957).
20. The expression "fighting fire with fire" was first used explicitly by Loewenstein in his second article from 1937, "Militant Democracy and Fundamental Rights," published in the *American Political Science Review*. It is then taken up and used at several junctions also in *Political Power and the Governmental Process*.
21. Loewenstein, *Political Power and the Governmental Process*, 49.
22. Ibid., 70–72.
23. C. Montesquieu, *The Spirit of the Laws* (Cambridge University Press, 1989).
24. D. Carrithers, M. Mosher, P. Rahe, eds., *Montesquieu's Science of Politics: Essays on The Spirit of the Laws* (Rowman and Littlefield, 2011). See also: Alexander Hirschmann, *The Passions and the Interests: Political Arguments for Capitalism Before Its Triumph* (Princeton, NJ: Princeton University Press, 1977).
25. Loewenstein, *Political Power and the Governmental Process*, 384.
26. Ibid., 384.
27. Loewenstein, "Militant Democracy and Fundamental Rights," 417–18.
28. Ibid., 418.
29. Ibid., 423.
30. Ibid., 424.
31. Ibid., 432.
32. As several commentators have already pointed out (Cf. Sajò), the most plausible way of making sense of the distinction between "emotionalism" and "constitutional government" in Loewenstein's work is in terms of the Weberian categories of "charismatic" and "legal–rational" forms of authority, which Loewenstein seems to allude to directly in his definition of constitutional government as a way of guaranteeing the "rationality and calculability of administration." However, the comparison with Weber also reveals precisely what is wrong with Loewenstein's attempt to use such categories as juridical tools. For in Weber's work, "legal–rational" and "charismatic" authority are posited as "ideal-types," not as concrete

phenomena in the world. Their purpose is therefore to provide categories for a sociological interpretation of reality, not for drawing juridical distinctions. Thus, Weber makes clear that most concrete cases usually involve elements of *both* legal–rational and charismatic authority.

33. Schmitt, *Constitutional Theory*.
34. Ibid., 238.
35. For a further analysis of the complex intellectual—but also historical—relationship between Loewenstein and Schmitt, see also Sollors, "Dilemmas of Denazification."
36. Loewenstein, "Militant Democracy and Fundamental Rights," 418.
37. On the absence of a theory of democratic legitimacy in Max Weber, see T. Show, "Max Weber on Democracy: Can the People Have Political Power in Modern States?," *Constellations* 15, 1 (2008): 33–45.
38. Loewenstein, "Militant Democracy and Fundamental Rights," 418
39. Ibid., 428.
40. Ibid.
41. Ibid., 657
42. Recent scholars have traced this idea to the work of other contemporaneous German émigrés. See, for example, D. Bessner and N. Guilhot, "How Realism Waltzed Off," *International Security* 40, no. 2 (2015): 41–79; D. Bessner, *Democracy in Exile* (forthcoming)
43. Loewenstein, "Militant Democracy and Fundamental Rights," 659.
44. See, for example, C. Rossiter, *Constitutional Dictatorship* (Princeton, NJ: Princeton University Press, 1948).
45. Robert Kostal, "The Alchemy of Occupation: Karl Loewenstein and the Legal Reconstruction of Nazi German, 1945–1946: *Law and History Review* 29, no 1 (2011): 3.
46. Greenberg, "Individual Liberties and Militant Democracy," 194. This section in general is highly indebted to Greenberg's book.
47. Ibid., 190.
48. Ibid., 191. Karl Loewenstein, "Legislation against Subversive Activities in Argentina," *Harvard Law Review* (1943): 1261–1306; Karl Loewenstein, "Legislation in the Defense of the State in Chile," *Columbia Law Review* (1944): 366–407; Karl Loewenstein, *Brazil under Vargas* (New York: Macmillan, 1942), 133–234.
49. Greenberg, "Individual Liberties and Militant Democracy," 195.
50. Ibid., 198. See also: K. Hanshew, *Terror and Democracy in West Germany* (Cambridge University Press, 2012), 34–67 and Kostal, "Alchemy of Occupation."
51. Kostal, "Alchemy of Occupation," 52.

Bibliography

Bessner, Daniel. *Democracy in Exile: Hans Speier and the Rise of the Defense Intellectual*. Ithaca, NY: Cornell University Press, forthcoming.

Bessner, Daniel, and Nicolas Guilhot. "How Realism Waltzed Off," *International Security* 40 no. 2 (2015): 41–79.

Bourne, Angela. "The Proscription of Parties and the Problem with Militant Democracy," *The Journal of Comparative Law* 7, no. 1 (2012): 196–213.

Capoccia, Giovanni. "Militant Democracy: The Institutional Bases of Democratic Self-Preservation," *Annual Review of Law and Social Sciences* 9 (2013): 207–226.

Carrithers, Davic, Michael Mosher, and Paul Rahe, eds. *Montesquieu's Science of Politics: Essays on the Spirit of the Laws*. Lanham, MD: Rowman and Littlefield, 2011.

Evans, Carolyn. "Islamic Scarf in the European Court of Human Rights." *Melbourne Journal of International Law* 52 (2006): 52–73.

Friedrich, Carl Joachim. *Constitutional Reason of State*. Providence, RI: Brown University Press, 1957.

Greenberg, Udi. "Individual Liberties and Militant Democracy: Karl Loewenstein and Aggressive Liberalism." In Udi Greenberg, *The Weimar Century: German Emigrés and the Ideological Foundations of the Cold War*, Princeton, NJ: Princeton University Press, 2014: 169–210.

Hanshew, Karrin. *Terror and Democracy in West Germany*. Cambridge, UK: Cambridge University Press, 2012.

Harvey, Paul. "Militant Democracy and the European Convention on Human Rights." *European Law Review* 29 (2004): 407–420.

Hirschmann, Alexander. *The Passions and the Interests: Political Arguments for Capitalism Before Its Triumph*. Princeton, NJ: Princeton University Press, 1977.

Invernizzi-Accetti, Carlo, and Ian Zuckerman. "What's Wrong with Militant Democracy." *Political Studies* 65, no 1 (2017): 182–199.

Issacharoff, Samuel. "Fragile Democracies." *Harvard Law Review* 120, no. 6 (2007): 1405–1467.

Kelly, Duncan. *The State of the Political: Conceptions of Politics and the State in the Thought of Max Weber, Carl Schmitt and Franz Neumann*. Oxford: Oxford University Press, 2003.

Kirshner, Alexander. *A Theory of Militant Democracy: The Ethics of Combatting Political Extremism*. New Haven, CT: Yale University Press, 2014.

Klamt, Martin. "Militant Democracy and the Democratic Dilemma: Different Ways of Protecting Democratic Constitutions." In *Explorations in Legal Cultures*, edited by F. Bruinsma and D. Nelken, 133–159. The Hague: Elsevier, 2008.

Kornhauser, Anne. *Debating the American State: Liberal Anxieties and the New Leviathan 1930–1970*. Philadelphia: University of Pennsylvania Press, 2015.

Kostal, Robert. "The Alchemy of Occupation: Karl Loewenstein and the Legal Reconstruction of Nazi Germany, 1945–1946." *Law and History Review* 29, (2011): 1–52.

Lang, Markus. "Karl Loewenstein: From Public Law to Political Science." In *German Scholars in Exile*, edited by A. Fair-Schulz and M. Kessler, 19–50. Lanham, MD: Lexington Books, 2011.

Loewenstein, Karl. *Brazil under Vargas*. New York: Macmillan, 1942.

———. "Dictatorship and the German Constitution." *University of Chicago Law Review* 4, no. 4 (1937): 537–574.
———. "Legislation against Subversive Activities in Argentina." *Harvard Law Review* (1943): 1261–1306.
———. "Legislation in the Defense of the State in Chile." *Columbia Law Review* (1944): 366–407.
———. "Legislative Control of Political Extremism in European Democracies." *Columbia Law Review* 38, no. 4 (1938): 725–774.
———. "Militant Democracy and Fundamental Rights." *American Political Science Review* 31, nos. 3 and 4 (1937): 417–432.
———. *Political Power and the Governmental Process*. Chicago, IL: University of Chicago Press, 1957.
———. *Volk und Parlament nach der Staatstheorie der Französischen Nationalversammlung von 1789*. Munich: Drei Masken Verlag, 1922.
Macklem, Patrick. "Guarding the Perimeter: Militant Democracy and Religious Freedom in Europe." *Constellations* 19, no. 4 (2012): 575–590.
McCormick, John. *Carl Schmitt's Critique of Liberalism: Against Politics as Technology*. Cambridge, UK: Cambridge University Press, 1995.
Montesquieu, Charles de Secondat. *The Spirit of the Laws*. Cambridge, UK: Cambridge University Press, 1989.
Muller, Jan-Werner. "A 'Practical Dilemma Which Philosophy Alone Cannot Resolve'? Rethinking Militant Democracy." *Constellations* 19, no. 4 (2012): 536–539.
Niesen, Peter. "Anti-Extremism, Negative Republicanism, Civil Society: Three Paradigms for Banning Political Parties." *German Law Journal* 3, no. 7 (2002), reprinted in *Annual of German and European Law 2003*, eds. Peer Zumbansen & Russell A. Miller, 81–112. Oxford: Berghahn 2004.
Nolte, Georg, and Gregory Fox. "Intolerant Democracies." *Harvard International Law Journal* 36, no. 1 (1995): 1–70.
Plache, Ben. "Soldiers for Democracy: Karl Loewenstein and John H. Herz, Militant Democracy and the Defense of the Democratic State." *Virginia Commonwealth University Scholars Compass* (2013). Retrieved 19 July 2018 from https://scholarscompass.vcu.edu/cgi/viewcontent.cgi?referer=https://www.google.it/&httpsredir=1&article=3994&context=etd.
Rossiter, Clinton. *Constitutional Dictatorship*. Princeton, NJ: Princeton University Press, 1948.
Sajò, Andras, ed. *Militant Democracy*. Utrecht: Eleven International Publishing, 2004.
Schmitt, Carl J. *Constitutional Theory*. Durham, NC: Duke University Press, 2008.
Shklar, Judith. "The Liberalism of Fear." In *Political Thought and Political Thinkers*, edited by Judith Shklar, 3–21. Chicago, IL: University of Chicago Press, 1998.
Show, Tamsin. "Max Weber on Democracy: Can the People Have Political Power In Modern States?" *Constellations* 15, no. 1 (2008): 33–45.
Sollors, Werner. "Dilemmas of Denazification. Karl Loewenstein, Carl Schmitt, Military Occupation, and Militant Democracy." In *The Temptation*

of Despair, edited by Werner Sollors: 216–254. Cambridge, MA: Harvard University Press, 2014.

Thiel, Markus, ed. *The "Militant Democracy" Principle in Modern Democracies*. London: Ashgate, 2007.

Weber, Max. "Politics as a Vocation." In *From Max Weber: Essays in Sociology*, edited by H. H. Girth and C. Wright Mills, 77–128. London: Routledge 1991.

 3

Parliamentary and Electoral Decisions as Political Acts
Kari Palonen

The term "decisions" has two different connotations in studies of political thought. The first one is that of closing an open situation by an irrevocable, final decision, a fait accompli that forever alters the conditions of political action. Carl Schmitt's *Politische Theologie* provides a paradigm for it.[1] It is, however, equally possible to insist on the necessity of a choice in combination with the contingency of the decision, and the absence of sufficient grounds for the choice then marks the freedom of political action.[2]

Even if these two aspects may in some respects be two sides of the same coin, their political context is highly different. In the first case, a dramatic and extraordinary decision is committed by an authorized entity; in the second case, the decisions can be frequent and multiple, and they are available to a great number of political agents. In the first setting, the question is whether the decision is necessary or even possible at all; in the second perspective, contingent decisions are treated as a regular part of parliamentary and democratic polities.

In this chapter, I want to discuss the character and political quality of parliamentary and electoral decisions. My point of departure is Max Weber's booklet "Wahlrecht und Demokratie in Deutschland," in which he discusses electoral and parliamentary politics in the context of the acceptance of the democratization of suffrage.[3] I shall, however, complement the analysis with the procedural literature around the Westminster Parliament in order to illustrate the multistage and multilayer character of parliamentary decisions and their close links to the preceding debates of the items on the parliamentary agenda.[4]

The combination of debate and decision by voting is one of the original features that make the Westminster Parliament a close approximation of the parliamentary ideal type of politics. Gilbert Campion, a twentieth-century Clerk of the House of Commons, formulates the point thus: "Motion, Question and Decision are all parts of a process that may be called the elementary form of debate."[5]

What Campion writes about debate is a remarkable extension of the concept, marking the singularity of the parliamentary style of politics. Parliamentary debate is the opposite of a polite conversation to reach a consensus, but neither does it simply repeat already existing stands of the government and opposition. In parliament, opposite standpoints alternate and the dissensus between perspectives enriches the understanding of the question on the agenda. The Canadian rhetoric scholar James De Mille put it as follows: "The aim of parliamentary debate is to investigate the subject from many points of view which are presented from two contrary sides. In no other way can a subject be so exhaustively considered."[6] Here we can see a kind of methodological justification of debate as political action: a question can be properly understood if and only if it is approached from opposite points of view. Parliamentary procedure and rhetoric are forms of thinking politically. From this perspective, neither the authority of the best argument nor the decisionistic separation of vote from debate appear plausible.

Decisions Versus the "Best Argument"

Before discussing the relationship between "debate" and "vote" in parliamentary and electoral contexts, a few words are needed on the broader context of debate, namely on the dualism between the ultrarationalistic and the decisionistic tradition. Ultrarationalists from Hegel to Habermas regard making a decision per se as something suspicious. They are instead looking for the "best argument" in a discussion, something "inexpugnable" (to quote Thomas Hobbes's term[7]), something that silences the audience.

This setting is based on the assumption that everyone has recognized a priori the "unforced force of the best argument," as Habermas's favorite phrase goes. In an early formulation, Habermas connected this to the idea of emancipation into adulthood (*Mündigkeit*) as the given structure of the human language. With this is "the intention of a general and unforced consensus unmistakable formulated"—translations without reference are my own.[8]

Against Weber and others, Habermas once formulated his point of criticism as follows: "In the last resort political action cannot be justified rationally, but rather take place by a decision between competing orders of values and powers of belief, which escape compelling arguments and remain inaccessible to a binding discussion."[9] In other words, he accused them of replacing "rationally justified" political action by a decision between "competing orders of values and beliefs," which would be inaccessible to the force of argument and to a "binding discussion" allowing the participants to arrive at a consensus.

When such a force is presupposed, there is no need to ascribe decision-making either to an entity or a person or to recourse to a vote. Such a setting of the question is highly partisan. Behind it—and this is also explicit in the view of *Mündigkeit* as a given structure of language—is obviously the classical contractarian paradigm of a transition from the "state of nature" to the "state of civilization" or "state of society." This move is formally voluntary, but it still does not constitute a genuine decision, because staying in the state of nature is not a serious alternative. Only within this paradigm could discussion lead to a "binding" solution as a quasilogical move accepted by all. In other situations, however, what counts as an argument and what should be the criteria of the "best argument" can be seen as controversial in principle, and subject to change as well, due to new moves in the discussion.

From the existentialist or Weberian tradition, the possibility of making a political decision will be seen as an expression of human freedom of choice. Following his critical evaluation of the entire Frankfurt school's inability to deal with politics, my late colleague, Michael Th. Greven, sketched "democratic decisionism" in a series of articles during the 1990s, later collected into his book *Kontingenz und Dezision* and in his monograph *Die politische Gesellschaft*.[10] He insists both on the necessity and the importance of decisions in democratic and parliamentary politics and on removing the authoritarian tone from the concept of decisionism. Similarly to such existentialist authors as Karl Jaspers and Jean-Paul Sartre, Greven strongly insists on a close connection between decision and responsibility, with a special emphasis on its political significance.[11] From a different angle, the rhetorical tradition, for its part, sees that in politics there is always the possibility to argue *in utramque partem* (being able to see validity in both sides of an argument), and therefore the choice is left to the political agents themselves.[12]

The Habermasian ideal of a consensus also gives the impression of a religious conversion: the ideal discussion appears as if it would convert the last "pagan" participant and draw her into the community of believers. John Stuart Mill offers a rhetoric-inspired counter-position for this conversion-by-consensus in *On Liberty*:

> If all mankind minus one, were of one opinion, and only one person were of the contrary opinion, mankind would be no more justified in silencing that one person, than he, if he had the power, would be justified in silencing mankind. ... But the peculiar evil of silencing the expression of an opinion is, that it is robbing the human race; posterity as well as the existing generation; those who dissent from the opinion, still more than those who hold it. If the opinion is right, they are deprived of the opportunity of exchanging error for truth: if wrong, they lose, what is almost as great a benefit, the clearer perception and livelier impression of truth, produced by its collision with error.[13]

For Mill, not only the arguments and the criteria for judging their goodness are contested. The very ideal of consensus is nothing worth striving for. In matters of opinion, no binding decisions are needed, for dissensus has a value of its own. However, political matters are not merely questions of opinion, but also struggles for power that are incompatible with each other. Mill, of course, undertook to change the existing power relationships when he was a member of the House of Commons. In the 1867 debate on parliamentary suffrage, he moved his famous amendment for female suffrage by replacing the word "man" with "person."[14]

Besides the ultrarationalists, an intellectual current opposed to them, the German romantic tradition of the early nineteenth century, also failed to recognize the political necessity of decisions. Carl Schmitt's *Politische Romantik* (1919) — published before his better-known works, *Die Diktatur* (1921) and *Politische Theologie* (1922) — identified the counter-position to his own thinking in German romanticism. For Schmitt, romanticism was not merely a philosophical or literature current, but also a militantly anti-political style of thought, even if the romantics might have thought otherwise. Schmitt famously blamed the German romantic conservative Adam Müller for indulging in an "eternal conversation" — *ewiges Gespräch*.[15]

Indeed, if Habermas wants to avoid an unending moment of conversation, looking for the best argument without any limits is liable to lead precisely there. Political action takes place in time and operates with time, and the scarcity of time makes decisions necessary. Søren Kierkegaard's point against Hegel's self-development of reason in history was exactly the idea that sooner or later, we are faced with the necessity of making a decision, choosing either one side or the other (*enten-eller*). For Kierkegaard the theologian, the choice was for or against God.[16]

Schmitt, the Catholic jurist, was indebted to the Lutheran Kierkegaard. His paradigm is the pure and absolute decision, created *ex nihilo*, "a pure, non-justified, non-reasoned, undiscussed, illegitimate decision, thus one created out of nothing."[17] The sovereign dictator is the instance of the making of this decision, as formulated in the first words of Schmitt's *Politische Theologie* on the decision to declare a state of exception. "The sovereign is one who decides on the state of exception."[18]

Contrary to both Hegel and the Romantics, Kierkegaard and Schmitt had excellent grounds to affirm that decisions are necessary in a polity. No decision arrives by itself, as a result of a consensual conversation. The appeal for the consensus is, rather, a rhetorical justification for silencing adversaries or prolonging the discussion ad infinitum. Both Kierkegaard and Schmitt refer to limit situations in which decisions are unique, dramatic, and irreversible. Yet, such situations do not help much in understanding other kinds of politically important decisions, such as voting in Parliament and in elections.

Decisions by Vote

The paradigmatic form of political decision-making in democratic and parliamentary practice is the vote. The German terms *Abstimmung* and *Wahl* both refer to decisions by a counting of votes. The former concerns an item on the agenda in a Parliament or a meeting; the second, in voting for a person in an election.

Weber makes the important distinction between election and acclamation. A referendum is an example of acclamation. "A plebiscite is not an election but a one-time or … repeated recognition of the position of a pretender as a personally qualified charismatic ruler."[19] Following the rules of epideictic rhetoric, the voters in a referendum or a plebiscite have only the choice between a given yes and no, between acclaiming or refusing to do so. The second round of the presidential elections in the French and Finnish systems resembles a referendum, although a yes for one candidate marks a no for the other. Voting blank, that is against both, might make more sense in such an election than in a referendum. For Schmitt, acclamation is the only way for "the people" to act politically, and he supports both referenda and presidential regimes.[20]

For Weber, it is possible to transform acclamation into a genuine election by regularization, whatever the final exact method of the election. "The acclamation by the ruled can … also develop into a regular 'election procedure,' including by norms of regulated direct or indirect 'suffrage, with local or regional elections, classes of voters, and electoral districts.'"[21] A regularization of the electoral system increases both the contingency of the choice between alternatives and the fairness of the electoral procedure. Fair elections are opposed to governmental support for the yes side in a referendum and to a no side that turns into a plebiscite against the government. Weber sees a transformation from acclamation to election to be present both in the US with its semidirect presidential elections and in the British-type parliamentary representation. "Only in the occident has the election of rulers step by step developed into a representative system."[22]

In the older electoral systems, the number of votes and voters is by no means always the same. On the contrary, the votes of different voters might have a different weight, based on varying grounds. In contrast, counting votes is a major aspect in the democratization of a polity or an institution. This political transition is the main topic of Weber's *Wahlrecht* booklet, published during World War I late in 1917. At this stage, the transition to parliamentary government was already on the agenda of German parliamentary and public debate, while in opposition to it, various antidemocratic and antiparliamentary modes of thinking were militantly advocated by war hawks.

Weber's targets of criticism include plural voting, as practiced at his time in Belgian parliamentary elections, and what he called the "plutocratic" tripartite division of the electorate in the elections of the Prussian lower house. Both cases operated with male-only suffrage and the votes were counted and not weighted. However, in Belgium, extra votes on the basis of certain criteria (family, degrees, property, etc.) were given to some voters, while in Prussia, the electorate was divided into three classes on the basis of taxation, and votes had varying weights in deciding the composition of the parliament. A partisan distribution of parliamentary seats in favor of the old order was predetermined, although the exact distribution of votes was not.

In such elections, a lesser importance is attached to voter choice than in equal suffrage, in which a radically contingent distribution of votes is the ideal. Weber regards both types of unequal elections as expressions of the cowardice of the bourgeoisie in the face of democracy,[23] of its unwillingness to acknowledge democratic equality and the political contingency of electoral results.

For Weber, suffrage by numbers (*Ziffernwahlrecht*) is, furthermore, an indispensable part of the "mechanical nature of the modern state." The independence of citizens (*Staatsbürger*) is manifested in equal suffrage, in which all citizens are treated equally as political agents, as opposed to the plural voting and the tripartite division of voters in the Prussian *Abgeordnetenhaus*.

> The modern state is the first to have the concept of the citizen of the state [*Staatsbürger*]. Equal voting rights mean in the first instance simply this: at this point in social life the individual, is *not*, as everywhere else, considered in terms of a particular professional or family position, nor in terms of differences in material or social station, but purely and simply as a *citizen*.[24]

Equality of suffrage has for Weber an "anthropological" justification in the equality of citizens before the state, whose representatives do have power over life and death.

The "one person, one vote" principle as well as the equal weight of votes in general elections mark for Weber a decisive break with the regimes of the estates of the realm. A political consequence of this break was the profound contingency it brought to the voting. Even if parties try to bind voters to their own viewpoints, the procedure of elections and intraparliamentary votes ensures that the votes are counted one by one. The decisions of voters are singular acts that result in contingent numerical constellations in elections, out of which parliamentary majorities will be formed and revised through debates and intraparliamentary votes.[25] In this sense, parliamentary and electoral votes are far from the existential decisions before God à la Kierkegaard, the groundless decisions of the Schmittian "sovereign," and the "non-decisions" based on "best argument" à la Habermas.

The second and even more important target of Weber's polemics is the call of numerous literati in wartime Germany to replace universal and equal suffrage with a corporative representation, *berufsständische Vertretung*. The point of such proposals is to replace decision by vote with diplomatic-style negotiations between professional corporations.

For Weber, such principle corresponds to the feudal system of estate representation. The division of persons according to specific interests or occupations was to some degree possible in a regime of separate estates. In the estate assemblies, there was neither a vote nor a binding decision, but a complex of compromises serving as the juridical basis for decisions. "Only when compromise was the *legal* basis of political action did the estate structure based on occupation inherently have a proper place."[26]

For example, in the four-estate Swedish Riksdag—which persisted until 1866, and in Finland (as part of the Russian empire) until 1906—the final decision was found in the negotiations between the estates' representatives. Even if the peasants and the burghers represented a much broader section of the population, their weight was similar or lesser to that of the "higher estates" of the nobility and the clergy. In some cases, a majority of three estates was sufficient to put through a motion; in others, an agreement between the four estates was necessary. Although the imperative mandate for members within the estates was rejected in the Swedish 1810 Constitution (Instrument of Government) and in the Finnish 1869 Diet's procedure, compromise between estates persisted as the basis for decision-making in the Diet.[27] Without an agreement between estates, no decision was possible.

Political representation must, in contrast, be built on *competition* between parties. According to Weber, in the Germany of his time, party competition increasingly governed the decision-making not only of municipal assemblies, but also of cooperative bodies, health service boards, and so on. Nowadays, in an open and constantly changing market economy, no natural division of occupations or trades is possible. For Weber, party struggle was the appropriate political form for every type of electoral contest. "Wherever one finds rule by means of ballot and elections, the *political* parties as such are already predisposed to become the bearers of the struggle."[28]

In a regime of estates, neither a debate before the voters (*Agitation*) nor a decision by vote makes sense. Modern elections are characterized by a competition between "voluntaristic" parties, based on the free recruitment of supporters: "*Political parties* in the modern state are organizations which have as their starting point the (legally) free recruitment of supporters, while their goal is to determine policy through the *number* of their supporters. The *ultima ratio* of modern party politics is voting or the ballot slip."[29] The struggle in Parliament and in electoral campaigns is based on numerical strength. Reasons and arguments as well as compromises are important, but the final decision is based on the number of votes.

The vote by ballot (*Stimmzettel*) is the most important qualification of the modern Parliament and its mode of election. The competition between parties as voluntary organizations regulates the general election and parliamentary voting—their contingency is no hazard or random phenomenon, but an expression of party strength. In Parliament, contingency arises from agenda setting and debate on motions. The agenda setting itself could perhaps be understood also as a preventive vote, by which the topics of debate are selected. The debates, with their aim of persuading the adversary, are focused on an estimation of the relative strengths of the parties, and the previous elections and parliamentary votes serve as a background for determining which questions provide a *Spielraum* for change and in which ones further agitation would be vain and fruitless.

Compromises in Parliament are possible and frequently desirable, but these are conducted against the background of counting of the votes.

> This means that, when compromises are reached, it is under pressure from the fact that, if no compromise is reached, the subsequent election or ballot may produce a result that is more or less undesirable for *all* concerned. There is no getting away from the fact that a real or an approximate *counting* of votes is an integral and essential element both of modern electoral contests and of the conduct of business in parliament.[30]

In electoral campaigns, the diplomatic instruments—threats of war, breaks in diplomatic relations, and so on—or their analogs in labor markets—e.g., strikes and boycotts—do not make sense. To boycott an election or a vote in Parliament might be imaginable in extreme cases—for example, one in which fair procedures have been conspicuously violated.

In short, the party competition helps to reduce the contingency of elections to a limited number of realistic alternatives. This holds true independent of whether the competition is between individual candidates in single-member constituencies, or between closed party lists, or whether there is a second-level competition between candidates within a party in an electoral district. The art of contingency and the strategic role that parties play in regulating it are different in these three basic cases, but the competition of candidates for the votes of the electorate is common to all of them.

Election day constitutes a deadline for the political time of campaigns. For incumbent parliamentarians, it serves as a timeframe for needing to decide upon the questions on its agenda. If a prime minister or a president has the power to dissolve the parliament, the danger of a sudden interruption of the parliamentary debates before the elections could be understood as a more immanent threat than in a fixed-term electoral system.[31]

The Political Significance of Electoral Decisions

The point of general elections with universal suffrage is that although the casting of votes is highly important for individual citizens, voters remain practically powerless in the face of the contingent results. One vote hardly ever is decisive in broader electorates, and voters misunderstand electoral politics when they complain that their vote does not count. Of course, politically literate voters might, for example, refrain from voting for splinter groupings that have no chance of getting their candidates elected.

However, the electoral decisions may be judged in terms of their political significance for the voter. John Stuart Mill recommended that the voter "give his vote, to the best of his judgment, exactly as he would be bound to do if he were the sole voter, and the election depended upon him alone."[32] Even if it is pretty clear that your vote does not make a difference in the final outcome, you should vote as if it would; this is the point of Mill's thought experiment.

Jean-Paul Sartre, in his planned Cornell lectures of 1965 (cancelled due to his opposition to US policy in Vietnam) made another thought experiment to explain individual electoral choices. His point was that voters do not only choose between the candidates, but by this very choice they also choose their own political image or self-identity. Discussing the primaries of the US Democratic Party between John F. Kennedy and Hubert Humphrey 1960 in West Virginia, the self-choice for Sartre explained why the Catholic Kennedy won over the Protestant Humphrey in a state dominated by Protestants. Every election offers a chance to dissolve one's past prejudices and to recast individual political identity and judgment. The West Virginian Democrats chose Kennedy in order to show that they were tolerant, not bound by their past prejudices.[33] Sartre's point holds true mutatis mutandis for parliamentary elections, although strategic voting is equally legitimate: Is it better to choose an excellent candidate with no chances than a mediocre one among those who do have chances?

This corresponds to Weber's view that in parliamentary elections, the individual considers herself just as a *Staatsbürger*. In other words, the citizens can see the elections as an extraordinary occasion to act, in Weber's words, as an "occasional politician" (*Gelegenheitspolitiker*). Voting is the first activity that Weber mentions when in "Politik als Beruf," he characterizes the ideal type of occasional politician, which "we all are," in contrast to the professional politician.[34] For the occasional politician, the point is not the result of the elections, but the right to vote as a chance to participate in the election of parliamentarians.

The Parliamentary Link between the Debate and the Vote

When Weber sees the number of votes as the *ultima ratio* of parliamentary debate, he recognizes that the final vote in Parliament cannot be separated from the preceding debate and that the arguments in the debate might at any moment alter the majority. Even if he speaks only of party compromises, he by no means underestimates the significance of the debate. The Parliament's main power for Weber lies in the possibility of controlling the administration. "In all mass states democratization leads to bureaucratic administration, and, without parliamentarization, to pure *rule* by officials."[35] In the control of the officialdom, parliaments are much more efficient than direct democracy.

Weber sees in the possibility of debating the strengths and the weaknesses of a motion a major opportunity in which parliamentarians can show their competencies: "A member of Parliament can learn to weigh the *power of words* in a party *conflict*."[36] The possibility of parliamentarians to control the knowledge of officials is further developed in Weber's academic pamphlet, "Parlament und Regierung im neugeordneten Deutschland." He mentions three rhetorical tools of this control, namely, the cross-examination of officials by parliamentarians, the possibility to conduct on-the-spot examination of the sources of the officials' knowledge, and the forms of scrutiny enabled by parliamentary examination commissions.[37] This view is closely connected to Weber's reinterpretation of "objectivity" in terms of a fair debate between opposed points of view, for which the Westminster parliamentary procedure offers the historical model.[38]

As quoted in the beginning, Gilbert Campion regards the vote as a stage in the debate in the Westminster parliament. "When a motion is moved (and seconded), the Speaker proposes the Question (in the same terms as the motion), as the subject of debate, and at the conclusion of the debate puts the Question for eliciting the immediate decision of the House."[39] In the Westminster-style of parliamentary politics, the vote is part of debate at the same time as it terminates it.

The point of the decision arrives when the time for debate is recognized to be at its limit. Also, in Parliament, an eternal prolongation of debate would appear as a pretext against the recognition that at a certain point it is time to move on and vote. The famous obstruction cases of the nineteenth-century even necessitated procedures such as the *clôture* in order to vote on terminating the debate.[40] Similar timelines can be agreed on for the intraparliamentary negotiations between parties.

A Westminster specialty is to connect debate with a vote on a resolution. The time limits for debate were recognized already in the tracts on parliamentary procedure in the sixteenth and seventeenth century. The main measure to guarantee that the members speak "to the matter" is to connect the debate to a resolution, posing a definite question to which the member must take a stand in both the debate and the vote. This is still the case with the latest tract on the Westminster procedure:

> The process of debate ... is the main process used for most House business. ... The process is essentially simple: a member proposes a motion ... that proposal is repeated by the Speaker in the same form; debate arises, the proposal is put for decision; it is agreed or negatived ... if agreed a resolution (expressing an opinion) or an order (requiring action by the House, or a committee, or individual Members or officers) results.[41]

An old Westminster rule to prevent a senseless prolongation of debate is that in the plenum, members are allowed to speak only once to the item on the agenda. Henry Scobell, a Clerk of the House of Commons, formulated this in his tract from the Cromwellian period:

> If the Matter moved do receive a Debate pro & contra, in that Debate none may speak more than once to the Matter; And after some time spent in the Debate, the Speaker collecting the Sense of the House upon the Debate, is to reduce the same into a Question, which he is to propound, to the end, the House in their Debate afterwards may kept to the Matter of that Question, if the same be approved by the House to contain the substance of the former Debate.[42]

In a strict sense, a debate that includes alteration between replies and counter-replies took place only in committee, including in the Committee of the whole House. Later on, the rule partially lost its significance due to the parliamentary time budget, because more effective instruments of delay were invented. Since the nineteenth century, replies have received their place also in the plenum, although on certain conditions, as formulated by Campion:

(a) A right to reply is granted to the mover of a substantive motion. ... The rule is relaxed
(b) in the case of a Bill under consideration as amended by a standing committee, in favour of the Member in charge and also of the mover of an amendment in respect to that amendment;
(c) in favour of a Member who complains that his meaning has been misinterpreted by another speaker;
(d) to allow a Member, whose conduct or character has been impugned in the debate, to make a personal declaration;
(e) to allow a Member to raise a point of order;
(f) by indulgence of the House (especially when a reply is desired from a Minister).[43]

The priority of the debate over the vote is thus recognized in the aim of avoiding a premature vote. The main historical instrument for preventing an overly hasty vote—i.e., one without thorough debate—is adjournment, either of debate or of the House itself. Jeremy Bentham already distinguished three types of adjournments: *sine die, in diem,* and *post quam*.[44] Adjournment thus does not mean merely a postponement to give the members more time to think about the matter on the agenda; it also interrupts the ongoing debate, allowing members to avoid taking a stand on the item on the agenda if they have not already formed a stand or are insecure about the possible outcome of a sudden vote.

An interesting twentieth-century innovation is the creation of adjournment debates without a vote to serve as an extraordinary occasion for the members to take a stand on questions that are not on the ordinary agenda. Different occasions exist for the opposition, the government, and the backbenchers.[45] This can be seen as another example of the priority of the debate over the vote in the Westminster practice.

Parliamentary politics operate with multiple stages (three readings) and layers (plenum and committees) of debate. Each stage and layer offers an institutionalized occasion to evaluate a motion on the agenda from a different perspective in order to reevaluate its strengths and weaknesses.[46] The Westminster-style of parliamentary debate contains decisions at every stage: they may concern whether to continue the debate at all, whether to accept amendments, or whether to adjourn the debate. The final vote on the surviving formulation of a motion is only the last decision. Parliamentary votes are irrevocable in the short term in so far as a decision on a motion cannot be reversed in the same parliamentary session.

The multiple debates and the subsequent decisions by voting appear much less dramatic than the paradigms of the decisionists, such as declaration of war or a state of emergency. The votes in the first and second reading as well as in the committees concern the question of whether or not a motion shall be allowed to move to the next stage of debate. Most motions never reach the final stage, but many members may, in the name of a fair debate, allow a motion to proceed to the next stage, although they firmly intend to vote against it. In contemporary parliaments, with an ever stronger pressure on time, such fairness as to the motions of the opposite side might be more seldom, but it is not the case that all opposition or backbenchers' motions are killed before they are allowed to go to committee.

The parliamentary votes in Westminster are of an either–or character. It is impossible to vote both for and against the same motion or to reject both. Unlike many other parliaments, no blank vote is allowed, and being absent from the vote leaves the decision to others. Therefore, parliamentarians have learnt to choose between evils, often on insufficient grounds.

However, the Westminster practice contains an important modification of this "absolute" character of the votes, namely the amendment. The political alternatives are formed in terms of amendments that include "Alteration, Addition or Omission," as Henry Scobell put it.[47] Moving an amendment both interrupts the debate on an ongoing motion and originates a new one on the amendment, which also allows those who have already spoken on the original motion to speak again on the amendment. Originally, amendments could not be radically opposed to the sense of the original motion, but in the course of time, this restriction has been loosened. Accepting an amendment to the original motion is, in procedural terms, something different than a straightforward rejection, an adjournment *sine die*, or stopping a motion in the early stages of debate.[48] The parliamentary practice of constructing alternatives in terms of amendments can be seen as a both formally and politically important relativization of decisions of the either–or type.

Even more than adjournment, the amendment as a focused alternative to the original motion affirms the priority of debate over the vote. The main point is to challenge the strengths of the original motion rather than present an exact alternative and to insist on the possibility to change the resolution on the basis of the debate.

This priority of debate over vote (decision) holds thus for the Westminster-type of parliamentary politics. If we look at the tracts on the French parliamentary procedure, the tradition is rather the opposite. Vallette and Saint-Marsy during the Orléans monarchy regard the parliament above all as a legislature. For a representative assembly, making laws is the aim of parliamentary work.[49] Although debate is necessary, its role is clearly subordinated to law making and it has no other value than gaining power.[50]

Also, other features in the French parliamentary *procédure* tend to give the impression that the debates themselves are not, unlike in Westminster, the main focus of politics. This is the case, for example, in the replacement of the tacit rejection by means of an adjournment *sine die* by an explicit rejection, when Poudra and Pierre write in their authoritative tract from 1878.[51] Even in the Third République, praised rightly by Roussellier as *parlement de l'éloquence*, the debate remained subordinated to the vote, as clearly manifested in the frequent falls of government as the major manifestation of the powers of the *Assemblée nationale*.[52]

The Search for One Big Decision

However, there exist also important either–or decisions in the Westminster Parliament. Their paradigm is the vote of no confidence in the government, initiated by Sandys's motion in 1741 on the basis of pure political expediency.[53] The question of confidence in the government is also preceded by a single debate in the plenum, which concludes in a vote concerning dismissal of the government. In this vote, policy questions or the government's style of acting politically are subordinate to the chance of dismissing or maintaining the government. Whereas debates and decisions on substantial motions are, in rhetorical terms, of the deliberative genre, the vote on the fate on the government is rather a matter of epideictic rhetoric, which increases the pressure on backbenchers to show party loyalty.

It has been the interests of government to focus parliamentary politics on the either–or decisions between government and opposition. The stable majorities created by election results and the governmental aims to obtain a quasi-monopoly of parliamentary initiative have, since the nineteenth century, contributed to a tendency toward the presidentialization of parliamentary government, resulting in the focus on such either–or decisions.[54] There are, however, good grounds to contest this tendency at Westminster. The multistage and multilayer procedure for debates matters, and the official recognition of the independence and powers of the backbenchers, has limited both governmentalization and presidentialization.[55] Recent reforms have again increased the powers of backbenchers at the expense of party whips.[56]

Another way to combine parliamentary government with a linear up-or-down style of decision-making has involved the electoral majority of the government. In the electoralist perspective, parliamentary politics appears to be restricted to the question of realizing or not realizing the electoral program of the majority parties, against which, however, parliamentary procedure and debate serve as constraints. In an electoralist view, the Parliament itself appears as a mere rubber stamp of registration and ratification. Such electoralization is as radical as presidentialization in devaluating parliamentary powers.

The decisive argument against this view is, however, why then keep parliaments with a broad agenda and full-time members at all? Why not replace it with a cheaper, more efficient system with rotating loyal government supporters enjoying the parliamentary rituals and ceremonies and voting always for the government's case?

Indeed, this is not a new idea. Joseph Cowen, a Radical MP for Newcastle, as early as the 1882 debate on the Gladstone government's procedural reform, presented a thought experiment. He was engaged in a polemic against the famous Birmingham Caucus of the Liberals, formed by Joseph Chamberlain. The idea of the Caucus was to subordinate Parliament to parties and elections.[57] Cowen asks why an institution as large and costly as the House of Commons should be maintained at all, if it has been reduced to a registry office.

> If we are merely to vote as we are told—which is the motto of the Caucus—why are we sent here? It is a great waste of power, of health, of time, and of temper. Instead of 600, 60, or, indeed, 6 would suffice. All that is wanted is a body of experts to whom the decisions taken in the different constituencies might be sent. They might be tabulated, and formulated, and summarized— – handed first to a draftsman to embody in Bills, and then to an Executive to put in operation. The Prime Minister desires to lessen the amount of speaking. This is an easy plan of doing it. The work of legislation might be greatly simplified by such a course of procedure. Government shrinks from such a result; but it is the logical, inevitable, and irresistible outcome of their course of action.[58]

Even if, for example, De Gaulle radically reduced the powers of the Assemblée Nationale in the constitution of the Fifth Republic, he still recognized the importance of the opposition and the forms of thorough parliamentary procedure and debate.[59] From populists of a different variety, we hear now and then proposals to reduce the parliament's agenda, to shorten its sitting time, to reduce the number of members or to get rid of full-time MPs with their monthly salaries and professional staff. With Cowen, I don't think such proposals to devaluate parliaments have any real chance.

While post-war political science has treated parliaments mainly as arenas for parties and government versus opposition struggles, an increasing scholarly interest in parliaments as parliaments has risen anew in the recent years.[60] The core idea is that Parliament as a deliberative assembly also incarnates a distinct parliamentary style of thinking politically based on *pro et contra* debate. It sees, as I quoted Campion, decision as an inherent part of multistage and multilayer parliamentary debate. We could also move to the opposite direction and include voting in elections as a part of parliamentary debate, marking election day as the time when membership in Parliament is extended to all voters.[61]

Dedramatizing of Decisions

The democratic decisionism of Michael Th. Greven deals with situations in which the decisions are based on the confrontation of a plurality of opposed views, out of which, through debate and voting, a decision must be reached that is also regarded as legitimate by the opponents.[62] In sharp contrast to the sovereign dictator paradigm, democratic decisionism requires an extended participation by those who are concerned with the decisions in the debates preceding the concluding decision.[63]

In this chapter, I have continued Greven's dedramatization of decisions with the focus on parliamentary and electoral votes, their political quality and their significance.[64] The political role of decisions in parliamentary and democratic politics is based on both the relatively rare decisions of voters in parliamentary elections and the very frequent intraparliamentary decisions of a different type and political significance. Neither type of decision is understandable without preceding parliamentary debates on the questions on the agenda as well as on those of the agenda itself.

For the debater, the need to terminate debates with decisions by vote illustrates, above all, that all politics operates with limited times. This is also the main reason for the Westminster practice of connecting debates with resolutions to be voted on.

One of the frequent critiques in the name of making democracy "more participative" is that the system of holding parliamentary elections only every fourth year or so makes voting in them a rare event. In fact, the municipal, local, European, and so on elections contain opportunities for citizens to vote on the basis of campaign-type rhetoric, which dedramatizes the electoral choices and allows more complex political profiles. The Sartrean argument that in elections, voters also choose their own political profile supports the idea of keeping elections relatively rare and in contrast to the Swiss type semi-plebiscitarian regime with frequent referenda.

The current tendency goes, in the name of efficiency, toward greater units in local politics and, correspondingly, reduces the number of parliamentary-type assemblies and committee-type boards on the local level. The "participatory" model wants to add citizens' consultations in order to render the bureaucratic decision-making more efficient and legitimate. This practice not only tends to increase the "rule of officialdom," but also to weaken citizens' knowledge of parliamentary-style debate-based decision-making.[65] An alternative would consist of offering additional occasions for the citizens to engage themselves in parliamentary-type debates and decisions, independent of elections. How this can and should be done is a different topic.

Kari Palonen is Professor Emeritusof Political Science at the University of Jyväskylä, Finland. Currently, he is the editor-in-chief of the journal *Redescriptions*, the cochair of the ECPR Standing Group *Political Concepts*, and coeditor of the book series *Politics, Debate, Concepts*. Recents books include: *From Oratory to Debate: Parliamentarisation of*

Deliberative Rhetoric in Westminster (Budrich, 2016); *Parliament and Parliamentarism* (Berghahn, 2016, coedited with Pasi Ihalainen and Cornelia Ilie); *A Political Style of Thinking: Essays on Max Weber* (ECPR Press, 2017); *Debates, Rhetoric and Political Action* (Palgrave, 2017, with Claudia Wiesner and Taru Haapala) and *Parliamentary Thinking: Procedure, Rhetoric and Time* (Palgrave, 2018).

Notes

1. Carl Schmitt, *Politische Theologie* (Berlin: Duncker & Humblot, 1979).
2. See, for example, Helmuth Plessner, "Macht und menschliche Natur," in *Gesammelte Schriften*, vol. 5 (Frankfurt-am-Main: Suhrkamp, 1981), 135–234; Michael Th. Greven, *Kontingenz und Decision* (Opladen: Leske+Budrich, 2000).
3. Max Weber, "Wahlrecht und Demokratie in Deutschland," in *Max-Weber-Studienausgabe*, I/15, ed. Wolfgang J. Mommsen (Tübingen: Mohr, 1988): 155–89.
4. See in more detail Kari Palonen, *The Politics of Parliamentary Procedure: The Formation of the Westminster Procedure as a Political Ideal Type* (Leverkusen: Budrich, 2014); Kari Palonen, *From Oratory to Debate: Parliamentarisation of Deliberative Rhetoric in Westminster* (Baden-Baden: Nomos, 2016).
5. G. F. M. Campion, *An Introduction to the Procedure of the House of Commons* (London: Allen & Co., 1929), 143.
6. James De Mille, *Elements of Rhetoric* (New York: Harpers & Brothers, 1878), 473, http://tinyurl.com/mhps972.
7. Quoted in Quentin Skinner, *Reason and Rhetoric in the Philosophy of Hobbes* (Cambridge, UK: Cambridge University Press, 1996), 300.
8. "ist die Intention eines allgemeinen und ungezwungenen Konsenses umißverständlich ausgesprochen." Jürgen Habermas, *Technik und Wissenschaft als "Ideologie"* (Frankfurt am Main: Suhrkamp, 1968), 163.
9. "In letzter Instanz kann sich das politische Handeln nicht rational begründen, es realisiert vielmehr eine Dezision zwischen konkurrierenden Werteordnungen und Glaubensmächten, die zwingenden Argumenten entraten und einer verbindlichen Diskussion unzugänglich bleiben." Habermas, *Technik*, 121.
10. Michael Th. Greven, *Kritische Theorie und historische Politik* (Opladen: Leske+Budrich, 1994); *Die politische Gesellschaft* (Opladen: Leske+Budrich, 1999); *Kontingenz und Decision* (Opladen: Leske+Budrich, 2000).
11. Karl Jaspers, *Philosophie II. Existenzerhellung* (Heidelberg: Springer, 1932 [1973]); Jean-Paul Sartre, "Qu'est-ce que la littérature?" in *Situations* II (Paris: Gallimard, 1948), 55–330.
12. See, for example, Skinner, *Reason and Rhetoric*.
13. John Stuart Mill, "On Liberty," in *On Liberty and Other Writings*, ed. Stefan Collini (Cambridge: Cambridge University Press, 1989), 20.

14. *Parliamentary Debates*, House of Commons, 3rd ser., vol. 187 (1867): cols. 779–852.
15. Carl Schmitt, *Politische Romantik* (Berlin: Duncker & Humblot, 1968), 40.
16. On Kierkegaard's concept of decision, see Burkhard Conrad, *Der Augenblick der Entscheidung* (Baden-Baden: Nomos, 2008).
17. "Eine reine, nicht räsonnierende und nicht diskutierende, sich nicht rechtfertigende, also aus dem Nichts geschaffene absolute Entscheidung." Schmitt, *Theologie*, 83.
18. "Souverän ist, wer über den Ausnahmezustand entscheidet." Schmitt, *Theologie*, 11. See also Carl Schmitt, *Die Diktatur* (Berlin: Duncker & Humblot, 1978).
19. "Das Plebiszit ist keine 'Wahl,' sondern erstmalige oder ... erneute Anerkennung eines Prätendenten als persönlich qualifizierten, charismatischen Herrschers." Max Weber, *Wirtschaft und Gesellschaft*, ed. Johannes Winckelmann (Tübingen: Mohr, 1980), 665.
20. Carl Schmitt, *Verfassungslehre* (Berlin: Duncker & Humblot, 1970), 83–84, 242–52.
21. "Die Akklamation der Beherrschten kann sich aber umgekehrt zu einem regulären 'Wahlverfahren' entwickeln, mit einem durch Regeln normierten 'Wahlrecht,' direkten oder indirekten, 'Bezirks'- oder 'Proportionalwahlen', 'Wahlklassen' und 'Wahlkreisen.'" Weber, *Wirtschaft*, 666.
22. "Zum Repräsentativsystem ist die Herrscherwahl nur im Okzident allmählich entwickelt worden." Weber, *Wirtschaft*, 666.
23. "Feigheit des Bürgertums vor der Demokratie."
24. Max Weber, *Political Writings*, ed. Peter Lassman and Ronald Speirs, trans. Speirs (Cambridge, UK: Cambridge University Press, 1994), 103. In original: "Dem modernen Staat erst gehört der Begriff des '*Staatsbürgers*' an. Und das gleiche Wahlrecht bedeutet zunächst schlechterdings nichts anderes als: daß an diesem Punkt des sozialen Lebens der einzelne einmal *nicht*, wie sonst überall, nach seiner Besonderung in beruflichen und familienhaften Stellungen und nach den Verschiedenheiten seiner materiellen oder sozialen Lage in Betracht kommt, sondern eben nur: *als Staatsbürger*." Weber, "Wahlrecht und Demokratie," 170. Emphasis in original.
25. On the majority principle, see Egon Flaig, *Die Mehrheitsentscheidung* (Paderborn: Schöningh, 2013).
26. Weber, *Writings*, 102. In original: "Nur als das Kompromiß die *rechtliche* Grundlage politischen Handelns war, war auch die ständische Berufsgliederung ihrem Wesen nach am Platze." Weber, "Wahlrecht und Demokratie," 169. Emphasis in original.
27. See Jussi Kurunmäki, "Representation, Nation and Time: The Political Rhetoric of the 1866 Parliamentary Reform in Sweden" (PhD diss., University of Jyväskylä, 2000); Onni Pekonen, "Debating the ABCs of Parliamentary Life: The Learning of Parliamentary Rules and Practices in the Late Nineteenth-century Finnish Diet and the Early Eduskunta" (PhD diss., University of Jyväskylä, 2014).

28. Weber, *Writings*, 94. In original "Daß überall, wo Wahlzettel und Agitation herrscht, die *politischen* Parteien als solche schon jetzt dazu prädisponiert sind, Träger des Kampfes zu werden." Weber, "Wahlrecht und Demokratie," 164.
29. Weber, *Writings*, 99. In German: "*Politische Parteien* sind dagegen im modernen Staat Organisationen, welche auf (rechtlich) '*freie*' Werbung von Anhängern ausgehen und deren Ziel ist: durch die *Zahl* ihrer Anhänger die Politik zu bestimmen: die ultima ratio aller modernen Parteipolitik ist der Wahl- oder Stimmzettel." Weber, "Wahlrecht und Demokratie," 167. Emphasis in original.
30. Weber, *Writings*, 102. In the original: "Unter dem Druck, daß in Ermanglung des Zustandekommens des Kompromisses die dann stattfindende Wahl oder Abstimmung ein vielleicht *allen* Beteiligten annähernd gleich unerwünschtes Resultat haben werde. Wirkliche und schätzungsweise *Stimmenzählung* gehört nun einmal zum eingeborenen Wesen des modernen Wahlkampfes sowohl als der parlamentarischen Geschäftsführung." Weber, "Wahlrecht und Demokratie," 169. Emphasis in original.
31. See the discussion in Kari Palonen, *The Politics of Limited Times* (Baden-Baden: Nomos, 2008).
32. John Stuart Mill, *Considerations on Representative Government* (Buffalo, NY: Prometheus Books, 1991), 208.
33. Jean-Paul Sartre, "Kennedy and West Virginia," in *Sartre Alive*, ed. Ronald Aronson and Adrian van den Hoven (Detroit, MI: Wayne State University Press, 1991), 37–52.
34. Max Weber, "Politik als Beruf," in *Max-Weber-Studienausgabe* I/17, ed. Wolfgang Schluchter and Wolfgang J. Mommsen (Tübingen: Mohr, 1994), 41; *Writings*, 316–17.
35. Weber, *Writings*, 127. In German: "In jedem Massenstaat führt Demokratie zur bürokratischen Verwaltung, und, ohne Parlamentarisierung, zur reinen Beamten*herrschaft*." Weber, "Wahlrecht und Demokratie," 187. Emphasis in original.
36. Weber, *Writings*, 127. In German: "Daß ... ein Parlamentarier im *Kampf* der Parteien zu lernen vermag, die *Tragweite des Wortes* zu wägen." Weber, "Wahlrecht und Demokratie," 187. Emphasis in original.
37. Max Weber, "Parlament und Regierung im neugeordneten Deutschland," in *Max-Weber-Studienausgabe* I/15, ed. Wolfgang J. Mommsen (Tübingen: Mohr, 1988), esp. 235–37; *Writings*, 177–80.
38. See the discussion in Kari Palonen, *"Objektivität" als faires Spiel: Wissenschaft als Politik bei Max Weber* (Baden-Baden: Nomos, 2010).
39. Campion, *Introduction*, 145.
40. See Josef Redlich, *Recht und Technik des Englischen Parlamentarismus* (Leipzig: Duncker & Humblot, 1905).
41. J. A. G. Griffith and Michael Ryle, *Parliament: Functions, Practices and Procedures*, 2nd ed., ed. Robert Blackburn and Andrew Kinnon (London: Sweet & Maxwell, 2003), 86.

42. Henry Scobell, *Memorials of the Method and Manner of Proceedings in Parliament in Passing Bills* (London: Hills and Fields / EEBO Editions, 1656), 22.
43. Campion, *Introduction*, 167.
44. Jeremy Bentham, "Essay on Political Tactics," in *Collected Works of Jeremy Bentham*, vol. 2, ed. John Bowring (Edinburgh: Tait, 1843), 298–378, § XII, http://oll.libertyfund.org/title/1921/113915.
45. See Campion, *Introduction*, 91–92; Griffith and Ryle, *Parliament*, 376, 379.
46. For this idea, see Gottfried Cohen, *Die Verfassung und Geschäftsordnung des englischen Parlaments mit Hinweis auf die Geschäftsordnungen deutscher Kammern* (Hamburg: Perthes-Besser & Mauke, 1861), http://tinyurl.com/o556sjt.
47. Scobell, *Memorials*, 22–23.
48. See Palonen, *Procedure*.
49. "La loi est encore le but final de l'œuvre parlementaire." Philippe Valette and Benoît Saint-Marsy, *Traité de la confection des lois, ou examen raisonnée des règlements suivis par les assemblées legislatives françaises, compares aux formes parlementaries de l'Angleterre, des États-Unis, de la Bélgique, de l'Espagne, de la Suisse, etc.* (Paris: Joubert, 1839), 4, http://tinyurl.com/zrfkw3o.
50. "Ces débats nous paraissent accessoires en ce sens qu'ils ne constituent jamais que des moyens pour arriver à un but: la conquête du pouvoir." Ibid.
51. "C'est par la voie du *rejet* formel et non par la voie indirecte du adjournement que la Chambre écarte un projet dont elle ne veut pas." Jules Poudra and Eugène Pierre, *Traité de droit politique, électoral et parlementaire* (Versailles: Cerf, 1878), 658, http://tinyurl.com/nvkt9r9.
52. Nicolas Roussellier, *Le parlement de l'éloquence* (Paris: Presses de Sciences-Po, 1997).
53. Tapani Turkka, *The Origins of Parliamentarism: A Study of Sandys' Motion* (Baden-Baden: Nomos, 2007).
54. On this thesis, see Pierre Rosanvallon, *Le bon gouvernement* (Paris: Seuil, 2015).
55. This aspect was already emphasized by the Whittaker Committee of 1913–14, discussed in Palonen, *Oratory*.
56. See Tony Wright, *Doing Politics* (London: Biteback, 2012); Emma Crewe, *The House of Commons: An Anthropology of the MPs at Work* (London: Bloomsbury, 2015).
57. On the Caucus see Weber, *Politik*, 63–65.
58. *Parliamentary Debates*, House of Commons, 5th ser., vol. 274 (1882), cols. 1206–87.
59. On the procedural reform to strengthen the parliament under Sarkozy, see Tuula Vaarakallio, "Re-Activating the Parliament of Eloquence? Sarkozy's Reform of Procedure in the French Assemblée Nationale," in *The Politics of Dissensus: Parliament in Debate*, ed. Kari Palonen, José María Rosales, and Tapani Turkka (Santander: University of Cantabria Press and McGraw Hill, 2014), 375–98.

60. See Jean Garrigues, ed., *Histoire du Parlement de 1789 à nos jours* (Paris: Colin, 2007); Cornelia Ilie, ed., *European Parliaments under Scrutiny* (Amsterdam: Benjamins, 2010); Andreas Schulz and Andreas Wirsching, eds., *Parlamentarische Kulturen in Europa: Das Parlament als Kommunikationsraum* (Düsseldorf: Droste, 2012); Pasi Ihalainen, Cornelia Ilie, and Kari Palonen, eds., *Parliament and Parliamentarism: A Comparative History of a European Concept* (Oxford: Berghahn, 2016).
61. On this thought experiment, see Kari Palonen, "The Parliamentarisation of Elections," *Redescriptions* 14, no. 1 (2010): 133–56.
62. Greven, *Kontingenz*, 57.
63. Ibid., 62.
64. See also my discussion on electoral and parliamentary contingency in Kari Palonen, "Parlament und Freiheit: Eine rhetorische Perspektive zur Kontingenz," in *Politik und Kontingenz*, ed. Katrin Toens and Ulrich Willems (Wiesbaden: Springer VS, 2012), 99–115.
65. Weber, "Parlament und Regierung im neugeordneten Deutschland."

Bibliography

Bentham, Jeremy. "Essay on Political Tactics." In *Collected Works of Jeremy Bentham*, vol. 2, 298–378, edited by John Bowring. Edinburgh: Tait, 1843.
Campion, G. F. M. *An Introduction to the Procedure of the House of Commons*. London: Allen & Co., 1929.
Cohen, Gottfried. *Die Verfassung und Geschäftsordnung des englischen Parlaments mit Hinweis auf die Geschäftsordnungen deutscher Kammern*. Hamburg: Perthes-Besser & Mauke, 1861.
Conrad, Burkhard. *Der Augenblick der Entscheidung*. Baden-Baden: Nomos, 2008.
Crewe, Emma. *The House of Commons: An Anthropology of the MPs at Work*. London: Bloomsbury, 2015.
De Mille, James. *Elements of Rhetoric*. New York: Harpers & Brothers, 1878.
Flaig, Egon. *Die Mehrheitsentscheidung*. Paderborn: Schöningh, 2013.
Garrigues, Jean, ed. *Histoire du Parlement de 1789 à nos jours*. Paris: Colin, 2007.
Greven, Michael Th. *Die politische Gesellschaft*. Opladen: Leske+Budrich, 1999.
———. *Kontingenz und Decision*. Opladen: Leske+Budrich, 2000.
———. *Kritische Theorie und historische Politik*. Opladen: Leske+Budrich, 1994.
Griffith, J. A. G., and Michael Ryle. *Parliament: Functions, Practices and Procedures*, 2nd ed., edited by Robert Blackburn and Andrew Kinnon. London: Sweet & Maxwell, 2003.
Habermas, Jürgen. *Technik und Wissenschaft als "Ideologie."* Frankfurt am Main: Suhrkamp, 1968.
Ihalainen, Pasi, Cornelia Ilie, and Kari Palonen, eds. *Parliament and Parliamentarism: A Comparative History of a European Concept*. Oxford: Berghahn, 2016.
Ilie, Cornelia, ed. *European Parliaments under Scrutiny*. Amsterdam: Benjamins, 2010.
Jaspers, Karl. *Philosophie II. Existenzerhellung*. Heidelberg: Springer, 1973 [1932].

Kurunmäki, Jussi. "Representation, Nation and Time: The Political Rhetoric of the 1866 Parliamentary Reform in Sweden." PhD diss., University of Jyväskylä, 2000.
Mill, John Stuart. "On Liberty." In *On Liberty and Other Writings*, edited by Stefan Collini. Cambridge, UK: Cambridge University Press, 1989 [1859].
Palonen, Kari. *From Oratory to Debate: Parliamentarisation of Deliberative Rhetoric in Westminster*. Baden-Baden: Nomos, 2016.
———. "Objektivität" als faires Spiel. Wissenschaft als Politik bei Max Weber. Baden-Baden: Nomos, 2010.
———. "Parlament und Freiheit. Eine rhetorische Perspektive zur Kontingenz." In *Politik und Kontingenz*, edited by Katrin Toens and Ulrich Willems, 99–115. Wiesbaden: Springer VS, 2012.
———. "The Parliamentarisation of Elections." *Redescriptions* 14, no. 1 (2010): 133–56.
———. *The Politics of Limited Times*. Baden-Baden: Nomos, 2008.
———. *The Politics of Parliamentary Procedure: The Formation of the Westminster Procedure as a Political Ideal Type*. Leverkusen: Budrich, 2014.
Parliamentary Debates. House of Commons. 3rd ser., vol. 187. 1867.
Parliamentary Debates. House of Commons. 5th ser., vol. 274. 1882.
Pekonen, Onni. "Debating the ABCs of Parliamentary Life: The Learning of Parliamentary Rules and Practices in the Late Nineteenth-century Finnish Diet and the Early Eduskunta." PhD diss., University of Jyväskylä, 2014.
Plessner, Helmuth. "Macht und menschliche Natur." In *Gesammelte Schriften*, vol. 5, 135–234. Frankfurt-am-Main: Suhrkamp, 1981 [1931].
Poudra, Jules, and Eugène Pierre. *Traité de droit politique, électoral et parlementaire*. Versailles: Cerf, 1878.
Redlich, Josef. *Recht und Technik des Englischen Parlamentarismus*. Leipzig: Duncker & Humblot, 1905.
Rosanvallon, Pierre. *Le bon gouvernement*. Paris: Seuil, 2015.
Roussellier, Nicolas. *Le parlement de l'éloquence*. Paris: Presses de Sciences-Po, 1997.
Sartre, Jean-Paul. "Kennedy and West Virginia." In *Sartre Alive*, edited by Ronald Aronson and Adrian van den Hoven, 37–52. Detroit, MI: Wayne State University Press, 1991.
———. "Qu'est-ce que la littérature?" In *Situations II*, 55–330. Paris: Gallimard, 1948.
Schmitt, Carl. *Die Diktatur*. Berlin: Duncker & Humblot, 1921 [1978].
———. *Politische Romantik*. Berlin: Duncker & Humblot, 1919 [1968].
———. *Politische Theologie*. Berlin: Duncker & Humblot, 1922 [1979].
———. *Verfassungslehre*. Berlin: Duncker & Humblot, 1928 [1970].
Schulz, Andreas, and Andreas Wirsching, eds. *Parlamentarische Kulturen in Europa: Das Parlament als Kommunikationsraum*. Düsseldorf: Droste, 2012.
Scobell, Henry. *Memorials of the Method and Manner of Proceedings in Parliament in Passing Bills*. London: Hills and Fields / EEBO Editions, 1656.
Skinner, Quentin. *Reason and Rhetoric in the Philosophy of Hobbes*. Cambridge, UK: Cambridge University Press, 1996.

———. *Considerations on Representative Government*. Buffalo, NY: Prometheus Books, 1861 [1991].

Turkka, Tapani. *The Origins of Parliamentarism: A Study of Sandys' Motion*. Baden-Baden: Nomos, 2007.

Vaarakallio, Tuula. "Re-Activating the Parliament of Eloquence? Sarkozy's Reform of Procedure in the French Assemblée Nationale." In *The Politics of Dissensus: Parliament in Debate*, edited by Kari Palonen, José María Rosales, and Tapani Turkka, 375–98. Santander: University of Cantabria Press and McGraw Hill, 2014.

Valette, Philippe, and Benoît Saint-Marsy. *Traité de la confection des lois, ou examen raisonnée des règlements suivis par les assemblées legislatives françaises, compares aux formes parlementaries de l'Angleterre, des États-Unis, de la Bélgique, de l'Espagne, de la Suisse, etc*. Paris: Joubert, 1839.

Weber, Max. "Parlament und Regierung im neugeordneten Deutschland." In *Max-Weber-Studienausgabe* I/15, edited by Wolfgang J. Mommsen. Tübingen: Mohr, 1918 [1988].

———. *Political Writings*, edited by Peter Lassman and Ronald Speirs. Cambridge, UK: Cambridge University Press, 1994.

———. "Politik als Beruf." In *Max-Weber-Studienausgabe* I1/17, edited by Wolfgang Schluchter and Wolfgang J. Mommsen. Tübingen: Morh, 1919 [1994].

———. "Wahlrecht und Demokratie in Deutschland." In *Max-Weber-Studienausgabe*, I/15, 155–189, edited by Wolfgang J. Mommsen. Tübingen: Mohr, 1917 [1988].

Weber, Max. *Wirtschaft und Gesellschaft*, edited by Johannes Winckelmann. Tübingen: Mohr, 1922 [1980].

Wright, Tony. *Doing Politics*. London: Biteback, 2012.

 **4**

DECISION AND DECISIONISM
Nomi Claire Lazar

When urgent matters press the state, it is necessary for a leader to act decisively. Rights and procedures thought definitive of a liberal–democratic form of government may be held in abeyance, the law bent or broken. In the wake of a resurgence of interest in the work of Carl Schmitt, such critical decisions are often conflated with decisionism. Among political theorists, decisionism denotes a theory of law and action whereby a law's originary force is coextensive with the force of the person who makes the law, such that that person may also cancel or subdue the law at will. As Schmitt argued in his 1934 defense of the Night of the Long Knives, "The true leader [Führer] is always also *Judge*. From the power inherent in the leader [Führertum] emanates the power to judge [Richtertum]."[1] That person who makes and protects the law is the person at whose discretion the law is silent. This person is, according to Schmitt, sovereign. But because decisions and power are invariably constrained and their context complex, decisionism, conceptualized in these terms, relies on a fallacious dichotomy between individual rule and rule of law with no counterpart in the real politics of a liberal polyarchy. It is only by isolating the moment of a decision, committing a *temporal fallacy*, that decisionism can appear coherent.

It is, then, a striking fact that many political theorists have taken decisionism as a descriptive feature of executive power in liberal polyarchies, such as the United States. Critical theorists like Giorgio Agamben, drawing Schmitt's claim to its natural conclusion, have found in decisionism grounds for the rejection of law-based regimes.[2] States are either incompetent and in peril or else mere fronts for absolute power, which can render citizens, at any moment, naked and helpless before raw, sovereign violence. In that case, what recommends the liberal polyarchy as a form of organization?

In what follows, I argue for a principled distinction between critical decision in a liberal polyarchy and decisionism. While all decisions are made, fundamentally, on their own authority, the decisionist decision, in Schmitt's words "emanates from nothingness."[3] That is, it exists independent of any normative, legal, or other considerations. By contrast, in liberal polyarchies, a range of prelegal principles and powers, partially codified, eternally expanding and contracting, exist alongside the range of prelegal (self-evident) rights. Powers like prerogative and police enable the flexibility necessary for critical decisions within a rich normative context. It is only by committing a temporal fallacy—isolating the decision from the events which lead up to and away from it—that critical decisions in a polyarchy can be mistaken for acts of independent, sovereign power. Ultimately, because a leader is accountable for her decisions, regardless of the power on the basis of which the decision was taken, critical decision is not decisionism and executive power is not sovereign. I illustrate my argument with examples of critical, *accountable* decisions made on the authority of both prerogative and police.

Decisionism in Political Theory

As the chief exponent of decisionism in twentieth-century political thought, Carl Schmitt argued that the parliamentary system under the Weimar constitution was ineffective in the face of threats from Nazi and communist parties, whose explicit aim was to dismantle the system which would bring them to power. Principled neutrality forbade the exclusion of these parties and rejected the fundamental distinction between friend and enemy that constitutes, for Schmitt, politics at its core. Liberal parliamentary regimes attempted to eradicate the role of sovereign power, marked, as Schmitt famously claimed, by the important capacity to decide on the exception.[4] It is the height of dangerous naiveté, for Schmitt, to insist on the continuous operation of neutral, liberal norms. Norms depend on a guarantor of order who holds near mythic power, can recognize a threat, and destroy it with neither hesitation nor burden of normative restriction.[5] Moreover, because such a threat may come about at any time, someone must have permanent responsibility for the identification of a state of exception, when the norms applicable to a normal situation are nullified. As opposed to a simple emergency (*Notstand*), a state of exception

(*Ausnahmezustand*) is a condition of "extreme peril, a danger to the existence of the state."[6] While an emergency may pose a threat to some characteristic, some predicate of the state (e.g., its GDP), exception pertains to the state as subject, which either exists or does not exist in a binary measure. Such a threat, according to Schmitt, is to a collective way of life, an identity, a tradition of governance, and not just to the preservation of life and limb.[7]

It is no easy matter to distinguish a passing emergency from an existential threat. The first warnings of the downfall of a state are rarely sudden or obvious. A condition of fundamental enmity, which is to say a properly political condition, has no determinate or objective metaphysical status; it could manifest in an infinite number of ways. So, there are no necessary and sufficient conditions warranting a state of exception. If no norms and legalized criteria clearly distinguish the normal situation from the exception, then someone, not some law, must decide when norms apply and when they do not. This means that Schmitt's conception of exception negates the possibility of a law-governed order.[8] No technocratic or discursive practice could determine what is merely *Not* and what *Ausnahmezustand*, so the law must be in a permanent condition of potential suspension, the person who so judges permanently above the law. This is an epistemological, rather than ontological, perspective on crisis.

Schmitt claims, "All law is 'situational law'"[9]—norms apply only to the normal situation. This person at whose discretion law operates or not, this decider, Schmitt defines as sovereign. The sovereign who must take command in the constantly potential state of exception must have "unlimited authority, which means the suspension of the entire existing order."[10] It is this sovereign power that renders norms possible—that is, the sovereign who decides is the *source and guarantor* of norms: "To create tranquility, security, and order, and thereby establish the normal situation, is the prerequisite for legal norms to be valid. Every norm presupposes the normal situation and no norm can be valid in an entirely abnormal situation."[11] The sovereign can be bound by no restriction except the end-appropriateness of the means he chooses.[12] Even here, the sovereign is his own judge. This is the meaning of sovereignty, and it is what separates this form of decision from others.

The separation of decision from legal and super-legal norms is always opposed to liberal and parliamentary perspectives centered on the rule of law. Schmitt says: "The precondition as well as the content of jurisdictional competence in such a case [i.e., a state of exception] must necessarily be unlimited. From a liberal constitutional point of view, there would be no jurisdictional competence at all."[13] Parliaments busy themselves with talk and normative debate when what is really required is decisive action in the moment of crisis. The liberal, faced with "Christ or Barabbas?" convenes a committee and a discussion.[14] It cannot be left to a committee to manage existential matters.

Schmitt speaks often of war in the context of enmity, but it is not restricted to external war, as Schmitt's sustained interest in revolutionary politics confirms.[15] At the sovereign's discretion, recognizing the enemy may require the extermination of some internal element of the state. Anyone can be declared the enemy of the state, because the Sovereign, as such, need give no reasons nor answer to any authority. Because the enemy can be killed, the Sovereign holds, at his discretion, the life of each in his hands. At the Sovereign's will, one can be rendered outside the law. And because the Sovereign refers to no norms and is not responsible for giving a reason, we are all always potentially outside the protection of the law—which is to say, it is as though we are already beyond the law's protection. These consequences of the theory of sovereign decision were brought home to Schmitt in the most visceral way. After joining the Nazi party in 1933 and accepting the Berlin chair of Hermann Heller (his Jewish colleague in exile), along with an appointment, courtesy of Göring, as State Counselor for Prussia, Schmitt later found himself under attack for hypocrisy and opportunism and backed away from politics in fear for his life.[16]

Schmitt's conception of law and protection at the will of the sovereign creates conceptual opportunities at the extreme right and the extreme left. Schmitt's service to the right, the action-orientation of his work, and its rejection of parliamentarism was very attractive to fascists. In addition to his early favor with the Nazis, he was a friend to the Franco regime, developing his theory of the Partisan in the course of invited lectures in Spain in the early 1960s.[17] But his conception of politics—its disdain for liberal neutrality, its valorization of energy—has been influential in left political thought too. Walter Benjamin was drawn to its theological seriousness.[18] And since the 1990s, with the rise of post-modernism undermining left grand-narratives, the European left has also felt the draw of Schmitt's notion of the divine power of decisive, originary action. Schmitt's sovereign decisionism has also been put to work toward critical theory's core task of diagnosing the times, particularly in the work of Giorgio Agamben.

Agamben has argued that Schmitt's insight into the state of exception reveals the violence and lawlessness at the heart of liberal democracy. The facade of law conceals the reality of always-potential exception. This means that anyone can, at any time, become *homo sacer*—a Roman legal category that Agamben uses to mean a person placed outside the protection of the state who can be freely killed.[19] No system of rights protects individuals precisely because sovereign power can render those rights irrelevant at any moment. Agamben thus takes Schmitt's characterization of government as the actually existing state of affairs, and uses the normative revulsion this generates to ground a case for the fundamental rejection of law as such.[20] The force of law, a term Agamben adapts from Derrida, is all there ever is, because the content or meaning of law has no relevance if, at any moment, it can be rendered as though it were not. The constant possibility of a state of exception is functionally equivalent to a constantly existing state of exception. Law is really only force, and we are all always potentially *homo sacer*, free to be killed at any moment.[21] So long as there is law, there is this sovereign power masquerading as justice. In this way, Schmitt's decisionism becomes a platform for a strange new form of revolutionary politics. Relying on Schmitt's argument with respect to sovereignty and the state of exception, it follows that both the Law and the State must die. What we need is to open up the possibility of "nonjuridical politics and human life," a politics of love where sovereignty and right do not intrude.[22]

Schmittian decisionism thus unwittingly opens up a new ground for radical and revolutionary politics of the left whose practitioners see in decisionism precisely the moral impetus for the liberal polyarchy's necessary destruction, or else for a principled withdrawal. Anyone skeptical of such a "politics of love" in place of law will see a variety of reasons to regret this form of left politics. I want now to show that, in conflating critical *decisions* in a liberal polyarchy with *decisionism*, there are reasons to reject this form of politics as unfounded.

Decisions and Decisionism

What distinguishes decisionism from decision? The first necessary condition of a *decisionist* decision is that it is ontologically self-contained. Schmitt claimed that the sovereign decision "emanates from nothingness."[23] What does it mean to make a decision that emanates from nothing? Decisions, generally, do have a peculiar ontological status. A decision takes place in a moment. A decision has no truth-value, but rather is always a spontaneous reification, changing the field in which it emerges by generating an intervention in the causal mesh of events. While a decision can be arbitrary, reasoned, intuitive, or impulsive, it cannot, by definition, be necessary or compelled. To claim that one was compelled to make a certain decision is to speak metaphorically: the reasons in favor of the decision were so strong that it would have been foolish to choose otherwise, but this is not necessity, per se. Even compelling reasons are not, literally, a form of compulsion. And, one cannot say that a decision, in itself, is incorrect, though one can judge its instrumental value with respect to some further goal, or its moral value according to some further normative considerations. That is, a decision can be wrong with respect to some criterion beyond itself, but qua decision, it is a self-emanating fact.

While some decisions are arbitrary—as when one decides between equally preferred ice cream flavors—others rest on instrumental, normative, or preferential grounds. In the case of sovereign decision, to claim that this decision emanates from nothing is not to claim that the sovereign decides without reasons, but rather that the reasons are entirely the sovereign's own, they form part of the sovereign self from which the decision emerges, and they do not stand as *justifications* drawn from outside. The sovereign cannot be compelled, morally or legally, to give these reasons. She, with her decision, stands alone. The decisionist decision is independent.

This self-contained character is a necessary but not sufficient condition for a decision to be decisionist. For example, the originary basis of a marriage is precisely this kind of ontological decision, willed into existence by means of a self-contained action. While legal criteria must be met thereafter, a marriage that lacks this force of self-generated will, without reason or justification, can be annulled, deemed never to have existed, despite the presence of the proper legal form. So, not all decisions that call something originary into existence are, purely by means of themselves, decisionist decisions. They must also be independent of law, which a marriage is not, and they must pertain to the protection of the state and its way of life.

These criteria mark a decisionist decision. The decisionist decision pertains to a political matter, and it stands on its own, divorced from any external law or reason. Again, this does not mean that the person who makes the decision is not guided by reasons, but those reasons are internal and cannot be forced into the open. That is to say, a decisionist decision is precisely *not* an accountable decision—no reasons can be demanded. This is why the decisionist decision is sovereign and why it is to be feared: with no external connection to reasons, there is no predictability and no accountability.

With this distinction in mind, we turn to political decision-making in those liberal polyarchies that Agamben and others consider particularly vile. Are these regimes actually reliant on decisionism, rendering us all *homo sacer*? Schmitt thought, on the example of Weimar, that liberal democracies were incapable of decisive action, but this is, evidently, empirically false. Within this framework, one might then conclude, with Agamben, that there is in fact some sovereign power at work behind the facade of liberal democracy. If a state requires sovereign power to survive, then either liberal polyarchies do not survive, which is evidently false, or sovereign power is surreptitiously at work making political decisions in isolation from external norms — that is, making decisionist decisions which render individuals *homo sacer*. But decisions on exceptions to the normal protection and enforcement of rights and law are evidently part of the liberal democratic governance toolkit. And these decisions, while political, are distinctly *not* decisionist.

Decision in a Polyarchy

A brief example: in the course of the 2013–16 Ebola outbreak, New Jersey Governor Chris Christie ordered Kaci Hickox quarantined for four days in a locked tent outside Newark Airport in New Jersey. A nurse with the humanitarian organization Doctors Without Borders, she was returning from caring for Ebola patients in Sierra Leone. Released from custody at Newark Airport and travelling to her home in Maine, Hickox was then ordered by the Public Health Board, under their authority in Title 22 S. 802, to remain in her house for the three-week incubation period characteristic of the Ebola virus. Hickox defied this order, arguing that, because she was not symptomatic, she posed no risk to the public. The Chief Judge of the Maine District Court, Charles LaVerdiere, found for Ms. Hickox on the basis that while the scientific evidence presented to the Court supported intensive daily monitoring for symptoms, it did not necessitate quarantine.[24] But the judge did not question the Public Health Board's authority to quarantine Hickox should she become symptomatic. For not only is the health board's power to do so explicit in the intentionally broadly worded public health laws of the State of Maine, but these laws in turn rest on the established authority of the police power, whose long history in American jurisprudence and European political thought has been strangely ignored in contemporary scholarship on limitation, derogation, and violation of rights in the context of crisis. In Ms. Hickox's case, the court quickly corrected the Public Health Board's use of police power. Within days, Ms. Hickox was able to bring her case before a judge. And in line with the limitations that have—through America's flexible institutions—grown up around the police power, her liberty to move about was restored. Hickox subsequently sued Governor Christie for the critical decision he took to quarantine her, violating her civil rights and defaming her.[25] A rich normative context led up to the decision to quarantine Ms. Hickox, and a rich normative context informed the layers of accountability that followed: technocratic input, institutional norms, and democratic passions bolstered and countered one another in a polyarchic reach (however flawed) for the public good.

This complexity illustrates how it is only in the face of a false and excessively abstract dichotomy between rule by law and individual rule that the notion of sovereign decision could be made appealing. This blunt dichotomy ignores the myriad and messy ways in which written law; prerogative and police power; principle, moral normativity; legal interpretation and reinterpretation; layers of individual discretion; and diffuse individual-power, civil, legal, and political accountability interact in a polyarchy. A polyarchy, following Dahl, is a system of government in which citizens can express preferences both through voting and through civil action and free speech, where nearly anyone can run for office, but in which elites compete for election, and interest groups compete for the attention and support of these elites.[26] In this kind of regime, there is no stark zero sum between law and individual power. Rather, power has many sources and is checked in many ways, influencing the development, interpretation, enforcement, and reinterpretation of law, including constitutional law.[27] All these forces aim not just for personal advantage, but also to advocate for different visions of how to define and achieve three common aims of any state: to paraphrase Ernst Freund, its preservation, the pursuit of right and justice, and the public welfare.[28] Nobody, in a polyarchy, is sovereign. If the buck stops, it is only for a moment. As a result, the shape of government, the way its institutions operate in practice, changes and develops with context.

Liberal democracies are built to be flexible. In particular, in common law regimes, there are two forms of prelegal power that specifically impact legal and moral decision-making in crises, obviating the need for sovereignty. These serve as resources for decisions made on their own, not on legal, authority. But this is not decisionism, because such decisions remain tightly entwined with external legal and moral norms. While they are not determined by external norms, and while they may violate these norms, the decision maker is never independent from norms. In the vibrant cacophony of moral life in a polyarchy, she must ultimately give reasons, accept responsibility, submit to judgment, and, in some cases, pay the penalty for that judgment in a crisis.

Flexibility is inherent in the operation of rights. Most rights in international charters and most rights in domestic constitutions and jurisprudence come replete with limitations and, usually, broadly worded conditions for derogation. Within polyarchies, there are those who persistently claim the absoluteness of rights, claims which form an important part of the civic constraint on abuse. But in practice, there are few absolute rights and no, or nearly no, laws that are uniformly and consistently enforced. The practice of law and the practice of rights are always fluid. That flexibility and fluidity sometimes come at a high cost, and I make no claim with respect to the uprightness or purity of any specific derogation practice or decision in a flexible regime. My claim is descriptive, not normative: these regimes are flexible *and* accountable, enabling security while eschewing sovereignty.

One way to think of this is that prelegal rights may be self-evident, flowing naturally and logically from the very idea of liberal democracy. But prelegal power to limit rights is just as organic and, in a crisis, self-evident. It is as much a core duty of government to preserve the public welfare and the existence of the state as it is to preserve justice and rights. It is only together that these three legs of liberal democratic government support individuals within a state. The public good is best served when rights are not only protected but enjoyed. This requires both the persistence of a working state which can enforce those rights and the persistence of conditions of public welfare which enable their enjoyment. These conditions are protected by prelegal powers to derogate rights, specifically the powers of prerogative and police. While these three state aims conflict, as I have argued elsewhere, good judgment and after-the-fact accountability aid navigation among them.[29]

Just as liberal democracies, particularly in a common law tradition, have used law and written constitutions to codify, confer, and constrain prelegal rights, they have done the same with prerogative and police power. But just as the legal codification of rights does not supersede their natural expression, the powers of prerogative and police persist regardless of their legally codified form. The law may be stretched or even silenced for the achievement of public aims, just as the law can be altered or made more pliant where these powers press too hard on rights.

Prerogative

Locke defined prerogative as "power to act according to discretion, for the public good, without prescription of the law, and sometimes even against it."[30] In the United Kingdom, the power was a means of protecting against foreign incursion as well as the residue of power the King could use to promote the *salus populi*, or public good. In the course of the seventeenth century, tension between parliament and the Crown led to Petition of Right (1641) and later the Bill of Rights (1689), which, along with the fresh threat of royal execution or expulsion, served to check royal prerogative by formal and informal means. Through parliamentary reform in the nineteenth century, many of the prerogative powers that had inhered in the Crown came to adhere in the Ministers of the Crown and the cabinet, although some powers do continue to inhere in the Royal Person. While many prerogative powers are clearly defined, others, particularly those meant for managing contingencies, are intentionally delineated only vaguely. All are, in theory, governed by common law precedent and subject to incorporation or supersession in a statute. By reference to statute and precedent, the scope of prerogative is justiciable. In addition, since *Council of Civil Service Unions v Minister for the Civil Service* (1983), executive action in the UK on the basis of prerogative that touches individual liberties is subject to judicial review, not only with respect to the scope of power, but also with respect to the action taken. Furthermore, Ministers who exercise prerogative are answerable, after the fact, both to Parliament and Departmental Select Committees.[31] They must also stand for reelection. While the prerogative power is the subject of considerable contemporary debate with respect to scope, constraint, and the degree to which it should be codified in statute, two points are evident: first the prerogative offers flexibility to act decisively in the absence of explicit statute or sanction, or even, in certain cases, against statute. Second, the prerogative power, in the United Kingdom, remains enmeshed in normativity and subject to accountability (of variable adequacy).

In the United States, questions about prerogative power, its enablement and constraint, infused Madison's discussion of the separation of powers in the *Federalist*.[32] The framers of the American constitution left scope for executive prerogative through a combination of the vagueness of the description of presidential powers and commitments undertaken in swearing the Oath of Office. When a President acts through her prerogative, she acts in a unilateral, quasi-legislative manner. The justification she gives may be explicitly constitutional, as when George W. Bush justified his actions in the aftermath of the attacks of September 11, 2001, on the basis of reinterpretation of vague presidential power. Or, he may invoke some overarching need implicit in the Oath of Office, as when Lincoln questioned, in response to the Supreme Court's Ruling on his suspension of Habeas Corpus, whether "all the laws but one" should go unexecuted.[33]

Lincoln followed in the tradition of Jefferson, who provides perhaps the most explicit example of prerogative power in American history. Jefferson purchased Louisiana from France with no legal warrant. Jefferson wrote, "France possessing herself of Louisiana ... is the embryo of a tornado which will burst on the countries on both shores of the Atlantic and involve in its effects their highest destinies."[34] With Napoleon's eye on North America, and access to the Mississippi compromised, France's foothold on the continent was a dramatic threat not only to the security of the United States, but to its commerce and to national unity. Jefferson sent James Monroe to Paris to negotiate an agreement, and when Napoleon gave up his North American ambitions in the face of military pressures elsewhere, Monroe pressed this advantage, agreeing to purchase the whole territory, doubling the size of the United States and securing access to critical waterways, for the sum of $15 million. The deal was announced in July 1803 with an October deadline for ratification. Jefferson deliberated intensively with his cabinet, concerned over his lack of constitutional authority to execute such an undertaking. As he famously wrote to his friend Breckenridge in September of 1803:

> The Executive in siesing [sic] the fugitive occurrence which so much advanced the good of their country, have done an act beyond the constitution. The legislature in casting behind them Metaphysical subtleties, and risking themselves like faithful servants, must ratify & pay for it, and throw themselves on their country for doing for them unauthorised what we know they would have done for themselves had they been in a situation to do it. It is the case of a guardian, investing the money of his ward in purchasing an important adjacent territory; & saying to him when of age, I did this for your good; I pretend to no right to bind you. You may disavow me, and I must get out of the scrape as I can. I thought it my duty to risk myself for you. But we shall not be disavowed by the nation, and their act of indemnity will confirm & not weaken the constitution, by more strongly marking out its lines.[35]

Jefferson acted decisively in sending Monroe to negotiate the agreement and in following through without constitutional authority. But his decision was not sovereign. It was situated amid normative, legal, strategic, and political considerations, preceded by deliberation and followed by ratification on the part of Senate, and then by the people as

Jefferson stood for reelection the following year. Years later, he wrote to John Colvin:

> A strict observance of the written laws is doubtless one of the high duties of a good citizen: but it is not the highest. The laws of necessity, of self-preservation, of saving our country when in danger, are of higher obligation. To lose our country by a scrupulous adherence to written law, would be to lose the law itself, with life, liberty, property & all those who are enjoying them with us; thus absurdly sacrificing the end to the means.[36]

Prerogative efforts like these, conducted in a spirit of accountability to the American people, yield, when there is popular approval, what scholars of presidentialism call a "frontlash," spurring expansion of executive power, however temporarily.[37] Locke himself recognized this when he said that the greatest danger of prerogative was its use by a good and trusted prince who may leave this expanded power to a bad successor.[38] In the American context, misuse of prerogative has sometimes generated a backlash, as when Truman attempted to seize American steel mills during the Korean War, and Nixon impounded billions of dollars of funds that Congress had approved for domestic programs.[39] But again, as in the United Kingdom, uses of prerogative demonstrate the inherent flexibility of liberal polyarchy, and the extensive field of normativity and accountability in which any executive who would act on the basis of prerogative is situated.

In both the American and UK contexts, there have been moves toward and away from the legal codification of unilateral executive action. Nixon's counsel claimed, "Essentially, this concept of 'executive power' [is the] overall duty to run the government responsibly and efficiently"; and hence, any power that served that end was implied in the grant of executive power to the President.[40] In the US, George W. Bush famously appealed to strained legal interpretations, unwilling to act without explicit legal sanction. Jack Goldsmith has argued that this is typical: the expansion of executive power in the twentieth and twenty-first centuries means legalization is now the norm.[41] In the UK, the last decade has seen substantial engagement with the question of the codification of prerogative power, including concerns about the limitation of flexibility.[42] Regardless of codification, there will remain a residue of power under the common law for confronting crises with decisive action, without the need for sovereign power.

I have argued elsewhere that it is because of after-the-fact accountability, which evidence suggests factors into before-the-fact deliberation, that the use of prerogative or other expansive and extraordinary executive measures can stand in the spirit of liberal democracy.[43]

Jefferson faced Congress and received its blessing. Nixon was mired in the courts. In addition to the threat of impeachment and domestic (or, in certain cases, international) prosecution, there are the threats of electoral failure or infamy. The wide range of political and normative constraints, in addition to legal constraints, on extraordinary executive action supplement or supersede the constraint of law and precedent.[44] Again, it is not my claim that accountability is always adequate or effective in preventing abuse, nor do I minimize the human cost of such lapses. Rather, my claim is that no decision on the grounds of prerogative or its expansive legally sanctioned cousins is sovereign. To attempt to radically distinguish law and exception to law is to remain blind to the realities of politics, particularly in complex polyarchies like that in the United States. Law, politics, and moral normativity all accompany, even while they do not determine, any decision in a liberal polyarchy made on the grounds of that prelegal power to serve the public good and preserve the state.

Police

Even more damning to the claim of sovereign exception is the fact that, in liberal democracies, flexibility with respect to rights extends well beyond extreme situations. The limitation and derogation of rights is neither rare nor restricted to conditions of existential risk. In promoting and protecting the public welfare, rights derogations are common. As with prerogative power and its legalized expressions, these more quotidian practices of exception are surrounded by a substantial jurisprudence and public discourse which, while not determining a leader's decision, negate any suggestion of sovereignty. Day-to-day protections of the public welfare that require limitation and derogation of rights are conducted on the authority of the prelegal power of police; and here, too, we see the inherent flexibility of liberal polyarchy.

Police power is not the power of *"the police,"* as in Peel's police, but rather "the authority to provide for the public health, safety, and morals."[45] In the US context, police power rests with the states, unless the pertinent matter affects interstate commerce. Though ignored in contemporary political theory (if not in legal history),[46] the police power was a common concern in political treatises of the decades surrounding America's founding. It was prescribed and described in a family of versions by the likes of Adam Smith, Blackstone, Bentham, and even Kant.[47] For Bentham, "Police applies itself to the prevention both of offences and calamities; its expedients are, not punishments but precautions; it foresees evils, and provides against wants."[48] For Adam Smith, the police "comprehends: ... to preserve the cleanlyness of the roads, streets, etc. and prevent the bad effects of corrupting and putrefying substances" and ensures "cheapness and plenty."[49] Blackstone, a likely direct source for American founders and legislators, describes the police as concerned with matters "such as are against the public health of the nation; a concern of the highest importance."[50] In both *Federalist* 17 and 34, Hamilton makes reference to "domestic police" with the same apparent meaning, though both times he diminishes its importance and contrasts it with those great matters of state that prompt ambition or expense.[51] With some variation, these theorists describe police as the power to prevent harm by securing order and sanitation, and promoting affluence, clearly interrelated.[52] Ernst Freund explains: "The state ... exercises its compulsory powers for the prevention and anticipation of wrong by narrowing common law rights, through conventional restraints and positive regulations which are not confined to the prohibition of wrongful acts. It is this ... which constitutes the essence of police power."[53] A wide range of government action can only be understood as issuing from this power: keeping the peace regulating the safety of infrastructure, the management of dangerous animals, the preparation of food, the practice of medicine, and of death and burial, gambling, lotteries, urban planning and liquor licensing, sanitation and quarantine, labor laws, weights and measures, prostitution, marriage, delinquency, and the protection of minors.[54] All these government actions involve infringements on liberty, from minor to substantial.

We accept the exercise of any power on the basis of claims, verbal or symbolic, for its legitimacy. Rhetorically successful power claims rest partly on the grounds of the normative standing of the person exercising that power and partly on the basis of the normative legitimacy of the use to which she sets her power. From this perspective, there is nothing sinister about supra- or prelegal power, which, like every form of power, makes normative claims for itself. What legitimates a specific use of police power is that it is exercised in accordance with the boundaries of existing jurisprudence, along with any supra-legal normative justification of its use. In some cases, this normative justification may expand the power, altering the jurisprudence going forward. But in such cases, there is no reason to assume any sovereign or pseudo-theological source. Protecting the public welfare is a charge we give to *whomever* governs, it is one reason why we seek to have and maintain a government at all, and police is a key tool to meet that charge.

Because police is less discussed than prerogative, I provide an extended example: the management of a smallpox outbreak. Both rights limitation and serious rights derogations are widespread in cases of epidemic disease, because the physical safety of each necessitates the safety of all, and the safety of all demands constraints on each. The control of epidemic diseases touches core liberties: of physical integrity in the case of compulsory vaccination, of liberty of movement in the case of quarantine and isolation, of property in case of destroying contaminated materials, of freedom of assembly in the case of shutting houses of worship and schools and banning public meetings to minimize contagion. And, unlike the liberty restrictions brought about, for instance, by criminal conviction, quarantine and isolation are imposed on an epidemic's *victims*.

Epidemics are a permanent fixture of human life. In addition to the annual influenza outbreak, historically, the major epidemic killer in the United States was smallpox. Smallpox has ravaged human communities for thousands of years. Virulent and—in close quarters—airborne, without the benefit of vaccination, it kills around 30 percent of affected adults and 80 percent of affected children, horribly disfiguring survivors.[55] There have been two main means of managing smallpox outbreaks: quarantine/isolation and inoculation, and each involves both preventive and reactive rights derogation. Smallpox was the disease for which inoculation was first developed; but in its first iteration, variolation, it had a fatality rate of 0.5–2 percent.[56] It was only when Edward Jenner discovered that a cousin virus, cowpox, could provide the same protection with a much lower risk that the modern era of vaccination really began in the West. Even this new vaccination procedure was not without risk, however, as a lack of regulation, inadequate sanitation, and irregular production and storage led to deaths: American children, for example, sometimes contracted tetanus from contaminated vaccines.[57] Nonetheless, the use of vaccination dramatically decreased the number of deaths from smallpox across the United States, and (notably, also as a matter of police) regulation of the vaccine industry has made the process safer and safer.

We now turn to the 1901–03 Boston epidemic to illustrate how the flexibility of rights and the role of law and normativity after the fact separate decisive action from decisionism. In this epidemic, the last great American smallpox outbreak, mass vaccination campaigns led to fatality rates that were dramatically lower than average. Between 1901 and 1903, 1,596 cases were diagnosed, an attack rate of three cases per one thousand citizens and a mortality rate of 17 percent.[58] All Boston school children had been required to undergo vaccination since 1827, and all American soldiers had been required to be vaccinated since 1834.[59] This made sense from a military perspective because even with the benefits of smallpox vaccination, historically, deaths from disease vastly outnumbered deaths from battle wounds in American military encounters.[60] Disease, in war, was the greatest killer. Compulsory vaccination of school children and soldiers constitutes a mass rights derogation to *prevent* a potential existential crisis.

The head of Boston's Board of Health at the turn of the twentieth century was the Harvard Medical School professor Dr Samuel Holmes Durgin. In late 1901, he took a number of police measures to mitigate the epidemic, including isolation of the sick and quarantine of the exposed on an island in Boston Harbor. The Board called for the "thorough disinfection, vaccination and revaccination of all persons who have been in contact or exposed to [a] patient and surveillance of the suspects for two weeks."[61] While the Board offered free vaccination clinics, and while four hundred thousand people were vaccinated or revaccinated in the Boston area in 1901 and 1902, cases continued to erupt. As the *New York Times* reported, "Over 500 people have been vaccinated in the last two days. ... [But m]any refuse to be vaccinated, while others evade the doctors when they call at the houses."[62] And so in the face of widespread fear, misinformation, and resistance to vaccination, the Public Health Board sent gangs out into the streets and to rooming houses, forming mobile forced vaccination clinics. As they went, they not only vaccinated with violent restraint where necessary, but sought out and forcibly confined the sick and exposed, burning any potentially infected property.[63]

These apparent violations of the fourteenth amendment met with vigorous debate both in the legislature and in the media, where opponents of the measures—members of the nascent anti-vaccination movement still with us today—aptly noted the use of excessive force and the "autocratic power" the Public Health Board attempted to wield.[64] Yet as the New York Court of Appeals had noted in the then recent (1895) case *In re Smith*, "I think no one will dispute the right of the legislature to enact such measures as will protect all persons from the impending calamity of a pestilence, and to vest in local authorities such comprehensive powers as will enable them to act competently and effectively."[65] Indeed, it is arguably a state government's *duty* to do so.[66] In the late nineteenth and early twentieth centuries, where a locality failed to contain disease, state or federal officials often assumed control in their stead.[67]

Exceptional times may call for exceptional police measures, but not for sovereignty. The Boston smallpox epidemic led to several court decisions, including a cornerstone case in American public health jurisprudence: *Jacobson v. Massachusetts*. Henning Jacobson, a pastor, claimed to have suffered after a childhood inoculation and refused to be vaccinated or to pay the consequent five-dollar fine.[68] Jacobson argued that compulsory vaccination violated "the inherent right of every freeman to care for his own body and health in such a way as to him seems best."[69] The Supreme Court held in its 1905 decision that public health trumps individual liberties, and that while the state could not force vaccination on a person for *her own good*, it certainly could do so for the *public good*. But there were important caveats: " If a statute purporting to have been enacted to protect the public health, the public morals or the public safety, has no real or substantial relation to those objects, or is, beyond all question, a plain, palpable invasion of rights secured by the fundamental law, it is the duty of the courts to so adjudge, and thereby give effect to the Constitution."[70] Justice Harlan delivered the decision for the majority, arguing that while a Public Health Board could reasonably grant a medical exemption, particularly to a child, there would have to be compelling scientific grounds, which there were not in the case of Jacobson. Furthermore, while the State could enforce a penalty for refusing vaccination, it could not force vaccination.

The Court found that because the Public Health Board had acted on the basis of the police power neither unreasonably nor arbitrarily, this had not been a violation of Jacobson's fourteenth amendment rights. The Court compared protection against epidemic disease to self-defense since, after all, "There are manifold restraints to which each person is necessarily subject for the common good."[71] And so Jacobson was ordered to pay his fine of five dollars.

The executive's power—whether as police or prerogative—to make exceptions to quotidian rights protections to serve the public good is part of the organic fabric of every liberal democracy. But the effectiveness of police and prerogative, as well as the police *of* police and prerogative, depend on institutional safeguards and after-the-fact accountability. Boards of Public Health have sweeping powers to decide on derogations of rights, but courts, then, limit police power on the basis of what is rational with respect to scientific evidence, what is reasonable with respect to the end in view, and what is nondiscriminatory. Boards of Public Health must match means of prevention and control to the particular disease in question, its mechanism of transmission, its level of contagion, and the seriousness of its effects. The measures taken must be supported by the best available science, and they must not be discriminatory. They require that states minimize the negative effects of necessary rights derogations, and treat those quarantined, isolated, or required to submit to vaccination with dignity and respect, as ends in themselves, not as means only. The members of Boards of Public Health must be aware of and must anticipate correctives and consequences of any abuse or miscalculation, and must bear this in mind even as they maintain the scope for flexible judgment in rapidly changing circumstances. This is rich normative soil for decisions, even crisis decisions. All of this is robustly evident, for example, in the preamble to the Model State Emergency Health Powers Act, by now adopted by most American states.[72]

When the use of police power does not support the *salus populi*, it meets its limit. In *Jew Ho v. Williamson* (1900), the Court held that a quarantine around San Francisco's Chinatown on suspicion of bubonic plague, which excluded certain houses owned by non-Chinese persons "cannot be continued, by reason of the fact that it is unreasonable, unjust, and oppressive, and therefore contrary to the laws limiting the police powers of the state and municipality in such matters; and … that it is discriminating in its character, and is contrary to the provisions of the fourteenth amendment."[73] And in *Holden v. Hardy*, the Supreme Court found that "the police power cannot be put forward as an excuse for oppressive and unjust legislation," and on this basis, upheld a Utah law limiting the length of miners' workdays.[74] When there is overreach, a combination of normative and legal principle, together with the cacophonous politics of a healthy polyarchy, intervene to press for accountability.

In protecting the public good, both prerogative and police power protect the necessary conditions for the enjoyment of rights. They do so by providing normative grounds alongside other considerations, which together inform (but do not determine) political agents' decisive, but still accountable, action. In this temporal context, it is clear that even world rattling decisions in liberal democracies are not evidence of Schmittian decisionism. They only appear so when removed from their temporal context, from the political, scientific, normative, and legal deliberation that led up to the point of decision, and from the legal, political, and normative fallout that comes next. It is only by committing what we might call the temporal fallacy, by isolating the moment of decision, that he who decides on the exception might appear to be sovereign.

Conclusion

In Schmitt's famous formulation: "There exists *no norm* that is *applicable* to chaos. For a legal order to make sense, a *normal situation* must exist."[75] But in challenging situations in particular, decision-makers look to norms to help navigate the often conflicting requirements of protecting the public: both rights and the conditions for their enjoyment. The public, in turn, hold decision-makers accountable on the basis of norms. Decisionism isolates the moment of decision, ignoring this range of ways in which norms and laws feed into a decision, however autonomous in its moment, and then inform mechanisms of accountability after the fact. Decision is not decisionism. The illusion of decisionism depends upon the temporal fallacy.

In chaos and in calm, decision makers in liberal polyarchies act in this rich normative context. While this cacophonous mode of crisis management does not, of course, consistently yield morally optimal results (after all, it is driven by people), it has the resources both to be effective and often self-correcting, and it is incumbent on denizens of such states to work to improve those mechanisms of self-correction. However, decisionism has caught the imagination of many political thinkers who see in it not only a fundamental insight into the nature of emergencies but a clear view, in this isolated instant, of the true nature of law and power. If all law exists only by leave of sovereign decision, then we are all not only the subjects of that sovereign, but its objects also. This persistent rhetoric—of decisionism, exception, and sovereignty—is a dangerous fiction, encouraging fantasies of anomic freedom. These distract from the important work of a critical study of law and institutions as they are with a focus on improving what they might be. There is nothing in the messy, plural environment of crisis that necessitates sovereign exception. To claim otherwise is an abdication of responsibility. It is time that straw Leviathan blew over.

Nomi Claire Lazar (PhD, Yale 2005) is Associate Dean of Academic Affairs and Associate Professor of Politics at Yale-NUS College in Singapore. She is the author of *States of Emergency in Liberal Democracies* (Cambridge University Press, 2009) and of *Out of Joint: Power, Crisis, and the Rhetoric of Time* (Yale University Press, 2019). Lazar has been Harper-Schmidt Collegiate Assistant Professor at the University of Chicago, Canadian Bicentennial Visiting Fellow at Yale University, and, prior to graduate school, served in the Criminal Law Policy section of the Department of Justice, Canada.

Notes

The research for this chapter was supported by the Social Sciences and Humanities Research Council of Canada.

1. Carl Schmitt, "Der Fuhrer Schützt das Recht," *Deutsche Juristen-Zeitung* 15 (1934): 946–47. My translation.
2. Giorgio Agamben, *Means Without End*, trans. Vincenzo Binetti and Cesare Casarino (Minneapolis: University of Minnesota Press, 2000), 112.
3. Carl Schmitt, *The Crisis of Parliamentary Democracy*, trans. Ellen Kennedy (Cambridge, MA: MIT Press, 1988), 31–32.
4. Schmitt, *The Crisis of Parliamentary Democracy*, 36.
5. On the importance of mythic power, see Carl Schmitt, *The Leviathan in the State Theory of Thomas Hobbes*, trans. George Schwab (Westport, CT: Greenwood Press, 1996).
6. Carl Schmitt, *Political Theology*, trans. George Schwab (Cambridge: MIT Press, 1985), 6.
7. Carl Schmitt, *The Concept of the Political*, trans. George Schwab (Chicago, IL: University of Chicago Press, 2007), 27, 49.
8. See the interesting discussion in Marc de Wilde, "Uncertain Futures and the Problem of Constraining Emergency Powers: Temporal Dimensions of Carl Schmitt's Theory of the State of Exception," in *Temporal Boundaries of Law and Politics: Time Out of Joint*, ed. Lyana Francot and Luigi Corrias (London: Routledge, 2018), 107–125.
9. Schmitt, *Political Theology*, 13.
10. Schmitt, *Political Theology*, 12.
11. Schmitt, *The Concept of the Political*, 46.
12. Schmitt, *Die Diktatur* (Berlin: Duncker & Humblot, 2007), xvii ff.
13. Schmitt, *Political Theology*, 7.
14. Schmitt, *Political Theology*, 62. Schmitt is discussing the views of Donoso Cortès here.
15. Carl Schmitt, *The Theory of the Partisan: Intermediate Commentary on the Concept of the Political*, trans. G. L. Ulmen (New York: Telos Press Publishing, 2007).
16. See George Schwab's apologist introduction in Schmitt, *Leviathan*, xiv ff.
17. Schmitt, *Partisan*.
18. On some interesting affinities between Benjamin and Schmitt, see Marc de Wilde, "Meeting Opposites: The Political Theologies of Walter Benjamin and Carl Schmitt," *Philosophy and Rhetoric* 44 (2011).
19. Giorgio Agamben, *Homo Sacer*, trans. Daniel Heller-Roazan (Stanford, CA: Stanford University Press, 1998).
20. Agamben, *Homo Sacer*, 28–29; Giorgio Agamben, *State of Exception*, trans. Kevin Attell (Chicago, IL: University of Chicago Press, 2005), 40, 63.
21. "The camp, which is now securely lodged within the city's interior, is the new biopolitical *nomos* of the planet." Agamben, *Homo Sacer*, 176.
22. Agamben, *Means Without End*, 112, 114–15.
23. Schmitt, *Political Theology*, 32.

24. Mary C. Mayhew, Commissioner State of Maine Department of Health and Human Services v. Hickox, State of Maine District Court Docket No: CV-2014-36.
25. The suit is ongoing. "Quarantined Nurse Opposes Christie's Attempt to End Case," ACLU, 15 March 2016, https://www.aclu-nj.org/news/2016/03/15/quarantined-nurse-opposes-christies-attempt-end-case.
26. Robert Dahl, *Polyarchy: Participation and Opposition* (New Haven, CT: Yale University Press, 1972).
27. I develop this argument for the importance of power pluralism in emergencies in Nomi Claire Lazar, "Making Emergencies Safe for Democracy," *Constellations* 13 (2006): 506–21.
28. Ernst Freund, *Police Power, Public Policy, and Constitutional Rights* (Chicago, IL: Callaghan & Co, 1904), 3.
29. Nomi Claire Lazar, *States of Emergency in Liberal Democracies* (Cambridge, UK: Cambridge University Press, 2009), 18ff.
30. John Locke, *Second Treatise of Government*, chapter 14, http://www.constitution.org/jl/2ndtreat.htm.
31. Lucinda Maer and Oonagh Gay, *The Royal Prerogative*, House of Commons Library SN/PC/03861, 30 December 2009.
32. Alexander Hamilton, John Jay, and James Madison, *Federalist Papers* (New York: Signet Classics, 2003), 47–51.
33. Abraham Lincoln, *Message to Congress in Special Session*, 4 July 1861, http://www.fjc.gov/history/home.nsf/page/tu_merryman_doc_5.html. See also *Ex Parte Merryman*, 17 F. Cas. 144 (C.C.D. Md. 1861) (No. 9487).
34. Thomas Jefferson to Pierre Samuel Du Pont de Nemours, Letter of 25 April 1802, http://founders.archives.gov/documents/Jefferson/01-37-02-0263.
35. Thomas Jefferson to John Breckenridge, Letter of 12 August 1803, http://founders.archives.gov/documents/Jefferson/01-41-02-0139.
36. Thomas Jefferson to John Colvin, Letter of 20 September 1810, http://founders.archives.gov/documents/Jefferson/03-03-02-0060.
37. Richard Pious, *The American Presidency* (New York: Basic Books, 1977), 46ff.
38. Locke, *Second Treatise*, s. 166.
39. On Truman, see Maeva Marcus, *Truman and the Steel Seizure Case: The Limits of Presidential Power (New York: Columbia University Press, 1973)*. Truman's move was adjudicated in Youngstown Sheet & Tube Co. v. Sawyer, 343 U.S. 579 (1952). On Nixon, see Neil Soltman, "The Limits of Executive Power: Impoundment of Funds," *Catholic University Law Review* 23 (1973): 359.
40. Pealo v. Farmers Home Administration, 361 F. Supp. 1320 (D.D.C. 1973) at 15. Cited in Soltman, "The Limits of Executive Power," 364.
41. Jack Goldsmith, "The Irrelevance of Prerogative Power, and the Evils of Secret Legal Interpretation," in *Extra-Legal Power and Legitimacy*, ed. B. Kleinerman and C. Fatovic (Oxford: Oxford University Press, 2013).
42. Ministry of Justice (United Kingdom), *Review of the Executive Royal Prerogative: Final Report* (15 October 2009).

43. Lazar, *States of Emergency*, 132. On the effectiveness of oversight regimes, see, for instance, Christoph Schreuer, "Derogation of Human Rights in Situations of Public Emergency: The Experience of the European Convention on Human Rights," *Yale Journal of World Public Order* 9 (1982).
44. Political constitutionalism, as it pertains to emergency powers, is discussed in the contributions of Lazar and Tushnet in *Emergencies and the Limits of Legality*, ed. V. Ramraj and Mark Tushnet. (Cambridge, Cambridge University Press, 2008) and in Mark Tushnet, "Emergency Powers and Terrorism-Related Regulation Circa 2012," in *Extra-Legal Power and Legitimacy*, ed. B. Kleinerman and C. Fatovic (Oxford: Oxford University Press, 2013).
45. It is noteworthy, however, that Sir Robert Peel prioritized the *prevention* of crime and disorder as the job of the police, and the gauge of "efficient" policing was, for Peel, precisely the absence of crime and the invisibility of those officers of police. Charles Reith, *A New Study of Police History* (London: Oliver & Boyd: 1956), 140; Barnes v. Glen Theatre, 501 U.S. 569 (1991), 569.
46 48. William Novak, *The People's Welfare: Law and Regulation in Nineteenth-Century America* (Chapel Hill: University of North Carolina Press, 2006).
47. Kant says, "Police provide for public *security, convenience*, and *decency*." *Metaphysics of Morals*, trans. Mary Gregor (Cambridge: Cambridge University Press), 6:325.
48. Jeremy Bentham, *Theory of Legislation*, vol. 2 (Boston, MA: Weeks, 1840), 7.
49. Adam Smith, *Lectures on Justice, Police, Revenue, and Arms* (Oxford: Clarendon, 1869), 154.
50. William Blackstone, "Blackstone's Commentaries on the Laws of England: Book the Fourth—Chapter the Thirteenth: Of Offenses Against the Public Health, and the Public Police or Economy," Yale Law School, http://avalon.law.yale.edu/18th_century/blackstone_bk4ch13.asp.
51. Hamilton, Jay, and Madison, *Federalist Papers*, 114, 205.
52. It is interesting to note how consistently these theorists associate security and order with prosperity, because it makes the federal extension of police in the form of the commerce clause more natural.
53. Freund, *Police Power*, 6.
54. Freund, *Police Power*, iii.
55. In the twentieth century alone, smallpox killed somewhere between 300 and 500 million people before it was eradicated in 1977 with the help of a massive, global vaccination campaign. For contrast, it is estimated that 109.7 million deaths resulted from military conflicts in the twentieth century. Etienne Krug, *World Report on Violence and Health* (Geneva: WHO, 2002), 218.
56. The intentional exposure to dead smallpox virus seems to have first been practiced in China during the tenth century, and had become common practice by the Ming Dynasty, as it was, too, in the Ottoman Empire at least by the beginning of the eighteenth century. It may also have been practiced in India. F. Fenner, *Smallpox and Its Eradication* (Geneva: WHO, 1988), 246ff.

57. D. E. Lilienfeld, "The First Pharmacoepidemiologic Investigations: National Drug Safety Policy in the United States, 1901–1902," *Perspectives in Biology and Medicine* 51 (2008): 188–98; Charles Armstrong, "Tetanus following Vaccination against Smallpox, and Its Prevention: With Special Reference to the Use of Vaccination Shields and Dressings," *Public Health Reports* 42 no. 50 (1927): 3061–71.
58. Of these, apparently due to the benefits of vaccination even to those who did get sick, only 17 percent died. Michael R. Albert et al., "Smallpox Manifestations and Survival during the Boston Epidemic of 1901 to 1903," *Annals of Internal Medicine* 137 no. 12 (2002): 993–1000. It is noteworthy that one effect of police-mandated compulsory vaccination of schoolchildren was that 19 percent of cases occurred in pre-school aged (and therefore unvaccinated) children, while recently vaccinated six–ten year olds, though representing a similar overall number of Bostonians, accounted for only 3 percent of cases.
59. *James Hodge Jr. and L. O. Gostin, "School Vaccination Requirements: Historical, Social, and Legal Perspectives," Kentucky Law Journal 90 (2001): 8331.*
60. Vincent Cirillo, *Bullets and Bacilli: The Spanish-American War and Military Medicine* (New Brunswick, NJ: Rutgers University Press, 2004). See also Michael Willrich, *Pox: An American History* (New York: Penguin, 2011), 117ff.
61. *Thirty-First Annual Report of the Health Department of the City of Boston for the Year 1902* (Boston, MA: Municipal Printing Office, 1903), 83.
62. "Smallpox in Cambridge: Schools Close and Church Services Are Suspended in Consequence of Prevalence of the Disease," *The New York Times*, 21 June 1902: 6.
63. "Smallpox Decreasing," *Boston Globe*, 27 December 1901: 7.
64. M. R. Albert, "The Last Smallpox Epidemic in Boston and the Vaccination Controversy, 1901–1903," *New England Journal of Medicine* 344 (2001): 375–79.
65. The Justices go on to underline that this power must, nonetheless, rest on facts that support the action taken. In Re Smith 146 N.Y. 68, 77 (1895).
66. L. O. Gostin and Lindsay Wiley, *Public Health Law: Power, Duty, Restraint* (Berkeley: University of California Press, 2008), 91ff.
67. Willrich, *Pox*, 63ff.
68. This is about US$150 in today's (2018) money.
69. Jacobson v. Massachusetts, 197 U.S. 11 (1905), 26.
70. Ibid., 31.
71. Ibid., 26–27.
72. *The Model State Emergency Health Powers Act*, Preamble, https://www.aapsonline.org/legis/msehpa2.pdf.
73. Jew Ho v. Williamson, 103 F. 10 (1900), 26.
74. Holden v. Hardy, 169 U.S. 366 (1898), 392.
75. Schmitt, *Political Theology*, 13.

Bibliography

Agamben, Giorgio. *Homo Sacer*. Translated by Daniel Heller-Roazan. Stanford, CA: Stanford University Press, 1998.
———. *Means Without End*. Translated by Vincenzo Binetti and Cesare Casarino. Minneapolis: University of Minnesota Press, 2000.
———. *State of Exception*. Translated by Kevin Attell. Chicago, IL: University of Chicago Press, 2005.
Albert, Michael R. "The Last Smallpox Epidemic in Boston and the Vaccination Controversy, 1901–1903." *New England Journal of Medicine* 344 (2001): 375–79.
Albert, Michael R., Kristen G. Ostheimer, David J. Liewehr, Seth M. Steinberg, and Joel G. Breman. "Smallpox Manifestations and Survival during the Boston Epidemic of 1901 to 1903." *Annals of Internal Medicine* 137, no. 12 (2002): 993–1000.
American Civil Liberties Union. "Quarantined Nurse Opposes Christie's Attempt to End Case." ACLU. Retrieved 19 July 2018 from https://www.aclu-nj.org/news/2016/03/15/quarantined-nurse-opposes-christies-attempt-end-case.
Armstrong, Charles. "Tetanus following Vaccination against Smallpox, and Its Prevention: With Special Reference to the Use of Vaccination Shields and Dressings." *Public Health Reports* 42, no. 50 (1927): 3061–71.
Bentham, Jeremy. *Theory of Legislation*. Boston, MA: Weeks, 1840.
Blackstone, William. "Blackstone's Commentaries on the Laws of England: Book the Fourth—Chapter the Thirteenth: Of Offenses Against the Public Health, and the Public Police or Economy." Yale Law School. Retrieved 19 July 2018 from http://avalon.law.yale.edu/18th_century/blackstone_bk4ch13.asp.
Gostin, L., J. Sapsin, S. Teret, S. Burris, J. Mair, J. Hodge, and J. Vernick, *The Model State Emergency Health Powers Act*. The Center for Law and the Public's Health at Georgetown and Johns Hopkins Universities. Retrieved 19 July 2018 from https://www.aapsonline.org/legis/msehpa2.pdf.
Cirillo, Vincent. *Bullets and Bacilli: The Spanish-American War and Military Medicine*. New Brunswick, NJ: Rutgers University Press, 2004.
Dahl, Robert. *Polyarchy: Participation and Opposition*. New Haven, CT: Yale University Press, 1972.
De Wilde, Marc. "Meeting Opposites: The Political Theologies of Walter Benjamin and Carl Schmitt." *Philosophy and Rhetoric* 44 (2011): 363–81.
———. "Uncertain Futures and the Problem of Constraining Emergency Powers: Temporal Dimensions of Carl Schmitt's Theory of the State of Exception." In *Temporal Boundaries of Law and Politics: Time Out of Joint*, edited by Lyana Francot and Luigi Corrias, 107–125. London: Routledge, 2017.
Fenner, F. *Smallpox and Its Eradication*. Geneva: WHO, 1988.
Freund, Ernst. *Police Power, Public Policy, and Constitutional Rights*. Chicago, IL: Callaghan & Co, 1904.
Gostin, L. O., and Lindsay Wiley. *Public Health Law: Power, Duty, Restraint*. Berkeley: University of California Press, 2008.
Hamilton, Alexander, John Jay, and James Madison. *Federalist Papers*. New York: Signet Classics, 2003.

Hodge, James Jr., and L. O. Gostin. "School Vaccination Requirements: Historical, Social, and Legal Perspectives." *Kentucky Law Journal* 90 no. 4 (2001): 831–90.

Holden v. Hardy, 169 U. S. 366 (1898).

In Re Smith, 146 N.Y. 68, 40 N. E. 497 (1895).

Jacobson v. Massachusetts, 197 U.S. 11 (1905).

Jefferson, Thomas. *Letter to John Breckenridge*. 12 August 1803. Retrieved 10 July 2018 from http://founders.archives.gov/documents/Jefferson/01-41-02-0139.

———. *Letter to John Colvin*. 20 September 1810. Retrieved 19 July 2018 from http://founders.archives.gov/documents/Jefferson/03-03-02-0060.

———. *Letter to Pierre Samuel Du Pont de Nemours*. 25 April 1802. Retrieved 19 July 2018 from http://founders.archives.gov/documents/Jefferson/01-37-02-0263.

Jew Ho v. Williamson, 103 F. 10 (1900).

Kant, Immanuel. *Metaphysics of Morals*. Translated by Mary Gregor. Cambridge, UK: Cambridge University Press, 1991.

Kleinerman, Benjamin, and Clement Fatovic, eds. *Extra-Legal Power and Legitimacy*. Oxford: Oxford University Press, 2013.

Krug, Etienne. *World Report on Violence and Health*. Geneva: WHO, 2002.

Lazar, Nomi Claire. "Making Emergencies Safe for Democracy." *Constellations* 13 (2006): 506–21.

———. *States of Emergency in Liberal Democracies*. Cambridge, UK: Cambridge University Press, 2009.

Lilienfeld, D. E. "The First Pharmacoepidemiologic Investigations: National Drug Safety Policy in the United States, 1901–1902." *Perspectives in Biology and Medicine* 51 (2008): 188–98.

Lincoln, Abraham. *Message to Congress in Special Session*. 4 July 1861. http://www.fjc.gov/history/home.nsf/page/tu_merryman_doc_5.html.

Locke, John. *Second Treatise of Government*. Retrieved 19 July 2018 from http://www.constitution.org/jl/2ndtreat.htm.

Maer, Lucinda, and Oonagh Gay. 2009. *The Royal Prerogative*. House of Commons Library SN/PC/03861. 30 December 2009.

Marcus, Maeva. *Truman and the Steel Seizure Case: The Limits of Presidential Power*. New York: Columbia University Press, 1973.

Mayhew, Mary C. Commissioner State of Maine Department of Health and Human Services v. Hickox, State of Maine District Court Docket No: CV-2014-36.

Ministry of Justice, United Kingdom. *Review of the Executive Royal Prerogative: Final Report*. 15 October 2009.

Novak, William. *The People's Welfare: Law and Regulation in Nineteenth-Century America*. Chapel Hill: University of North Carolina Press, 2006.

Pious, Richard. *The American Presidency*. New York: Basic Books, 1977.

"Quarantined Nurse Opposes Christie's Attempt to End Case." ACLU. 15 March 2016. Retrieved 19 July 2018 from https://www.aclu-nj.org/news/2016/03/15/quarantined-nurse-opposes-christies-attempt-end-case.

Ramraj, Victor, and Mark V. Tushnet, eds. *Emergencies and the Limits of Legality*. Cambridge, UK: Cambridge University Press, 2008.

Reith, Charles. *A New Study of Police History*. London: Oliver & Boyd, 1956.

Schmitt, Carl. *The Concept of the Political*. Translated by George Schwab. Chicago, IL: University of Chicago Press, 2007.
———. *The Crisis of Parliamentary Democracy*. Translated by Ellen Kennedy. Cambridge, MA: MIT Press, 1988.
———. *Die Diktatur*. Berlin: Duncker & Humblot, 2007.
———. "Der Fuhrer Schützt das Recht." *Deutsche Juristen-Zeitung* 15 (1934): 946–47.
———. *The Leviathan in the State Theory of Thomas Hobbes*. Translated by George Schwab. Westport, CT: Greenwood Press, 1996.
———. *Political Theology*. Translated by George Schwab. Cambridge, MA: MIT Press, 1985.
———. *The Theory of the Partisan: Intermediate Commentary on the Concept of the Political*. Translated by G. L. Ulmen. New York: Telos Press, 2007.
Schreuer, Christoph. "Derogation of Human Rights in Situations of Public Emergency: The Experience of the European Convention on Human Rights." *Yale Journal of World Public Order* 9 no. 1 (1982): 113–132.
Smith, Adam. *Lectures on Justice, Police, Revenue, and Arms*. Oxford: Clarendon, 1869.
Soltman, Neil. "The Limits of Executive Power: Impoundment of Funds." *Catholic University Law Review* 23 (1973): 359.
Thirty-First Annual Report of the Health Department of the City of Boston for the Year 1902. Boston, MA: Municipal Printing Office, 1903.
Willrich, Michael. *Pox: An American History*. New York: Penguin, 2011.

 5

How Having Reasons Became Making a Decision
The Cold War Rise of Decision Theory and the Invention of Rational Choice

Philip Mirowski

> An elaborate theory of rational decision has been developed by economists and statisticians, and put to widespread use in theoretical and policy studies. This is a powerful, mathematically precise, and tractable theory. Although its adequacy as a description of actual behavior has been questioned, it stands as the dominant view of the conditions that a rational decision should satisfy: it is the dominant normative theory.
>
> —Robert Nozick, *The Nature of Rationality*

There are abundant reasons to be dissatisfied with the current state of intellectual history; one version happens when some concerned bystanders begin to suspect that a gaggle of historians have skittered off on a wild goose chase after something has addled their normally refined historical sensibilities, producing narrative accounts that no longer seem to illuminate much of anything at all. One such interlude happened with Kuhn and his paradigms, as so trenchantly demonstrated by Nicolas Guilhot's paper "The Kuhning of Reason."[1] I am going to risk what remains of my reputation among historians of economics to suggest the current fascination with rationality itself threatens to tempt the unwary to yet another mad dash to bedlam. Basically, my qualms can be traced to the fact that, like Kuhnian paradigms, "rationality" doesn't really exist. (Fiction writers have known this for a very long time, but they will remain beyond the bounds of this chapter. Also, I acknowledge that many academics predicate their activities upon the presumption that it exists.) I sympathize that this cuts against the grain in a world currently transfixed with fear of the irrational; but as historians, we really must try and rise above such idols of the crowd.

Various intellectual formations may have become fascinated with rationality because they believe it serves as a portmanteau for many of their favored explanatory devices; but both paradigms and rationality share the very bad attribute of encouraging every tyro acolyte to be over-confident that there abides some coherent ontological stability that just isn't there to be found. One might think that the denizens of science studies would be especially attuned to this delusion; but some recent work by STS scholars leaves much to be desired.[2] Every academic is usually convinced she personally knows in detail how her chosen discipline is structured and policed; and every self-identified intellectual thinks he knows the indispensable skeletons of a legitimate argument. And yet, and yet—push these creatures some distance out of their comfort zone, and all that seemed solid dissolves into the air. It gets worse when one ventures to appreciate just how much the term "rationality" is being cavalierly tossed around in widely divergent ways within different disciplines at any particular juncture in time.

The surest way to detect a shamelessly depleted concept is to observe both practitioners and outside observers when they try to transform the hollow shell into their ultimate badge of honor, constituting the touchstone in defining everything that deserves the honorific of legitimacy in their potted disciplinary histories. Here, I will mostly be concerned with the history of economics, with side glances toward philosophy and the surrounding social sciences. In that bailiwick, one cannot count the waves of lemmings who jostle to push the history of economics back to Adam, or at least Adam Smith, through an appeal to a putative science of the "rational agent." Although I am not one to usually lean on the wisdom of the Elect, even Ronald Coase knew: "It is wrong to believe, as is commonly done, that Adam Smith had as his view of man an abstraction, an 'economic man,' rationally pursuing his self-interest in a single-minded way. Smith would not have thought it sensible to treat man as a rational utility maximizer."[3] The short version of this objection was that such a dessicated vision of rationality simply did not exist back then. Enlightenment figures (especially after Kant) talked in terms of Reason, not rationality. One disturbing thought is that the Enlightenment world of reasons and sound reasoning have given way to an empty disenchanted world of spurious ungrounded rationality. Perhaps we might also date the watershed to the middle of the twentieth century.

Rational Choice Theory

I hasten to reassure my audience that I am not waxing pomo here. Both history and philosophy combine to reveal just how vertiginously insubstantial all those thousands of books and papers praised by Nozick on rationality really have been. Let us narrow the focus of what threatens to become an ungainly inquiry and restrict ourselves to the (still massive) subset of those books and papers that propound something called "rational choice theory." It may come as a shock to those who believe in timeless canons of rationality, but the unbearable lightness of "rational choice" as an intellectual movement has been the subject of elaborate repeated commentary for a very long time now. Once thought to be securely rooted in the province of neoclassical economics, something very similar to rational choice theory in the latter twentieth century seems to have now migrated throughout the latter-day social sciences.[4] Although called by many names, in economics, decision theory and rational choice theory were treated as synonyms until the turn of the millennium—this in itself will soon constitute an important piece of evidence. Given its shape-shifting character, some philosophers and social scientists have sought to pin down its definition more precisely, even if only for the plucky purpose of seeking to refute it.[5] These observers frequently characterize it as comprising three components: (1) a consistent, well-behaved preference ordering reflecting the mindset of some individual; (2) the axiomatic method employed to describe mental manipulations of (1) as comprising the definition of "rational choice"; and (3), reduction of all social phenomena to decisions, that is, to be attributed to the activities of individual agents applying (2) to (1). These three components may be referred to in shorthand as utility functions, formal axiomatic definitions (including maximization provisions and consistency restrictions), and some species of methodological individualism.

Whether this fanciful scenario actually exists between anyone's ears in any normal vernacular sense (something admitted by Nozick) is a question we shall sidestep; for the nonce, the immediate response is to marvel how anyone could have confused this extraordinary contraption with human rationality, however loosely defined. Start with component (1). The preexistence of an inviolate preference ordering rules out-of-bounds most phenomena of learning, as well as the simplest and most commonplace of human experiences, that feeling of changing one's mind. I have had the disconcerting experience of discovering late in life that I really do seem to like bacon and the Beach Boys, after shunning them most of my life; perhaps you have stumbled upon similar epiphanies. People have frequently been known to make personally inconsistent evaluations of events both observed and unobserved; yet in rational choice theory, committing such a solecism is the only real mortal sin, one that gets you harshly punished at minimum, and summarily drummed out of the realm of the elect in the final analysis.[6] The ukase does not involve conforming to the canons of logic, as such, as much as maintaining a certain rigid invariance of attitudes. It thus forbids any contextual framing effects of rational thought, or what has been called bounded rationality, and even evolutionary approaches to epistemology. Now let's contemplate component (2). This stipulates that the best way to enshrine rationality is by mimicking a formal axiomatic system—as if that were some sterling bulwark against human frailty and oblique hidden flaws of hubris. One would have thought Gödel's Theorem might have chilled the enthusiasm for this format, but curiously, the opposite happened. Every rational person within this tradition is presupposed to conform to his or her own impregnable axiom system, something that comes preloaded, like Microsoft on a laptop. This cod-Bourbakism ruled out many further phenomena which one might otherwise innocently call rational: an experimental or pragmatic stance toward the world; a life where one understands prudence as behaving different ways in different contexts; a self predicating action on the possibility that much personal knowledge is embodied, tacit, inarticulate, and heavily emotionally driven. Furthermore, it strangely banishes many computational approaches to cognition: for instance, it simply elides the fact that much algorithmic inference can be shown to be noncomputable in practice; or a somewhat less daunting proposition, that it is intractable in terms of the time and resources required to carry it out. Then contemplate component (3): complaints about methodological individualism are so drearily commonplace in intellectual history it would be tedious to reproduce them here.[7] Suffice it to say that (3) simply denies the very existence of social cognition in its many manifestations as deserving of the honorific "rational."

There is nothing very new about any of these observations. Veblen's infamous quote from *The Place of Science in Modern Civilization* summed them up more than a century ago: "The hedonistic conception of man is that of a lightning calculator of pleasures and pains, who oscillates like a homogeneous globule of desire of happiness under the impulse of stimuli that shift him about the area, but leave him intact."[8] Although Veblen was himself ridiculing a certain species of utilitarian psychology back at the beginning of the twentieth century, he did not live to see it become baked into a "decision theory" of "rational choice." That came later, as did the chorus of reproach and disdain. The roster of latter-day dissenters is similarly illustrious, from Herb Simon to Daniel Ellsberg to Amartya Sen to Gerd Gigerenzer to Ian Shapiro, although none are perhaps quite up to Veblen's snuff in stylish prose or withering skepticism.

Why anyone would come to mistake this virtual system of billiard balls careening on the baize as capturing the white-hot conviction of rationality in human life is a question worthy of a few years of hard work by competent intellectual historians; but that does not seem to be what we have been bequeathed of late.[9] In its place, I would argue, is the work of (mostly) historians of economics and some historians of science treating these three components of rationality as if they were more or less patently obvious, while scouring over fine points of dispute concerning the formalisms involved, and in particular, an inordinate fascination for rival treatments of probability theory within the framework. What we get are histories of ordinal versus cardinal utility, game theory, "behavioral" peccadilloes, preferences versus "capacities," social choice theory, experimental interventions, causal versus evidential decision theory, formalized management theory, and so forth, all situated within a larger frame tale of the inexorable rise of neoclassical economics. If and when this rat choice complex is observed taking root within political science, or sociology, or biology, or some peripheral precincts of psychology, it is often treated as though it had migrated wholesale over from the economists' citadel.[10] If that option is declined, then instead it is intimated that "science" and the "mathematical tools" made the figures in question revert to certain stereotypic caricatures of rationality.[11]

As if this weren't bad enough, there is the even more vexing phenomenon that this abstruse definition of rationality is simply taken for granted as a prelude for making further generalizations about the trajectory of economics after 1980, most of which enthuse that, in the interim, the current generation of economists has providentially become the most open-minded, subtle, and psychologically sophisticated researchers in all the annals of economic thought, in that they have now managed to perform the astounding conjuring trick of somehow augmenting and reconciling the previously rigid construct of rationality with all manner of behavioral quirks, sociological idiosyncrasies, mental peccadilloes, and outright irrationalities that beset the cognitive makeup of *homo economicus*. With the help of some hefty hardware, such as PET scanners and magnetic resonance imagers, they have the brain in their crosshairs, when previously they had abjured any consideration of the mind.[12] The impression is thus conveyed that neoclassical economics has finally sworn off its previous boisterous imperialistic tendencies, and now is united in sweet concord with all the other social and natural sciences in developing a grand, unified portrait of what it means to be rational.[13] This brave new world of "behavioral economics" thus somehow manages to square the circle of subsuming supposedly irrational agents under the continued sovereignty of old-fashioned rational choice theory, seemingly without breaking a sweat. I will not have much occasion in this chapter to explore this post-1980 travesty in elaborate detail, other than to insist that if the original understanding of rational choice theory in the period of 1940–80 has been flawed, then the contemporary magic realism of behavioral economics is *a fortiori* built upon sand.

This pattern of historical narrative—one that takes complex questions of rationality as effectively reducible to rational choice—even extends to writers who might otherwise consider themselves critics of the rational choice tradition. I resort for purposes of illustration here to Nicola Giocoli's book *Modeling Rational Agents*.[14] He starts by acknowledging that in the first half of the twentieth century, neoclassical economic theorists had approached their model as a system of forces (and not ratiocination), but because they harbored a residual predilection to refer to minds, they were bedeviled by two strange (and unexplained) obsessions: to escape any reliance upon academic psychology of any stripe, and to eschew their seeming reliance on a presumption of perfect foresight of the future in their little agents. Those motives were internally inconsistent, says Giocoli, and furthermore, could never have been reconciled on their own terms. Lacking an appreciation for reflexivity, and perhaps a sense of irony, Giocoli therefore argues that the prophets of rational consistency were inconsistent in their own reasoning. The deliverance from the dilemma was providentially provided by a few mathematicians and logical positivist philosophers, or so he claims, by reducing the meaning of "rationality" to consistency of an empty set of formal relations, viz., what we have identified above as the formal axiomatic component of rat choice. The axiomatic method thus absolved them from any commitments to disciplinary psychology, whilst the marriage of probability theory and utility (attributed by all and sundry initially to von Neumann and Morgenstern) putatively absolved the agents from perfect foresight. The new prophets of rationality proceeded to pronounce their project rational by fiat, and beyond all reasonable expectations, were stunningly successful in convincing others. The rest of the book then becomes a long meditation on the history of game theory as one necessary consequence of this reconceptualization of rationality.

While Giocoli does strive to bring his argument to bear on many different texts, in the final analysis, his story just does not hang together. The biggest complaint one might make is that the narrative takes place in an amazingly arid vacuum: other than the *deus ex machina* of the logical positivists, no attention is accorded to anything happening outside of the narrowly conceived coterie of neoclassical economists. Giocoli stumbles when he effectively sets out to write a history of decision theory (and *not* price theory) over the course of the twentieth century, *when there was no such intellectual formation before World War II*. Betraying the bad habit of reading current obsessions back into innocent predecessors, and presuming everyone in economics was concerned with an ahistorical entity called "rationality," he imagines that his early prewar protagonists agonized persistently over the character of the decision in much the same way as they did after 1945—but there is no substantial evidence of that. Indeed, if they shared anything in those halcyon days, it was a peremptory dismissal of "mind"; if and when cognitive matters did come up, they were dealt with as issues of intelligence (with the usual eugenic implications) rather than rationality.[15] Simply having resort to similar mathematics is nowhere tantamount to being driven by the same conceptual questions. The only way to begin to gain some perspective on this is to venture outside of narrowly conceived economics: Where did the earlier neoclassicals derive their questions from, and what was happening in the other sciences that caused them grief and aggravation?

A superior historical story must begin with the fact that the original neoclassical model was copied from energy physics.[16] The early neoclassicals were by and large agnostic about the mind: all that mattered for them was to equate the formalisms of energy with something they diffidently called "utility" so that they could portray the market as deterministic and law-governed, as the rolling of a ball to the bottom of a bowl. If there was any appeal to the rational, it was summarily conflated with conformity to the laws of nature. First and foremost, the neoclassicals were drawn like moths to the flame of science; almost none of them were avid acolytes of the fine points of utility. Only a very few card-carrying mathematical neoclassical economists of the first three generations could be bothered to follow up on the mathematical metaphor and ask what it may have explicitly implied for psychological predispositions; and those inquiries were ignored by the newly professionalizing cadre.[17] It is revealing that Giocoli opts to call this a "System of Forces" approach to economics—somehow he cannot bring himself to go the whole nine yards and admit it was merely a bowdlerized physics. Furthermore, the physics inspiration reveals why "perfect foresight" was not the dreaded albatross that Giocoli paints dangling from economists in the prewar era: the theory was purely static, as nearly every figure freely admitted; and moreover, many realized that classical mechanics itself had no need of perfect foresight, since it was purely time reversible. One of the quaint characteristics of prewar neoclassical economics was that it was concertedly *backward-oriented*: events in the past were thought to determine realized prices and quantities in the present—think of the Austrians and their capital theory, or the endless Marshallian fascination with cost structures inherited from the past. Causality was assumed to obey time's arrow. It was only after World War II that neoclassical price theory swung around 180 degrees on the time axis, with occurrences in the *future* supposedly governing current choice and decisions. Absent that futurity, thinking was effectively minimized in most prewar neoclassical theory. What Giocoli paints as a source of deep anguish was thus merely a minor distraction for neoclassicals before the World Wars.

However, it is demonstrably true that neoclassical economists have *always* sought to absolve themselves from the strictures of formal or professional psychology.[18] If there is a constant throughout the history of neoclassical economics, that is surely it. It is curious that Giocoli cannot be bothered to glance at what was happening in psychology at the turn of the twentieth century, for then he would begin to grasp how very distressing the "science of the mind" was trending for the early neoclassicals. The new fascinating thing on the Continent was Freud and psychoanalysis; the enthusiasm in America was "habit psychology." In both cases, the preferred stance in most social sciences tended to stress the great extent to which the irrational governed people's behavior: conscious rationality was portrayed as a weak, thin vessel tossed about the surface of a roiling set of instincts, urges, and inaccessible unconscious. Indeed, most early neoclassicals did *not* tend to characterize their theories as expressions of generic rationality for the very important reason that the median attitude in the social sciences circa 1920 was that the great mass of humanity was *not rational*; the proud breakthrough of the social sciences was having the courage to demonstrate the pervasive yet bitter truth of this stricture. Indeed, in the alternative narrative we shall shortly explore, *this was the premier "fact" of prewar social science*.[19]

This scientific distrust of the ability of the masses to reason is the prime motivation for the rise of decision theory from the mid-twentieth century; it is also the missing protagonist in contemporary attempts in science studies to account for the rise of Cold War rationality.[20] Curiously, historians and STS scholars tend to retreat to a species of technological determinism, asserting that The Bomb and intercontinental missiles rendered the demands of reason hapless in the face of the speed of nuclear war and the necessity to suppress emotions; but in fact, the fear of the reasoning abilities of the masses predated that fact by at least four decades. Thus, the citation of the Cold War as immediate cause tends to put the cart before the horse: "Humans in this era fell far short of the standards presumed by Cold War rationality. This growing recognition ... ultimately brought about the privileging of 'irrationality' as the prime characteristic of human decision making."[21] The editors of the current volume in their Introduction date these misgivings back to Walter Lippmann and Carl Schmitt in the 1920s; the importance for our current thesis is that, first and foremost, the rise of rational choice notions in economics was a response to a political problem, and not, in the first instance, an epistemological one.

Returning to the history of neoclassical economics: to promote their nascent project as construction of a theory of rational choice capacity in the common human would have been extremely quixotic, at least prior to the 1940s; discretion being the better part of valor, most neoclassical theorists did not go there. The least discreet among them, Vilfredo Pareto, in his *Manuele*, did suggest that economics was the province of "logical" action, whereas sociology was stuck with the "non-logical" dregs; but even he immediately got tied up in knots over where this dividing line could be drawn: "non-logical action does not mean illogical; a non-logical action may be one which a person could see, after observing the fact and the logic as the best way to adapt the means to the end; but that adaptation has been obtained by a procedure other than that of logical reasoning."[22] In claiming the mantle of logic for neoclassical economics, Pareto in no way was asserting that the great mass of people adhered to logical behavior—far from it.

By and large, neoclassical economics propounded neither a theory of choice nor of decision in the prewar era. That is the first clue that the raft of internalist histories and philosopher narratives (like those of Giocoli, Blume, Nozick, and others) are deeply misleading for understanding the rise of rational choice theory. And if that was the case, then what caused the watershed around mid-twentieth century, the rise of the decision as the hallowed hallmark of our humanity, a tremor of tectonic proportions that even Giocoli detects? Was it the handiwork of the nefarious "positivists"? Not by a long shot. The billiard ball model of rational choice mostly came from outside economics: But where?

An Alternative Genealogy of "The Decision"

What follows might be regarded as a sketch in the larger program of what has been called "historical epistemology." Instead of presuming an ahistorical entity called "rationality" is present throughout, it seeks to portray the changes in what it meant to be an agent capable of reason over long stretches of time. In this frame tale, transmutations don't happen so much within disciplines as between them, thus eluding the grasp of standard historiographies. In this instance, I will seek to suggest that the rise of the decision, ably documented by contributors to this volume, was due to the interplay of the natural sciences, war, politics, and the computer. However, to write such a Universal History in fifteen thousand words is an impossible task, so I will arbitrarily confine my sketch to the ways in which the larger intellectual trends manifested themselves in and around the field of economics.

I have already set out with an insistence that utility theory in the modern mode did not actually begin with Bernoulli, or Bentham, nor indeed with any concerted theory of mind to be found in the contemporary literatures of psychology.[23] The "utility function," which enjoys pride of place in neoclassical economics, was first proposed in the 1870s and was a direct transfer from field theory in energy physics, and this tells us quite a bit concerning its initial relationship to the problem of rationality. The earliest proponents, such as Jevons and Walras, did not even stress the maximization of the quantum—although this may have been due to their weaknesses when it came to mathematical manipulation. Walras in his *Elements* insisted "pure" economics dealt with economic phenomena free of all human intentionality. Instead, they appropriated the formalism to demonstrate the law-governed character of the *market*, and not the amazing powers of measured deliberation and virtual calculation of each individual to search out their maximum advantage, however they might conceive it.

The lack of direct connection of these utility functions to vernacular notions of reason and judgment would have been obvious to anyone who understood the source context of the mathematics. It was recognized in physics that particles did not choose the path of least energy when they traversed an energy field; the few historical attempts to portray extremum theories as rational tended to attribute the Principle of Least Action to a Deity or Maker or some wispy Wisdom of Nature, and not the humble centers of gravity looping through the field. The test particle did not decide to navigate the field in any sense that was permissible in science; the field did not choose to direct the particle to equilibrium. Attempts to attribute intentionality to inanimate nature had been largely prohibited in the history of rational mechanics: this was one heritage of the Enlightenment. Thus, by extension, in the formalism brought over from physics, the economic agent who purportedly possesses the utility function does not make a choice when his consumption bundle moves from initial position to rest point; he simply obeys a parallel natural law. Precisely because the model describes a deterministic equilibrium, there abides, strictly speaking, no actual conscious choice in canonical neoclassical microeconomic theory—something that has been pointed out repeatedly in the history of economics (to no avail).

Thus, recourse to the physics model had already effectively dispensed with the Enlightenment world of Reason by the later nineteenth century. The earlier mathematical neoclassicals were quite clear on this. Leon Walras, for instance, defined "pure economics" as a consequence of the "blind and ineluctable forces of the universe," devoid of human will, and insisted, "we need not concern ourselves with the morality or immorality of any desire which a useful thing answers or serves to satisfy. From other points of view, the question of whether a drug is wanted to cure a patient, or by a murderer to kill his family is a serious matter, but from our point of view, it is totally irrelevant."[24] This was the beginning of an unabashed disdain for any reasons nominally held by the agent: all that mattered was that they behaved like a physical particle, viz., they were "rational." But it is important to insist this was not yet a theory of rational choice.

The rise of rational choice theory was the confluence of at least four major intellectual trends, which had more or less tenuous grounding in the narrowly defined field of economics. Our list of trends is chronological; but also, the trends occupy progressively shorter time spans. Luckily, each has been the subject of extensive research by historians and, as such, can be summarized tersely, in the following outline:

[1] *The long-term displacement of human reason and judgement by rote rules and algorithmic notions of rationality within mathematics and philosophy.* This is the bailiwick of Lorraine Daston, best expressed

in her lecture.[25] This pan-European trend can be observed in the history of philosophy, mathematics, and calculation devices. Although she herself cites the Cold War as watershed, the actual narrative stretches over centuries. It is primarily a story grounded in the natural sciences.

[2] *The twentieth-century struggle over the relationship of epistemically unreliable masses and the role of politics in both democracies and dictatorships.* Curiously, this starts out as a German and Austrian story, but migrates over to the United States during and after World War II. It can be found throughout the social sciences as it grows in importance. The representative historian for this story is one of the editors of this volume: Nicolas Guilhot.

[3] *In reaction to the first two trends, there is the rise of a new political formation, best summarized as "Neoliberalism."* It is born in the 1930s, but really only consolidates as an important political economy during the Cold War. It innovated a new approach to the problem of epistemology by attempting to offload its onus onto "The Market." Recent efforts by myself and others to describe the trajectory of the Neoliberal Thought Collective will provide the main input on this intellectual trend.

[4] *Finally, in reaction to the above three trends, and with extensive input from Cold War sciences such as Operations Research and Cybernetics, a subset of the American economics profession elevates "The Decision" to pride of place in the Cold War formation of "Rational Choice Theory."* In conventional histories of economics, it is only this stream that is graced with attention as the original incubator of rational choice. It begins in the Cowles Commission, which was explicitly concerned to refute the Neoliberal challenge mentioned above; one of the historians who intently insists upon the importance of operations research and cybernetics in the narrative is Hunter Heyck. The culmination of all the combined trends is the reification of an abstract "decision" as an analytical object, an unprecedented caricature of human reason.

Rather than recapitulate the vast internalist literature on the history of rational choice, the remainder of this chapter is devoted to sketches of the above overarching intellectual trends, with side glances at how they influenced the trajectory of economics.

Daston's *Longue Durée*

Daston begins by circumscribing the target of her history as theories of rational choice, which she deems to encompass such subsets as formal decision theory, game theory, operations research, artificial intelligence, formal logic, and Bayesian inductive inference. However, as befits one of the premier proponents of the practice of historical epistemology, she does not undertake to write conventional history of the models, techniques, or theoretical disputes in any of those areas; instead, she asks: What is it that each of these takes for granted when it comes to the characterization of the performance characteristics of human reason? Furthermore, although she considers herself primarily a historian of the eighteenth century, and in the past having exerted great concentration on the early travails of the probability literature, she is motivated by the fact that very few authors back then would have endorsed anything like modern rational choice approaches. This stance is diametrically opposed to the internalist histories cited herein that attempt to draw direct connections between Bernoulli and Kenneth Arrow. Moreover, it is the kind of history of the *longue durée*, passing easily over centuries, something that does not curry much favor in modern intellectual history.

Daston sets out to paint the discrepancy between the Enlightenment and the Cold War as the former version of reason grounded fundamentally in human judgment, moral considerations, emotional maturity, and wisdom, versus a modernist rationality consisting of finite well-defined rules, applicable indifferently to almost any setting without recourse to faculties of judgement or appeals to human reason. Daston has a tendency to attribute the former as mindful reason of a warm and fuzzy *Gemeinschaft*, while the latter is disparagingly dubbed "mindless rationality" and equated rather too much with the appearance of algorithms. Nevertheless, because the story is intimately bound up with the mechanization of arithmetic and logic and the later appearance of computers, one can appreciate that the engineering mechanization of mind in its various guises inevitably came to alter what it meant to provide reasons for action.

Daston proceeds to argue that earlier forays into the transmutation of reason into rationality had been roundly disparaged in the nineteenth century, and that in her opinion, by 1860, the entire project of a "calculus of reason" was considered a dead letter. This verdict tends to ignore a few major figures who were closely associated with economics, especially Charles Babbage and William Stanley Jevons.

The former, with his Analytical Engine, and the latter, with his logical piano, were not stirring successes in their own day, but later were fondly remembered as anticipators of the later development of algorithmic rationality.[26] Nonetheless, Daston does provide an edifying history of the very notion of a rule in the sphere of reason, arguing that *regula* started out as a moral and political category, but later morphed into exemplars or models, and by the nineteenth century started to assume the trappings of algorithms. In the process, arithmetic lost its association with the higher intellectual faculties, only to become something to be contracted out to uneducated workers, and then finally, outsourced to machines.

This downward mobility of the performers of calculation over the centuries had an ironic effect in Daston's account of rationality. If performance of calculations increasingly could be carried out without refined judgment or seasoned reflection or even understanding, then how did the comparable algorithms of rational choice come to represent the epitome of epistemology in the twentieth century? This is where the Cold War enters into Daston's narrative. She suggests that earlier reliance upon seasoned judgment and elaborate reasoning began to appear too threatening in the context of nuclear war and confrontation of the Communist enemy. Humans couldn't reason fast enough, or reliably enough, to be trusted with the launch keys. Human attributes such as emotion, self-deception, inconsistency, ad hoc adjustments to contingencies, the pervasiveness of indeterminacy, and the bugaboo of paradox left the paragons of reason terminally afraid of large-scale dependence upon human reason. In effect, the human being became portrayed as the enemy of reason in the mid-twentieth century; the way out was to elevate an inhuman algorithmic reason to pride of place in the cultural hierarchy.

Consequently, Daston asserts that the deskilled and deracinated version of rationality, once untethered from human attributes, then became projected back upon a new vision of what it meant to be human. The reification of the algorithm as the all-purpose definition of rationality—reliably definite, conclusive, and general—became identified as the paragon of human credibility because it was always the same, no matter where it was deployed.

Although this story nicely dovetails with the timing of the appearance of rational choice theory, we might suggest it is insufficient on its own to fully account for its shape and content. Clearly, Daston omits the earlier physics origins of neoclassical theory, as I pointed out earlier. The reification of context-free calculation had already partially taken hold in some precincts of economics; the Cold War only served to elevate it into a grander cultural trope. Yet too much weight is resting on the nuclear standoff to support her thesis. In her narrative, there is also the trademark habit of science and technology studies eliding the politics of the situation, in deference to the shiny missiles, obscure mathematical symbols, and blinking computers. Here is where the intellectual history of politics can be inserted to solidify both the timing and the outlines of the "decision."

The Unruly Electorate and the Ungrounded Decision

Providentially, the editors of this volume have proposed one of the main generalizations concerning intellectual history to be accessed as a foundation for our thesis. Nicolas Guilhot has documented how a Germanophone critique of democracy, growing out of the Weimar years, eventually made an alliance with an American critique of the capacity of the public to even understand the issues of the day, much less to make a considered opinion into some coherent public will. The avatar of the German critique was Carl Schmitt; while the most prominent representative of the American critique was Walter Lippmann. American social science in the 1920s had been already deeply conflicted over the implications of the pervasive ignorance it had uncovered amidst the masses; they could not reconcile their commitments to democracy with the epistemic shambles they believed they had discovered in the electorate. The pragmatists around John Dewey proposed that more education was the answer; but the suspicion grew (especially in the 1930s) that the person in the street was simply far too irrational to place much faith in that remedy.

Lippmann and Schmitt are almost never cited in existing histories of rational choice theory; this is unfortunate, because a major influence upon the development of "the decision" was a strain of German/Austrian thought on the problem of the political. Not only did the duo play a part in the reification of the decision in a way that was not found in previous political thought, but they also provided major resources for the invention of Neoliberalism: Lippmann directly through the famous Lippmann Colloquium of 1938, and Schmitt somewhat more indirectly in the political thought of Friedrich Hayek.[27] For the sake of concision, we will briefly deal with Schmitt here, and Neoliberalism in the subsequent section.

Carl Schmitt is today notorious as the Nazi thinker who redefined the sphere of the political as constituted by the friend/enemy distinction. As our editors point out, an important corollary of his critique of liberal democracy was the need for the leader to decide upon the "exception" in cases of political emergency. He insisted, "Sovereign is he who decides on the exception." The sovereign is deemed capable of instilling order in a people if he has the capacity to make a decision based purely upon the friend/enemy distinction, and not upon any set of nonpolitical determinants: he must act in order to affirm the existence of authority. Early commentators interpreted Schmitt as propounding a doctrine of decisionism in the 1920s: for instance, Karl Löwith, in 1935, asserted that Schmitt had rendered the decision "purely formal" and "indifferent to any kind of political content."[28] In the case of political extremity, all that matters is that some decision is made, and it is irrelevant whether the decision was prompted by context or, indeed, was based upon some epistemic principles of truth. If the decision is primarily a matter of expression of resolute will, then the mere act of choice becomes its own justification and only bears analysis in the very moment of its assertion. In a manner unprecedented from previous appeals to reason, the Schmittian decision was cut off from everything that came before it and, indeed, everything that followed from it. If the electorate really were as inept as social science was suggesting in the 1920s, one can appreciate this might have been regarded as a virtue of decisionism rather than as some perverse attribute of tyrants. This artificial isolation of the decision was a subject of much commentary in the 1930s, whether the topic was Schmitt's political theory, or else some other parallel but unrelated approaches to analysis of the decision. For instance, Hayek's understanding of Schmitt consisted almost entirely of equating his notion of order with this isolated conception of the decision.[29]

One example of this style of Austrian/German discussion can be found in a figure widely acknowledged as a progenitor of rational choice theory, Oskar Morgenstern, joint author with John von Neumann of *The Theory of Games and Economic Behavior*.[30] Oskar Morgenstern figures in our narrative not because he read Carl Schmitt (there is no evidence of that), but rather because he harbored ambitions to be the premier philosopher of economic life in 1930s Vienna. Under the patronage of Hayek, he was named head of the Institut fur Konjunkturforschung at Vienna from 1928–38; but rather than working on business cycles, he published a series of articles on the limitations of rationalization and the impossibility of forecasting in social life.[31] From 1928 onward, he was fascinated with the Sherlock Holmes story "The Final Problem," wherein Holmes and Moriarty struggle to outwit one another by taking (or not) various trains from London to the Continent by striving to anticipate what the rival would do. The fundamental interdependence of rationality was a recurring theme in his work. For instance, it exemplified for him the fact that, should perfect foresight exist, it would never neutralize risk, since:

> always there is exhibited an endless chain of reciprocally conjectural reactions and counter-reactions. This chain can never be broken off by an act of knowledge, *but always only by an arbitrary act, by a decision*. Unrestricted foresight and economic equilibrium are therefore incompatible. But can the equilibrium come about with defective, dissimilar, arbitrarily distributed foresight?[32]

Morgenstern was struggling with the notion that physical (neoclassical) equilibrium seemed at odds with the existence of a thinking economic agent attempting to anticipate and outwit other such similar agents; in this, he was very prescient. Reasons and reasoning had always seemed in pitched conflict with the physical neoclassical model; epistemic considerations had been banished prior to that time in economics, as argued in my first section. This postulate of "the decision" as something standing above and beyond the normal utility calculus was Morgenstern's favored vehicle to reintroduce questions of ratiocination and social interaction into a theory apparently devoid of those attributes. Although he personally made no contributions to the formalization of later rational choice theory (other than prompting an addendum to *The Theory of Games* where von Neumann formalized expected utility theory), there is a sense in which Morgenstern was one major conduit whereby the Germanic concept of the decision made its way over into political economy. He realized that a more plausible economic theory would require the decision to be lifted out of its social context and reified as a purely self-justified break with reason.

Hostility to classical liberal notions of reason were a dime a dozen in the interwar German culture sphere, and thus one can recognize the family resemblance of Schmitt and Morgenstern's recourse to decisionism to solve thorny theoretical problems in politics and economics. For Schmitt, the irrationality of the masses (in parliamentary democracy) was countered by the decisionist super-rationality of the Führer. In a sense, a similar move can be detected in Morgenstern's quest to transcend the hopeless tangle of inferences concerning the future on the part of the economic agent in the 1930s. At first, recourse to the new-fangled ungrounded decision might offer to restore order in the addled head of the economic agent.

Yet the Germanic conception of the decision did not survive entirely unscathed in its migration across the Atlantic. By the time he settled in Princeton, Morgenstern thought "modern logic" could help solve the dilemma of the decision: he was therefore eventually drawn to collaborate with John von Neumann, and is thus credited in most conventional internalist histories of rational choice theory as jointly sparking the field through the axiomatization of Expected Utility Theory (1947) and his supporting role in the promulgation of game theory.[33] This folk tale represses the significant fact that von Neumann's game theory was explicitly intended to displace neoclassical economics, not save it. But nevertheless, the German connection does provide one link for the Austrian fascination with the decision to be freighted into the American genesis of the mathematical side of rational choice theory.

Early game theory bore the marks of the German decisionist temperament in that it still reified the decision as relatively free of context and prior reason: it broke the stalemate of uncoordinated action. The von Neumann/Morgenstern "stable set" solution concept went part way down that road; the embrace of the Nash equilibrium later reinforced the static isolation of the decision from context.[34] In America, the decision was thus extracted from the dire state of exception to become the essence of mechanical choice. The lion could lay down with the lamb. This happened in many different postwar American social sciences. The average person was therefore eventually to be declared "rational" by fiat *because they made an ungrounded decision*—the ultimate Schmittian move to rebuke Schmitt. This was the final victory over German thought: no more worries over Weimar.

Neoliberalism and the Decision

The political economy of the Neoliberal Thought Collective (NTC) was the next major influence on the rise of decisionism in twentieth-century economics. We can only provide the briefest caricature of the doctrine in order to describe how rationality was further shaped by their interventions.

Neoliberalism as a body of thought itself did not exist before World War II, and is only now beginning to be the subject of scholarly research in the history of economics.[35] The most important fact about the Neoliberals, at least after they got over their earlier interwar interval of disarray, was that they were *not* advocates for a simplistic *laissez-faire*: that is one of the crudest canards concerning the contours of late twentieth century political economy. The political goal of the Neoliberal project has been to redefine the shape and functions of the state, not to hobble or destroy it. In the interests of brevity, we will list a subset of four principles of Neoliberalism developed jointly and severally by members of the Mont Pelerin Society (MPS) over the last half of the twentieth century, relevant to our history. These four precepts nowhere exhaust the intellectual innovations of the NTC.

[1] What sort of "market" do the neoliberals want to foster and protect? While one wing of the Mont Pelerin Society (the Chicago School of Economics) has made its career attempting to reconcile one version of neoclassical economic theory with neoliberal precepts, other subsets of MPS have innovated entirely different characterizations of the market. The "radical subjectivist" wing of the Austrian School of economics attempted to ground the market in a dynamic process of discovery by entrepreneurs of what consumers did not yet even know that they wanted, due to the fact that the future is radically unknowable. Perhaps the dominant version within the MPS (and later, the dominant cultural doctrine) emanated from Friedrich Hayek himself, wherein *the Market is posited to be an information processor more powerful than any human brain, but essentially patterned upon brain/computation metaphors.*[36] This is a key point in the history of rational choice theory. This doctrine had three distinctly different interpretations in Hayek's own career alone (covered below), but is often inadequately expressed by neoclassical economists associated with the MPS as the proposition that prices in an efficient market "contain all relevant information" and therefore cannot be predicted by mere mortals, whose powers fail to measure up. Whatever the version, the moral is always the same: *the Market always surpasses the state's ability to process information,* and this constitutes the kernel of the argument for the necessary failure of socialism.

[2] *Neoliberalism thoroughly revises what it means to be a human person.* Many quote Michel Foucault's prescient observation from over three decades ago: "In neoliberalism ... Homo Economicus is an entrepreneur, an entrepreneur of himself."[37] Not only does Neoliberalism deconstruct any special status for human labor to ground the legitimacy of property rights, but it lays waste to older distinctions between production and consumption rooted in the labor theory of value, and reduces the human being to an arbitrary bundle of "investments," skill sets, temporary alliances (family, sex, race), and fungible body parts. "Government of the self" becomes the taproot of all social order. And more to the point, knowledge as a cognitive state becomes hopelessly conflated with knowledge as a thinglike commodity in human capital theory.

[3] *Most neoliberals insist that they value freedom above all else; but more hairs are split in the definition of freedom than over any other neoliberal concept. It is axiomatic that freedom can only be "negative" for neoliberals,* for one very important reason. Freedom cannot be extended from the use of knowledge *in* society to the use of knowledge *about* society, because self-examination concerning why one passively accepts local and incomplete knowledge leads to contemplation of how market signals create some forms of knowledge and squelch others. Meditation upon our limitations imposed by dependence upon markets leads to inquiry into how markets actually work and to meta-reflection on our place in larger orders, something that neoliberals warn is beyond our ken. Knowledge in that eventuality assumes global dimensions, and is no longer "local," and this undermines the key doctrine of the market as transcendental superior information processor. This implies that decisions should be made without full comprehension of their context.

[4] *Neoliberals regard inequality of economic resources and political rights not as an unfortunate byproduct of capitalism but as a necessary functional characteristic of their ideal market system.* Inequality is not only the natural state of market economies from a neoliberal perspective, but it is actually one of its strongest motor forces for progress. Hence, the rich are not parasites, but a boon to mankind. People should be encouraged to envy and emulate the rich. Demands for equality are merely the sour grapes of the losers, or if they are more generous, the atavistic holdovers of older images of justice which must be extirpated from the modern mindset. As Hayek wrote, "The market order does not bring about any close correspondence between subjective merit or individual needs and rewards."[38] Indeed, this lack of correlation between reward and personal effort is one of the major inciters of (misguided) demands for justice on the part of *hoi polloi*. Social justice is blind, because mere humans can never comprehend the true consequences of their market activity. *Note well this severs the decision from any close relationship to its consequences.*

Inequality in resources is paired with ineradicable inequality in knowledge: in a well-functioning economy, most people are simply doomed to be mired in stupidity. Thus the early twentieth century skepticism concerning the epistemic capacities of the masses from Lippmann onward were simply accepted as necessary prerequisites for a theory of politics.

These generalizations may seem dauntingly abstract building blocks with which to construct a narrative history of rational choice (although they are absolutely central to it). In order to render the neoliberal approach to decisions more palpable, we can briefly track the trajectory of one of the most important Neoliberal thinkers: Friedrich Hayek.

Only recently, with the explosion of historical literature on Hayek, have we begun to encounter serious scholarly work on Hayek's struggles with epistemology.[39] As with every other major intellectual figure, Hayek changed his position on key theoretical terms over the course of his career; and none was more consequential than his treatment of knowledge. Interestingly, in Hayek's last book, *The Fatal Conceit*, he admits, "I confess it took me too a long time from my first breakthrough, in my essay 'Economics and Knowledge' through the recognition of 'Competition as a Discovery Procedure' and my essay on 'The Pretense of Knowledge' to state my theory of the dispersal of information, from which follows my conclusions about the superiority of spontaneous formations to central direction."[40] So while we have his frank admission that his system did not congeal around the concept of *information* until rather late in his career, at least in his own mind, we do not have a historical schematic of how it changed from his own hand. Leaning on the secondary literature, we could summarize it as a symphony in three movements.

In the first movement of this symphony, Hayek displaced the rather cryptic position of Mises in the Socialist Calculation controversy with the notion that knowledge is dispersed in such a way that bringing it all together in a central planning authority would be difficult—but, note well, *not impossible*. There seemed to be a special kind of slippery knowledge, qualitatively different from more conventional scientific conceptions, which was *local*, characterized by special conditions of time and place. It was almost as if this species of knowledge was something *entropic*: an energy which grew too diffuse to be readily gathered up and consolidated into a useful form. Not all knowledge shared this character, said Hayek; but the mere fact it existed at all was a club he could use to beat the market socialists of the world. Sometimes, Hayek hinted that the dispersed character had something to do with subjective experience, but he stayed well clear of issues of cognitive capacities or capacities to articulate this knowledge to others during this phase. At this stage, there was very little in the way of actual epistemology or formal psychology standing behind the concept; there was as yet no treatment of the decision.

The next movement in Hayek's Surprise Symphony happened sometime around his own return to psychology, published in 1952 as *The Sensory Order*. At this stage, Hayek entertained the notion that much of human knowledge is not only non-articulable, but also tacit and inaccessible to self-examination. Much of his revised attitudes concerning knowledge seems to have occurred during his stint at the Committee on Social Thought at the University of Chicago. In brief, Hayek there sought to revive the old discredited associationist psychology of the late eighteenth/early nineteenth centuries by suggesting mind was little more than sets of hierarchies of systems of classifier algorithms. He also had been in contact with Michael Polanyi at the early MPS meetings, and had come across Gilbert Ryle's distinction between "knowing how" and "knowing that" in Ryle's *Concept of Mind*.[41] He began to explore variations on tacit or non-articulable knowledge, not so much by explicitly following Polanyi or Ryle on this topic, as through building his own theory of mind upon a foundation of classifier systems about which the subject was not even aware of knowing, but regularly made use of in order to interact with the environment.[42] From this point forward, Hayek began to play fast and loose with the concept of consciousness, inverting the then popular Freudian frametale that the unconscious was a soup of barely accessible urges upon which rested a fragile vessel of rational thought; for Hayek, it was *rationality that was largely unconscious*, with conscious perception and drives constituting the thin veneer of intentionality and desires floating on top of the sea of obscure and inaccessible rule structures. Thus the types of knowledge that mattered most were inarticulate and largely inaccessible to the thinking agent. It was also precisely at this point that Hayek began making explicit references to evolutionary theory as the basis of his entire philosophy. The reason behind this shift was that Hayek sought to propound that the individual mind did not actually choose the rules that worked the best: that was done either through a sort of quasi-evolutionary selection of life success at the individual level reinforcing the relevant classifier rules, or more frequently, natural selection weeding out the individuals with unfit rules in favor of those individuals lucky enough to come previously equipped with superior classifiers. Note well, the decision now lives at the supra-personal level. It was, not to mince words, a harsh version of social Darwinism.

It is important to understand how this refracted the very notion of knowledge in the later political economy of Hayek. In this conception, the process of coming-to-know was largely disengaged from the knower, with most of the action happening at the subconscious level. As he wrote in his "Primacy of the Abstract," "the formation of a new abstraction seems *never* to be the outcome of a conscious process, not something at which the mind can deliberately aim, but always a discovery of something which *already* guides its operation."⁴³ Here, the philosopher of freedom postulated a species of predestination which would make even Calvin blush. Reason was losing all the trappings of ratiocination. The political implication was clear: if an individual mind could not even reliably plan or organize its own pathway of learning through life, it would exhibit contemptible *hubris* to think it could ever plan the lives of others, much less a whole economy. Knowledge was no longer like entropy, or pixie dust; it now resembled a great submerged iceberg, nine-tenths invisible, and frozen into place eons ago, with only minor changes around the margins when it jostled up against other similar icebergs.

How did these lumbering monads ever manage to communicate, much less live in societies which displayed any reliable level of organization? That question was finally answered in the third movement of Hayek's Surprise Symphony. Strangely, for a doctrine that started out so concerned over respect for individuals, the late Hayek rendered his system internally coherent by admitting that knowledge did not really persist in the level of the individual mind, but was processed and invested with meaning at the supra-personal level. In a catchphrase, since so much that people actually knew was inaccessible to them, the only entity that really was capable of judging and validating human knowledge was the Market. The key turning point, as Hayek informs us in *The Fatal Conceit*, was his essay "Competition as a Discovery Procedure":⁴⁴

> [Epistemology is governed by] competition as a procedure for the discovery of such facts as, without resort to it, *would not be known to anyone*. ... The knowledge of which we speak consists rather of a capacity to find out the particular circumstances, which becomes effective *only if the possessors of this knowledge are informed by the market* which kinds of things or services are wanted, and how urgently they are wanted. ... Knowledge that is used [in a market] is that of *all its members*. Ends that it serves are the separate ends of all those individuals, in all their variety and contrariness.⁴⁵

No longer was knowledge treated as a thing by Hayek, scattered about in an inconvenient matter, because not only is much human knowledge unable to be retrieved from within by the individual in question, but, indeed, there exists a species of *knowledge not "known" by any individual human being at all*. Note well, the decision has now been extracted entirely out of any psychological context. The place of the rational individual is therefore to acquiesce in signals conveyed by the Market, which hint at deeper truths that most humans will never know. But what is this depersonalized and deracinated supra-human knowledge but a new virtual kind of *information*? This, we think, explains Hayek's rather uncharacteristic reversion to the term "information" in his last work, *Fatal Conceit*. Sometimes, when it came to this ectoplasmic information, the late Hayek lapsed into his scientistic mode, where evolution had winnowed the elusive truth out of human frailty; but other times, he reverted to full religious mystery: "spontaneous order ... cannot be properly said to have a purpose ... known to any single person, or relatively small group of persons."[46] Some latter-day Austrians have argued that entrepreneurs are smarter than any dedicated intellectual since they are marinated in this information, and thus quicker to respond to market signals. Almost by definition, there is no instrument available to mankind to test this proposition. As with all the great world religions, the final destination for the skeptic was to surrender to Faith. The Market, as Super Information Processor, knows more than we could ever begin to divine.

The decision takes on an ineffable yet heroic character in this particular construction of knowledge. Indeed, the individual market participant cannot know very much, including their own true interests and desires, so most choice is driven by unconscious motives. In this sense, Hayekian theory conformed to the prewar consensus of the social sciences. However, in his particular case, order and progress are thought to be guaranteed by entrepreneurs who exercise the decision to create new commodities and opportunities out of nothing: the Schmittian decision personified.

In the neoliberal (by contrast with the neoclassical) solution to the conundrum of choice, almost all agents are irrational; only the supra-personal market can embody the rationality inadequately characterized by neoclassical economic theory. Instead of the Fuhrer, citizens were enjoined to prostrate themselves before an ineffable Market and its high priests, the entrepreneurs. This solution also had its Schmittian overtones, since a few neoliberals like Hayek invoked an exception that they (somehow) understood the imperatives of this rationality sufficiently to intervene politically in the state to help bring about a suitably constrained and chastened democracy subservient to the Market.

One cartoon characterization of this split within the Austrian camp might be $Schmitt_M$ (for Morgenstern) versus $Schmitt_H$ (for Hayek). It pitted Morgenstern's resort to the ungrounded decision to break various paradoxes of treating neoclassical utility theory as a cognitive theory of choice, against a Hayekian appeal to the decision as a means of rejecting neoclassical theory in favor of a market-based notion of rationality. Neither of these options was especially attractive for Americans in the immediate postwar era; so they went to work to tame the decision.

From Operations Research to Decision Theory

Since the more conventional history of neoclassical rational choice theory, forged at RAND and the Cowles Commission, is better known than our previous thumbnail sketches, we will opt to dispense with its summary here. However, the fact that the Cowles economists were almost exclusively market socialists, and developed their decision theories of rational choice in order to refute Hayek and the Neoliberal Thought Collective, is the indispensable starting point of any comprehensive history of "the decision."

Postwar Americans were desperate to be seen to be refuting the trope that democracy led to Nazism, and by extension Schmittian decisionism, through subordination of the act of the decision itself to a framework of science-like algorithms. As our editors have argued, "generations of postwar social scientists embraced a form of technocratic politics in which decisions were made by systems of equations, not people." What has not been appreciated, as yet, is the extent to which the return of the repressed happened first in military research, of which operations research during World War II was the exemplar, and then spread throughout the rest of the social sciences during the Cold War.[47] What the military had thought it was paying for at RAND and the ONR was a science of war and planning; what it got was a science of rational choice. My argument will be that the rise of decision theory was first and foremost an expression of a conscious rejection of a charismatic construction of leadership and rationality, best exemplified by Schmitt, at first within the military itself, and then, with a lag, in the social sciences. The success of the army was no longer attributed to the brilliance of a few top brass or elitist *esprit de corps*; it was due rather to the fact that it was a smooth, well-oiled, cybernetic feedback mechanism: the very icon of rationality. Nuclear strategy was portrayed as a series of games played out on computers. The average citizen and the market participant alike would be portrayed as coming equipped with a natural algorithmic rationality, if unfortunately perhaps bereft of wisdom; political democracy and market purchases would be the public manifestations of that rationality. The rise of the computer out of the very same research units that first produced operations research cemented the connections. In other words, *pace* Giocoli, "decision theory" was not an obvious extrapolation of prewar themes in economics, however much there abided certain similarities in the mathematics; instead, it was the utter repudiation of pre–World War II social science altogether. Rationality stopped being about actual human reasons altogether, just as Lorraine Daston has suggested, and was recast as mere transitivity and consistency of unexplained preferences, under the joint aegis of logic and cybernetics. The major contribution of the economists was to make it seem as if there had been continuity within scientific economics, where in fact, there had been drastic rupture.

The historian Hunter Heyck has given the deepest explanation of this phase of the American reconstruction of "rationality."[48] It was a complete transmogrification of the essence of humanity: "We are [no longer] defined by our bodies, our souls, our hopes or our dreams. We are defined by our choices."[49] This both finally renounced the older Enlightenment construct of reasons and understandings, passions and interests; it also neutralized the prewar fears that the masses were not fully rational by insisting only their choices could be subject to a rationality audit. Democracy was no longer threatened, since almost anything could clear this low bar of rationality:

> In many cases a type of behavior may be explained as rational if one introduces uncertainty and the need for learning. ... The economist is usually not interested in choices or preferences themselves. There is little investigation of the utility function itself. ... [It is permissible for] choice theory to consider it applicable to unconscious or at any rate unreflective choices, as well as decisions in the narrower sense.[50]

From the perspective of Cowles scholars like Kenneth Arrow, Hayek was comprehensively defanged: even if the unwashed market participant might be a bit scattered and irrational, as Lippmann and others insisted, their choices were not, by definition. Of course, democracy never did as good a job of aggregating choices as the market managed to do: but this left open a role for elites to maintain their political sovereignty over the system.[51] In the final analysis, what mattered was the reified *choice*, and not the shambolic *chooser*. Decisions grew so hypostasized that they could be made by anything: a person, a firm, a legislator, a nation, a gene, and even a machine. Note well this was Schmittian decisionism inflated to a truly heroic scale, politics blown up into a Theory of Everything. Consumer sovereignty was guaranteed by the mere act of the isolated choice, without any evaluation of its content—a curious spawn of Schmitt and constrained optimization. As Heyck has insisted, "The new study of decisionmaking offered an opportunity to save reason while admitting unreason."[52] It accomplished this by banishing almost every connotation of reason inherited from the eighteenth and nineteenth centuries.

The initial uptake of this innovation was not just discipline-centered, but happened on a number of fronts simultaneously, all of which happened in areas affiliated to a greater or lesser degree with postwar operations research units. Take, for instance, postwar analytic philosophy. Some might be surprised to learn one of the canonical early axiomatizations of rational choice theory appeared in the journal *Philosophy of Science*.[53] Indeed, the career of philosopher Donald Davidson has yet to be adequately appreciated as one long meditation upon the implications of the decisionist move, which began in his early apprenticeship at RAND, exploring the belief-desire nexus of this species of folk psychology, to his pivotal doctrine of the so-called "principle of charity," which counsels that we should deploy a principle of interpretation with regard to the actions of others, which attributes to them true beliefs and rational desires as a default option. (This is precisely the methodological mandate of decisionism.) Nothing expresses better the utter rejection of prewar social science which continually attributed irrational desires and beliefs to the masses, and consequently elevates the folk psychology of desire or utility to a causal status on par with the natural sciences.

Other key contributions to the stabilization of rational choice were made in the first decade by mathematicians (R. M. Thrall, Merrill Flood), statisticians (Frederick Mosteller, Leonard Savage) and of course, a subset of psychologists. Ward Edwards was particularly important in bringing the work on rational choice to the attention of his colleagues, especially in his 1954 review essay in the *Psychological Bulletin*. Especially in psychology and statistics, human beings were being reconfigured as little betting machines, coming in at least two different "models," one equipped with Neyman-Pearson hypothesis testing, and the other with a Bayesian inference engine.[54] One thing that stands out in this first postwar decade is the extent to which *everyone else but the economists* were briefly open to the notion that human experimentation was one legitimate way to get at the vexed question of rationality—this includes mathematicians, statisticians, and philosophers who might otherwise have abjured experimentation as foreign to their home research protocols. Another noteworthy aspect of the history was that the moment of empiricist enthusiasm was unexpectedly fleeting, primarily because the preponderance of evidence produced was that the popular versions of axioms of rational choice, and particularly von Neumann-Morgenstern expected utility, were repeatedly violated in experimental settings. This empiricist fervor only seemed to impinge upon the consciousness of the economists in one special case: that of the so-called Allais paradox.[55] But even in that instance, all notions that choice theory was subject to falsification were effortlessly repressed among the economists.

The reactions of major players to this disappointment after the brief flowering of empiricism is another major part of the as-yet unwritten history of rational choice theory; it has close connections to the retreat from operations research and return to disciplinarity and the attendant impenetrable boundaries between the academic professions in the postwar American university. It seems clear that the philosophers were quickest to exit the military rational choice complex: Davidson, for one, never again participated in experiments, abjured further axiomatizations, and retreated to abstract lucubrations composed solely for his fellow analytical philosophers. Many of the mathematicians also withdrew from the field, retreating to the consolations of the purity of a Bourbakist approach to mathematics. The mathematicians working on game theory in the later 1950s tended to drift away from any conceptual dependence upon utility theory, with the exception of a very few figures like John Nash.

The response of many psychologists was more interesting. Even early enthusiasts for utility formalisms, such as Ward Edwards, tended to turn against them later in life. Utility was never wholly taken on board as a serious psychological theory in American profession; empirical research on "the decision," however, did continue apace, in many cases under the guise of research into judgment processes.[56] Almost alone in resisting the blandishments of the decisionist program, psychologists perversely kept trying to reintroduce context and history into the constitution of "the choice." Increasingly, psychologists focused their attentions on how people (mis)understood probabilities and risks, rather than possessed preset preferences. After the mid-1950s, various operations research-flavored decisionist themes tended to fragment into multiple noncommunicating variants, confined primarily within individual disciplinary research programs. It might be called judgment theory in some precincts of psychology, or behavioral science or risk theory in business schools, or decision theory in International Relations, but much of it tended to display aspects of their origins in wartime operations research, while wandering off into parochial disciplinary concerns.

Conclusion

This chapter has sketched an alternative history of the origins of rational choice theory, downplaying the more conventional narrative that it mostly occurred within neoclassical economics following an internalist logic, and instead, highlighting the role of both long term trends in the sciences, as well as the central pivot located in the Cold War and the military in the promotion of operations research. It gains its inspiration from a newer literature mostly found in science studies that identifies the rise of an unprecedented complex of meanings and motives all revolving around the mid-century construct of "rational choice" and "the decision." One could view it as an exercise in the exploration of historical epistemology: that is, a history built upon the presupposition that there never in history was a single correct way to approach the validation of reason and rationality.

The story, of course, continues, although that ventures beyond our self-imposed end point of 1968. After the 1960s, the military component of scientific research funding tended to diminish in magnitude and importance in general; that opened up the possibility that other patrons' concerns might also efface the original fascination with decisionism. Yet, contrary to such expectations, rational choice theory only grew stronger and more entrenched, but localized primarily within the American economics profession in the 1960s–80s. Over time, the formalisms of decision theory became more and more associated with the orthodoxy of neoclassical economics, as microeconomics persisted immune from previous empirical disconfirmations and contemporary extra-disciplinary entanglements.

It is this curious sequestration of rational choice theory within economics in the post-1965 era, and its demonstrable success in perduring over multiple decades as a coherent doctrine, that requires further serious historical explication. Instead of being distracted by the perennial yet meaningless question of whether or not people are really rational in the economists' sense, the more pointed question should be: How did such a highly stylized and empirically bankrupt theory, cut off from intellectual support from most other relevant disciplines and drifting away from military patronage, come to be the icon of rationality for subsequent generations of social theorists? In other words, the immediate Cold War setting can go some distance in explaining the spread of decisionism throughout many postwar American social sciences in the late 1940s and 1950s. The more interesting question is how did neoclassical economics provide the citadel for it to become unquestioned cultural wisdom in the later twentieth century?

Philip Mirowski is Carl Koch Professor of Economics and the History and Philosophy of Science at the University of Notre Dame. He is the author of, among others (with co-author Edward Nik-Khah) *The Knowledge We Have Lost in Information* (Oxford University Press, 2017), *More Heat than Light* (Cambridge University Press, 1989), *Machine Dreams* (Cambridge University Press, 2001), *ScienceMart* (Havard University Press, 2011), and *Never Let a Serious Crisis Go to Waste* (Verso, 2013).

Notes

1. Nicolas Guilhot, "The Kuhning of Reason," *Review of International Studies* 42, no. 1 (2016): 3–24.
2. One thinks here especially of Paul Erickson, et al., *How Reason Almost Lost Its Mind* (Chicago, IL: University of Chicago Press, 2013); and Paul Erickson, "Mathematical Models, Rational Choice, and the Search for Cold War Culture," *Isis* 101, no. 2 (2010): 386–92; Paul Erickson, *The World the Game Theorists Made* (Chicago, IL: University of Chicago Press, 2015); they are reviewed by economist Roy Weintraub in Roy Weintraub, "Game Theory and Cold War Rationality: A Review Essay," ERIC Working Paper no. 208 (2016), retrieved 18 July 2018 from https://www.scribd.com/document/317686595/JEL-Review-Essay-SSRN. To be fair, the work of Hunter Heyck—such as Hunter Heyck, "Producing Reason," in *Cold War Social Science: Knowledge Production, Liberal Democracy, and Human Nature*, ed. Mark Solovey and Hamilton Cravens (New York: Palgrave Macmillan, 2012), 99–116; and Hunter Heyck, *The Age of System* (Baltimore, MD: Johns Hopkins University Press, 2015)—is more historically promising, as we shall observe below. Unbeknownst to me when I first composed a draft of this chapter, Lorraine Daston, "The Rule of Rules, or How Reason Became Rationality," lecture 21 November 2010 in Berlin, https://vimeo.com/18497646, had begun to explore similar themes.
3. Ronald Coase, *Essays on Economics and Economists* (Chicago, IL: University of Chicago Press, 1994), 116.
4. For some examples chosen at random from my bookshelf: Will Thomas, *Rational Action* (Cambridge, MA: MIT Press, 2015); S. M. Amadae, *Prisoners of Reason* (New York: Cambridge University Press, 2016); Erickson, *World the Game Theorists Made*.
5. See Kaisa Herne and Majia Setala, "A Response to the Critique of Rational Choice Theory," *Inquiry* 47, no. 1 (2004): 67–85; Donald Green and Ian Shapiro, *Pathologies of Rational Choice Theory* (Cambridge, UK: Cambridge University Press, 1994); Paul Weirich, "Causal Decision Theory," in

The Stanford Encyclopedia of Philosophy, ed. Edward N. Zalta (Winter 2012 Edition), http://plato.stanford.edu/archives/win2012/entries/decision-causal/; Daniel Hausman, *Preference, Value, Choice and Welfare* (New York: Cambridge University Press, 2012); Maurice Lagueux, *Rationality and Explanation in Economics* (London: Routledge, 2010).

6. I am thinking here of Dutch Book style arguments, sometimes called "money pumps." Nozick's appeal to the normative suggests you will suffer these sorts of consequences if you don't shape up and conform to the rhythm of the neoclassical strictures.

7. Although, see Philip Mirowski, *Machine Dreams: Economics Becomes a Cyborg Science* (New York: Cambridge University Press, 2002), chapter 7; John Davis, *The Theory of the Individual in Economics* (London: Routledge, 2003).

8. See Thostein Veblen, *The Place of Science in Modern Civilization* (New York: Viking, 1930), 73.

9. For the cognoscenti, the comparison of rational choice to a billiard player computing as-if mechanics was a trope in the famous paper by Milton Friedman and Leonard Savage, "The Expected Utility Hypothesis and the Measurability of Utility," *Journal of Political Economy* 60, no. 6 (1952): 463–74.

10. It may seem ungenerous to name names, but a few exemplars will nevertheless focus the mind on the phenomenon: Roger Backhouse, Ann Cudd, Francisco Guala, Lawrence Blume, Mie Augier, Wade Hands, Maurice Lagueux, and Shira Lewin. Daniel Rodgers, *The Age of Fracture* (Cambridge, MA: Harvard University Press, 2011) tells a similar story, only by suggesting notions of rationality had become fractured in the other disciplines.

11. The brushing off of what is an essential ontological and epistemological stance as comprising a mere tool that might be dispensed with in the same way one might put down a screwdriver to pick up a hammer is one of the worst misrepresentations of what has been at stake in the intellectual history. For this tool excuse, see Erickson, "Models"; Erickson, *Game Theorists*; Joel Isaac, "Tool Shock: Technique and Epistemology in the Postwar Social Sciences," *History of Political Economic* 42, Supplement (2010): 133–64.

12. See, for instance, Floris Heukelom, *Behavioral Economics: A History* (New York: Cambridge University Press, 2014).

13. A major popularizer of this view is the former Marxist Herbert Gintis, as in Herbert Gintis, *Bounds of Reason* (Oxford: Oxford University Press, 2009).

14. Nicolas Giocoli, *Modeling Rational Agents* (Cheltenham, UK: Edward Elgar, 2003).

15. See, for instance, Matthias Klaes and Esther-Mirjam Sent, "A Conceptual History of the Emergence of Bounded Rationality," *History of Political Economy* 37, no. 1 (2005): 27–59.

16. This is discussed in detail in Philip Mirowski, *More Heat than Light* (New York: Cambridge University Press, 1989).

17. My prime test case would be Francis Ysidro Edgeworth; his stance toward utility is covered in Philip Mirowski, *Edgeworth on Chance, Economic Hazars and Statistics* (Totawa: Rowman & Littlefield, 1994).
18. Contrary to Shira Lewin, "Economics and Psychology: Lessons for Our Own Day," *Journal of Economic Literature* 34, no. 3 (1996): 1293–1323, there is nothing new about this. A transdiciplinary history of the mutual revulsion of the disciplines of political economy and psychology still awaits its historian.
19. This was the message of that classic work Edward Purcell, *The Crisis of Democratic Theory* (Lexington: University of Kentucky Press, 1973), and H. Stuart Hughes, *Consciousness and Society: The Reorientation of European Social Thought, 1870–1930* (New York: Vintage, 1958).
20. The key texts here would be Daston, "Rules"; Erickson, et al., *Reason*; Weintraub, "Game Theory."
21. Erickson, et al., *Reason*, 158.
22. Vilfredo Pareto, *Manuel d'économie Politique* (Geneva: Droz, 1981), 41.
23. This argument would be based upon the fact that neither Bernoulli nor Bentham allowed for a general single-valued utility function defined over commodity space. Nevertheless, the canard is repeated incessantly within the economics profession, viz., Lawrence Blume and David Easley, *New Palgrave Dictionary of Economics* (London: Macmillan, 2008), s.v. "Rationality."
24. Leon Walras, *Elements of Pure Economics*, trans. William Jaffe (Homewood, IL: Irwin, 1954), 65.
25. Daston, "Rules."
26. See Mirowski, *Dreams*, 31–43.
27. For the former, see Philip Mirowski and Dieter Plehwe, eds., *The Road from Mont Pèlerin* (Cambridge, MA: Harvard University Press, 2009), 444; for the latter, see F. R. Christi, "Hayek and Schmitt on the Rule of Law," *Canadian Journal of Political Science* 17, no. 3 (1984): 521–35.
28. See Karl Löwith, *Martin Heidegger and European Nihilism*, trans. Gary Steiner (New York: Columbia University Press, 1995), 143, 150.
29. See Christi, "Law," 531.
30. John von Neumann and Oskar Morgenstern, *Theory of Games and Economic Behavior*, rev. ed. (New York: Wiley, 1947).
31. See Philip Mirowski, "What Were Von Neumann and Morgenstern Trying to Accomplish?" in *Towards a History of Game Theory, History of Political Economy*, ed. E. Roy Weintraub (Durham: Duke University Press, 1992), 113–47.
32. Oskar Morgenstern, "Vollkommene Voraussicht und Wirtschaftliches Gleichgewicht," *Zeitschrift für Nationalokonomie* 6, no. 3 (1935): 344, emphasis added.
33. John von Neumann and Oskar Morgenstern, *Theory of Games and Economic Behavior* (Princeton: Princeton University Press, 1944). See, for instance, William Goldstein and Robin Hogarth, eds., "Judgment and Decision Research: Some Historical Context," in *Research on Judgment and Decision Making: Currents, Connections, Controversies* (Cambridge,

UK: Cambridge University Press, 1997), 3–65; Giocoli, *Modeling*; Robert Leonard, *Von Neumann, Morgenstern, and the Creation of Game Theory* (New York: Cambridge University Press, 2010); Mirowski, *Dreams*, chapter 3. As Arrow said, "The Von Neumann-Nash tradition had created the tools. Once the tools are there, somebody was bound to pick them up." Quoted in George Feiwel, ed., *Arrow and the Ascent of Modern Economic Theory* (New York: NYU Press, 1987), 195.

34. Indeed, the Nash equilibrium only really made sense if you knew so much about your opponent that you might as well be playing yourself—again, the solipsistic Schmittian conception of the decision. See Miroswki, *Dreams*, 341–49.
35. See Angus Burgin, *The Great Persuasion* (Cambridge, MA: Harvard University Press, 2012); Mirowski and Plehwe, *Road*; Philip Mirowski, "A History Best Served Cold," in *Uncertain Empire: American History and the Idea of the Cold War*, ed. Joel Isaac and Duncan Bell (Oxford: Oxford University Press, 2012): 61–74.
36. This is discussed in greater detail in Bruce Caldwell, *Hayel's Challenge: An Intellectual Biography of F. A. Hayek* (Chicago, IL: The University of Chicago Press, 2004); Mirowski, *Dreams*; Philip Mirowski, "Markets Come to Bits: Evolution, Computation, and Markomata in Economic Science," *Journal of Economic Behavior* 63, no. 2 (2007): 209–42; Philip Mirowski, *Science-Mart* (Cambridge, MA: Harvard University Press, 2011). Hayek himself admits the dependence upon brain metaphors in his Friedrich Hayek, "The Sensory Order after 25 Years," in *Cognition and the Symbolic Process*, vol. 2, ed. W. Weimer and D. Palermo (Hillsdale, NJ: Erlbaum, 1982): 287–93.
37. Michel Foucault, *Birth of Biopolitics* (London: Palgrave MacMillan, 2008), 226.
38. Friedrich Hayek, *The Constitution of Liberty* (Chicago, IL: University of Chicago Press, 1960), 172.
39. Pride of place goes to Fuat Oguz, "Hayek on Tacit Knowledge," *Journal of Institutional Economics* 6, no. 2 (2010): 145–66.
40. Friedrich Hayek, *The Fatal Conceit* (Chicago, IL: University of Chicago Press, 1988), 88.
41. Gilbert Ryle, *The Concept of Mind* (New York: Barnes and Noble, 1949).
42. It has not been clear to subsequent commentators just how different, and even opposed, were Polanyi's and Hayek's philosophies of knowledge. This has been occluded by assertions that they both believed in similar notions of "tacit knowledge." On this, see Philip Mirowski, "Economics, Science and Knowledge: Polanyi vs Hayek," *Tradition and Discovery* 25, no. 1 (1998): 21–42; Oguz, "Hayek."
43. Friedrich Hayek, *New Studies in Philosophy, Politics, Economics and the History of Ideas* (London: Routledge, 1978), 46.
44. Ibid.
45. Hayek, *Studies*, 179, 182, 183, emphasis added.
46. Ibid., 183.
47. For some histories of Operations Research, see Mirowski, *Dreams*, chapter 4; Thomas, *Rational Action*. For a survey of the history of cybernetics,

see Ronald Kline, *The Cybernetic Moment* (Baltimore, MD: Johns Hopkins University Press, 2015).
48. In Heyck, "Producing"; Heyck, *Age*.
49. Heyck, "Producing," 99. I must insert a personal aside here. When did movies and TV shows start using the insipid phrase, "He made some bad choices," when having a protagonist denounce what formerly used to be the moral constitution of another character? In my impression, it began in the 1980s.
50. Kenneth Arrow, "Utilities, Attitudes, Choices: A Review Note," *Econometrica* 26, no 1 (1958), 10, 8, 1.
51. I am referring here to the so-called Arrow Impossibility Theorem.
52. Heyck, "Producing," 106.
53. Donald Davidson, J. C. C. McKinsey, and Patrick Suppes, "Outline of a Formal Theory of Value," *Philosophy of Science* 22, no 2 (1955): 140–60.
54. See Nicola Giocoli, "From Wald to Savage," *Journal of the History of the Behavioral Sciences* 49, no. 1 (2013): 63–95; Gerg Gigerenzer and David Murray, *Cognition as Intuitive Statistics* (Hillsdale, NJ: L. Erlbaum Associates, 1987).
55. See Maurice Allais, "Le comportement de l'homme rationnel devant le risque," *Econometrica* 21, no. 4 (1953): 503–46.
56. This history is covered in Goldstein and Hogarth, "Judgment."

Bibliography

Allais, Maurice. "Le comportement de l'homme rationnel devant le risqué." *Econometrica* 21 (1953): 503–46.
Amadae, Sonia. *Prisoners of Reason*. New York: Cambridge University Press, 2016.
———. *Rationalizing Capitalist Democracy*. Chicago, IL: University of Chicago Press, 2003.
Arrow, Kenneth. "Utilities, Attitudes, Choices: A Review Note." *Econometrica* 26 (1958): 1–23.
Arrow, Kenneth, E. Columbatto, M. Perlman, and C. Schmidt, eds. *The Rational Foundations of Economic Behaviour*. London: Macmillan, 1996.
Bartolotti, Lisa. "The Epistemic Benefits of Reason Giving." *Theory and Psychology* 19 (2009): 624–45.
Bessner, Daniel. *Democracy in Exile: Hans Speier and the Rise of the Defense Intellectual*. Ithaca, NY: Cornell University Press, 2018.
Blume, Lawrence, and David Easley. *New Palgrave Dictionary of Economics*. London: Macmillan, 2008.
Burgin, Angus. *The Great Persuasion*. Cambridge, MA: Harvard University Press, 2012.
Christi, F. R. "Hayek and Schmitt on the Rule of Law." *Canadian Journal of Political Science* 17 (1984): 521–35.
Coase, Ronald. *Essays on Economics and Economists*. Chicago, IL: University of Chicago Press, 1994.

Colander, David, Ric Holt, and J. B. Rosser, eds. *The Changing Face of Economics*. Ann Arbor: University of Michigan Press, 2004.
Cudd, Ann. "Game Theory and the History of Ideas about Rationality." *Economics and Philosophy* 9 (1993): 101–33.
Daston, Lorraine. "The Rule of Rules, or how reason became rationality." Lecture 21 November 2010 in Berlin, https://vimeo.com/18497646.
Davidson, Donald. *Essays on Action and Events*. Oxford: Oxford University Press, 2001.
Davidson, Donald, J. C. C. McKinsey, and Patrick Suppes. "Outline of a Formal Theory of Value." *Philosophy of Science* 22 (April 1955): 140–60.
Davidson, Donald, Patrick Suppes, and Sid Siegle. *Decision Making: An Experimental Approach*. Stanford, CA: Stanford University Press, 1957.
Davis, John. *The Theory of the Individual in Economics*. London: Routledge, 2003.
Edwards, Ward. "The Theory of Decision Making." *Psychological Bulletin* 51 (1954): 380–417.
Erickson, Paul. "Mathematical Models, Rational Choice, and the Search for Cold War Culture." *Isis* 101 (2010): 386–92.
———. *The World the Game Theorists Made*. Chicago, IL: University of Chicago Press, 2015.
Erickson, Paul, Judy Klein, Lorraine Daston, Rebecca Lemov, Thomas Sturm, and Michael Gordin. *How Reason Almost Lost Its Mind: The Strange Career of Cold War Rationality*. Chicago, IL: University of Chicago Press, 2013.
Feiwel, George, ed. *Arrow and the Ascent of Modern Economic Theory*. New York: NYU Press, 1987.
Friedman, Milton, and Leonard Savage. "The Expected Utility Hypothesis and the Measurability of Utility." *Journal of Political Economy* 60 (1952): 463–74.
Gigerenzer, Gerd. "What Can Economists Know?", https://www.youtube.com/watch?v=DdEEwoKkfMA, 12 April 2012.
Gigerenzer, Gerd, and David Murray. *Cognition as Intuitive Statistics*. Hillsdale, NJ: L. Erlbaum Associates, 1987.
Gintis, Herbert. *Bounds of Reason*. Oxford: Oxford University Press, 2009.
Giocoli, Nicola. "From Wald to Savage." *Journal of the History of the Behavioral Sciences* 49 (2013): 63–95.
———. *Modeling Rational Agents*. Cheltenham, UK: Edward Elgar, 2003.
Gleick, James. *The Information*. New York: Vintage, 2012.
Goldstein, William, and Robin Hogarth, eds. "Judgment and Decision Research: Some Historical Context." In *Research on Judgment and Decision Making*. Cambridge: Cambridge University Press, 1997.
Goodwin, Craufurd. *Walter Lippmann*. Cambridge, MA: Harvard University Press, 2014.
Green, Donald, and Ian Shapiro. *Pathologies of Rational Choice Theory*. Cambridge, UK: Cambridge University Press, 1994.
Guilhot, Nicolas. "Cyborg Pantocrator." *Journal of the History of the Behavioral Sciences* 47 (2011): 279–301.
———. "The Kuhning of Reason." *Review of International Studies* 42, no. 1 (2016): 3–24.

Hausman, Daniel. *Preference, Value, Choice and Welfare.* New York: Cambridge University Press, 2012.
Hayek, Friedrich. *The Constitution of Liberty.* Chicago, IL: University of Chicago Press, 1960.
———. *The Fatal Conceit.* Chicago, IL: University of Chicago Press, 1988.
———. *Individualism and Economic Order.* Chicago, IL: Regnery, 1948.
———. *New Studies in Philosophy, Politics, Economics and the History of Ideas.* London: Routledge, 1978.
———. "The Sensory Order after 25 Years." In *Cognition and the Symbolic Process.* Edited by W. Weimer and D. Palermo. Hillsdale, NJ: Erlbaum, 1982.
Herne, Kaisa, and Majia Setala. "A Response to the Critique of Rational Choice Theory." *Inquiry* 47 (2004): 67–85.
Heukelom, Floris. *Behavioral Economics: A History.* New York: Cambridge University Press, 2014.
Heyck, Hunter. *The Age of System.* Baltimore, MD: Johns Hopkins University Press, 2015.
———. "Producing Reason." In *Cold War Social Science.* Edited by Mark Solovey and Hamilton Cravens. New York: Palgrave Macmillan, 2012.
Hughes, H. Stuart. *Consciousness and Society: The Reorientation of European Social Thought, 1870–1930.* New York: Vintage, 1958.
Isaac, Joel. "The Human Sciences in Cold War America." *Historical Journal* 6 (2007): 397–424.
———. "Tool Shock: Technique and Epistemology in the Postwar Social Sciences." *History of Political Economy* 40, Supplement (2010): 133–64.
Isaac, Joel, and Duncan Bell eds. *Uncertain Empire: American History and the Idea of the Cold War.* Oxford: Oxford University Press, 2012.
Klaes, Matthias, and Esther-Mirjam Sent. "A Conceptual History of the Emergence of Bounded Rationality." *History of Political Economy* 37 (2005): 27–59.
Kline, Ronald. *The Cybernetic Moment.* Baltimore, MD: Johns Hopkins University Press, 2015.
Lagueux, Maurice. *Rationality and Explanation in Economics.* London: Routledge, 2010.
Leonard, Robert. *Von Neumann, Morgenstern, and the Creation of Game Theory.* New York: Cambridge University Press, 2010.
Lewin, Shira. "Economics and Psychology: Lessons for our own day." *Journal of Economic Literature* 34 (1996): 1293–1323.
Löwith, Karl. *Martin Heidegger and European Nihilism.* Translated by Gary Steiner. New York: Columbia University Press, 1995.
Luce, R., and H. Raiffa. *Games and Decisions.* New York: Wiley, 1957.
Marschak, Jacob. "Rational Behavior, Uncertain Prospects, and Measurable Utility." *Econometrica* 18 (1950): 111–41.
Mirowski, Philip. *Edgeworth on Chance: Economic Hazard and Statistics.* Totawa: Rowman & Littlefield, 1994.

———. "A History Best Served Cold." In *Uncertain Empire: American History and the Idea of the Cold War*. Edited by Joel Isaac and Duncan Bell. Oxford: Oxford University Press, 2012.
———. *Machine Dreams*. New York: Cambridge University Press, 2002.
———. *More Heat than Light*. New York: Cambridge University Press, 1989.
———. "What Were Von Neumann and Morgenstern Trying to Accomplish?" In *Towards a History of Game Theory*. Edited by E. Roy Weintraub. Annual Supplement to *History of Political Economy* 24 (1992): 113–47.
———. "When Games Grow Deadly Serious: The Influence of the Military on the Evolution of Game Theory." In *Economics and National Security*. Edited by Craufurd Goodwin. Annual Supplement to *History of Political Economy* 23 (1991): 227–55.
———. "Why There Is (As Yet) No Such Thing as an Economics of Knowledge." In *Oxford Handbook of the Philosophy of Economics*. Edited by Harold Kincaid and Don Ross, 99–156. Oxford: Oxford University Press, 2009.
Mirowski, Philip, and Dieter Plehwe, eds. *The Road from Mont Pèlerin*. Cambridge, MA: Harvard University Press, 2009.
Mirowski, Philip, and Edward Nik-Khah. *The Knowledge We Have Lost in Information*. New York: Oxford University Press, 2016.
Morgenstern, Oskar. *The Limits of Economics*. London: Hodge, 1937.
———. "Vollkommene Voraussicht und Wirtschaftliches Gleichgewicht." *Zeitschrift für Nationalokonomie* 6, no. 3 (1935): 337–57.
Nozick, Robert. *The Nature of Rationality*. Princeton: Princeton University Press, 1993.
Oguz, Fuat. "Hayek on Tacit Knowledge." *Journal of Institutional Economics* 6 (2010): 145–66.
Pareto, Vilfredo. *Manuel d'économie politique*. Geneva: Droz, 1981.
Purcell, Edward. *The Crisis of Democratic Theory*. Lexington: University of Kentucky Press, 1973.
Rancan, Antonella. "Modigliani's and Simon's Early Contributions to Uncertainty." *History of Political Economy* 45 (2013): 1–38.
Rodgers, Daniel. *The Age of Fracture*. Cambridge, MA: Harvard University Press, 2011.
Sen, Amartya. "Rational Behaviour." In *Utility and Probability: The New Palgrave*. London: Macmillan, 1987.
Sent, Esther-Mirjam. "The Tricks of the No Trade Theorem." *History of Political Economy* 38, Supplement (2006): 305–21.
Solovey, Mark. *Shaky Foundations: The Politics-Patronage-Social Science Nexus in Cold War America*. New Brunswick: Rutgers University Press, 2013.
Solovey, Mark, and Hamilton Cravens, eds. *Cold War Social Science*. New York: Palgrave Macmillan, 2012.
Thomas, Will. *Rational Action*. Cambridge: MIT Press, 2015.
Thrall, R. M., C. H. Coombs, and R. L. Davis, eds. *Decision Processes*. New York: Wiley, 1954.
Veblen, Thorstein. *The Place of Science in Modern Civilization*. New York: Viking, 1930.

Von Neumann, John, and Oskar Morgenstern. *Theory of Games and Economic Behavior*. Rev. ed. New York: Wiley, 1947.

Walras, Léon. *Elements of Pure Economics*. Translated by William Jaffe. Homewood, IL: Irwin, 1954.

Weintraub, Roy. "Game Theory and Cold War Rationality: A Review Essay." CHOPE Working Paper (2016). Retrieved 18 July 2018 from https://www.scribd.com/document/317686595/JEL-Review-Essay-SSRN.

Weirich, Paul. "Causal Decision Theory." *The Stanford Encyclopedia of Philosophy*. Edited by Edward N. Zalta. Winter 2012 Edition. http://plato.stanford.edu/archives/win2012/entries/decision-causal/.

6

COMPUTABLE RATIONALITY, NUTS, AND THE NUCLEAR LEVIATHAN

S. M. Amadae

> Liberal democracy was saved only by nuclear weapons. ... NATO adopted the doctrine of MAD (mutual assured destruction), according to which even conventional Soviet attacks would be answered by an all-out nuclear strike. ... Without nukes, there would have been no Woodstock, no Beatles and no overflowing supermarkets.
> —Yuval Noah Harari, *Homo Deus: A Brief History of Tomorrow*

> A *rational decision process* will be understood ... to refer to the *entire* reasoning activity that intervenes between the receipt of a decision stimulus and the ultimate decisions. ... Such an approach forces rational behavior to be thought of as essentially algorithmic. This makes it natural to model a rational player as a suitably programmed computing machine.
> —Ken Binmore, *Essays on the Foundations of Game Theory*

> As the case of nuclear strategy makes clear, there was no straightforward way of adding the mind back into questions of rationality. The appeal of the algorithmic definition of rationality was precisely that it avoided the messes that ensued when one attempted to account for the fact that decision makers had personalities, histories, and prejudices.
> —Paul Erickson et al., *How Reason Almost Lost Its Mind*

Recent Cold War historiography has demonstrated how military security concerns drove the development of decision technologies such as game theory, bounded rationality, operations research, and systems analysis.[1] Recollecting such history is important because it enables us to see how these decision theories—game theory in particular—were well-suited to the logistics and strategy of conflict. In their reliance on computational techniques that abandon the need for a conscious subject, prominent decision-theoretic tools sharply broke with previous understandings of human reasoning. Under these new frameworks, neither the agents modeled nor the analysts using the models need an intelligible grasp of the problems they are solving in order to identify solutions. The *mindless* strategic rationality of game theory came to define the nuclear security dilemma and, as this chapter argues, is profoundly entangled with the strategic posture it recommends.

Nuclear strategy is ostensibly more effective the less intelligible it is to observers because deterrent threats achieve credibility at the price of absurdly endangering constituents with apocalyptic terror. Far from the popular conception of the public and journalists, the nuclear strategy sanctioned by game theory is not MAD (Mutual Assured Destruction), but rather NUTS (Nuclear Utilization Targeting Selection), referring to a nuclear war-fighting posture.[2] Whereas MAD is structured to symmetrically hold nuclear weapons in reserve to multilaterally counter a nuclear attack, NUTS entails developing asymmetric advantage based on coercive bargaining, threatening to introduce nuclear warheads into conflict, and preparing to achieve escalation dominance at all levels of engagement. The mindless quality of game theory is useful in nuclear security because, according to strategic rationality, credible deterrence depends on preparing and intending to wage an omnicidal nuclear war, an action that would strike the casual subject as not only recklessly immoral but also pointless. Thus, the fact that strategic rationality jettisons intelligibility, or understanding of the problem it aims to solve, enables it to rationalize mobilizing and maintaining resources for ends that defy both moral reasoning and purposive action. This alienating logic of unintentional, and not necessarily intelligible, choice informing nuclear deterrence has been elevated to the standard understanding of classical western instrumental rationality, with detrimental consequences. Such strategic rationality now informs modeling and decision-making spanning from nonhuman actors to individuals' choices and collective action, including the exercise of national sovereignty.

Section one introduces recent historiography to show how Cold War strategic rationality—also referred to as rational deterrence, game theory, and rational choice—erased the role of understanding, or a thinking subject, in rational decision-making. This reconceptualization of rational choice foreclosed on the idea of informed citizens who participate in a process of democratic will formation to oversee executive decisions. Section two investigates the entanglement of the content of game theory with the nuclear security posture it recommends. The substance of game theory grounds nuclear strategy, finding that the most effective form of deterrence is to prepare to fight and win a nuclear war. Section three investigates how prominent social theorists use game theory as a way to unify our understanding of decision-making across actors, encompassing biological organisms, persons, and collectives. Corporate agency, the artificial product of collective action, has been subject to theorization at least since Thomas Hobbes's *Leviathan*. Game theory, which served dual Cold War roles of grounding nuclear deterrence and rethinking the intellectual bases of democratic governance and free markets, offers a way to model and enact corporate agency without the need for actors to be aware of their role in realizing inferred joint goals.[3] Given the limited view of agency and choice offered by strategic rationality, this general acceptance of game theory as a tool for institutional design and public policy formation treats individuals as intentionless subjects and governance as a technocratic exercise of steering equilibrium outcomes through the introduction of appropriate incentives.[4] The conclusion counters contemporary complacency over game theory and atomic warfare, emphasizing that both strategic rationality and the US nuclear weapons program are more entrenched than ever.[5] As this paper shows, game theory's demotion of decision-making, whether individual or collective, to intentionless action makes it theoretically consistent for nations to prepare omnicidal measures to engage in nuclear combat in which they can only achieve their end by perpetually threatening, or actualizing, the complete destruction of humanity. The alternative is to invest in intentional decision-procedures that sustain individual rationality and interpersonal social commitments that insist on intelligibility as a criterion of purposive agency.

How Rationality Lost Its Mind

Nuclear deterrence, as a topic of analysis, is typically left to experts. During the early years of the Cold War, the ground for strategic expertise shifted from seasoned military commanders to blackboard consultants with mastery of abstract decision theory.[6] Although their decision-theoretic tools encompassed operations research, linear programming, and cost-benefit analysis, the most articulated coherent decision theory was game theory, formalized by John von Neumann and Oskar Morgenstern in their 1944 *Theory of Games and Economic Behavior*.[7] Game theory spans both strategic rationality, which refers to individualistically vying against others to achieve one's aims, and a theory of expected utility, which provides a technique to build exhaustive single-scale rankings of outcomes.[8] A rational actor must know how to consistently exhibit preferences over whether, for example, she prefers to travel to London, Singapore, or Cairo in all pairwise comparisons. Her choices must also be consistent over lottery tickets, such as making a rational choice between visiting Singapore for sure, or receiving a 20 percent chance of going to London and an 80 percent chance of traveling to Cairo. Game theory puts forward a comprehensive explanatory, normative, and prescriptive theory of rational choice that could be integrated into systems analysis and operations research, as well as a distinctive and well-codified body of mathematics.[9]

The embrace of game theory had a defining impact on Cold War strategy and social science writ large. First, without knowledge of rational decision theory, or rational deterrence theory, it has been difficult to contribute to or influence debates over nuclear strategy. By the 1970s, nuclear deterrence was synonymous with strategic rationality, which included the calculated use of probabilistic decision-making.[10] Second, the concept of action proposed by game theory, mandatory individualistic strategic competition, became the widely accepted standard for purposive action throughout American social science and the professional programs of law, public policy, and business by the 1980s.[11] There is no widely accepted alternative for formalizing instrumental rationality, and strategic rationality is notorious for not leaving room for other approaches, such as the deliberative approach of Jürgen Habermas or various forms of collective intention.[12] The reconceptualization of theories of markets and governance according to game theory undermined essential pieces of once-conventional wisdom, such as the rationality of voting and voluntary collective action.[13] Third, rational deterrence theory, which is at best amoral, and potentially even immoral, provided the means to "think the unthinkable," to use the phrase of Herman Kahn.[14] This meant matter-of-factly and routinely contemplating the exercise of nuclear threats in the form of flexible-response, lower-yield, first-strike weapons or second-strike counterforce without regard for the intrinsic value of human life.[15] Thus, fourth, the sense of urgency which rationalizes nuclear deterrence and the command-and-control structure it necessitates supported a theory of agency and intelligence that in principle leaves no distinction between human beings and artificial intelligences.[16] Philip Mirowski makes this point repeatedly: "Because the computer so readily trespasses upon the self-image of man as the thinking animal, it has become equally commonplace to believe that the mind is nothing more than a machine; that is, it operates like a computer."[17]

Although the first three points have been addressed to varying degrees in the literature, the last point, and its particular poignancy with respect to nuclear deterrence, remains unexplored. The oblivious character of rational choice permeates the nuclear security state at all levels of function, from justifying nuclear doctrine and theories of collective choice to normalizing a specific form of rational action and rendering politics the unintended outcome of individuals' preference satisfaction. Hence, blind steering predicated on formulaic maximization of expected utility rationalizes nuclear strategy despite its unintelligibility to the population it allegedly, although not actually, secures from harm.

Game theorists pursue "the quest for algorithmic rationality ... the complete and consistent calculation of the strategies of the opponent."[18] A benefit of this seamless transition from human to machine actors is that the maintenance of command and control could be decentralized, and in principle could be distilled to "a complete set of instructions that tells every individual what to do in every conceivable circumstance" that could be executed even without a consciously present human decision-maker.[19] Thus, in erasing the line demarcating a consciously present decider with Kantian autonomy, and in postulating that insofar as people think, strategize, and calculate, so can computers, it then became possible to build a complex, diversified, and extended command-and-control network that would carry the burden of prosecuting modern warfare.[20] The newly minted strategic actor obeys a structure of agency limited by the consistency conditions characterizing rational choice theory.[21] Rationality becomes algorithmic. Computer simulations of action and causal implications replaced experimentation, and military command-and-control needs led to the "diffusion of the computer throughout all levels of military command structure."[22]

Despite the plethora of research on the entanglement of game theory with Cold War nuclear strategy, mainstream economics and social science more broadly continue to rely on rational choice theory without examining this rich intellectual and contextual heritage.[23] This oversight neglects the potential synergy between game theory and conflict, thus proliferating a model for action that is best suited to antagonistic encounters. However, the development of and fascination with strategic rationality is inseparable from the continued US embrace of nuclear weapons at the apex of its military and strategy of full-spectrum dominance.[24] Strategic rationality loses the quality of *mind*, or the characteristic of intelligible grasp of the problem it is harnessed to solve. The very credibility of nuclear deterrence depends on demonstrating the intention and capability to fight and win a nuclear war among superpowers, even though such victory is impossible due to the cataclysmic destructive power of these weapons. Indeed, the United States and Russian Federation have thousands of thermonuclear bombs when a war fought with even only one hundred could, or even much less is likely to, end known civilization. This provocative stance furthermore entails privileging preparing for, and hence rendering more plausible, nuclear war rather than countering the risks of accidental or intentional nuclear war and pursing means to rescind the use of thermonuclear bombs.[25] Game theory, in other words, helps to normalize a nuclear security state in which a "nuclear eternity" is preferable to actively negating the historically demonstrated tendency to, sooner or later, employ deadly technologies on hand.[26] Hence rational choice rationalizes that we all live under, and strategists contribute to, a regime that permanently equates security to living with the doomsday clock at under three minutes to midnight. Thousands of nuclear weapons remain on an unceasing alert status that will only be abrogated by either the launching of these weapons or a comprehensive rethinking of the logic underlying this exercise of national power.[27]

By discounting the role of anxiety-ridden nuclear nightmares as a primary background to, and motive underlying, strategic rationality, we fail to come to terms with how profoundly the practice of nuclear deterrence, informed by and justifying game theory, continues to shape the cognitive landscape of human geopolitical and economic systems.[28] Thus with every passing year, we further embrace a concept of intelligence that accepts mindless computation and automates social interactions alongside the pedestrian normalization of nuclear weapons with unfathomable destructive potential.[29] Accommodating nuclear weapons relies on algorithmic decision technologies for rationalizing deterrence, and on hybrid AI-human agency to maintain national sovereignty through command-and-control systems prior to and during nuclear war wherein casualties likely will interrupt human command chains and communication channels.[30] Both computable rationality and hybrid AI-human decision-making systems deviate from privileging a sovereign human subject, instead turning to algorithmic rule-following punctuated by randomized number generation to ground strategy and carry out commands. So important did defense analysts estimate the significance of command-and-control that it received an additional 90 billion US dollars over and above the 100 billion that were concurrently spent on military hardware throughout the Cold War years.[31]

Erickson et al.'s volume documents the far-reaching transformation during the Cold War of what had formerly been human reason, which connoted a role for consciousness and possibly even a soul in animating decision-making. The authors observe:

> In the two decades following World War II, human reason was reconceptualized as rationality. Philosophers, mathematicians, economists, political scientists, military strategists, computer scientists, and psychologists sought, defined, and debated new norms for "rational actors," a deliberately capacious category that included business firms, chess players, the mafia, computers, parents and children, and nuclear superpowers.[32]

Rationality, in other words, became synonymous with what had formerly been deemed the lowest level of cognition: routine calculation. Whereas during the Enlightenment and up until the Cold War, reason had referred to evaluative judgments and the formation of ideas, with the innovation of game theory, rationality merely came to connote calculation subject to rules.[33] These rules, also referred to as algorithms, could be followed by low-level human workers or even machines. Initially, it seemed to 1940s contemporaries that even permitting calculation to be conducted by low-paid laborers denigrated "calculation from a mindful to a mindless exercise."[34] However, with the embrace of game theory, following a rule, with definitive and predictable machine-like exactness, came to be the hallmark of rationality. There is no need for a subject with intelligible grasp of the significance of the instructions or their legitimacy. Moreover, the instructions are self-executing in the sense that they ideally specify a singular (or randomized) outcome independent of the faculties of the computor.[35] Unaccounted for and rendered obsolete is the sense of cognizance that could invent rules, understand them, and apply them to diverse and yet unknown circumstances. This ingenuity typified, for example, Immanuel Kant's attempt to establish rules to differentiate between art and technique, or Isaac Newton's discovery of the rules of motion that then could serve as models for understanding mass, momentum, and energy.[36] Thus, rule-following becomes the mindless and exacting execution of a set of instructions, with the rule itself reduced to to a mechanically executable algorithm.[37]

Rationality loses mindfulness, or a conscious subject with intelligible and existential grasp of the problems it solves.[38] This foreclosure on the merits of understanding represents one side of an enduring philosophical divide over whether mind and intelligibility play any causal role in actualizing behavior. Whereas some theorists argue that humans exhibit freedom of will in making deliberate choices, game theorists put forward a theory of rationality that is wholly determined by a set of instructions, or an algorithm, that is enacted as causal process.[39] This renders intelligence, or purposive agency, in principle subject to automated computation in carbon- or silicon-based systems. This has the added benefit, as game theory textbook authors Duncan Luce and Howard Raiffa observe, of making rational decision-making achievable by human or artificial intelligence.[40]

The definitive aspect of such algorithmic rule-following is its exacting production, over and again, of precisely the same outcome for identical sets of input data. This is the opposite of Ludwig Wittgenstein's approach to rule-following, according to which rules do not by themselves specify the outcome of their application.[41] John Searle, who explicitly acknowledges his philosophical affinity to Wittgenstein, challenges both the classical model of rationality encompassing game theory and the view that AI performs intelligence on par with human agents.[42] In differentiating between human and machine intelligence, he sides with Wittgenstein in pointing out the importance of mindful judgment, based on understanding of intelligibility and recognition of veracity. In contrast, promoters of rational choice and game theory view rationality as one concept, whether exhibited by a human, a nonhuman organism, or a machine. Insofar as game theory represents the orthodox statement of instrumental rationality, Alan Turing's conceptualization of intelligence has prevailed.[43] According to the Church-Turing thesis, there are four criteria of programmable rationality.[44] First, it can be stipulated by a finite set of precise instructions stated in a finite set of symbols. Second, if executed without error, it always produces the same result in a limited number of steps. Third, it can be completed by a human without machine assistance. Fourth, and most significantly, no intelligible grasp or understanding of the instructions is necessary for the one who calculates.[45] Procedures meeting these criteria are deemed to be logically and mechanically computable.[46]

Cold War rationality was integrally connected to military problem solving. George Dantzig's linear programming, which was mathematically equivalent to von Neumann and Morgenstern's two-person, zero-sum game theory, was developed to solve military logistics problems such as the Berlin Airlift operation.[47] Von Neumann and Morgenstern's game theory was used to provide solutions for military duels and other strategic problems, including nuclear brinkmanship and escalation in the Vietnam War.[48] Herbert Simon's bounded rationality was applied to resource allocation problems.[49] According to Erickson et al., "[Herman] Kahn [author of *On Thermonuclear War*] believed that everything about nuclear war could be understood using the core principles of rational-choice theory."[50] Not only did Thomas

Schelling rely on the Prisoner's Dilemma game to develop his theoretical defense of mutual assured destruction, but other Cold War intellectuals working at the Arms Control and Disarmament Agency also used the Prisoner's Dilemma to model Nixon's dilemma of whether or not to escalate in Vietnam, and to structure bargaining during conflict and over weapons in arms control.[51]

Herman Kahn, whose NUTS position on nuclear deterrence prevailed by 1980 and still governs US policy, believed that "axiomatic, formalized rationality was the only way to prepare for the vicissitudes of conflict."[52] Even though RAND's staff grew disenchanted with game theory for its failure to generate a science of warfare by the 1960s, the Pentagon still established the Studies Analysis and Gaming Agency dedicated to gaming simulations to analyze how conflicts may be prosecuted.[53] In 1977, RAND analyst Jack Snyder wrote a report identifying the American national security state as a quintessential rational actor.[54] Nuclear strategists modeled deterrence itself using game theory, and the body of thought comprising it was and remains strategic rationality.[55] Game theory thus provided decision makers with a means of making onerous policy decisions without emotion, context, and even moral judgment or ethical principle and understanding.[56] Without the military decision-making context to sponsor the initial development of game theory to solve logistical and strategic problems, it is unlikely that rational choice theory would have eventually won over economists who, although skeptical at first, were by the 1980s among its greatest proponents, contributing to its preeminence in the American social sciences by the 1980s.[57] Possibly their enthusiasm followed from their propensity to believe that market coordination arises without actors' intentional effort to achieve mutual prosperity or equilibrium, as though by an invisible hand.

Von Neumann and Morgenstern formalized game theory to be an all-encompassing science of choice, applicable to every decision in all conceivable circumstances throughout the lifetime of rational agents.[58] Every consideration of worth, insofar as it impinges on choice, can be, the authors insist, encapsulated into this formalism. Strategic rationality is perfect to capture "calmly aggressive selfishness."[59] Game theory, as a decision technology, only recognizes that consequences matter and demands that only individualistic competition is rational.[60] Therefore, only outcomes, and not principled or ethical means, matter to decision-makers.[61] Even if individuals can form coalitions to compete against other actors, once spoils are obtained, every group must disintegrate into individuals who compete among each other. Although game theory promises to deliver a "crystalline definiteness, generality, and conclusiveness" with which to define rational action, it can only guarantee single solutions in contexts of zero-sum competition.[62] In a non-zero-sum game with multiple possible equilibria, rational actors would no longer have a clear template for action that results in predictable outcomes. To address this obvious limitation, game theorists consider repeating interactions in which a history of engagement may enable actors to reach a Nash equilibrium: a single point outcome from which no single actor has any incentive to diverge given the choices that all other actors made.

Wittingly or not, by reducing agency to mindless action, game theorists end up endorsing these characteristic limitations. Rules and norms are not deemed to guide action, but rather to merely describe behavioral regularities.[63] We need to ask *how* our dominant form of social science and public policy analysis has so roundly accepted that purposive agency can dispense with the meaning of action as a primary motivator.[64] The fact that we use this theory of rationality to inform our nuclear security posture and to solve the challenge of credible deterrence is inseparable from social scientists' and policy analysts' embrace of its potential to explain all human action, individual and collective. It is no coincidence that the theory of rationality governing the US nuclear arsenal under the nuclear war fighting protocol is also the template for rational action used to inform individual and collective action, as well as theories of sovereign decision-making. As a unified theory of action, strategic rationality accounts for the most prosaic choices and the most consequential: to engage in nuclear combat.

MAD, NUTS, and Game Theory

Whereas strategic rationality elides the need for an agent who deliberately makes decisions, nuclear war raises numerous existential quandaries. In particular, the now ever-present potential for nuclear war rewrites the social contract between citizens and government. Daniel Deudney argues that after World War II, the modern social contract predicated on the state's ability to take its citizens out of harm's way was only able to maintain the *appearance* of legitimacy given the impossibility of realizing this promise.[65] The state achieves such an appearance by downplaying the role of nuclear weapons in projecting state power and giving citizens the false impression that its nuclear program is oriented toward an anti-nuclear goal.[66] Whereas most sectors of even US civil society are under the impression that nuclear policy has been and is structured to the end of deterring nuclear war consistent with a policy of mutual assured destruction (MAD), its actual policy stance is, in fact, NUTS. Deudney notices that which has otherwise gone unrecognized: "the doctrine of mutual assured destruction gradually became supplemental and then supplanted by nuclear utilization targeting theory and strategies—known among nuclear strategists as ... NUTS."[67] The reality of NUTS—i.e., the US preparedness to engage in all levels of nuclear combat regardless of the risks of error, accident, cyber hacking, proliferation, and escalation—is not made manifestly clear to the public because this would erode the remaining legitimacy from the social contract.[68] Not only does government hold citizens hostage as the potential casualties of the failure of nuclear brinkmanship, but the momentum of the state's nuclear program also proliferates the risk of nuclear engagement far beyond the outcome that would result from jointly and progressively reducing nuclear capabilities and attenuating their alert status.

There are four bodies of literature that provide evidence that nuclear deterrence and game theory are coextensive with each other: that rational deterrence theory is the same as rational decision theory. One is the historical record of practice and engagement.[69] The second is the internal perspective of international relations theory that makes clear on the one hand that the abstract formal theory of rational deterrence is game theory and on the other that the war gaming simulations used to make arguments for different strategies were game-based models and simulations that were indistinguishable from how actual scenarios would be handled.[70] Third is the literature of strategic practice that provides retrospective vision, making clear the extent to which the problem of deterrence was viewed in terms of strategic rationality.[71] Fourth, and finally, strategic rationality developed in conjunction with theoretically exploring problems of nuclear deterrence, most importantly the credibility problem.[72]

Schelling's *Strategy of Conflict* is important to all four bodies of literature. Those who follow his lead modeled the nuclear security dilemma and arms race using the recalcitrant Prisoner's Dilemma game.[73] Within the context of strategic arms control, as addressed by the US Arms Control and Disarmament Agency, "the prisoner's dilemma *did* become a key theoretical framework for thinking about 'the problem of the bomb,' and the game matrix could leap from the mathematics of optimization to psychological laboratories to problems of war and peace writ large."[74] The significance of this is twofold. On the one hand, the Prisoner's Dilemma game, which was originally developed by Merrill Flood and Melvin Drescher at RAND to reflect two prisoners who are each given the choice by a jailor to confess or remain silent, seemed apt to capture the problem of the "Reciprocal Fear of Surprise Attack," and an arms race.[75] However, on the other hand, the fact that hard-nosed strategic rationality led to an unambiguously suboptimal result in this game signified a deep puzzle at the core of game theory.[76] Given their inability to intentionally collaborate, rational actors achieve suboptimal, and therefore inscrutable, results.

In the Prisoner's Dilemma, a district attorney gives two inmates suspected of having committed a crime each two choices: to remain silent, or to confess. Four possible outcomes obtain, depending on the inmates' individual choices of what to do. If both remain silent, they both serve a short sentence. If both confess, they both serve a long sentence. If one confesses and the other remains silent, then the confessor goes free while the one who remains silent serves a lifetime sentence. In orthodox game theory, the moral of the Prisoner's Dilemma is that each individual is better off defecting, regardless of what the other decides to do. Thus both actors achieve a worse outcome (a long jail sentence) than if they had been able to cooperate (shorter sentences). If the other remains silent, then it is better to confess, thereby achieving freedom. If the other confesses, then it is still better to confess to save oneself from the worst outcome of lifetime imprisonment (Table 6.1).

Applied to the Cold War, either in terms of the preemptive fear of surprise attack (Table 6.2) or a nuclear arms race (Table 6.3), each country is better off pursuing unilateral success, because this secures at best dominance and at worst mutual ruin rather than singular defeat. As the analysis goes, in an arms race, regardless of what the USSR does, the US is better off building arms without limit, because this will either grant it supremacy or prevent it from being dominated. In the Prisoner's Dilemma both actors seek unilateral advantage, securing the worst possible outcome for the other agent. These preferences are consistent with an aggressor or revisionist state.[77]

		Joe Silent	Joe Talk
Bob	Silent	1 year, 1 year	life in jail, freedom
	Talk	freedom, life in jail	10 years, 10 years

Table 6.1: Standard Prisoner's Dilemma

		USSR	
		Defend	Attack
US	Defend	security, security	surrender, victory
	Attack	victory, surrender	destruction, destruction

Table 6.2: Reciprocal Fear of Surprise Attack (see, e.g., Schelling, *Strategy of Conflict*)

		USSR	
		Disarm	Arm
US	Disarm	peace, peace	submission, dominance
	Arm	dominance, submission	precarity, precarity

Table 6.3: Nuclear Arms Race (see, e.g., Campbell and Sowden, *Paradoxes of Rationality and Cooperation*)

However, few seem to have asked whether an endless nuclear arms race, such as what the US has pursued even after the Cold War ended, makes sense, unless it is both possible to achieve military supremacy and meaningful to exercise it. Similarly, with respect to actually waging war, experts note that the US strategic policy meets the specifics of striving to realize being "a nuclear-armed state ... planning to have the capacity to fight and win a nuclear war by disarming enemies [including Russia with its seven thousand nuclear warheads] with a surprise first strike."[78]

Game theorists originally argued that one possible way out of the reciprocal fear of surprise attack is to ensure a second-strike counterattack that would neutralize the adversary's advantage with what would end up being mutual assured destruction.[79] The hope is that issuing a threat of counterattack, or the certainty of mutual assured destruction, will be sufficient to secure safety from nuclear attack. However, given the severity of the nuclear threat and the fact that all that would remain for the preemptively attacked power is to issue a counterattack amid the ashes of destruction, game theorists worried that issuing a credible threat of retaliation is as impossible as counting on the two prisoners to follow through on promises to remain silent. In each case, actors' actual interests diverge from their promises or threats, rendering both incredible: I promise to remain silent, but, according to game theory's model of the Prisoner's Dilemma, I really prefer to go free. I seek to deter nuclear attack and hold my arsenal in reserve to prevent the enemy's attack, yet once the attack has occurred, I no longer have a reason to counterattack, according the game theoretic modeling. Thus, the wrenching problem of nuclear deterrence—how to issue a credible threat of mutual destruction after deterrence has failed—was mapped into the conceptual space of the irresolvable Prisoner's Dilemma paradox and explored in the related problems of the Toxin puzzle.[80] The Prisoner's Dilemma modeling of nuclear deterrence renders a nuclear war-fighting posture necessary because the only way to shore up the credibility of deterrence is to perpetually threaten to wage nuclear war with the aim to win.[81]

In this thought experiment designed by Gregory Kavka, a being with acute predictive powers offers the protagonist one million dollars if she can form an intention today to drink a vial of toxin tomorrow that will cause no long-term harm but would make her feel terribly ill for one day. The supernatural being offers a large sum of money if she can promise, and follow through on that promise, to drink nonlethal poison, even if the money is already in her bank account prior to the act of drinking. No matter how many times theorists investigated this puzzle, they could not identify a means by which the rational person could form an intention at time t_1 to perform an action at time t_2 that would be costly at that time and simultaneously would serve no function in promoting the protagonist's goals. Why would the rational agent actually follow through on drinking the toxin *after* the million dollars is already in the bank? Kavka initially reached that conclusion, and David Gauthier similarly reached the same conclusion a few years later.[82] Both saw this thought experiment as equivalent to that of nuclear deterrence in the context of issuing an "apocalyptic threat."[83]

The toxin puzzle has a similar logical structure to the Prisoner's Dilemma as it relates to nuclear deterrence. Forming a credible threat to retaliate with a devastating second strike is an intention that at the time of acting would both be repugnant and serve no instrumental role in furthering the agent's goal. Thus, in terms of game theoretic analysis, no threat of mutual assured destruction is credible: What could motivate a counterstrike that would only wreak further damage after deterrence has already failed? Following this logic, analysts argued that the only way to ensure that deterrence is credible is to integrate it into a plan to prevail in nuclear war at all levels of engagement.[84] This is consistent with the position of escalation dominance in which the US seeks to have sufficient nuclear capability to win on any rung on the escalation ladder of potential conflict. The fact that game theory was designed to be computable and demands that its instructions for action in principle lack intelligibility to agents carrying them out is well-suited to legitimize nuclear strategy without any need for the actual comprehension of that strategy. This possibly underlies the reality that citizens, who may resist endorsing an unintelligible nuclear procurement and deployment posture, are largely left in the dark about US nuclear policy, naively believing that MAD prevails—i.e., that nuclear weapons are on hand to deter attack, and not to vie for dominance.[85]

It is not yet clear why the policy of flexible response, or being the first to deploy nuclear weapons *prior* to their introduction into arenas of conflict by hostile parties, need be invoked given the US's dominance in conventional forces.[86] According to NUTS strategic doctrine, however, in flagrant disregard for the "nuclear taboo," holding that nuclear weapons are categorically different from conventional arms and should remain off the table on a first-use basis, the US should build small tactical nuclear weapons to be launched in lesser conflicts, thus introducing nuclear weapons in an otherwise conventional war.[87] This strategic stance of flexible response, although consistent with Kahn's escalation dominance and preparedness to fight to win nuclear combat of any scale conceivable, outright contradicts the position of maintaining nuclear weapons only for the sake of deterring a nuclear strike. Proponents of flexible response perceive the need to thoroughly integrate nuclear arms into the US military's standard operating procedure.[88] Thus, the aim of making nuclear threats credible at the highest level of nuclear attack and counterattack merges with assuring other nations that much less provocation could be met with a nuclear strike, including efforts to achieve their own deterrent posture. Hence, against the idea that nuclear weapons are useless, apart from hopefully serving to avoid nuclear war, flexible response seeks to keep them as an option perpetually on the table either to directly strike terror into, or to signal the US's willingness to engage in nuclear war to, potential adversaries, with the overall aim of compelling them to acquiesce to US demands.[89]

Political maneuvering to appease domestic political supporters by projecting strength, and business interests associated with the nuclear weapons industry, may both contribute to the US's reliance on nuclear weapons in its security protocol. However, rational deterrence theory is at least equally complicit. There are, of course, exceptions: Thomas Schelling, Robert Jervis, and Steven Brams deserve recognition as experts who were fluent in game theory but supported a deterrent position consistent with respecting the nuclear taboo and hoping to gradually reduce nuclear arsenals in staged rounds of reciprocal arms reduction under conditions of mutual surveillance. However, from the perspective of pure strategic rationality, the position of using nuclear threats only to counter nuclear aggression and the aim of reducing arms to a reciprocated minimum deterrent stance have not been successfully sustained within rational choice theory.[90]

The position which has prevailed is unmistakably NUTS. Deudney captures the essence of this view, which he calls nuclear strategism, in his 2007 book *Bounding Power*:

> This view takes states as given, conflict as endemic, and holds that the quintessential state activity of preparing for and making war defines world politics regardless of the type of weaponry prevalent. Nuclear strategism postulates that states seeking security in a nuclear world will—and should—prepare themselves to exercise a full range of nuclear use options and seek to gain political advantage from relatively small differences in nuclear force levels.[91]

He sketches out four possible deterrence positions: disarmament, automatic deterrence, institutional deterrence, and the assertive stance of escalation dominance, which he calls nuclear strategism. According to strategic rationality, which is presented as a comprehensive and all-inclusive theory of rational choice, the lack of credibility of following through on a deterrent threat requires demonstrating the capability and intention to wage nuclear war. Additional features of nuclear strategism, also known as NUTS, include manipulating opponents' perception of the risk of nuclear war for various actions, and limited nuclear options, both of which violate a no first use pledge. Originally, forgoing the assurance of renouncing first use served to deter a Soviet land invasion into Europe. However, now that US conventional arms are deemed sufficient to the task, the US still reserves the prerogative of first use because doing otherwise would maintain the categorical separation of nuclear weapons from conventional weapons.[92] This would result in the same problem: without constant announcement of the preparedness and capability to resort to nuclear warfare, deterrence—or, similarly, the power to compel others to comply with the state's demands—would lack credibility. Similarly, with the goals of achieving escalation dominance in any conflict or engaging in coercive bargaining to negotiate settlements, the state relies on its ability to threaten harm. Actors are motivated to avoid harm because it is directly contrary to their interests. The overall strategy of developing and maintaining the physical and institutional infrastructure to perpetuate nuclear threats itself need not be and is not intelligible because it interminably risks the existence of all human life. However, demanding intelligibility requires exiting the framework of strategic rationality and heeding that meaning, understanding, and recognition can provide reasons and causes for action.

From a Unified Social Ontology to a Unified World Order

Although game theory's roots of application lie in the nuclear dilemma, in the subsequent decades, theorists have used strategic rationality to explain all levels of agency, from the biological and human to the corporate and sovereign. Theorists posit that *all* coherent purposive agency must obey the dictates of rational choice. The nation state, originally analyzed by Thomas Hobbes as an artificial person or Leviathan, is now formally modeled as the outcome of rational self-interest expressed in markets and politics.[93] In particular, the contemporary American state becomes a nuclearized Leviathan whose greatest purview of decision-making, that exerting the most singular impact on life planetwide, is how and when to project power using nuclear arms. Power, in such a situation, can be understood as the ability to influence others' actions by issuing devastating and credible threats of harm. The rational choice approach to politics, collective action, and warfare is realist in the sense that it shuns moralizing justification of action, rather deferring to the unbridled strategic pursuit of ends.[94] This realism permeates the analytic decision technology of strategic rationality itself because it promotes an understanding and practice of communication that denies intention, meaning, and intelligibility. Instead, communication becomes a science of signaling asymmetric information of what world states obtain, and calculating whether costly signals or cheap talk, true or false, best achieves actors' goals.[95]

In their conclusion to *How Reason Almost Lost Its Mind*, Erickson et al. propose that worries about nuclear security have receded hand-in-hand with the abandonment of mindless rationality.[96] However, just as the nuclear security dilemma remains as pressing as during any time of the Cold War, rationality has never been as mindless as in the first two decades of the twenty-first century.[97] Now strategic rationality not only provides a tool for decision-making in national security and logistical planning, as well as a paradigm for rational action, but also serves as a means to provide a unifying logic of action that spans across all levels and types of agency. Thus, rational decision theory is applied to evolving organisms, cognition, language, individual agency, collective agency, hybrid systems of human and robotic actors, formal and informal institutions, and arriving at sovereign decisions. The theorist Fancesco Guala refers to this broad application of rational choice as a "unified social ontology."[98] Economist Herbert Gintis claims that game theory unifies the behavioral sciences, which encompass both animal and human behavior.[99] Rather than being a relic of the past, robotic rationality has become so normal that those promoting alternative forms of reason—Wittgensteinian rule-following, commitment to principles as opposed to only being incentivized by outcomes, solidarity and team reasoning, shared intention, and virtue-inspired action, for example—must persistently advocate to maintain these heterodox actions' academic relevance. The greatest prospective casualties are mind, intention, and intelligibility.

The paradigm of computational rationality comfortably sustains the position that mind is an illusion that will gradually fall away.[100] Some urge us to grasp that we are in the midst of a fourth revolution. Just as humans' beliefs that the earth is in the center of the universe, and that humans are of a different order of creation than animals, have given way, so too will our view that we are categorically distinct from artificial intelligence.[101] However, as soon as we settled on using strategic rationality as a template for human intelligence, we *already* conceded that the conscious presence of a decision-maker with comprehension of the meaning of actions is irrelevant to rational choice.[102] Furthermore, insofar as this model of rationality presents a normative standard, it accepts the premise that subjects need have no comprehension of how following the rules they are incentivized to follow serves the purpose of coordinating their actions for mutual benefit.[103] Rules, alternatively called equilibria by game theorists, are no longer motivating reasons for action. Instead, they reflect regularities of action caused by individuals' automatic preference satisfaction.

The titles of two recent papers convey the trend toward viewing the brain as an organ functioning on par with a computer: "Computational Rationality: Linking Mechanism and Behavior through Bounded Utility Maximization" and "Computational Rationality: A Converging Paradigm for Intelligence in Brains, Minds, and Machines."[104] This branch of research, referred to as computational rationality, uses expected utility theory as the basis for how organisms, including people, register external states of the world in brain states.[105] Life forms are further postulated to have probability estimates of the likelihood of various action-dependent outcomes and act as "information-processing mechanisms by selecting an optimal program for a bounded machine that maximizes utility in some environment."[106] According to a broad review of this new field published in *Science*, "the fields of artificial intelligence (AI), cognitive science, and neuroscience are reconverging on a shared view of the computational foundations of intelligence."[107] Along the same lines, economist Herbert Gintis argues that game theory can explain action all the way down to the way that cognition functions. He observes that "expected utility maximization is not simply an 'as if' story" because "neuroscientists increasingly find that an aggregate decision making process in the brain synthesizes all available information into a single unitary value."[108] These scientific results, and interpretations of them, remain tentative, but at the same time reflect how the Cold War view of rationality maintains its currency and continues to blur artificial and human intelligence, relegating subjective understanding of the meaning of acts and events to insignificance.[109]

Game theory has become ubiquitous as an explanatory tool. Game theoretic modeling has been applied extensively in evolutionary biology, and lessons learned from these models have been used to draw conclusions about the possibility of and basis for human cooperation.[110] Game theoretic accounts of individual human and collective action are integrated into public policy.[111] Rational choice theory informs the applied schools of law and economics, public choice, and institutional design.[112] Game theory has also been extensively applied in international relations theory spanning nuclear deterrence and hegemonic stability theory, to analyzing treaties as cheap talk insofar as they are not enforceable.[113]

As a method, game theory simply offers a means to model, and possibly predict, political and economic phenomena. However, from the time of its founding, game theory also stood as a normative theory of rational choice with prescriptive implications for individual and collective decision-making.[114] Thus, if, as its advocates propose, game theory is both a normatively valid theory of instrumental action and a descriptively informative account of agency, then it is not surprising that game theorists find it possible to conceive of all levels of agency, from the nonhuman biological to individual and collective action to superordinate action of organized groups including companies and states, and hybrid human-AI systems, as each embodying the same tenets of rational action.[115] However, the question is to what extent descriptive modeling of agency and normative theories of agency could influence the performative dimension of action. This question can be addressed in depth by focusing on various levels of agency: (1) individual action; (2) large-scale collective action; (3) human agency within institutions designed using (a) analytic rational choice and (b) behavioral experiments that rely on orthodox game theory to provide a template for perfectly rational conduct; and (4) sovereign bodies which are structured to conform to the theoretical results learned from rational choice modeling.

Game theorists address all these expressions of agency with their singular model for action.[116] Modeling individual competition, collective action, and institutions as games is staple in rational choice. More interesting for purposes here is the application of rational choice theory to the sovereign function of governance, particularly by way of the Prisoner's Dilemma.[117] Revisiting the conceptualization of the state as Leviathan, contemporary political theorists have used game theory to provide an analysis of the state of nature and the maintenance of social order offered by Hobbes.[118] According to this new assessment, strategic rationality governs all purposive conduct and must account for the exercise of collective sovereignty from the micromotives of individual choice.[119] Game theorists view Hobbes as a realist, finding common ground with him in their approach, which associates motivation with rational self-interest void of any types of deontological commitment or political obligation. However, Jeremy Bentham is a more fitting forbearer than Hobbes since the former viewed talk of rights and obligations as nonsense, and the latter had a complex approach to natural law, agents' duty to abide by agreements made, and forging the Artificial Man or commonwealth.[120]

A more in-depth inquiry is necessary to discern the nuances between Hobbes's theory of sovereignty and that offered by game theory.[121] Here, it is sufficient to point out that Hobbes's theory bases the sovereign's authoritative rule on individuals' covenants with one another to lay down their rights to all things. Whereas Hobbes identifies gain, safety, and reputation as individuals' primary, and unlikely rational, motivating forces, game theorists impute to individuals the all-encompassing aim of maximizing expected utility.[122] Where Hobbes's *Leviathan* depends on both subjects' sense of allegiance in exchange for the sovereign's promise of security, and the sword to threaten rule-breakers, game theorists assess individuals' calculated gain against the cost of rule-breaking to identify the impetus underlying stable governance. For Hobbes, achieving the threshold of security will secure the stability of a sovereign. For rational choice theorists, subjects may vigilantly engage in cost-benefit analysis to determine whether to obey or break laws on a case-by-case basis.[123]

Leaving aside individuals' motives and choices to comply with or challenge the rule of law, rational choice also offers the means to both analyze and rationalize government policies. This is because strategic rationality is useful for both assessing what outcomes will obtain from individual choices, and for formalizing the conditions that must be met for collective political will formation to be legitimate in reflecting individuals' interests. As is by now common lore, Kenneth J. Arrow's generation of his impossibility theorem, proving the irrationality of all collective decision-procedures for more than two individuals selecting among three or more alternatives, was at least in part inspired by his early Cold War assignment of formulating an expected utility function conveying Soviet citizens' preferences over nuclear war.[124] The rich body of social choice theory that followed Arrow's 1951 proof remains central to the design of voting procedures, and has been incorporated into search engines such as Google that rely on ranking systems to reflect multiple-criteria decision problems.[125] Constitutional design has also been methodically studied using game theory to ascertain which fundamental principles will structure a society that upholds attractive conditions, such as citizens' sovereignty, efficient use of resources, and egalitarian commitments.[126] Thus, with respect to institutional design of governing bodies, rational choice theory has played a significant role in providing a means to analyze how to achieve desired outcomes, assuming that strategic rationality best reflects purposive agency.

The particular view of collective agency offered by game theory was perfectly attuned to the early Cold War hostility toward organic collective action and collectivism.[127] Recent literature has drawn attention to the distrust of intentionally organized collective agency, now referred to as conspiracy. Alfred Moore, for example, argues that Friedrich Hayek opposed social theories which accept the possibility of either collective rationality or intentional collective action.[128] Orthodox game theory, which demands thoroughly individualistic interaction and unintended consequences, was thus a fitting social scientific methodology for followers of Hayek and those who sought to help maintain an individualistic market order.

Rational choice offers a comprehensive theory for legitimation. Once we accept orthodox game theory as the best statement of the conditions that individual and collective rational agency must obey, if individuals' preferences are complete and consistent, then the only question about strategic interactions is what equilibrium will obtain.[129] In other words, it comes down to whether an equilibrium outcome is Pareto optimal—i.e., a state of affairs in which no single individual can be made better off without making anyone worse off. Individuals can be compelled to accept less through processes of coercive bargaining in which preemptive threats can incentivize actors to make concessions. Rational choice models generally accept that scarce tangible physical resources, as in natural social dilemmas, are interpersonally salient sources of value that individuals alike seek to amass or consume in competition with others.[130] Orthodox game theory thus resonates with realism by anchoring the source of value underlying individuals' preferences in concrete goods, and accepting as necessary de facto outcomes.

Game theory likewise offers a realist approach to politics. Insofar as it claims to be an all-encompassing theory of rational choice, it invalidates types of agency and collective intentionality that are inconsistent with its assumptions, such as reflexive governance based on voluntary rule-following to realize joint goals informed by shared meanings.[131] Nuclear security policy is ratified by game theory three times over. First, game theory offers no means to theorize about legitimate collective agency other than to provide accounts of how collective will formation reflects individuals' choices. Nuclear security policy is no different. Achieving a US strategic policy different from NUTS would require a different institutional arrangement, one which must privilege intelligibility, commitment, and reflexive governance over computable rationality and rational choice. Second, given that nuclear war has been modeled as a strategic game, this exercise offers clear guidance for action: specifically, it privileges NUTS over MAD as the surest means to achieve credible deterrence. This guidance follows as a computable solution to a "game" that requires no intelligible grasp of its validity, implications, or assumptions. Third, the entire command-and-control structure, which integrates human decision-makers into a hybrid world of telecommunications, computation, and military hardware, invites agents to operate on a level commensurate with computable rationality. Even with a keen sense of oversight, anthropomorphic qualities are easily lost in humans' contribution to a platform of action in which sustainability is defined as the propagation of a war plan and control over military operations.

The realism underlying the sheer destructive power of existing nuclear arms is inseparable from the realism inherent in the game theoretic assessment of value, typically as fungible, interpersonally transferable utility, and its estimation of power with respect to actors' ability to either directly achieve ends, or achieve ends by manipulating others' choices with incentives.[132] Nuclear security expert Daniel Deudney argues that the US nuclear security state cannot meet its basic legitimation demand, and thus it shies away from openly proclaiming its readiness to engage in nuclear war attendant with its bid for global nuclear supremacy.[133] This may seem to be a distinct consideration from examining how rational choice is used to assess legitimacy; however, it is tightly aligned because the US security state purchases its license to act recklessly abroad and to violate civil liberties at home by threatening "the core of the core, the limited government constitution of the United States itself."[134]

Realism can be constructive in demystifying power relations. However, in the case of rational choice, strategic rationality is restrictive because it denies the coherence of alternative means of acting, such as commitment, intrinsic interests, and joint instrumental agency.[135] This, in effect, ends up rationalizing the de facto exercise of power without due process that must be upheld by commitment to constitutional principles.[136] The exigencies of nuclear deterrence and the nuclearized Leviathan who must channel authority to exercise a planetary death warrant and interface with AI systems rendering intelligibility superfluous, facilitate an expression of agency that must, by design, be complicit with this exercise of authority. The ground for legitimation for this NUTS strategy inherently forfeits guaranteeing humans security from nuclear annihilation. This renders denial and unintelligibility the core ingredients of maintaining the sprawling, resource-engulfing, and perpetually endangering nuclear security complex.

The triumvirate of nuclear arms, strategic rationality, and hybrid command-and-control systems threatens constitutional order.[137] One reason that the realism underlying game theory is insufficient to unmask this unsettling fact is that it coopts our theory of linguistic communication, eviscerating it of intelligibility and meaning. Instead, communication is solely based on a strategic platform of signaling, with calculated decisions over whether to be truthful or deceptive. Language itself, when serving the programmed needs of AI and information technologies, becomes purely syntactic with a minimal semantic bridge that associates a physically detectable world state, such as temperature, with a symbol, in this case a numeric temperature scale. This theory of language is consistent with computational rationality and its application to brains, as well as to integrated information processing theory.[138] Runciman recognizes the role played by Cold War military initiatives in generating the "true roots of the digital revolution."[139] Also, much to the point, he quotes political theorist John Gray who notes, "cyberspace is a site of unceasing warfare." Gray likewise muses that "while they are being used as weapons, electronic technologies may also be creating a terrain on which intelligent life forms could evolve independent of human control."[140] As game theory is developed to accommodate agent-based modeling in contexts of conflict and economic transactions, the transmission of information as the primary means of communication increases in salience. Warfare is described in terms of "the achievement of Information Superiority with characteristics of gross asymmetries and a diversity of 'players.'"[141] Strategic rationality and information theory merge to be pivotal in the projection of power in twenty-first century warfare.

We must wake up to a potential threat that the rational choice revolution, wedded at the hip to the nuclear security state, poses in its theory of rationality that is individualistic, anchors utility in scarce, competitive resources, and, most importantly, denies intelligibility a role in judgment. A constitutional order that rests on game theory, which necessarily neglects the fact that "intrinsic interests" and commitments may animate actors, must by its analytic structure posit "rationalist, interest-based mechanisms of political behavior."[142] The realism of game theory, which presupposes a common world by imputing that environments afford value independent from and prior to sociability, ignores that human communication is predicated on intention and intelligibility, and that a joint social order regulated by a legitimate rule of law "is both a *mechanism* of political commitment and *itself* a political commitment."[143]

This treatment of communication as thoroughly strategic, which represents a recent trend in research into treating communication as signaling and cheap talk without implications for outcomes, views human actors as on par with computing devices that send signals and calculate whether received signals are credible or not.[144] Jürgen Habermas worried that nondialogic market transactions threaten the life-world of human inhabitants, but even his analysis is insufficient to grasp the full implications of accepting a theory of agency and communication that is wholly strategic.[145] Envisioning a vibrant potential for cultural reproduction through authentic dialogue can open our eyes to the significance of viewing rationality as mindless and computable, and simultaneously treating communication as reducible to strategic signaling that facilitates strategic action. Thus, we can be sensitive to forms of AI that "automate the social," drawing humans into complexes of interaction and communication as though they are governed by either computable rationality or predictable habituated behavioral patterns.[146] We can also recognize, against the reductionist realism of orthodox game theory, that an intelligible grasp of decision-making, which depends on recognition of validity conditions underlying truth claims and the acknowledgment of other like actors, could be positioned to challenge the cogency of a permanent nuclear Leviathan and rule of law reduced to compelling compliance with incentives.[147] Resonating with Habermas's critical stance, even the legal positivist H. L. A. Hart held that "legal validity ultimately rests on a social practice among officials (if not citizens more broadly) of recognizing and accepting certain rules or practices as obligatory."[148]

A unified ontology consistent with orthodox game theory legitimates a nuclear security stance that holds all of humanity hostage.[149] This theory of action indiscriminately applies to animal action, human action, collective action, governance, and hybrid action systems with human and artificial agents. Throughout, intelligibility, intention, and commitment are jettisoned in favor of a simplistic protocol for action: maximizing expected utility. Its convenience for modeling and managing social institutions, in addition to its eschewal of collective intentionality, make it attractive to policy analysts and useful for structuring environments that can force people to reduce their own expressions of selfhood to conform to the prerogatives of AI.[150] As yet, it remains unknown what possibilities lie in a collective rationality that embraces intelligibility, commitment, and shared intention. However, it is clear that strategic rational action makes it possible to mindlessly contribute to systems that neither place an intrinsic value on life, nor have any concern for whether human civilization is obliterated in a miscarriage of every individual's natural right "to use his own power, as he will himselfe, for the preservation of his own ... Life; and consequently of doing any thing, which in his own Judgement, and Reason, hee shall conceive to be the aptest means thereunto."[151]

Conclusion

The unified social ontology of game theory, its normative clout as the dominant standard of rational choice, and its long-established role in policy-making underlie the contemporary world order in which the United States pursues escalation dominance, negates a no-first-use pledge, and develops flexible nuclear alternatives in the form of limited nuclear options.[152] This is not to say that critiques of this unified social ontology and unified world order do not exist. Nye's *Nuclear Ethics* and Deudney's *Bounding Power* present views of agency and collective security that are not limited to strategic rationality. Nye contrasts strategic rationality with moral judgment. Deudney emphasizes the universal pursuit of "security from predatory violence and for political liberty."[153] Finding "human corporeal vulnerability and the fundamental value of life as prerequisite for all other ends" as a basis for common ground, he calls for a federated international solution to the nuclear security dilemma.[154] These points all resonate as well with Elaine Scarry's

Thermonuclear Hegemony, which argues that legitimate government arises from the visceral and shared recognition of what it means to be harmed. The social contract must both be intelligible to its constituents and protect its members from wrongful harm to be legitimate.

Thus, it shades from ludicrous to alarming that the decision technologies that were first developed to address nuclear security, then applied to modeling all manner of individual and collective decisions, and developed to construct public policies and design institutions, presuppose at the outset that there is no comprehending subject in the decision-maker's seat.[155] The fact of mindless rationality is consistent with its design. Game theory's prominence is inseparable from its generative application to the nuclear security dilemma that selected the strategy of NUTS—preparing to fight and win a nuclear war—as the only way to solve the supposed paradox of MAD deriving from the lack of credibility of a mutually suicidal retaliatory strike. But any fact, including the reality of mutual assured destruction, cannot be a paradox. The paradox of deterrence was generated internal to rational decision theory, which, having jettisoned intelligibility as a distinguishing feature of human reasoning, then proposed an incredible and omnicidal solution to its logical reconstruction of a security dilemma. As Deudney observes, given how rapid the decision to pull the nuclear trigger would be, strategic rationality not only takes us from MAD to NUTS, but further to DEAD: Destructive-Entrusted Automation Devices.[156] There is no pretense of a conscious decision-maker in strategic games. Moreover, under US strategic protocol and also that of the Russians, potentially and even necessarily the decision to actualize a nuclear confrontation will be assisted with, if not implemented by, algorithmic decision machines.[157] This current situation invites us to question whether we should leave the future of humanity to strategic and computable rationality, which presents the greatest challenges as those of maintaining credibility and strategic parity in a world of overkill nuclear strike capability. We are thus poised to pursue a security posture that is intelligible and serves humans worldwide in affording security by minimizing the chances of intentional and accidental nuclear conflict.

S. M. Amadae is the author of *Prisoners of Reason* (Cambridge University Press, 2016) and the award winning *Rationalizing Capitalist Democracy* (University of Chicago Press, 2003). This research trajectory investigates the political theoretical implications of rational decision theory for classical liberal and neoliberal theories and practices. Amadae holds appointments as a University Lecturer of World Politics in the Dept.

of Economic and Political Studies, University of Helsinki; Associate Professor of international political economy in Swansea University's Department of Politics and International Relations and Research Affiliate in Science, Technology, and Society Studies, Massachusetts Institute of Technology.

Notes

1. Paul Erickson, Judy L. Klein, Lorraine Daston, Rebecca Lemov, Thomas Sturm, and Michael D. Gordin, *How Reason Almost Lost Its Mind: The Strange Career of Cold War Rationality* (Chicago, IL: University of Chicago Press, 2013); Paul Erickson, *The World the Game Theorists Made* (Chicago, IL: University of Chicago Press, 2015); William Thomas, *Rational Action: The Sciences of Policy in Britain and America, 1940–1960* (Cambridge, MA: MIT Press, 2015).
2. Yuval Noah Harari, *Homo Deus: A Brief History of Tomorrow* (New York: Random House, 2016).
3. On the former, see S. M. Amadae, *Rationalizing Capitalist Democracy: Cold War Origins of Rational Choice Liberalism* (Chicago, IL: University of Chicago Press, 2003); Alvin E. Roth, "The Economist as Engineer: Game Theory, Experimentation, and Computation as Tools for Design Economics," *Econometrica* 70, no. 4 (2002): 1341–78.
4. Philip R. Cohen and Hector J. Levesque, "Intention Is Choice with Commitment," *Artificial Intelligence* 42, no. 2–3 (1990): 213–61, see esp. 217, 257.
5. On the former, see, for example, Erickson et al., *How Reason Almost Lost its Mind*.
6. Amadae, *Prisoners of Reason*, 76–79; Thomas, *Rational Action*, 135.
7. On the former, see Thomas, *Rational Action*, 201, 203; Philip Mirowski, *Machine Dreams: Economics Becomes a Cyborg Science* (New York: Cambridge University Press, 2002); Amadae, *Rationalizing Capitalist Democracy*; Erickson, *The World the Game Theorists Made*.
8. John von Neumann and Oskar Morgenstern, *Theory of Games and Economic Behavior* (Princeton, NJ: Princeton University Press, 1947).
9. Keith Krause, "Rationality and Deterrence in Theory and Practice," in *Contemporary Security and Strategy*, ed. Craig A. Snyder, 120–49 (New York: Routledge, 1999).
10. See, for example, Thomas Schelling, *Strategy of Conflict* (Cambridge, 1960). The most optimistic statement of Schelling's influence apart from Schelling himself comes from Richard Ned Lebow who writes that "his ideas have also had considerable impact in the policy community, where they continue to shape the way in which policymakers seek to influence adversaries." In *Coercion, Cooperation and Ethics in International Relations* (London: Routledge, 2007), 255. [The essay was originally published in 1996]. Marc Trachtenberg, Richard Betts, and Francis J. Gavin are much

more sceptical of Schelling's influence and critical of his overstatement on this issue. See Marc Trachtenberg, "Social Scientists and National Security Policymaking," paper presented at Notre Dame University, 22–23 April 2010, 8 available at http://www.sscnet.ucla.edu/polisci/faculty/trachtenberg/cv/notre%20dame(2010).pdf; Richard Betts, "Should Strategic Studies Survive?" *World Politics* 50, no. 1 (1997): 9–11; Francis J. Gavin, *Nuclear Statecraft* (Ithaca, NY: Cornell University Press, 2012), 4 and chapter 6 on the limited impact of game theory on American policymakers. My argument is compatible with this caution about overemphasizing the role of game theory in constructing nuclear policy because, as Schelling originally observed, game theory has impact as more of a mentality and approach than the demand to provide a formal payoff matrix and decision tree for every choice. Thus, so long as game theory provides the widely accepted standard for instrumental rationality, then its overarching approach to rational choice remains implicit in mainstream strategic policies.

11. Daniel Ellsberg, "Theory of the Reluctant Duelist," *The American Economic Review* 46, no. 5 (1956); Amadae, *Rationalizing Capitalist Democracy*; Mirowski, *Machine Dreams*, 114–15. In Mirowski's close reading of the development of game theory within the context of military purpose and purview, game theory—along the lines of what would become the orthodox Nash equilibrium approach of mutual-best-reply, which postulated a calculable (machine representable) agent with hallmark consistent preferences—increasingly yielded ground to John von Neumann's post-1940s view of mechanism design as itself a form of algorithmic governance that spans from military command and control to markets (94–152, 536–45).

12. Jürgen Habermas, *The Theory of Communicative Action*, vol. 1, *Reason and the Rationalization of Society*, trans. Thomas McCarthy (Boston, MA: Beacon, 1984); Jürgen Habermas, *The Theory of Communicative Action*, vol. 2, *Lifeworld and System: A Critique of Functionalist Reason*, trans. Thomas McCarthy (Cambridge: MIT Press, 1987). On Habermas, see Joseph Heath, *Communicative Action and Rational Choice* (Cambridge, MA, 2001); Margaret Gilbert, *How We Together Make the Social* World (New York, 2015); John R. Searle, *Making the Social World: The Structure of Human Civilization* (Oxford, UK, 2010); Raimo Tuomela, *Social Ontology: Collective Intentionality and Group Agents* (New York, 2013). Alternatives within the rationality paradigm may include Herbert Simon's bounded rationality (Mirowski, *Machine Dreams*, 529–32; Crowther-Heyck, *Herbert A. Simon: The Bounds of Reason in Modern America*. Baltimore, MD: JHU Press, 2005) and Norbert Wiener's cybernetics (Peter Galison, "The Ontology of the Enemy: Norbert Wiener and the Cybernetic Vision," *Critical Inquiry* 21, no. 1 [1994]: 228–66), but Mirowski makes clear that not only were these programs similarly inspired by military aims, but also that they share with game theory the view of agency as programmable or algorithmic.

13. Amadae, *Rationalizing Capitalist Democracy*; Richard Tuck, *Free Riding* (Cambridge, MA, 2008).

14. Joseph S. Nye, *Nuclear Ethics* (New York, 1988); Herman Kahn, *Thinking the Unthinkable*, (New York: Avon, 1962).
15. Daniel Deudney, "Whole Earth Security: A Geopolitics of Peace," *Worldwatch Paper 55* (Washington, DC: Worldwatch Institute, 1983); on the economic value of a statistical human life, see Thomas C. Schelling, "The Life You Save May Be Your Own," in *Problems in Public Expenditure Analysis*, ed. Samuel B. Chase, Jr. (Washington DC: Brookings Institution, 1968).
16. On command and control, see Erik Gartzke and Jon R. Lindsay, "Thermonuclear Cyberwar," *Journal of Cyber Security* 1–2 (2017); on the principle computability of strategic rationality, see Amadae, "The Computability of Rational Choice."
17. Mirowski, *Machine Dreams*, 532.
18. Mirowski, *Machine Dreams*, 512.
19. Von Neumann and Morgenstern, *Theory of Games and Economic Behavior*, 31.
20. Desmond Ball, "US Strategic Forces: How Would They Be Used?" *International Security* 7, no. 3 (1982): 39, 56–58.
21. Mirowski, *Machine Dreams*, 440.
22. Mirowski, *Machine Dreams*, 190; see also Gartzke and Lindsay, "Thermonuclear Cyberwar."
23. See, for example, Ken Binmore, *Natural Justice* (Oxford, UK, 2005); Herbert Gintis, *The Bounds of Reason: Game Theory and the Unification of the Behavioral Sciences* (Princeton, NJ, 2009); Daniel H. Hausman, *Preference, Value, Choice and Welfare* (Cambridge, UK, 2011); Francesco Guala, *Understanding Institutions: The Science and Philosophy of Living Together* (Princeton, NJ, 2016).
24. U.S. Department of Defense, *Joint Vision 2020*, (Washington, DC: Publisher, 2000), https://web.archive.org/web/20011129104507/. Here I share ground with Erickson et al.'s recent assessment that nuclear security and other military concerns set the stage for economizing decision-making using game theory, and other means of algorithmic calculation, during the early Cold War, Erickson et al., *How Reason Almost Lost Its Mind*.
25. Ken Berry et al., *Delegitimizing Nuclear Weapons: Examining the Validity of Nuclear Deterrence* (Monterey, CA, 2010); Benoît Pelopidas, "The Oracles of Proliferation: How Experts Maintain a Biased Historical Reading That Limits Policy Innovation," *Nonproliferation Review* 18, no. 1 (2011); Benoît Pelopidas, "A Bet Portrayed as a Certainty: Reassessing the Added Deterrent Value of Nuclear Weapons," in *The War That Must Never Be Fought: Dilemmas of Nuclear Deterrence*, ed. J. Goodby and G. P. Shultz (Stanford, CA, 2015); Benoît Pelopidas, "The Unbearable Lightness of Luck: Three Sources of Overconfidence in the Manageability of Nuclear Crises," *European Journal of International Security* 2, no. 2 (July 2017): 240–62.
26. Benoît Pelopidas, "The Birth of Nuclear Eternity," *The Future: Interdisciplinary Perspectives*, ed. by Jenny Andersson and Sandra Kemp (Oxford: Oxford University Press, forthcoming 2019).

27. Daniel Deudney, *Bounding Power: Republican Security Theory from the Polis to the Global Village* (Princeton, NJ: 2007).
28. Frank C. Zagare and D. Marc Kilgour, *Perfect Deterrence* (Cambridge: Cambridge University Press, 2000), "classical deterrence theory remains a potent intellectual force shaping the policy debates in the US ... and elsewhere" (36).
29. Mark Coeckelbergh, "The Automation of the Social: What Robots Can Teach Us about the Social," in *Robo-Philosophy: Philosophy of, for, and by Social Robotics*, ed. J. Seibt, R. Hakli, and M. Nørskov (Cambridge, MA, 2018 forthcoming); Elaine Scarry, *Thermonuclear Monarchy: Choosing between Democracy and Doom* (New York, 2014).
30. Desmond Ball and Robert C. Toth, "Revising the SIOP: Taking War-Fighting to Dangerous Extremes," *International Security* 14, no. 4 (1990): 65–92; Gartzke and Lindsay, "Thermonuclear Cyberwar." For a frank discussion of this potential reliance on AI to maintain the chain of command see Brent Scowcroft, "C3 Systems for the President and Military Commanders," in *National Security Issues 1981 Symposium: Strategic Nuclear Policies, Weapons, and the C3 Connection*, d. by Drexel M. Ace (Bedford, MA: Mitre Corporation, Mitre Document M82-30, 1981), 93–98.
31. Daniel Volmar, "The Power of the Atom: US Command Control and Communications, 1945–1965" (PhD dissertation, Harvard University, 2017).
32. Erickson et al., *How Reason Almost Lost Its Mind*, 29.
33. Erickson et al., *How Reason Almost Lost Its Mind*, 37; Amadae, "The Computability of Rational Choice."
34. Erickson et al., *How Reason Almost Lost Its Mind*, 43.
35. Although it is a fictionalized account of the historical book *Hidden Figures* by Margot Lee Shetterly (New York, 2016), the film by the same name (2016) accurately captures the difference between a computerized calculation without the demand of intelligibility on the part of a computing machine and a human "computor" who understands and can vouch for the meaning, purpose, and validity of a calculation, in this case astronaut John Glenn's reentry trajectory and landing coordinates.
36. Erickson et al., *How Reason Almost Lost Its Mind*, 40–41.
37. Erickson et al., *How Reason Almost Lost Its Mind*, 39.
38. Rationality itself is postulated to have been programmed via evolution into living beings so that they can survive and propagate: R. L. Trivers, "The Evolution of Reciprocal Altruism," *The Quarterly Review of Biology* 46, no. 1 (1971): 35–57; John Maynard Smith, *Evolution and the Theory of Games* (Cambridge, UK, 1982); Philip Pettit, *Rules, Reasons, and Norms* (Oxford, UK, 2002).
39. For discussion, see John R. Searle, *Rationality in Action* (Cambridge, MA, 2001); Alfred R. Mele, *Motivation and Agency* (Oxford, UK, 2003); Amadae, "The Computability of Rational Choice"; Brendan Markey-Towler, "I, Roboticus Oeconomicus: The Philosophy of Mind in Economics, and Why It Matters," *Cambridge Journal of Economics* 41, no. 1 (2017): 203–37.

40. R. Duncan Luce and Howard Raiffa, *Games and Decisions: Introduction and Critical Survey* (New York, 1957), 6.
41. Ludwig Wittgenstein, *Philosophical Investigations*, trans. G. E. M. Anscombe (New York, 1999).
42. See John Searle, *Rationality in Action*, as well as the following by Searle: "Minds, Brains and Programs," *Behavioral and Brain Sciences* 3 (1980): 417–57; "Wittgenstein and the Background," *American Philosophical Quarterly* 48, no. 2 (2011): 119–28; "Insight and Error in Wittgenstein," *Philosophy of the Social Sciences* 46, no. 6 (2016): 527–47.
43. Erickson et al., *How Reason Almost Lost Its Mind*, 30.
44. Amadae, "The Computability of Rational Choice."
45. Alfred Church, "A Set of Postulates for the Foundation of Logic," *Annals of Mathematics*, second series, 33 (1936): 346–66.
46. Alan Turing, "Intelligent Machinery" (London, 1948) in *Machine Intelligence 5*, ed. Bernard Meltzer and Donald Michie (Edinburgh, 1969), 7.
47. Erickson et al., *How Reason Almost Lost Its Mind*.
48. Erickson et al., *How Reason Almost Lost Its Mind*, 136; Amadae, *Prisoners of Reason*, 73–93.
49. This vision of algorithmic rule-following is sufficiently comprehensive that Herbert Simon argued that scientific discovery itself can be modeled, and hence has a determinist quality, in *Models of Discovery*, 1977. For a comprehensive analysis of Simon's contributions to cybernetics and bounded rationality, see Hunter Crowther-Heyck, *Herbert A. Simon*. See also Heyck's *Age of System: Understanding the Development of Modern Social Science* (Baltimore, MD, 2015).
50. Erickson et al., *How Reason Almost Lost Its Mind*, 87. See also Amadae, *Prisoners of Reason*, 76–84.
51. Schelling, *Strategy of Conflict*; Amadae, *Prisoners of Reason*; Erickson et al., *How Reason Almost Lost Its Mind*, 135; Robert J. Aumann et al., *Models of Gradual Reduction of Arms*, Arms Control and Disarmament Agency, ACDA/ST-116, Sept. 1, 1967; Amadae, *Prisoners of Reason*, 49–58.
52. Sharon Ghamari-Tabrizi, *The Worlds of Herman Kahn: The Intuitive Science of Thermonuclear War* (Cambridge, MA, 2005); Deudney, *Whole Earth Security*; Amadae, *Prisoners of Reason*, 65–140; quote from Erickson et al., *How Reason Almost Lost Its Mind*, 87.
53. Amadae, *Prisoners of Reason*, 106 fn19; Mirowski, *Machine Dreams*.
54. Jack L. Snyder, *The Soviet Strategic Culture: Implications for Limited Nuclear Options* (Santa Monica, CA, 1977). In a similar vein, see Glenn H. Snyder, "'Prisoner's Dilemma' and 'Chicken' Models in International Politics," *International Studies Quarterly* 15, no. 1 (1971): 66–103.
55. Amadae, *Prisoners of Reason*; Selmer Bringsjord et al., "Nuclear Deterrence and the Logic of Deliberative Mindreading," *Cognitive Systems Research* 28 (2014): 20–43; David A. Shlapak and Michael Johnson, *Reinforcing Deterrence on NATO's Eastern Flank: Wargaming the Defense of the Baltics* (Santa Monica, CA, 2016).
56. Nye, *Nuclear Ethics*.

57. Robert J. Leonard, "Creating a Context for Game Theory," in *Toward a History of Game Theory*, ed. E. Roy Weintraub (Durham, NC, 1992); Mirowski, *Machine Dreams*; Amadae, *Rationalizing Capitalist Democracy* and *Prisoners of Reason*; Erickson, *The World the Game Theorists Made*.
58. Von Neumann and Morgenstern, *Theory of Games and Economic Behavior*, 30–33.
59. Erickson et al., *How Reason Almost Lost Its Mind*, 29.
60. Amartya K. Sen, "Goals, Commitment, and Identity," *Journal of Law, Economics and Organization* 1 (1985): 2; Daniel H. Hausman, *Preference, Value, Choice and Welfare*, (Cambridge, UK, 2011); John Nash, "Non-cooperative Games," *Annals of Mathematics* (1951): 286–95.
61. See, for example, Deirdre N. McCloskey, *Bourgeois Equality: How Ideas, not Capital or Institutions, Enriched the World* (Chicago, IL: 2016).
62. Erickson et al., *How Reason Almost Lost Its Mind*, 30.
63. Francesco Guala and Frank Hindricks, "A Unified Social Ontology," *The Philosophical Quarterly* 65, no. 259 (2015): 177–201.
64. See, for example, McCloskey, *Bourgeois Equality*.
65. Daniel Deudney, "Political Fission: State Structure, Civil Society, and Nuclear Security Politics in the United States," in *On Security*, ed. Ronnie Lipschutz (New York: 1995), 87–123.
66. Deudney, "Political Fission," 102–9.
67. Deudney, *Whole Earth Security*, 33.
68. Ball and Toth, "Revising the SIOP: Taking War-Fighting to Dangerous Extremes"; Hans M. Kristensen, Matthew McKinzie, and Theodore A. Postol, "How US Nuclear Force Modernization Is Undermining Strategic Stability: The Burst-Height Compensating Super-Fuze." *Bulletin of the Atomic Scientists*, vol. 1(2017), available online at https://thebulletin.org/2017/03/how-us-nuclear-force-modernization-is-undermining-strategic-stability-the-burst-height-compensating-super-fuze/. Gartzke and Lindsay, "Thermonuclear Cyberwar"; Deudney, "Political Fission."
69. Fred Kaplan, *The Wizards of Armageddon* (Palo Alto, CA, 1991); Gregg Herken, *Counsels of War* (New York, 1985); David R. Jardini, "Out of the Blue Yonder: The RAND Corporation's Diversification into Social Welfare Research, 1946–1968" (PhD dissertation, Carnegie Mellon University, 1996); Mirowski, *Machine Dreams*; Amadae, *Rationalizing Capitalist Democracy* and *Prisoners of Reason*; Erickson et al., *How Reason Almost Lost Its Mind*.
70. Robert Jervis, "Deterrence Theory Revisited," *World Politics* 31, no. 2 (1979): 289–324; Frank C. Zagare, "Classical Deterrence Theory: A Critical Assessment," *International Interactions* 21, no. 4 (1996): 365–87; Krause, "Rationality and Deterrence in Theory and Practice"; Amadae, *Prisoners of Reason*, 106.
71. Lawrence Freedman, *The Evolution of Nuclear Strategy* (New York, 1981); Douglas P. Lackey, "The American Debate on Nuclear Weapons Policy," *Analyse & Kritik* 9, no. 1–2 (1987): 7–46.
72. Gregory S. Kavka, "Some Paradoxes of Deterrence," *The Journal of Philosophy* 75, no. 6 (1978): 285–302; "Deterrence, Utility, and Rational

Choice," *Theory and Decision* 12, no. 1 (1980): 41–60; "The Toxin Puzzle," *Analysis* 43, no. 1 (1983): 33–36; *Hobbesian Moral and Political Theory* (Princeton, NJ, 1986); *Moral Paradoxes of Nuclear Deterrence* (Cambridge, UK, 1987); David Gauthier, "Deterrence, Maximization, and Rationality," *Ethics* 94, no. 3 (1984): 474–95; "Assure and Threaten," *Ethics* 104, no. 4 (1994): 690–721; and Richmond Campbell and Lanning Sowden, eds. *Paradoxes of Rationality and Cooperation: Prisoner's Dilemma and Newcomb's Problem* (Vancouver, 1985).
73. Erickson et al., *How Reason Almost Lost Its Mind*, 134.
74. Erickson et al., *How Reason Almost Lost Its Mind*, 148. See also John Mayberry, "The Notion of Threat," in *Models of Gradual Reduction of Arms*, ed. Robert J. Aumann (Princeton, NJ, 1967).
75. Schelling, *Strategy of Conflict*; Amadae, *Prisoners of Reason*.
76. Anatol Rapoport and Albert M. Chammah, *Prisoner's Dilemma: A Study of Conflict and Cooperation* (Ann Arbor, MI: University of Michigan Press, 1965); Campbell and Sowden, *Paradoxes of Rationality and Cooperation*.
77. Randall L. Schweller, "Neorealism's Status Quo Bias: What Security Dilemma?" *Security Studies* 5, no. 3 (1996): 90–121.
78. Kristensen et al., "How US Nuclear Force Modernization Is Undermining Strategic Stability."
79. Schelling, *Strategy of Conflict*; Amadae, *Prisoners of Reason*.
80. Campbell and Sowden, *Paradoxes of Rationality and Cooperation*; Kavka, "The Toxin Puzzle"; David Gauthier, "Rethinking the Toxin Puzzle," in *Rational Commitment and Social Justice: Essays for Gregory Kavka*, ed. Jules L. Coleman, Christopher W. Morris, and Gregory S. Kavka (Cambridge, UK, 1998), 47–58
81. Frank C. Zagare and D. Marc Kilgour argue for updating classical deterrence theory to perfect deterrence based on game theory's perfect Bayesian equilibrium. Their case rests on embracing the PD preferences characterizing an aggressor state, *Perfect Deterrence* (Cambridge: Cambridge University Press, 2000).
82. Kavka, *Moral Paradoxes of Nuclear Deterrence*; Gauthier, "Assure and Threaten."
83. Gauthier, "Assure and Threaten," 719.
84. Ball and Toth, "Revising the SIOP," 66; Kristensen et al., "How US Nuclear Force Modernization Is Undermining Strategic Stability," 1.
85. New York Times Editorial Board, "The Finger on the Nuclear Button," *New York Times*, 5 February 2017, https://www.nytimes.com/2017/02/05/opinion/the-finger-on-the-nuclear-button.html?_r=0.
86. Michael S. Gerson, "No First Use: The Next Step for US Nuclear Policy," *International Security* 35, no. 2 (2010): 7–47.
87. Thomas C. Schelling, "An Astonishing Sixty Years: The Legacy of Hiroshima," *The American economic review* 96, no. 4 (2006): 929–37.
88. The term for this is SIOP, or single integrated operational plan. For discussion, see Ball, "US Strategic Forces: How Would They Be Used?"; Ball and Toth, "Revising the SIOP."

89. Thomas C. Schelling, *Arms and Influence* (New Haven, CT, 1966). For a recent statement of this concern see Edward Geist and Andrew J. Lohn, "How Might Artificial Intelligence Affect the Risk of Nuclear War?" (Santa Monica, CA: RAND Corporation, 2018), 11. Available at https://www.rand.org/pubs/perspectives/PE296.html.
90. Schelling, *Strategy of Conflict*; Schelling, *Arms and Influence*; Robert Jervis, *The Meaning of the Nuclear Revolution: Statecraft and the Prospect of Armageddon* (Ithaca, NY, 1989); Steven J. Brams, *Superpower Games: Applying Game Theory to Superpower Conflict* (New Haven, CT, 1985). For discussion see Amadae, *Prisoners of Reason*.
91. Deudney, *Bounding Power*, 246.
92. Gerson, "No First Use."
93. Thomas Hobbes, *Leviathan*, rev. ed., ed. by Richard Tuck (Cambridge, UK: Cambridge University Press, 1996).
94. Mayberry, "The Notion of Threat"; Amadae, *Prisoners of Reason*, 57.
95. This insight resonates with David Runciman's exploration of the implications of new information technologies for schools of political realism and idealism. See David Runciman, "Political Theory and Real Politics in the Age of the Internet," *The Journal of Political Philosophy* 25, no. 1 (2016): 3–21.
96. Erickson et al., *How Reason Almost Lost Its Mind*, 159–88.
97. On the nuclear security dilemma, see Kristensen et al., "How US Nuclear Force Modernization Is Undermining Strategic Stability."
98. Guala, *Understanding Institutions*.
99. Gintis, *Bounds of Reason*.
100. S. J. Gershman et al., "Computational Rationality: A Converging Paradigm for Intelligence in Brains, Minds, and Machines," *Science* 349, no. 6245 (2015): 273–78.; Paul M. Churchland, *Matter and Consciousness*, rev. ed. (Cambridge, MA, 1988), 43–49; 156–65
101. See, for example, Luciano Floridi, *The Fourth Revolution: How the Infosphere Is Reshaping Human Reality* (Oxford, UK, 2014)
102. Amadae, "The Computability of Rational Choice."
103. On the normative status of rational choice, see Roger B. Myerson, *Game Theory: Analysis of Conflict* (Cambridge, MA, 1991); and Shaun Hargreaves Heap and Yanis Varoufakis, *Game Theory: A Critical Introduction* (Abingdon, 2004). On institutions, see Douglass C. North, *Institutions, Institutional Change and Economic Performance* (Cambridge, UK, 1990); and Roth, "The Economist as Engineer." On the nonreflexive quality of norms and rule-following, see Guala, *Understanding Institutions*.
104. R. L. Lewis et al., "Computational Rationality: Linking Mechanism and Behavior through Bounded Utility Maximization," *Topics in Cognitive Science* 6, no. 2 (2014): 279–311; Gershman et al., "Computational Rationality," 273–78.
105. Herbert Simon's bounded rationality is used because it is computable in biological systems.
106. Lewis et al., "Computational Rationality: Linking Mechanism and Behavior through Bounded Utility Maximization," 281.

107. Gershman et al., "Computational Rationality," 273.
108. Gintis, *Bounds of Reason*, 3.
109. See also Todd Jones, "Uncovering 'Cultural Meaning': Problems and Solutions," *Behavior and Philosophy* 32, no. 2 (2004): 247–68.
110. Trivers, "The Evolution of Reciprocal Altruism"; John Maynard Smith, *Evolution and the Theory of Games*; Robert Axelrod, *Evolution of Cooperation* (New York, 1984); Robert Axelrod and R. O. Keohane, "Achieving Cooperation," in *Neorealism and Neoliberalism: The Contemporary Debate*, ed. David A. Baldwin (New York, 1993), 85–115.
111. Russell Hardin, *Collective Action* (Baltimore, MD, 1982); Dennis C. Mueller, *Public Choice III* (Cambridge, UK, 2003). See also, for example, Nicholas Stern, *The Economics of Climate Change: The Stern Review* (Cambridge, UK, 2007).
112. Gary S. Becker, *The Economic Approach to Human Behavior* (Chicago, IL, 1978); Mueller, *Public Choice III*; North, *Institutions, Institutional Change and Economic Performance*; and Roth, "The Economist as Engineer."
113. Duncan Snidal, "The Limits of Hegemonic Stability Theory," *International Organization* 39, no. 4 (1985): 579–614; Ana Espinola-Arredondo and Félix Munoz-Garcia, "Free-Riding in International Environmental Agreements: A Signaling Approach to Non-enforceable Treaties," *Journal of Theoretical Politics* 23, no. 1 (2011): 111–34.
114. Myerson, *Game Theory*, 22.
115. On systems with AI actors, see Yoav Shoham and Kevin Leyton-Brown, *Multiagent Systems: Algorithmic, Game-Theoretic, and Logical Foundations* (Cambridge, UK, 2008).
116. Pettit, *Rules, Reasons, and Norms*; Binmore, *Natural Justice*; Gintis, *The Bounds of Reason*; Guala, *Understanding Institutions*.
117. See, example, Hargreaves, Heap, and Varoufakis, *Game Theory*.
118. David P. Gauthier, *The Logic of Leviathan: The Moral and Political Theory of Thomas Hobbes* (Oxford, UK, 1969); Pettit, *Rules, Reasons, and Norms*, 308–43; Amadae, *Prisoners of Reason*, 153–74.
119. Thomas C. Schelling, *Micromotives and Macrobehavior* (New York, 2006).
120. Jeremy Bentham, *A Fragment on Government* (New York, 2001); Hobbes, *Leviathan*, 191–200, chap. 14. For discussion, see Runciman, "Political Theory and Real Politics in the Age of the Internet," 16.
121. Amadae, *Prisoners of Reason*.
122. Hobbes, *Leviathan*, 88; Myerson, *Game Theory*, 3.
123. See, for example, Becker, *Economic Approach to Human Behavior*.
124. Kenneth J. Arrow, *Individual Values and Social Choice* (New Haven, CT, 1951); S. M. Amadae, "Arrow's Impossibility Theorem and the National Security State," *Studies in History and Philosophy of Science Part A* 36, no. 4 (2005): 734–43.
125. Chevaleyre Yann et al., "A Short Introduction to Computational Social Choice," *International Conference on Current Trends in Theory and Practice of Computer Science* (Heidelberg, 2007), 51–69; Felix Brandt et al., "Computational Social Choice," in *Multiagent Systems*, ed. Gerhard Weiss (Cambridge, MA, 2012).

126. James M. Buchanan and Gordon Tullock, *The Calculus of Consent* (Ann Arbor, 1962); John Rawls, *Theory of Justice* (Cambridge, MA, 1970); James M. Buchanan, *The Limits of Liberty: Between Anarchy and Leviathan* (Chicago, IL, 1975); Andrew Reynolds, ed., *The Architecture of Democracy: Constitutional Design, Conflict Management, and Democracy* (Oxford, UK, 2002).
127. Amadae, *Rationalizing Capitalist Democracy*.
128. Alfred Moore, "Hayek, Conspiracy, and Democracy," *Critical Review* 28, no. 1 (2016): 44–62.
129. On the conditions rational action must obey, see von Neumann and Morgenstern, *Theory of Games and Economic Behavior*, 30–33; Myerson, *Game Theory*, 1–33; and Hargreaves Heap and Varoufakis. *Game Theory*, 8–12.
130. Myerson, *Game Theory*, 1–5
131. On rational choice theory's "all things considered preferences," see Hausman, *Preference, Value, Choice and Welfare*.
132. On fungible interpersonally transferable utility, see Nicola Giocoli, "Do Prudent Agents Play Lotteries? Von Neumann's Contribution to the Theory of Rational Behavior," *Journal of the History of Economic Thought* 28, no. 1 (2006): 95–109.
133. Deudney, "Political Fission." "Basic legitimation demand" is Runciman's vocabulary—see "Political Theory and Real Politics in the Age of the Internet," 10.
134. On acting recklessly abroad, see Runciman, "Political Theory and Real Politics in the Age of the Internet," 10; Daniel Deudney, "Losing the Constitution? Omniviolence, Arms Control, and Limited Government," in his *On Security* (Princeton, NJ, 2009), 298.
135. On commitment, see Heath, *Communicative Action and Rational Choice*, 86–92; Hausman, *Preference, Value, Choice and Welfare*, 57–62. On intrinsic interests, see Daryl J. Levinson, "Parchment and Politics: The Positive Puzzle of Constitutional Commitment," *Harvard Law Review* (2011): 657–746. On joint instrumental action, see Michael Bacharach, Natalie Gold, and Robert Sugden, *Beyond Individual Choice: Teams and Frames in Game Theory* (Princeton, NJ, 2006).
136. Levinson, "Parchment and Politics," 729.
137. Deudney, "Losing the Constitution?"; Deudney, "Political Fission"; Scarry, *Thermonuclear Monarchy*.
138. Gershman et al., "Computational Rationality"; Giulio Tononi et al., "Integrated Information Theory: From Consciousness to Its Physical Substrate," *Nature Reviews Neuroscience* 17, no. 7 (2016): 450–61.
139. Runciman, "Political Theory and Real Politics in the Age of the Internet," 16.
140. John Gray, *The Soul of the Marionette: A Short Enquiry into Human Freedom* (London, 2015).
141. J. Moffat, *Complexity Theory and Network Centric Warfare* (CCRP Publications Series, 2003), 55; A. Cebrowski, "Network Centric Warfare and Information Superiority," Keynote address from the proceedings, Royal United Services Institute (RUSI) conference "C4ISTAR Achieving

Information Superiority," (Whitehall, London, UK: 2000); J. Moffat, *Command and Control in the Information Age: Representing Impact* (London: 2002).
142. Levinson, "Parchment and Politics," 693, 690.
143. On the strategic account of sociability, see Amadae, *Prisoners of Reason*, 125–35; Levinson, "Parchment and Politics," 697.
144. Joseph Farrell and Matthew Rabin, "Cheap Talk," *The Journal of Economic Perspectives* 10, no. 3 (1996): 103–18; S. M. Amadae, "Game Theory, Cheap Talk and Post-Truth Politics," *Journal for the Theory of Social Behavior*, May 2018, 1–24, https://doi.org/10.1111/jtsb.12169.
145. Jürgen Habermas, *Between Facts and Norm: Contribution to Discourse Theory of Law and Democracy*, trans. William Rehg (Cambridge, MA, 1996).
146. Coeckelbergh, "Automation of the Social."
147. Searle, *Rationality in Action*.
148. Levinson, "Parchment and Politics," 698.
149. Amadae, *Prisoners of Reason*, 69–140.
150. On game theory and policy analysis, see Stern, *Economics of Climate Change*; Coeckelbergh, "Automation of the Social."
151. Hobbes, *Leviathan*, 91.
152. See, for example, the Congressional Commission on the Strategic Posture of the United States (2009), available at http://media.usip/reports/strat_posture_report.pdf. See Frank C. Zagare and D. Marc Kilgour's *Perfect Deterrence* or the statement of the long dure hold of rational deterrence theory over mainstream nuclear policy, as well as their effort to update the role of game theory in deterrence policy using the concept of the sub-perfect equilibrium.
153. Deudney, *Bounding Power*, xii.
154. Deudney, *Bounding Power*, 27.
155. On public policy, see Mueller, *Public Choice III*. On institutional design, see North, *Institutions, Institutional Change and Economic Performance*.
156. Deudney, *Whole Earth Security*, 36–37.
157. Geist and Lohn, "How Might Artificial Intelligence Affect the Risk of Nuclear War?," 18.

Bibliography

Amadae, S. M. "Arrow's Impossibility Theorem and the National Security State." *Studies in History and Philosophy of Science Part A* 36, no. 4 (2005): 734–43.
———. "Game Theory, Cheap Talk and Post-Truth Politics," *Journal for the Theory of Social Behavior*, May 2018: 1–24.
———. "The Computability of Rational Choice." *What Robots Can and Should Do*. Proceedings of Robo-Philosophy: IOS Press, 2016.
———. *Prisoners of Reason: Game Theory and Neoliberal Political Economy*. New York: Cambridge University Press, 2016.

———. *Rationalizing Capitalist Democracy: Cold War Origins of Rational Choice Liberalism*. Chicago, IL: University of Chicago Press, 2003.
Arrow, Kenneth. *Social Choice and Individual Values*. New Haven, CT: Yale University Press, 1951.
Axelrod, Robert. *Evolution of Cooperation*. New York: Basic Books, 1984.
Axelrod, Robert, and R. O. Keohane. "Achieving Cooperation." In *Neorealism and Neoliberalism: The Contemporary Debate*, edited by David A. Baldwin, 85–115. New York: Columbia University Press, 1993.
Bacharach, Michael, Natalie Gold, and Robert Sugden. *Beyond Individual Choice: Teams and Frames in Game Theory*. Princeton, NJ: Princeton University Press, 2006.
Ball, Desmond. "US Strategic Forces: How Would They Be Used?" *International Security* 7, no. 3 (1982): 31–60.
Ball, Desmond, and Robert C. Toth. "Revising the SIOP: Taking War-Fighting to Dangerous Extremes." *International Security* 14, no. 4 (1990): 65–92.
Becker, Gary S. *The Economic Approach to Human Behavior*. Chicago, IL: University of Chicago Press, 1978.
Bentham, Jeremy. *A Fragment on Government*. New York: The Lawbook Exchange, Ltd., 2001.
Berry, K., P. Lewis, B. Pélopidas, N. Sokov, W. Wilson. *Delegitimizing Nuclear Weapons: Examining the Validity of Nuclear Weapons*. Monterey, CA: Monterey Institute for International Studies, 2010.
Betts, Richard. "Should Strategic Studies Survive?" *World Politics* 50, no. 1 (1997): 9–11.
Binmore, Ken. *Essays on the Foundations of Game Theory*. Oxford: Blackwell, 1990.
———. *Natural Justice*. Oxford: Oxford University Press, 2005.
Binmore, Ken, and Hyun Song Shin. "Algorithmic Knowledge and Game Theory." *Knowledge, Belief, and Strategic Interaction* 141 (1992): 154.
Brams, Steven J. *Superpower Games: Applying Game Theory to Superpower Conflict*. New Haven, CT: Yale University Press, 1985.
Brandt, Felix, Vincent Conitzer, and Ulle Endriss. "Computational Social Choice." In *Multiagent Systems*, edited by Gerhard Weiss, 213–283. Cambridge, MA: MIT Press, 2012.
Bringsjord, Selmer, Naveen Sundar Govindarajulu, Simon Ellis, Evan McCarty, and John Licato. "Nuclear Deterrence and the Logic of Deliberative Mindreading." *Cognitive Systems Research* 28 (2014): 20–43.
Buchanan, James M. *The Limits of Liberty: Between Anarchy and Leviathan*. Chicago, IL: University of Chicago Press, 1975.
Buchanan, James M., and Gordon Tullock. *The Calculus of Consent*. Ann Arbor: University of Michigan Press, 1962.
Campbell, Richmond, and Lanning Sowden, eds. *Paradoxes of Rationality and Cooperation: Prisoner's Dilemma and Newcomb's Problem*. British Columbia: UBC Press, 1985.
Cebrowski, A. "Network Centric Warfare and Information Superiority." Keynote address from the proceedings, Royal United Services Institute (RUSI) conference "C4ISTAR Achieving Information Superiority." Whitehall, London: RUSI, 2000.

Church, Alfred. "A Set of Postulates for the Foundation of Logic." *Annals of Mathematics*, second series 33 (1936): 346–66.
Churchland, Paul M. *Matter and Consciousness*. Rev. ed. Cambridge, MA: MIT Press, 1988.
Coeckelbergh, Mark. "The Automation of the Social: What Robots Can Teach Us about the Social." In *Robo-Philosophy: Philosophy of, for, and by Social Robotics*, edited by Johanna Seibt, Raul Hakli, and Marco Nørskov. Cambridge, MA: MIT Press, forthcoming 2018.
Crowther-Heyck, Hunter. *Age of System: Understanding the Development of Modern Social Science*. Baltimore, MD: Johns Hopkins University Press, 2015.
———. *Herbert A. Simon: The Bounds of Reason in Modern America*. Baltimore, MD: JHU Press, 2005.
Deudney, Daniel. *Bounding Power: Republican Security Theory from the Polis to the Global Village*. Princeton, NJ: Princeton University Press, 2007.
———. "Omniviolence, Arms Control, and Limited Government," in *The Limits of Constitutionalism*, edited by Jeffrey Tulis and Stephen Macedo, 297–316. Princeton, NJ: Princeton University Press, 2010.
———. "Political Fission: State Structure, Civil Society, and Nuclear Security Politics in the United States." In *On Security*, edited by Ronnie Lipschutz, 87–123. New York: Columbia University Press, 1995.
———. "Whole Earth Security: A Geopolitics of Peace." *Worldwatch Paper 55*. Washington, DC: Worldwatch Institute, 1983.
Erickson, Paul. *The World the Game Theorists Made*. Chicago, IL: University of Chicago Press, 2015.
Erickson, Paul, Judy L. Klein, Lorraine Daston, Rebecca Lemov, Thomas Sturm, and Michael D. Gordin. *How Reason Almost Lost Its Mind: The Strange Career of Cold War Rationality*. Chicago, IL: University of Chicago Press, 2013.
Ellsberg, Daniel. "Theory of the Reluctant Duelist." *The American Economic Review* 46, no. 5 (1956): 909–23.
Espinola-Arredondo, Ana, and Felix Munoz-Garcia. "Free-Riding in International Environmental Agreements: A Signaling Approach to Non-enforceable Treaties." *Journal of Theoretical Politics* 23, no. 1 (2011): 111–34.
Farrell, Joseph, and Matthew Rabin. "Cheap Talk." *The Journal of Economic Perspectives* 10, no. 3 (1996): 103–18.
Floridi, Luciano. *The Fourth Revolution: How the Infosphere Is Reshaping Human Reality*. Oxford: Oxford University Press, 2014.
Freedman, Lawrence. *The Evolution of Nuclear Strategy*. New York: St. Martin's Press, 1981.
Galison, Peter. "The Ontology of the Enemy: Norbert Wiener and the Cybernetic Vision." *Critical Inquiry* 21, no. 1 (1994): 228–66.
Gartzke, Erik, and Jon R. Lindsay. "Thermonuclear Cyberwar." *Journal of Cyber Security* 3, no. 1 (March 2017): 37–48. doi: 10.1093/cybsec/tyw017.
Gauthier, David. "Assure and Threaten." *Ethics* 104, no. 4 (1994): 690–721.
———. "Deterrence, Maximization, and Rationality." *Ethics* 94, no. 3 (1984): 474–95.
———. *The Logic of Leviathan: The Moral and Political Theory of Thomas Hobbes*. Oxford: Oxford University Press, 1969.

———. "Rethinking the Toxin Puzzle." In *Rational Commitment and Social Justice: Essays for Gregory Kavka*, edited by Jules L. Coleman, Christopher W. Morris, and Gregory S. Kavka, 47–58. Cambridge: Cambridge University Press, 1998.

Gavin, Francis J. *Nuclear Statecraft*. Ithaca, NY: Cornell University Press, 2012.

Geist, Edward, and Andrew J. Lohn. "How Might Artificial Intelligence Affect the Risk of Nuclear War?." Santa Monica, CA: RAND Corporation, 2018. https://www.rand.org/pubs/perspectives/PE296.html.

Gerson, Michael S. "No First Use: The Next Step for US Nuclear Policy." *International Security* 35, no. 2 (2010): 7–47.

Gershman, Samuel J., Eric J. Horvitz, and Joshua B. Tenenbaum. "Computational Rationality: A Converging Paradigm for Intelligence in Brains, Minds, and Machines." *Science* 349, no. 6245 (2015): 273–78.

Ghamari-Tabrizi, Sharon. *The Worlds of Herman Kahn. The Intuitive Science of Thermonuclear War*. Cambridge, MA: Harvard University Press, 2005.

Gilbert, Margaret. *Joint Commitment: How We Make the Social World*. Oxford: Oxford University Press, 2015.

Gintis, Herbert. *The Bounds of Reason: Game Theory and the Unification of the Behavioral Sciences*. Princeton, NJ: Princeton University Press, 2009.

Giocoli, Nicola. "Do Prudent Agents Play Lotteries? Von Neumann's Contribution to the Theory of Rational Behavior." *Journal of the History of Economic Thought* 28, no. 1 (2006): 95–109.

Gray, John. *The Soul of the Marionette: A Short Enquiry into Human Freedom*. London: Allen Lane, 2015.

Guala, Francesco. *Understanding Institutions: The Science and Philosophy of Living Together*. Princeton, NJ: Princeton University Press, 2016.

Guala, Francesco, and Frank Hindricks. "A Unified Social Ontology." *The Philosophical Quarterly* 65, no. 259 (2015): 177–201.

Habermas, Jürgen. *Between Facts and Norm, Contribution to Discourse Theory of Law and Democracy*. Translated by William Rehg. Cambridge, MA: MIT Press, 1996.

———. *The Theory of Communicative Action*. Vol. 1, *Reason and the Rationalization of Society*, translated by Thomas McCarthy. Boston, MA: Beacon, 1984.

———. *The Theory of Communicative Action*. Vol. 2, *Lifeworld and System: A Critique of Functionalist Reason*, translated by Thomas McCarthy. Cambridge: MIT Press, 1987.

Harari, Yuval Noah. *Homo Deus: A Brief History of Tomorrow*. New York: Random House, 2016.

Hardin, Russell. *Collective Action*. Baltimore, MD: Johns Hopkins University Press, 1982.

Hargreaves Heap, Shaun, and Yanis Varoufakis. *Game Theory: A Critical Introduction*. Abingdon: Routledge, 2004.

Hausman, Daniel H. *Preference, Value, Choice and Welfare*. Cambridge, UK: Cambridge University Press, 2011.

Heath, Joseph. *Communicative Action and Rational Choice*. Cambridge, MA: MIT Press, 2001.

Herken, Gregg. *Counsels of War*. New York: Alfred A. Knopf, 1985.

Hobbes, Thomas. *Leviathan*. Rev. ed. Edited by Richard Tuck. Cambridge, UK: Cambridge University Press, 1996.

Jardini, David R. "Out of the Blue Yonder: The RAND Corporation's Diversification into Social Welfare Research, 1946–1968." PhD diss., Carnegie Mellon University, 1996.

Jervis, Robert. "Deterrence Theory Revisited." *World Politics* 31, no. 2 (1979): 289–324.

———. *The Meaning of the Nuclear Revolution: Statecraft and the Prospect of Armageddon*. Ithaca, NY: Cornell University Press, 1989.

Jones, Todd. "Uncovering 'Cultural Meaning': Problems and Solutions." *Behavior and Philosophy* (2004): 247–68.

Kahn, Herman. *Thinking the Unthinkable*. New York: Avon, 1962.

Kaplan, Fred. *The Wizards of Armageddon*. Palo Alto, CA: Stanford University Press, 1991.

Kavka, Gregory S. "Deterrence, Utility, and Rational Choice." *Theory and Decision* 12, no. 1 (1980): 41–60.

———. *Hobbesian Moral and Political Theory*. Princeton, NJ: Princeton University Press, 1986.

———. *Moral Paradoxes of Nuclear Deterrence*. Cambridge, UK: Cambridge University Press, 1987.

———. "Some Paradoxes of Deterrence." *The Journal of Philosophy* 75, no. 6 (1978): 285–302.

———. "The Toxin Puzzle." *Analysis* 43, no. 1 (1983): 33–36.

Krause, Keith. "Rationality and Deterrence in Theory and Practice." In *Contemporary Security and Strategy*, edited by Craig A. Synder, 120–49. New York: Routledge, 1999.

Kristensen Hans M., Matthew McKinzie, and Theodore A. Postol "How US Nuclear Force Modernization Is Undermining Strategic Stability: The Burst-Height Compensating Super-Fuze." *Bulletin of the Atomic Scientists*, vol. 1 (2017). Retrieved 19 July 2018 from https://thebulletin.org/2017/03/how-us-nuclear-force-modernization-is-undermining-strategic-stability-the-burst-height-compensating-super-fuze/.

Lackey, Douglas P. "The American Debate on Nuclear Weapons Policy." *Analyse & Kritik* 9, no. 1–2 (1987): 7–46.

Lebow, Ned. *Coercion, Cooperation and Ethics in International Relations*. London: Routledge, 2007.

Leonard, Robert J. "Creating a Context for Game Theory." In *Toward a History of Game Theory*, edited by E. Roy Weintraub, 29–76. Durham, NC: Duke University Press, 1992.

Levinson, Daryl J. "Parchment and Politics: The Positive Puzzle of Constitutional Commitment." *Harvard Law Review* (2011): 657–746.

Lewis, Richard L., Andrew Howes, and Satinder Singh. "Computational Rationality: Linking Mechanism and Behavior through Bounded Utility Maximization." *Topics in Cognitive Science* 6, no. 2 (2014): 279–311.

Luce, R. Duncan, and Howard Raiffa. *Games and Decisions: Introduction and Critical Survey*. New York: Courier Corporation, 1957.

Markey-Towler, Brendan. "I, Roboticus Oeconomicus: The Philosophy of Mind in Economics, and Why It Matters." *Cambridge Journal of Economics* 41, no. 1 (2017): 203–37.

Mayberry, John P. "The Notion of Threat." In *Models of Gradual Reduction of Arms*, co-authored by Robert J. Aumann, John C. Harsanyi, John P. Mayberry, Michael Maschler, Herbert E. Scarf, Reinhard Selten, and Richard Stearns, 29–46, Washington DC: Arms Control and Disarmament Agency, ACDA/ST-116, 1967.

Maynard Smith, John. *Evolution and the Theory of Games*. Cambridge, UK: Cambridge University Press, 1982.

McCloskey, Deirdre N. *Bourgeois Equality: How Ideas, not Capital or Institutions, Enriched the World*. Chicago, IL: University of Chicago Press, 2016.

Mele, Alfred R. *Motivation and Agency*. Oxford: Oxford University Press, 2003.

Mirowski, Philip. *Machine Dreams: Economics Becomes a Cyborg Science*. Cambridge, UK: Cambridge University Press, 2002.

Moffat, J. *Command and Control in the Information Age: Representing Impact*. London: The Stationary Office, 2002.

———. *Complexity Theory and Network Centric Warfare*. CCRP Publications Series, 2003. http://internationalc2institute.org/ccrp-books/.

Moore, Alfred. "Hayek, Conspiracy, and Democracy." *Critical Review* 28, no 1 (2016): 44–62. DOI: 10.1080/08913811.2016.1167405.

Mueller, Dennis, C. *Public Choice III*. New York: Cambridge University Press, 2003.

Myerson, Roger B. *Game Theory: Analysis of Conflict*. Cambridge, MA: Harvard University Press, 1991.

Nash, John. "Non-cooperative Games." *Annals of Mathematics* (1951): 286–95.

New York Times Editorial Board. "The Finger on the Nuclear Button." *New York Times*. 5 February 2017. https://www.nytimes.com/2017/02/05/opinion/the-finger-on-the-nuclear-button.html?_r=0.

North, Douglass C. *Institutions, Institutional Change and Economic Performance*. Cambridge, UK: Cambridge University Press, 1990.

Nye, Joseph S. *Nuclear Ethics*. New York City: Simon and Schuster, 1988.

Pelopidas, Benoît. "A Bet Portrayed as a Certainty: Reassessing the Added Deterrent Value of Nuclear Weapons." In *The War That Must Never Be Fought: Dilemmas of Nuclear Deterrence*, edited by George P. Shultz, and James E. Goodby, 5–55. Stanford, CA: Hoover Press, 2015.

———. "The Birth of Nuclear Eternity." In *The Future: Interdisciplinary Perspectives*, edited by Jenny Andersson and Sandra Kemp. Oxford: Oxford University Press, forthcoming 2019.

———. "The Oracles of Proliferation: How Experts Maintain a Biased Historical Reading That Limits Policy Innovation." *Nonproliferation Review* 18, no. 1 (2011): 297–314.

———. "The Unbearable Lightness of Luck: Three Sources of Overconfidence in the Manageability of Nuclear Crises." *European Journal of International Security* 2, no. 2 (July 2017): 240–62.

Pettit Philip. "Deliberative Democracy and the Discursive Dilemma." *Noûs* October 2001 (35): 268–99.

———. *Rules, Reasons, and Norms.* Oxford: Clarendon Press, 2002.
Rapoport, Anatol, and Albert M. Chammah. *Prisoner's Dilemma: A Study of Conflict and Cooperation.* Ann Arbor, MI: University of Michigan Press, 1965.
Rawls, John. *Theory of Justice.* Cambridge, MA: Belknap Press, 1970.
Reynolds, Andrew, ed. *The Architecture of Democracy: Constitutional Design, Conflict Management, and Democracy.* Oxford: Oxford University Press, 2002.
Roth, Alvin E. "The Economist as Engineer: Game Theory, Experimentation, and Computation as Tools for Design Economics." *Econometrica* 70, no. 4 (2002): 1341–78.
Runciman, David. "Political Theory and Real Politics in the Age of the Internet." *The Journal of Political Philosophy* 25, no. 1 (2016): 3–21.
Scarry, Elaine. *Thermonuclear Monarchy: Choosing between Democracy and Doom.* New York: W. W. Norton & Company, 2014.
Schelling, Thomas C. *Arms and Influence.* New Haven, CT: Yale University Press, 1966.
———. "The Life You Save May Be Your Own." In *Problems in Public Expenditure Analysis*, edited by Samuel B. Chase, Jr., 127–623. Washington D.C.: Brookings Institution, 1968.
———. "An Astonishing Sixty Years: The Legacy of Hiroshima." *The American Economic Review* 96, no. 4 (2006): 929–37.
———. *Micromotives and Macrobehavior.* New York: W. W. Norton & Company, 2006.
———. *Strategy of Conflict.* Cambridge, MA: Harvard University Press, 1960.
Schweller, Randall L. "Neorealism's Status Quo Bias: What Security Dilemma?" *Security Studies* 5, no. 3 (1996): 90–121.
Scowcroft, Brent. "C3 Systems for the President and Military Commanders." In *National Security Issues 1981 Symposium: Strategic Nuclear Policies, Weapons, and the C3 Connection*, edited by Drexel M. Ace, 93–98. Bedford, MA: Mitre Corporation, Mitre Document M82-30, 1981.
Searle, John R. "Insight and Error in Wittgenstein." *Philosophy of the Social Sciences* 46, no. 6 (2016): 527–47.
———. *Making the Social World: The Structure of Human Civilization.* Oxford: Oxford University Press, 2010.
———. "Minds, Brains and Programs." *Behavioral and Brain Sciences* 3 (1980): 417–57.
———. *Rationality in Action.* Cambridge, MA: MIT Press, 2001.
———. "Wittgenstein and the Background." *American Philosophical Quarterly* 48, no. 2 (2011): 119–28.
Sen, Amartya K. "Goals, Commitment, and Identity." *Journal of Law, Economics and Organization* 1 (1985): 2.
Shetterly, Margot Lee. *Hidden Figures: The Untold Story of the African American Women Who Helped Win the Space Race.* London: Harper Collins UK, 2016.
Shlapak, David A., and Michael Johnson. *Reinforcing Deterrence on NATO's Eastern Flank: Wargaming the Defense of the Baltics.* Santa Monica, CA: RAND Corporation, 2016. https://www.rand.org/pubs/research_reports/RR1253.html.

Shoham, Yoav, and Kevin Leyton-Brown. *Multiagent Systems: Algorithmic, Game-Theoretic, and Logical Foundations*. Cambridge, UK: Cambridge University Press, 2008.

Snidal, Duncan. "The Limits of Hegemonic Stability Theory." *International Organization* 39, no. 4 (1985): 579–614.

Snyder, Glenn H. "'Prisoner's Dilemma' and 'Chicken' Models in International Politics." *International Studies Quarterly* 15, no.1 (1971): 66–103.

Snyder, Jack L. *The Soviet Strategic Culture: Implications for Limited Nuclear Options*. Santa Monica, CA: RAND Corporation, 1977.

Stern, Nicholas Herbert. *The Economics of Climate Change: The Stern Review*. Cambridge, UK: Cambridge University Press, 2007.

Thomas, William. *Rational Action: The Sciences of Policy in Britain and America, 1940–1960*. Cambridge, MA: MIT Press, 2015.

Tononi, Giulio, M. Boly, M. Massimini, and C. Koch. "Integrated Information Theory: From Consciousness to Its Physical Substrate." *Nature Reviews Neuroscience* 17, no. 7 (2016): 450–61.

Trachtenberg, Marc. "Social Scientists and National Security Policymaking." Paper presented at Notre Dame University, 22–23 April 2010. http://www.sscnet.ucla.edu/polisci/faculty/trachtenberg/cv/notre%20dame(2010).pdf.

Trivers, Robert L. "The Evolution of Reciprocal Altruism." *The Quarterly Review of Biology* 46, no. 1 (1971): 35–57.

Tuck, Richard. *Free Riding*. Cambridge, MA: Harvard University Press, 2008.

Tuomela, Raimo. *Social Ontology: Collective Intentionality and Group Agents*. Oxford: Oxford University Press, 2013.

Turing, Alan. "Intelligent Machinery." National Physical Laboratory Report. In *Machine Intelligence 5*, edited by B. Meltzer and D. Michie. Edinburgh: Edinburgh University Press, 1969. Digital facsimile viewable at http://www.AlanTuring.net/intelligent_machinery.

U.S. Department of Defense. *Joint Vision 2020*. Washington, DC, 2000. https://web.archive.org/web/20011129104507/.

Volmar, Daniel. "The Power of the Atom: US Command Control and Communications, 1945–1965." PhD diss., Harvard University, 2017.

von Neumann, John, and Oskar Morgenstern. *Theory of Games and Economic Behavior*. Princeton, NJ: Princeton University Press, 1947.

Wittgenstein, Ludwig. *Philosophical Investigations*. Trans. GEM Anscombe. New York: The Macmillan Company, 1999.

Yann, Chevaleyre, Ulle Endriss, Jérôme Lang, and Nicolas Maudet. "A Short Introduction to Computational Social Choice." *International Conference on Current Trends in Theory and Practice of Computer Science*. Berlin, Heidelberg: Springer, 2007.

Zagare, Frank C. "Classical Deterrence Theory: A Critical Assessment." *International Interactions* 21, no. 4 (1996): 365–87.

Zagare, Frank C., and D. Marc Kilgour. *Perfect Deterrence*. Cambridge, UK: Cambridge University Press, 2000.

 7

THE UNLIKELY REVOLUTIONARIES
Decision Sciences in the Soviet Government
Eglė Rindzevičiūtė

> When a glorious moment arrives
> Do trust yourself no more.
> A changing world, a complex world,
> Yet simple is the model of yours.
> —Oleg Larichev, "Nekotorye problemy metodologii priniatiia unikal'nykh reshenii"

In this chapter, I propose that we need to reassess the development of the Soviet decision sciences after World War II as an important intellectual field where innovative and influential forms of conceptualizing the governance were created.[1] By decision sciences, I refer to different scientific, often quantitative techniques developed in the fields of the operations research, game theory, and systems analysis that offer a cognitive procedure for arriving at a better judgment. Decision sciences are part of a wider field that is often described as "policy sciences" and "management sciences" in Western literature. In the Soviet context, these terms are captured by a Russian notion *nauchnoe upravlenie* (best translated as *scientific governance*, which includes but is not limited to scientific management), an approach that emerged in the early twentieth century, was capitalized on during the communist revolution, cracked down by Stalin in the 1930s–40s to be rehabilitated from the mid 1950s.[2]

Somewhat counterintuitively, the development of Soviet decision sciences was not limited to aiding the Communist Party government to find the most preferable course of action. To the contrary, I show in this chapter that the history of Soviet decision-sciences of the 1960s–80s contains important moments that can be interpreted as reflecting the incremental liberalization of an authoritarian political regime. From the 1960s onward, several influential Soviet decision scientists used decision science to develop a kind of alternative social science, seeking to explain social order and social change and offering a much more complex representation of social processes than could, for instance, Soviet sociologists, restricted by Marxist–Leninist ideological dogmas.[3] Soviet decision scientists used insights from operations research and systems analysis to conceptualize government as a depersonalized process of continuous adaptation to an ever-changing environment. In so doing, Soviet decision scientists addressed many of the Western concerns discussed elsewhere in this volume, including human irrationality and mass participation in government.

Although this story of Soviet decision science is fascinating in itself, there is an important intellectual rationale behind extending our inquiry of modern intellectual technologies of government beyond Western case studies.[4] In order to understand a full range of political implications of decision sciences, it is important to address the transnational dimension of their history. On the one hand, while there is an important intellectual history emerging about the ways in which scientific models of complex order and control spilled over into political imagination, these works tend to focus mainly on the West. The developments in the state socialist bloc are analyzed as either a deviation from or a peculiar adaptation of "Western ideas."[5] On the other hand, many historians traced the conceptual and institutional origins of decision sciences in the West—primarily in the US, Britain, and France—seeking to deconstruct what is understood as a neoliberal governmentality, a governmental regime that relies on the notions of instrumental rationality, responsibilization of the individual, as well as extension of practices of calculation and market regulation to wide areas of social and political life.[6] In this context, decision sciences become a suspect form of scientific expertise, a form that seeks to limit popular participation in politics. However, as I show in my Soviet case, there is also another side of decision science—one that bridges scientific governance and the liberal idea of self-regulation in a way that is not limited to the genealogy of the late twentieth century's neoliberalism.

Thus, I propose that decision sciences, a quantitative technique of governance that tends to be attributed to neoliberal governmentality, have a political history of their own, which should not be reduced to either Cold War technocracy or neoliberal political economy. First, decision sciences are a large, internally heterogeneous field in which different methodologies put different emphasis on predictability, measurability, and uncertainty. Their implications to what is rational, to the notions of individual agency and structure and the character of social order, can therefore differ quite significantly. Second, as I show in this chapter, in different contexts, decision sciences can have different political effects. For instance, some Soviet decision scientists developed a rather liberal model of limited government, a model that in the context of personalist, authoritarian government of the Communist Party should not necessarily be interpreted as a precursor solely to neoliberal regime, but rather a moment in the development of late modern governmentality.

I draw on the Foucaultian governmentality approach to situate the history of Soviet decision sciences in the long evolution of what is described by Foucaultians as the art of government. According to Mitchell Dean, the art of government refers to "an activity which requires craft, imagination, shrewd fashioning, the use of tacit skills and practical know how, the employment of intuition and so on."[7] By using the governmentality perspective, we can begin to understand decision sciences as not only a formal exercise in designing quantitative applications, but also a multifaceted activity that is best approached as an assemblage of conceptual principles, institutions, and reflexive practices. In his series of lectures at the Collège de France, Michel Foucault links the emergence of the art of government with the advent of the modern liberal state, which developed intellectual and disciplinary techniques that enabled governance at a distance, made possible by acknowledging the power of self-regulation to the governed subjects and objects.[8] As I show, in the Soviet context, it was the field of decision sciences that was conducive to a more liberal governmental imagination that underscored the principles of self-regulation, limited central control, and governance at a distance.

This contention needs some clarification though. It is remarkable just how different the liberal effect of decision sciences could be in different political contexts. In order to appreciate this, I propose going beyond the generic criticisms of scientific technocracy. Many histories of the decision scientists' communities emphasize their fascination with and even fetishism of numbers, precision, determinism, and computer technology. However, there were other decision scientists who were less concerned with deterministic, technical solutions, instead focusing on problem making rather than solving. But this latter strand of decision sciences so far has received much less attention from historians. This becomes particularly clear when we consider the emerging concern with governing global biosphere both in East and West from the late 1960s. This concern drew on the ideas emerging across different disciplines, such as the traditional liberal idea of self-regulation in the political thought but also its siblings in the theories of biological systems and ecology, the emerging organization theory of bounded rationality in human decision-making developed by Herbert Simon, and the mathematical models of nonlinear dynamics developed in the complex systems sciences. Recent studies began to disentangle the genealogy of self-regulation under uncertainty: examples can be found in the recent work by Stephen Collier and Andrew Lakoff on the history of government of vital systems; Helga Nowotny's and Louise Amoore's work on reflexive, prediction-based governance and uncertainty; my own study on the global application of the systems approach; while others outlined genealogies of resilience.[9] In a similar vein, in this chapter, I show that according to Soviet decision scientists, to govern a complex system—and Soviet society was increasingly understood as a complex system that included human and nonhuman actors—meant to rely on qualitative methods and postpositivist epistemology abandoning the utopia of linear planning. Furthermore, there were strands of Soviet decision science that transcended the laboratory approach, according to which scientists delivered their ready-made models to policy makers. Instead, some Soviet scientists cultivated a study of decision as a reflexive social science, an art of participatory government, hoping that this would enable breaking the Party's and the bureaucratic monopoly on decision-making. It is precisely this thrust of Soviet decision science to which I want to draw attention as it constitutes an important correction in the existing debates on scientific technocracy as trajectory that leads to a nondemocratic regime of governance.[10]

This chapter is organized as following. First, I map the transnational development of decision sciences during the postwar period in order to demonstrate the parallels of the origins, spread, and institutionalization of decision sciences in both the East and West. In the 1940s, decision sciences were developed in both the Soviet and US military-industrial complexes, formed an important part of Cold War competition, and later spilled over into the civilian realm. In the Soviet Union, this spillover coincided with de-Stalinization: the abolishment of the personality cult of the leader, which led to a period characterized by the softening of internal ideological control and the reestablishment of connections with the West. Next, I trace this shift by describing the institutionalization of Soviet operations research (OR) and systems analysis during the post-Stalinist period of the 1950s–70s. The Soviet decision sciences were practiced not only by academics—decision sciences were introduced into the policy process after 1964 as part and parcel of the attempt to increase the scientific level of national planning, an initiative that was led by the Prime Minister Aleksei Kosygin.[11] Finally, I close the chapter with a discussion of an important contribution to the Soviet decision sciences: the writings and institutional entrepreneurship of the prominent Russian mathematician Nikita N. Moiseev, who promoted the fields of OR and computer-based modeling of the geophysical system, most famously in the case of the simulation of environmental effects of nuclear war in 1983–85. The case of Moiseev speaks volumes about both the institutional structure of Soviet science, which harbored islands of permissibility for maverick ideas, but also the internationalization of Soviet governmental thought where new notions of government and control were pursued in cooperation with Western counterparts.

Revisiting the History of Soviet Governance

Before we proceed, several important implications of my argument for Soviet history must be addressed. Studies of Soviet governance have been traditionally divided into two approaches. One approach concentrated on the role of dictatorial, personalized decision-making in the social system, focusing on the leaders of the Communist Party of the Soviet Union (CPSU) and the nomenclature, as scholars regarded them as the key governmental actors. Known originally as "Kremlinology," this approach was enriched by institutionalists in the 1990s who remained interested in the role of personalities, power struggles among individual Soviet actors and their coalitions.[12] Other scholars who emerged as early as in the 1970s, collectively comprising the so-called "modernization school," focused on lower-level actors, such as regional leaders, managers, and scientific experts, and dedicated themselves to investigating whether a new Soviet technocratic class capable of challenging the hegemony of the Party was emerging.[13] Both of these approaches emphasized the importance of personalities in political and organizational contexts, seeking to identify the "real" decision-makers in a given situation and assess their significance and impact in the future. This epistemological orientation left policy sciences, which I call the arts of governance, outside the scope of Soviet historiography. The history of Soviet science and technology, albeit well-developed, never made it into the mainstream political history of the Soviet regime. While historians and political scientists examined the strategic uses of Marxist-Leninist ideology in the framing of governmental programs and decisions, the complex role played by decision sciences in Soviet governance was completely left out. Even with the rising interest in Cold War technocracies in East and West but also the global South, the internal intellectual, institutional, and political diversity of the field of Soviet decision science has hardly ever been seriously considered as a defining feature of late Soviet governmentality.[14]

Therefore, to admit that the Soviet policy sciences were not hostage to communist ideology, but in fact represented relatively autonomous intellectual resource for heterogeneous notions of order and control, as I do here, is to question some of the central established narratives in Soviet history. My approach is close to those scholars, such as Stephen Collier, who have emphasized the complexity of Soviet governmentality, where power and control did not flow in a top-down, linear way, but was rather diffused, where expert knowledge and material infrastructure could shape and constrain the scope of the activity of the Party elites.[15] Indeed, a growing body of recent literature on Soviet governance has documented persistent discrepancies between the supposed prevalence of centralized planning and the actual use, or lack thereof, of scientific expertise and local management practices. We now know, for example, that the annual and five-year plans were not "decided" by the CPSU leadership, but rather settled through an informal bargaining process between the All-Union State Planning Committee (Gosplan) and representatives of branch ministries and industry enterprises.[16] Accordingly, while some prominent computer scientists, such as Viktor Glushkov—who initiated a technoutopian attempt to centralize and computerize information processing in this defunct Soviet system through OGAS, an All-Union Automation System—failed to formalize the Soviet institutions, other Soviet experts of decision-making commanded an increasing authority from the 1980s.[17] While I described such cases in the fields of regional and global modeling and strategic management in Soviet Russia, here I develop further my argument by demonstrating the way in which Soviet decision sciences were constructed as a critical social thought.[18]

Furthermore, to focus on political implications of decision sciences means to use a particular notion of power. There is a tendency among Soviet historians to study the relation between scientists, experts, and governing communist political elites as an unfolding conflict, a zero-sum power game. Consider, for example, the many studies of scientific autonomy in such fields as physics or mathematical economics, which posit that this autonomy was only achieved at the cost of a "real," demonstrable influence on actual governmental decisions.[19] In turn, increasing authority and power over decision-making of scientists was interpreted as the loss of power of the Party's governing elites. Consider the fate of Soviet cybernetics. From the 1960s, according to Slava Gerovitch, the principles of cybernetic theory of predictive control were used to reconceptualize Soviet policy frameworks as an informational process of goal-setting and control through feedback loops. Cybernetics was officially acclaimed as *the* Soviet science of governance. However, cybernetics failed to structurally reform Soviet policy: a severe shortage of computer technology prevented automation.[20] Furthermore, the widespread practice of informal bargaining and economy of favors that thrived in Soviet ministries and enterprises was not conducive to any form of increased transparency and accountability.[21] Managers resisted cybernetic automation of systems of communication and accounting, because it was perceived as a risk of revealing their illicit activities.[22] If we were to apply this assumption on decision scientists, we would arrive at a similar conclusion: that decision sciences failed to undermine the personalist decision-making practice in the Soviet Union.

Nonetheless, it would be a mistake to interpret the incomplete cybernetization of the Soviet economy as a zero-sum game, thus as a failure. As I have argued elsewhere, Soviet cybernetics enabled the formation of a new normative understanding of what entails good, modern government. From the mid 1970s, conceptualizing governance in the Soviet Union meant referring to cybernetic principles of an adaptive self-regulation through feedback loops through administration of enterprise, national and global policy systems, and emerging new practices of personnel management as an interactive social process.[23] In this cybernetic governmental imagination, there was an intellectual and institutional place for decision sciences, which coexisted with the personalist world of decision-making, scrutinized by Kremlinologists.

We need to rediscover the intellectual history of the interdisciplinary field of Soviet decision science and understand the role of decision scientists, as they have been a rather neglected type of the Soviet governmental actor. In doing this, I propose that we can reconstruct the history of internal liberalization of Soviet governmental system, where decision science was used as a resource to limit the personalist but also institutional power of the Communist Party governing elites. It was through Soviet decision science that social, environmental, and system-cybernetic control systems were brought together to form a new constellation of power and rationality beyond ideology, patronage, and economy of favors; importantly, this process took place through an intense East-West circulation of people, technologies, and ideas. Conceived in this way, the Soviet case should be approached as an integral part of the transnational development of modern scientific governance.

Transnational Development of Postwar Decision Sciences: East-West

Existing literature outlines the history of decision sciences as a principally Western phenomenon, with its roots in the major military conflict: it is widely documented that operations research and systems analysis emerged from the military engineering, economic planning, and operations planning during World War II, while during the Cold War, American and European scientists applied their newly acquired expertise to aid decisions beyond military planning and strategy, turning to civil sectors of social and economic governance.[24] Historians, such as Philip Mirowski, David Jardini, and S. M. Amadae, have argued that decision sciences can be understood as an intellectual technology, instrumental in the struggle for world domination. As such, they assert, decision sciences were part of modern governmentality in the sense that they underscored the use of science in areas that previously relied on political and bureaucratic authority.[25] The political context for the rise of decision expertise, as suggested in the introduction to this volume, was crucial, because scientists and policy makers expected that decision sciences would serve as an antidote to a volatile, personalist decision-making, a structure of judgment associated with authoritarian dictatorships such as Nazi Germany and the Soviet Union.[26] It is important to note that the distinction between what was understood as an uninformed and personalist decision-making and scientific, disembodied decision-making was considered on both sides of the Iron Curtain. Indeed, the rise of Soviet decision sciences could also be understood as a response to informal, personalist decision-making and an attempt to limit this practice by ensuring participation of scientific experts in policy process.

The histories of the US cybernetics traced its particular career from the construction of automated weapon systems during the 1940s, such as antiaircraft missile systems that relied on computational processes to identify and attack targets, to the source of inspiration for attempts to fully automate decision-making in business, economic, and social planning. If automated servomechanisms could track and shoot a plane, perhaps a computer system could steer a factory, an industry, or even a national economy. Although the pioneers of cybernetics, particularly Norbert Wiener, were strictly against the use of cybernetic theory in social forecasting, the idea of information loops enabling surveillance and feedback-based control nonetheless spread throughout the disciplines and was reflected in the theories of political and social systems developed by Marshall McLuhan, Karl Deutsch, and David Easton, among others.[27] In comparison with the US, the extension of the Soviet cybernetics to automation of decisions in the wide societal sectors was also a complex technopolitical project, where multiple rationales intertwined.

The postwar development of East-West relations in the area of decision sciences can be divided into the following two stages: the height of the Cold War during the last seven years of Stalin's rule (1946–53) and the subsequent incremental reestablishment of contacts with the West and East-West technology transfers that were incrementally resumed after 1956.[28] Under Stalin, research on the military and technical applications of decision sciences was strictly limited to defense and technical applications and was conducted in complete secrecy.[29] Geopolitical tensions between the Soviet Union and United States pushed even the home-grown Soviet decision sciences into isolation: in 1946 Chairman of the Supreme Council Andrei Zhdanov banned any contacts with Western technoscience as part of the campaign against kowtowing to the West. Over the next five years, several major fields of scientific innovation, such as genetics, cybernetics, and relativity theory, were designated as pseudosciences and purged from Soviet academia. Nonetheless, as Gerovitch demonstrated, even under Stalin, the Soviet government realized that computer science was vital for defense: the engineering of large technical systems in defense and aviation just could not do without cybernetic automation. Accordingly, computer science was insulated from these ideological attacks; but then, computer technology was strictly classified in the Soviet Union until the mid 1950s.[30] Similarly, the early Soviet version of OR was developed in secret, experimental construction bureaus within the military-industrial complex.

The late 1950s and early 1960s were defined by intense Soviet efforts to establish international cooperation in the field of decision sciences. It was only after the death of Stalin in 1953 and Khrushchev's rejection of Stalin's personality cult in 1956 that the Soviet decision sciences would emerge into the daylight. The process of de-Stalinization resulted in manifold decision scientists returning from the secret science towns in which they had been sequestered to Moscow and other major cities in order to found new laboratories and institutes. The key turning point occurred in 1955, when the leading defense scientists and mathematicians Anatolii Kitov, Sergei Korolev, and Aleksei Liapunov published an article defending cybernetics as a genuine science, which, they proclaimed, had nothing to do with capitalist ideology.[31] The following decade saw the rapid development of Soviet research into computer technology and cybernetics, which were now praised in the press and policy programs as effective ways to modernize economic and social planning, management, and industrial production. Decision sciences became an integral part of an envisioned cybernetic future of communism.

With the exception of the ideological disputes that occurred between the end of World War II and Stalin's death, the trajectory of the Soviet decision sciences resembled the Western one. Mathematical methods—including OR and systems analysis, linear and nonlinear planning, and theories of optimal control and dynamic programming—were first transferred from the military-industrial complex to the realm of economic planning and management and, concomitantly, to the social sciences, which in the 1960s were still new disciplines in the Soviet Union.[32] The spread of decision sciences tapped into the modern belief, shared in both the East and West, in scientific rationalization and was assisted by international organizations, like the Organization for Economic Cooperation and Development, which disseminated the approach internationally from the early 1960s onward.[33] By that time, however, Soviet research policy elites had been learning from and interacting with leading Western institutions promoting the development of decision sciences.

As they were in the West, in the Soviet Union, decision sciences were expected to draw boundaries for personalist, dictatorial decisionism by creating a particular informational context and institutional legitimacy, defining what is a good decision. The institutional foundation for the Soviet decision sciences was established during the era of Nikita Khrushchev's leadership (1953–64), which was defined by a style of governance popularly and—ironically—known as "voluntarism," in which Khrushchev overrode expert suggestions, ruthlessly imposing what was described as his own "hare-brain schemes," such as corn planting campaigns across all climate zones in the Soviet Union.[34] However, as I have argued elsewhere, there were other actors in addition to Khrushchev who were centrally important to the development of late Soviet governmentality. One such key person was Khrushchev's minister and, later, prime minister, Aleksei Kosygin, a capable administrator who was crucially important for reintroducing scientific experts into economic planning and reestablishing East-West cooperation in the late 1950s.[35] When Khrushchev was ousted in 1964 to be replaced with Brezhnev, Kosygin acquired the central role in the Soviet policymaking. Decision sciences in particular were supported by Kosygin's son-in-law, Dzhermen Gvishiani, who served as a vice-chairman of the State Committee for Science and Technology (GKNT), the principal body in charge of the all-union policy of technoscientific development and East-West transfer. Gvishiani personally promoted management science and the emerging systems approach, having authored some of the first books on the subject in the Soviet Union.[36] It was under the leadership of Kosygin and Gvishiani in the 1960s–70s that Soviet decision science emerged as an academic field of applied and fundamental research, was institutionalized, and was used for East-West transfers of knowledge.

The Institutionalization of Soviet Decision Sciences

In the late 1950s and early 1960s, a wide array of different scientific approaches, developed to aid management and policy making, came to be publicly promoted and institutionalized in the Soviet Union. These approaches included cybernetics, linear and nonlinear planning, input-output modeling, OR, scientific forecasting, and what would become known as the systems approach. Sometimes these techniques were gathered under the umbrella of cybernetics, and sometimes they were promoted as "mathematical methods" of governance. Starting in 1957, the Soviet press presented computers as a new technology able to speed up decisions and, from 1960, widely promoted the automation of management, describing the national economy as an informational system.[37] Although, in reality, Soviet firms were severely underequipped with computer technology, a strong expectation of a computerized future was widely shared throughout the Soviet Union by the mid 1960s.[38]

The first Soviet research unit dedicated to OR and game theory was founded in 1961 at the Leningrad branch of the Soviet Academy of Sciences.[39] The laboratory had a high profile and was visited by prominent Western scientists, including Oscar Morgenstern, one of the fathers of game theory, who visited the unit in 1963.[40] East-West scientific exchanges had resumed in the late 1950s. In 1960, Norbert Wiener visited Moscow and gave a talk to an overcrowded auditorium; meanwhile, Soviet mathematicians, including the influential Vadim Trapeznikov, the director of the prestigious Institute of Automatics and Telemechanics, travelled to the US, returning deeply convinced of the need to apply OR and management science techniques to problems of governance.[41] In the same year, Vassily

Nemchinov, Leonid Kantorovich, and Andrei Kolmogorov pushed for introduction of mathematical modeling into economics and planning.[42] A fully-fledged network of Soviet OR institutes was initiated in 1964 when defense intellectuals E. Popov and Germogen S. Pospelov facilitated the establishment of OR as a research area in three major institutions: the Computer Centre in Moscow, the Mathematical Institute at Novosibirsk branch of the Academy of Sciences, and the Institute of Cybernetics in Kiyv, Ukraine.

Within the next few years, OR was institutionalized in the republic branches of the Soviet Academy of Sciences where OR was usually placed in computer science departments. Soviet universities also introduced OR into their curricula, while brochures, such as Georgii Smolian's *Operations Research: An Instrument of Effective Governance*, were published and disseminated widely by the main agency for the popularization of science, *Znanie* (knowledge). As Smolian's text shows, the Soviet scientific leadership identified OR with the optimization of decisions through quantitative methods—such as game theory—ideally using computer technology.[43] By the late 1960s, OR was entrenched in the Soviet academic system, and during the next decade, systems analysis would follow suit.

The institutionalization of OR and systems analysis was part of a larger governmental reform to launch national planning of infrastructure and research and development on a large scale. In 1966, the same scientists who institutionalized OR, Glushkov and Pospelov, proposed to introduce a complex forecasting of the Soviet economy and technoscientific progress for a five to ten year period into the state planning process. According to Dmitrii Efremenko, this proposal would have substantially increased the political role of scientific experts in the strategic decision-making. However, although the proposal was supported by Kosygin and Dmitrii Ustinov, who was in charge of the military industrial complex and who later became the minister of defense, it was turned down by the Politburo.[44] Yet, OR and systems analysis, and in particular the work on optimization, following Wassily Leontief, Leonid Kantorovich, and Vasily Nemchinov would later be used for the development of the complex planning program of technoscientific progress for 1980–2000, a giant document specifying national goals for the medium- and long-term with regards to the entire Soviet economy, including science, which was drafted over the 1970s.[45]

The use of decision sciences in economic planning had ambivalent consequences. As we will see, some pioneering scientists, such as Moiseev, became deeply disillusioned about the prospects of using these techniques to rationalize economic and social planning. Instead, they saw environmental governance as a more promising area of application for decision sciences. This environmental turn in Soviet system-cybernetic governmentality has so far escaped the attention of historians of Soviet economics, for these new developments took place not so much in the economics institutes, but in the institutes involved in computer modeling of large, complex systems, which were home to the scientists who employed home OR and systems analysis.[46]

While the 1950s–60s saw the rise of OR and game theory, the period beginning with the late 1960s and the 1970s was characterized by the advance of what was called "the systems approach" (in Russian, *sistemnyi podkhod*).[47] Like their Western counterparts, Soviet scientists developed a systemic approach to economic, industrial, environmental, and social analysis as an antidote to bureaucratic fragmentation and narrow-minded "technocratic" decision-making. The epistemology of the systems approach had both institutional and intellectual implications. First, the data and models of different industry branches, such as electric energy, mining, and machine building had to be integrated, because no single industry branch could be planned optimally in isolation from other branches: the expansion of an electric grid depended on the future factory siting, the construction of which had to take into consideration consumption and international trade forecasts. Second, system-based decision-making required a historical and long-term view. Fast changes in technoscientific and social development required an ever-greater capacity of prediction, but reliable prediction could only be made on the basis of extensive data sets about the past.[48] In practice, systems epistemology underpinned Soviet decision scientists' quest for increasing data transparency: scholars demanded wider access to different types of data, arguing that the sharing of data across disciplines, institutes, and governmental agencies was the only way to produce reliable scientific expertise. Thus, predictive epistemology forcefully introduced a new normative understanding of what constituted good governance, positing a need for new institutions capable of gathering and disseminating data not only within the Soviet Union, but also globally, exchanging the data with the West and developing countries.[49]

Both the Soviet and US cases of introducing decision science into policy process point to a symbiotic relation between OR and the systems approach, though the intertwining of these fields in the Soviet Union has a history of its own. It is important to consider this prehistory of the Soviet decision science in order to fully appreciate the political legitimacy of this field in the Soviet context (which remained wary of kowtowing before the West), because it explains the Soviet decision scientists' fervor and the strength of the feeling of a mission, which went beyond purely scientific inquiry. In the Soviet Union, the systems approach was rooted in local philosophical traditions, serving as a social glue for scientific communities. Soviet systems scholars were able to draw on the local legacy of systems thinking, which extended beyond Anglo-American OR to include interwar thought on geophysical, biological, and organizational systems.[50] It is remarkable that in some cases, Soviet systems thinkers saw the roots of their approach even in the nineteenth-century mystical tradition of Russian cosmism, a philosophical approach that sought to unite spirituality, human culture, and geophysical planetary system into one eschatological worldview.[51] In the context of policy sciences, the most influential thinker was Vladimir Vernadskii, whose ideas about the integration and even systemic unity of geophysical systems of space, Earth, and human society would become extremely influential in Soviet debates about the global biosphere in the 1970s and beyond. Another key thinker was Aleksandr Bogdanov (Malinovskii), whose grand, albeit cumbersome, theory of *tektology* was invoked by postwar Russian scientists as a genuinely home-grown, Russian theory of organization.[52]

It is important to notice that the key difference between inter- and postwar systems thinking was that, beginning in the 1960s, Soviet systems thinking fed directly into the policy sciences: a new normativity was coming into being, according to which one could not possibly make good decisions without considering complex systemic effects. While the Soviet OR field legitimized the introduction of mathematical methods into economic and social science, previously dominated by Marxism-Leninism, the systems approach posited a more complex view of governmental spheres where mathematical methods could be applied. The systems approach, in general, was a balancing act between philosophical theorizing and applied science. As a result, there was no single, homogenous Soviet school in systems thinking; rather, divergent attitudes to systems research prevailed. First, prominent systems philosophers such as Igor' Blauberg, Erik Iudin, and Vadim Sadovskii were predominantly interested in the development of General Systems Theory and what they called a more descriptive, empirical theory of systems. Others, such as Stanislav Emel'ianov, Iurii Popkov, and Viktor Gelovani, shared a background in OR and electronic engineering and were concerned with concrete applications of systems theory to scientific research, governmental problems, and computer-based modeling. Finally, some scholars, such as Boris Mil'ner, pursued the economic application of the systems approach.[53]

Systems analysis was institutionalized in the Soviet Union in response to what was perceived by scientists and policy makers as an emerging complex system: large scale infrastructure for oil and gas, industrial complexes such as nuclear power and chemical plants, but also large urban systems, as well as environmental projects, such as forestry, fisheries, and agriculture.[54] Now, the issues that emerged in all these very different sectors were understood as largely apolitical and, as such, suitable for international cooperation over the search for efficient solutions. It was to address all these complexities that new institutional frameworks for the production, processing, and analysis of data, and particularly its use for forecasting the future, were developed. Participation in international cooperation was of paramount importance in all areas of Soviet science and technology, and decision science was no exception. Convinced that the planning of Soviet systems had to benefit from computer-assisted decision-making, the Soviet government continuously sought to import both technology and know-how from large Western, mainly US, corporations.[55] The central actor in this process was the State Committee for Science and Technology (GKNT), whose directors regularly met with Western CEOs to learn about their experiences with decision-enhancement technologies. The first Soviet institutions dedicated to the systems approach appeared in the early 1970s, when the Committee for Systems Analysis was established at the Council of the Academy of Sciences, though the activities of this committee were limited to the circulation of information.[56] It was not until 1976 that the main center for systems analysis, the All-Union Institute for Systems Research (VNIISI), was established in Moscow. The VNIISI attracted scientists from some of the leading research organizations in the Soviet Union, such as the GKNT's institute and the Institute of Control Sciences.

Decision sciences also served as a channel for Cold War diplomacy. Beginning in the 1960s, the GKNT regarded the OR-based, quantitative systems approach as a strategically important field in East-West transfer. One of the key principles of nuclear or, indeed, any military strategy, is to ensure that one's opponent used the same forms of thought so that one is able to communicate with and respond predictably to an adversary.[57] This was made clear when, in 1966, Lyndon B. Johnson suggested to Kosygin that the United States and the Soviet Union establish an East-West think tank. It was American and Soviet decision scientists who were charged with realizing this diplomatic initiative. As a result, the International Institute of Applied Systems Analysis (IIASA) was established in Laxenburg, Austria, in 1972. Over the course of the 1970s, the IIASA became an important transnational space that brought together American and Soviet scholars in management science. In addition, Soviet scientists had regular contacts with the Cowles Foundation, MIT's Sloane School of Management, Stanford's Graduate School of Business, and Harvard Business School.[58] However, the internationalization of the Soviet decision sciences did not only proceed through Russian-directed organizations; scientists at the level of the satellite republics also actively sought East-West contacts. For instance, in Lithuania, an OR laboratory directed by Eduardas Vilkas, who specialized in game theory, econometrics, and decision science, was founded in 1967. Trained in Leningrad under Nikolai Vorob'ev, Vilkas spent four months as a visiting scientist at American universities, including the Cowles Foundation at Yale in 1976.[59] Such lengthy stays were common in fields associated with decision sciences, systems approach, and computing, and were crucial nodes for establishing informal ties that contributed to the transfer of knowledge. In this way, as I argue at length elsewhere, policy sciences were conducive to the emerging sociality and ethos of responsibility for global problems among the leading scholars from East and West.[60]

Here, the application of decision sciences to planning problems, including the regional and global environmental systems, turned out to be the most conducive area for East-West collaboration. A particularly important channel for East-West exchanges was UNESCO's program, *Man and Biosphere*, which was launched in 1971 to gather the scientific data about the multiple impacts on the environment. Soviet membership in this program was encouraged by environmental scientists, such as soil expert Viktor Kovda, who was a close friend of the research director of the Computer Centre, Nikita Moiseev. Now, Moiseev quickly realized that by participating in *Man and Biosphere*, Soviet scientists could lobby for an integration of environmental science with computer modeling. From the mid 1960s, Moiseev developed OR applications for participatory decision-making intended to combat the de facto existing fragmentation in the centralized planning.[61] But later, Moiseev became convinced about the need to change the entire conceptual apparatus of control. It is on this emerging thinking that I focus in the last section of this chapter.

Self-Regulation and Pluralistic Decisions in Soviet Systems Thinking

Perhaps the most prominent example of Soviet OR and systems thinking is found in the writings and institutional entrepreneurship of

Nikita Moiseev, a distinguished scientist who has left a deep legacy in the Russian science and intellectual culture, but has been overlooked in Western histories of science and technology. A mathematician by training, Moiseev was the long-standing vice-director for research of the Computer Centre at the All-Union Academy of Science and a patron of the Soviet OR community (a role reflected in his appointment as the honorary president of the first Russian OR Society, established in Moscow in 1996). Furthermore, Moiseev was a public figure and a prolific writer who extended the systems approach to what can be described as a philosophy of governance.

Moiseev's career was defined by a sustained effort to, first, foster the development of decision sciences in the Soviet academia and, second, encourage their internationalization. In 1966, Moiseev established an OR laboratory at the Computer Centre and appointed a young and distinguished military scientist, and his former university roommate, Iurii Germeier as the director. Starting in the 1970s, Moiseev initiated and developed one of the foremost computer laboratories at the Computer Centre, where the first three-dimensional computer model of the Earth system was created in the Soviet Union (this model contained subsystems reflexing land, atmosphere, and the ocean). However, due to space limitations, this section can only discuss Moiseev's writings about the role of decision sciences in what he described as a changing, increasingly complex world that posed unprecedented challenges—such as the exhaustion of natural resources, world population growth, and pollution—to the government. In contrast to narrow-minded Soviet technocrats who resorted to ill-conceived scientific schemes of rationalization that often caused human and environmental harm, Moiseev represented a rare, but influential, voice, championing uncertainty and complexity in the landscape of Soviet scientific expertise.

In his 1970 book *Mathematics, Government and Economics*, which was translated into German in 1973, Moiseev argued that decision sciences could not offer simple solutions to governmental problems. This was because decision sciences—which addressed real world concerns—could not be shut off in a sterile laboratory environment, but must instead engage with social practices and institutional design. Decision sciences, he continued, were just as much about problem making as problem solving. Here, Moiseev clearly posited decision sciences as a formative, productive governmental activity and not a mere aid, a devise for calculation and rationalization of political decision of the Party leaders. According to Moiseev, the first issue for decision sciences to consider was goal-setting, because defining what constitutes a desirable outcome was difficult to do in a policy and management context. Marrying theory and practice was another challenge, as finding an optimal solution to a problem did not mean solving it. The implementation of optimal planning required a well-functioning system of coordination, involving the effective feedback of information and clearly established decision procedures.[62] Optimal decision-making could not merely be imposed on chaotic, unregulated practices, such as, for instance, competing enterprises or inefficient management, but required wider institutional and management reform. Decision sciences were but one functional component in the government of large systems—at the national and world level.

From the 1960s, the mainstream Soviet decision sciences were legitimized by the strong hope that their economic applications would save the stalling economic growth. Soviet decision theorists argued that the Soviet government could uniquely benefit from computer-assisted decision systems, as these were most appropriate in large organizations: only in large-scale economies could the automation of decisions enable the economization of resources.[63] However, Moiseev recognized that even these economic planning-centered decisions could not be built "from simple blocks onto a complex whole," but instead required grasping complex reality, something which could only be achieved through interdisciplinary cooperation among economists, management theorists, mathematicians, and sociologists.[64] In this way, decision sciences, at least theoretically, were far from a detached intellectual technology, but were an integral component, if not a driving force, of social and organizational change.

An important part of decision sciences, particularly computer-based modeling, posited an epistemological connection between theoretical political economy and the practice of planning, in which the latter could challenge theoretical dogmas even in the Soviet Union. Hardly any Soviet scholar could get away with positing the superiority of computer-assisted decision sciences without making obligatory references to Marxism: even Moiseev wrote that Marx's model of production and consumption was "the first macroeconomic model" ever (although they hardly ever attributed much intellectual significance to these references, considering them a mere rhetoric convention).[65] Nonetheless, Moiseev went so far as to dismiss Marx's model as outdated and irrelevant to decision sciences:

> Karl Marx's model was created to study a specific process under specific conditions. ... Accordingly, it can not be used to study those processes, which are defined by different conditions. For example, Karl Marx's model cannot answer a question how to distribute investment in order

to achieve a certain level of consumption. As we have pointed out earlier, Karl Marx's model does not include governance: [for Marx] the initial state singularly determines all outcomes.[66]

Meanwhile, wrote Moiseev, "Contemporary macroeconomic models seek to study precisely the impact of 'governing' factors on the flow of economic processes."[67] Moiseev is very clear here, stating, "Highly aggregated models, such as Karl Marx's, cannot be used directly in planning" (he does add, then, that highly aggregated models can still be of practical use for very long-term planning).[68] Now, what is left after Marxist political economy is deemed insufficient? Moiseev proposes to bridge the gap between Marxist political economy and everyday decisions that are made by the Gosplan by the policy sciences: sophisticated modeling, offering aggregate models to enable long-term forecasting as they reveal general trends, while multi-branch models helped to shape the plan indicators of the economic development.[69]

Furthermore, because computer modeling was conceptually anchored in systems theory, it became possible for Moiseev to legitimately introduce the ideas of autonomy and heterogeneous purposive behavior in the models of Soviet society. For Moiseev, Soviet society was a system comprised of many different and autonomous decision makers, which social planning theories had to take into consideration. For instance, Moiseev wrote: "the economic organism of any state consists of a whole [set] of smaller economic organisms, which are to lesser or greater extent autonomous and are interlinked with each other into a complex hierarchical system of relations. Every element in this whole has both a certain will (ability to make decisions) and certain individual interests (goals)."[70] It is therefore only logical, Moiseev continued, that "society seeks to achieve multiple goals. These goals are not only incomparable, but they are also changing, because our society does not live in a thermostat, but on the Earth, where the conditions for life are not stable. The situations which emerge and influence life activities very often are not only out of [humans'] control, but also unpredictable."[71] Although Moiseev himself does not specify the political implications of his epistemological argument, this quote hints at his opinion that the existing practice of the Party ideological leadership in the setting of goals for long-term future and centralized planning are inconsistent with the basic organization of human society. Perhaps unwilling to push the boundaries too far, Moiseev restricted his argument to the criticism of the complete automation of decision-making. According to Moiseev, to delegate all decisions to a computer was impossible, partially because real time information processing could never be achieved: thus even a decision-making computer would never be able to "run with the system." But more importantly, Moiseev claimed that a viable system required what he called "a degree of freedom." A complex social system was not the sum of its parts, but rather a complex interaction, the complexity of which could never be known because it was changing continuously and, ultimately, chaotically. The only reasonable way for a decision-maker to deal with complexity, posited Moiseev, was to recognize that subsystems required autonomy for their activities, autonomy being a necessary condition for the emergence of "collective wisdom and collective energy" of the system as a whole.[72]

Moiseev's work suggests that, by the year 1970, Soviet decision scientists fundamentally transformed the Stalinist model of personalized governance. Governance was no longer understood as a personalized system where the leader or the Party gave direct orders to society. According to the point of view of decision science, the Soviet leadership could only function if it made use of proxies of scientific expertise. Economic planners required highly complex representations of the economy, multilevel models produced by scientific experts. Social planners had to consider society's view on the developmental goals set by the CPSU, but the social sciences and the humanities were needed to make sense of these views.[73] Did this scientific epistemology threaten the Party's monopoly over power? Moiseev made certain to avoid creating this impression: he cautioned that the scientific formulation of alternative decisions and their evaluation were merely "advisory," while only those "responsible for the country" could make the "final decisions."[74] Nevertheless, in spite of the subordinate role Moissev posited for scientific expertise, being both conceptual and institutional, this proxy of modeling became an increasingly significant field, nurturing ideas, practices, and actors that transformed Soviet governance.

While we need further studies on the impact of OR and systems analysis on Soviet economic and social planning, Moiseev's work suggests that the Soviet landscape of economic governance was highly polarized. Some scientists promoted mathematical applications as technical fixes for economic problems, while others doubted simple mathematical models could address such issues. Moiseev was one of the skeptics. As early as in 1970, he called into question the very idea that there could be an optimal planning of the national economy, writing that it was not possible to discern the optimal course of the Soviet economy because economies were relational and models of the world economy were not yet available.[75] Moiseev asserted that Soviet econometricians disregarded the fact that the notion of optimum is a fundamentally relational notion. It is only possible to establish an optimal value in one sector, such as machine production, while systematically considering the other values that emerge as a result of processes in related sectors, such as markets, energy, and natural resources. It is impossible to establish an optimal value in a subsystem of the economy without having a model of the whole national economy and, moreover, a model of the world economy. Pointing out this complexity, Moiseev did not argue against the idea of optimal planning as such, but rather called for conceptual consistency. An important implication of striving for such a conceptual consistency was a step toward a more integrated, relational, but at the same time more open vision of a firm, a region, and, finally, the entire Soviet Union.

However, when the first econometric models of the world economy were introduced in the 1970s, Moiseev continued to doubt if the Soviet government could benefit from this type of decision aid. In 1980, in his confidential letter to Dzhermen Gvishiani, the vice-chairman of GKNT, Moiseev could not be more blunt: "I think that the use of econometric methods for the evaluation of more or less long term evolution of economic situation is not particularly promising. Indeed, econometrics offers only a snapshot of a given situation. Accordingly, any extrapolation that is based on them, can only be more or less reliable in relatively short term, a quarter or one year."[76] To sum up, Soviet decision science posited the reality of multiple decision makers and the impossibility of decision-making in an institutionally fragmented context where data was not shared across sectors, countries, and time periods.

Conclusion

The Soviet decision sciences were much more than a Party instrument, being developed and promoted as an alternative social theory of order and change. Their development had important political and governmental implications. The very purpose of OR was to replace the everyday, ideological language used in government decision-making with a mathematical language and models that could be used to describe governmental problems and formulate solutions.[77] Whereas in the West, scientificization of governmental discourses was criticized as a problematic limitation of the possibility for nonspecialists to participate in decision-making, in the Soviet Union, the same process had an important, and potentially democratizing, side effect. Mathematical language of governance implicitly constrained the CPSU's capacity to make decisions single-handedly. Intermediaries—policy scientists—were required to step in. Accordingly, these intermediaries became increasingly aware of the importance of reflexive forms of scientific rationalization of governmental practices. Soviet decision sciences required social organization, enlightenment, and cooperation among different disciplinary actors, scientific and political elites. In the authoritarian context, this was a liberalizing revolution, albeit a quiet one; one that spoke in formulas and not ideological slogans and that developed in informal circles of scientific elites and not in public squares.

Similarly to the United States, the governmental revolution of Soviet decision sciences produced its avant-garde and rear-garde. Not all systems scientists were inclined to view the world as a reflexive, adaptive system; they sought instead safety in the authority of technoutopia: computers, mathematical models, and formal theorizing that took place in safe laboratory spaces. At the beginning of my chapter, I quoted a poem written by Oleg Larichev—who would become an academician and leading Russian scientist in artificial intelligence—that was published in a special issue of the principal systems research yearbook in the Soviet Union, published by VNIISI in the 1970s—80s. Larichev warns a systems engineer not to rely too heavily on results generated by computer modeling. These lines capture well the spirit of at least some Soviet scientists who adopted the systems approach and modeling as an open inquiry into the organization of society and nature, at the same time warning against a temptation to seek for quick fixes in decision sciences. This warning, albeit issued thirty-six years ago, is still valid today for policy makers both in East and West. It is also a reminder for historians of scientific governance to take into account reflexive and social construction of science, as abstract models may harbor quiet revolutions.

Dr Eglė Rindzevičiūtė holds a PhD in Culture Studies from Linköping University, Sweden, and is an Associate Professor (Reader) in Sociology at Kingston UniversityLondon, the UK. Dr Rindzevičiūtė has published widely on Soviet governance and scientific expertise. She is the author of *Constructing Soviet Cultural Policy: Cybernetics and Governance in Lithuania after World War II* (Linköping University Press, 2008) and *The Power of Systems: How Policy Sciences Opened Up the Cold War World* (Cornell University Press, 2016), and the co-editor of *The Struggle for the Long-Term in Transnational Science and Politics: Forging the Future* (Routledge, 2015).

Notes

I thank the editors, Nicolas Guilhot and Daniel Bessner, as well as the participants at the two workshops at the Centre for International Research in Humanities and Social Sciences (CIRHUS), New York University, in October 2015 and May 2013, for their helpful comments. The views and errors, however, are mine only.

1. "No v mig chudesnyi torzhestva/ty sam sebe ne ver'./Izmenchiv mir i slozhen mir,/prosta tvoia model'." Oleg Larichev, "Nekotorye problemy metodologii priniatiia unikal'nykh reshenii," in *Filosofskie aspekty sistemnykh issledovanii: VNII Sistemnykh issledovanii*, ed. D. Gvishiani, 24–32 (Moscow: VNIISI, 1980).
2. N. V. Ovchinnikova, ed., *Istoriia upravlencheskoi mysli* [*The History of the Management Thought*] (Moscow: RGGU, 2013), 287–88. It is important to note that the Russian word *upravlenie* is similar to the English word *governance*, whereas the English term *control* is translated into Russian as the term *regulirovanie* (which means regulating). V. G. Gorokhov, *Istoriia razvitiia avtomatizirovannykh sistem upravleniia v Sovetskom Soiuze, v 60-ee-70-ee gody* [*The History of the Development of Automated Management Systems in the Soviet Union in the 1960s–70s*]. Paper presented at the twelfth All-Russian Meeting on the Problems of Control, Moscow, 16–19 July 2014. For an important discussion of the Russian use of the terms *control* and *governance*, see Slava Gerovitch, *From Newspeak to Cyberspeak: The History of Soviet Cybernetics* (Cambridge, MA: MIT Press, 2002), 253.
3. Elizabeth A. Weinberg, *Sociology in the Soviet Union and Beyond: Social Enquiry and Social Change* (Aldershot: Ashgate, 2004); B. M. Firsov, *Istoriia sovetskoi sotsiologii 1950–1980 gg.: Kurs lektsii* (St. Petersburg: Izdatel'stvo Evropeiskogo universiteta v Sankt-Peterburge, 2001).
4. Daniel Bessner, "Organizing Complexity: The Hopeful Dreams and Harsh Realities of Interdisciplinary Collaboration at the RAND Corporation in the Early Cold War," *Journal of the History of the Behavioral Sciences* 51, no. 1 (2015): 31–53; Nicolas Guilhot, "Cybernetic Pantocrator: International Relations Theory from Decisionism to Rational Choice," *Journal of the History of the Behavioral Sciences* 47, no. 3 (2011): 279–301.
5. I criticized this approach proposing a coproductionist perspective on scientific governance, understood as an assemblage of ideas, institutions, and social networks, all of which were shaped across the Iron Curtain. Egle Rindzevičiūtė, *The Power of Systems: How Policy Sciences Opened Up the Cold War World* (Ithaca, NY: Cornell University Press, 2016).
6. S. M. Amadae, *Rationalizing Capitalist Democracy: The Cold War Origins of Rational Choice Liberalism* (Chicago, IL: The University of Chicago Press, 2003); Philip Mirowski, *Machine Dreams: Economics Becomes a Cyborg Science* (Cambridge, UK: Cambridge University Press, 2002); Will Davies, *The Limits of Neoliberalism: Authority, Sovereignty and the Logic of Competition* (London: Sage, 2014).
7. Mitchell Dean, *Governmentality: Power and Rule in Modern Society* (London: Sage, 1999), 18.

8. Michel Foucault, *Security, Territory, Population: Lectures at the Collège de France, 1977–1978*, trans. Graham Burchell, ed. Michael Senallart (Basingstoke, UK: Palgrave, 2009).
9. Rindzevičiūtė, *The Power of Systems*; Stephen Collier and Andrew Lakoff, "Vital Systems Security: Reflexive Biopolitics and the Government of Emergency," *Theory, Culture and Society* 32, no. 2 (2015): 19–51; Helga Nowotny, *The Cunning of Uncertainty* (Oxford: Polity, 2015); Louise Amoore, *The Politics of Possibility: Risk and Security Beyond Probability* (Durham, NC: Duke University Press, 2013). On the history of the concept of resilience, see Isabell Schrickel, "On Butterflies and Nuclear Reactors: Media and Politics of Resilience at the IIASA," *Behemoth: A Journal on Civilisation* 7, no. 2 (2014): 5–25.
10. I have developed a similar argument on the basis of economic forecasting in Egle Rindzevičiūtė, "A Struggle for the Soviet Future: The Birth of Scientific Forecasting in the Soviet Union," *Slavic Review* 75, no. 1 (2016): 52–76. See also Paul Erickson, "Mathematical Models, Rational Choice and the Search for Cold War Culture," *Isis* 101, no. 2 (2010): 386–92.
11. Rindzevičiūtė, "A Struggle for the Soviet Future," 62.
12. Such is one of early studies on Soviet decision makers edited by H. Gordon Skilling and Franklyn Griffiths, eds., *Interest Groups in Soviet Politics*; John Löwenhardt, *Decision Making in Soviet Politics* (Basingstoke: Palgrave, 1981). For an oversight of Kremlinology, see David C. Engerman, *Know Your Enemy: The Rise and Fall of America's Soviet Experts* (Oxford: Oxford University Press, 2009). For a recent personalist take on Soviet governance, see Oleg Khlevniuk and Nora Seligman, *Master of the House: Stalin and His Inner Circle* (New Haven: Yale University Press, 2009). For an example of a recent institutionalist approach, see Stephen Fortescue, ed., *Russian Politics from Lenin to Putin* (Basingstoke: Palgrave, 2010).
13. William Conyngham, *The Modernization of Soviet Industrial Management: Socioeconomic Development and the Search for Viability* (Cambridge, UK: Cambridge University Press, 1982); Erik Hoffmann and Robbin F. Laird, *Technocratic Socialism: The Soviet Union in the Advanced Industrial Era* (Durham, NC: Duke University Press, 1985); Mark Beissinger, *Scientific Management, Socialist Discipline and Soviet Power* (London: I.B. Tauris, 1988); Pekka Sutela, *Economic Thought and Economic Reform in the Soviet Union* (Cambridge, UK: Cambridge University Press, 1991).
14. Michal Kopeček and Piotr Wciślik, eds., *Thinking Through Transition: Liberal Democracy, Authoritarian Pasts, and Intellectual History in East Central Europe After 1989* (Budapest: Central European University Press, 2015); Eden Medina, *Cybernetic Revolutionaries: Technology and Politics in Allende's Chile* (Cambridge, MA: The MIT Press, 2011).
15. Stephen Collier, *Post-Soviet Social: Neoliberalism, Social Modernity, Biopolitics* (Princeton, NJ: Princeton University Press, 2011). For a relevant discussion of different types, Radical and Modernist, Communist approach to governance, see also David Priestland, *The Red Flag: Communism and the Making of Modern World* (London: Grove Press, 2009).

16. Peter Rutland, *The Myth of the Plan* (New York: Harper Collins, 1985); Paul Gregory, *The Political Economy of Stalinism: Evidence from the Soviet Secret Archives* (Cambridge, UK: Cambridge University Press, 2004); Yoram Gorlizki, "Scandal in Riazan: Networks of Trust and the Social Dynamics of Deception," *Kritika* 14, no. 2 (2013): 243–78.
17. Benjamin Peters, *How Not to Network a Nation: The Uneasy History of the Soviet Internet* (Cambridge, MA: The MIT Press, 2016).
18. Rindzevičiūtė, *The Power of Systems*; Eglė Rindzevičiūtė, "The Future as an Intellectual Technology in the Soviet Union: From Centralised Planning to Reflexive Management," *Cahiers du monde Russe* 56, no. 1 (2015): 111–34.
19. Philip Hanson, *The Rise and Fall of the Soviet Economy* (Harlow, UK: Longman, 2003); Loren Graham, *The Ghost of the Executed Engineer: Technology and the Fall of the Soviet Union* (Cambridge, MA: Harvard University Press, 1993); David Holloway, "The Political Uses of Scientific Models: The Cybernetic Model of Government in Soviet Social Science," in *The Use of Models in the Social Science*, ed. Lyndhurst Collins (Tavistock: Westview Press, 1976), 110–29.
20. Gerovitch, *From Newspeak to Cyberspeak*, 278–79. See also Manuel Castells and Emma Kiselyova, *The Collapse of Soviet Communism: A View from the Information Society* (Berkeley: University of California Press, 1995).
21. Alena Ledeneva, *Russia's Economy of Favours: Blat, Networking and Informal Exchange* (Cambridge, UK: Cambridge University Press, 1998).
22. Eglė Rindzevičiūtė, *Constructing Soviet Cultural Policy: Cybernetics and Governance in Lithuania After World War II* (Linköping: Linköping University Press, 2008), 143–47.
23. Eglė Rindzevičiūtė, "The Future as an Intellectual Technology in the Soviet Union: The Future as an Intellectual Technology in the Soviet Union".
24. Maurice W. Kirby, *Operations Research in War and Peace: The British Experience from the 1930s to 1970* (London: Imperial College Press, 2003); William Thomas, *Rational Action: The Sciences of Policy in Britain and America, 1940–1960* (Cambridge, MA: The MIT Press, 2015).
25. David R. Jardini, "Out of the Blue Yonder: The Transfer of Systems Thinking from the Pentagon to the Great Society, 1961–1965," in *Systems, Experts, and Computers: The Systems Approach in Management and Engineering, World War II and After*, ed. Agatha C. Hughes and Thomas P. Hughes, 385–412 (Cambridge, MA: The MIT Press, 2000); S. M. Amadae, *Prisoners of Reason: Game Theory and Neoliberal Political Economy* (Oxford: Oxford University Press, 2016); Paul Erickson, Judy L. Klein, Lorraine Daston, Rebecca Lemov, Thomas Sturm, and Michael D. Gordin, *How Reason Almost Lost Its Mind: The Strange Career of Cold War Rationality* (Chicago, IL: The University of Chicago Press, 2013).
26. Nicolas Guilhot, this volume.
27. Wiener was explicit on this. See also Ronald Kline, *The Cybernetics Moment: Or Why We Call Our Age the Information Age* (Baltimore, MD: Johns Hopkins University Press, 2015), 127.

    The political and cultural history of cybernetics is a growing field: Peter Galison, "The Ontology of the Enemy: Norbert Wiener and the Cybernetic

Vision," *Critical Inquiry* 21, no. 1 (1994): 228–66; Katherine Hayles, *How We Became Posthuman: Virtual Bodies in Cybernetics, Literature and Informatics* (Chicago, IL: The University of Chicago Press, 1999); Philip Mirowski, *Machine Dreams: Economics Becomes a Cyborg Science* (Cambridge, UK: Cambridge University Press, 2002); Slava Gerovitch, *From Newspeak to Cyberspeak: A History of Soviet Cybernetics* (Cambridge, MA: The MIT Press, 2002); Fred Turner, *From Counterculture to Cyberculture: Stuart Brand, the Whole Earth Network and the Rise of Digital Utopianism* (Cambridge, MA: The MIT Press, 2006); Eglė Rindzevičiūtė, *Constructing Soviet Cultural Policy: Cybernetics and Governance in Lithuania After World War II*; Eden Medina, *Cybernetic Revolutionaries: Technology and Politics in Allende's Chile* (Cambridge, MA: The MIT Press, 2011); Kline, *The Cybernetics Moment*; Orit Halpern, *The Beautiful Data: A History of Vision and Reason Since 1945* (Cambridge, MA: The MIT Press, 2015); Benjamin Peters, *How Not to Network a Nation: The Uneasy History of the Soviet Internet* (Cambridge, MA: The MIT Press, 2016); Rindzevičiūtė, *The Power of Systems*.
28. Sari Autio-Sarasmo and Katalin Miklóssy, eds. *Reassessing Cold War Europe* (New York: Publisher, 2011).
29. David Holloway, *Stalin and the Bomb: The Soviet Union and Atomic Energy, 1939–1956* (New Haven, CT: Yale University Press, 1996).
30. Gerovitch, *From Newspeak to Cyberspeak*, 159.
31. Ibid., 179.
32. For the impact of cybernetics on Soviet mathematical economics see Adam Leeds, "Dreams in Cybernetic Fugue: Cold War Technoscience, the Intelligentsia, and the Birth of Soviet Mathematical Economics," *Historical Studies in the Natural Sciences* 46, no. 5 (2016): 633–68.
33. Heyck Hunter, *Age of System: Understanding Development of Modern Social Science* (Baltimore, MD: John Hopkins University Press, 2015); Benoît Godin, "National Innovation System: The System Approach in Historical Perspective," *Sciences, Technology and Human Values* 34, no. 4 (2009): 476–501.
34. Melanie Ilic and Jeremy Smith, eds., *Soviet State and Society Under Nikita Khrushchev* (New York: Routledge, 2009).
35. Rindzevičiūtė, *The Power of Systems*.
36. Dzhermen Gvishiani and Richard Vidmer, "Management Science in the USSR: The Role of Americanizers," *International Studies Quarterly* 24, no. 3 (1980): 392–414.
37. Gerovitch, *From Newspeak to Cyberspeak*, 267.
38. See my argument in Rindzevičiūtė, "A Struggle for the Soviet Future."
39. This section draws on a chapter in my recent monograph. For more on the Soviet OR and systems analysis, see Rindzevičiūtė, *The Power of Systems*.
40. In 1970, the Russian translation of von Neumann's and Morgernstern's *Game Theory and Economic Behavior* was translated into Russian and published by the Nauka Press.
41. Gerovitch, *From Newspeak to Cyberspeak*, 272.
42. Ivan Boldyrev, "The Strategy of Getting Together, or How Mathematics Found its Way into Soviet Economic Discourse," paper presented at the

workshop *From Technocratic Socialism to Neoliberal Rule: Expert Cultures, Technocracy and Governance in East Central Europe 1960s–1990s*, Prague, 3–5 November 2016.
43. Although Soviet OR scientists did not identify themselves with the cybernetics movement, finding it too philosophical. An interview with an ex-Soviet OR scientist, 2007.
44. Dmitrii Efremov, *Ekologo-politicheskie diskursy: vozniknovenie i evoliutsiia* [*Ecological and Political Discourses: Emergence and Evolution*] (Moscow: INION, 2006), 43.
45. Major histories of Soviet planning skip forward from Kosygin's reforms of 1965 to Gorbachev's perestroika of 1986. However, the 1970s were an important period in Soviet planning, as it was at that time that scientific expertise was integrated in the planning process. For an example, see Michael Ellman, *Socialist Planning* (Cambridge, UK: Cambridge University Press, 2014).
46. For more on Moiseev's contribution to Earth system science, see Eglė Rindzevičiūtė, "Soviet Policy Sciences and Earth System Governmentality," *Modern Intellectual History* FirstView (2018): 1–30. For a good overview of the application of the systems approach in the late Soviet period see Pekka Sutela, *Economic Thought and Economic Reform in the Soviet Union* (Cambridge: Cambridge University Press, 1991).
47. Here the rise of the systems approach and modelling in the Soviet Union largely follows the trajectory of these sciences in the US, as detailed in Hunter Heyck, *Age of System*.
48. Jenny Andersson and Eglė Rindzevičiūtė, "Introduction," in *The Struggle for the Long-Term in Transnational Science and Politics: Forging the Future*, eds. Jenny Andersson and Eglė Rindzevičiūtė (New York: Routledge, 2015).
49. Rindzevičiūtė, *The Power of Systems*.
50. Nikolai Krementsov, *A Martian Stranded on Earth: Alexander Bogdanov, Blood Transfusions, and Proletarian Science* (Chicago, IL: The University of Chicago Press, 2011).
51. George M. Young, *The Russian Cosmists: The Esoteric Futurism of Nikolai Fedorov and His Followers* (Oxford: Oxford University Press, 2012).
52. For Vernadskii, see Jonathan Oldfield and Denis Shaw, "V. I. Vernadskii and the Development of Biogeochemical Understandings of the Biosphere, c. 1880s–1968," *British Journal for the History of Science* 46, no. 2 (2013): 287–310. For Bogdanov, also see John Biggart, Peter Dudley, and Francis King, eds., *Alexander Bogdanov and the Origins of Systems Thinking in Russia* (Aldershot, UK: Ashgate, 1998).
53. B. G. Iudin, "Iz istorii sistemnykh issledovanii: mezhdu metodologiei i ideologiei" ["From the History of Systems Research: Between Methodology and Ideology"], *Vestnik TGPU* 1, no. 75 (2008): 28–33.
54. Paul Josephson et al., *An Environmental History of Russia* (Cambridge, UK: Cambridge University Press, 2013); Stephen J. Collier, *Post-Soviet Social: Neoliberalism, Social Modernity, Biopolitics* (Princeton, NJ: Princeton University Press, 2011).

55. Sari Autio-Sarasmo and Katalin Miklóssy, eds., *Reassessing Cold War Europe* (New York: Routledge, 2011); Oscar Sanchez- Sibony, *Red Globalization: The Political Economy of the Soviet Cold War from Stalin to Khrushchev* (Cambridge: Cambridge University Press, 2014).
56. Interview with a systems scientist, November 2014.
57. See Karl E. Weick, *The Social Psychology of Organizing*, 2nd ed. (New York: McGraw-Hill, 1979); Fred M. Kaplan, *The Wizards of Armageddon* (Stanford, CA: Stanford University Press, 1991).
58. Boris Milner, "Application of Scientific Methods of Management in the Soviet Union," *Academy of Management Review* 2, no. 4 (1977): 560. For more on East-West relations in econometrics, see Johanna Bockman and Michael Bernstein, "Scientific Community in a Divided World: Economists, Planning and Research Priority during the Cold War," *Comparative Studies in the Society and History* 50, no. 3 (2008): 581–613.
59. Mifodijus Sapagovas et al., *Matematikos ir informatikos institutas* [The Institute of Mathematics and Informatics] (Vilnius: Matematikos ir informatikos institutas, 2006). See also Eduardas Vilkas, "On a General Approach to Optimality in Game Theory," *Cowles Foundation Discussion Paper* No. 419 (20 January 1976), available at http://cowles.yale.edu/publications.
60. Rindzevičiūtė, *The Power of Systems*. See also Johanna Bockman and Michael A. Bernstein, "Scientific Community in a Divided World: Economists, Planning, and Research Priority during the Cold War," *Comparative Studies in Society and History* 50, no. 3 (2008): 581–613.
61. N. N. Moiseev and A. G. Schmidt, "Some Problems of Centralized Economy," *Cowles Foundation Discussion Paper* No. 358 (5 April 1973), 28.
62. Nikita Moiseev, *Matematika, upravlenie, ekonomika* [*Mathematics, Governance, Economics*] (Moscow: Znanie, 1970), 4.
63. Ibid., 4-5.
64. Ibid., 7.
65. Ibid., 11.
66. Ibid., 15.
67. Ibid., 15.
68. Ibid., 15.
69. Ibid., 23.
70. Ibid., 25,
71. Ibid., 29.
72. Ibid., 59.
73. Ibid., 31.
74. Ibid., 31.
75. Ibid., 28.
76. Moiseev to Gvishiani (31 July 1980), The Archives of the Russian Academy of Sciences (ARAN), f. 1918, op.1, d. 463, l.1.
77. Ovchinnikova, *Istoriia upravlencheskoi mysli*, 295.

Bibliography

Amadae, S. M. *Prisoners of Reason: Game Theory and Neoliberal Political Economy.* Cambridge, UK: Cambridge University Press, 2016.

———. *Rationalizing Capitalist Democracy: The Cold War Origins of Rational Choice Liberalism.* Chicago, IL: The University of Chicago Press, 2003.

Amoore, Louise. *The Politics of Possibility: Risk and Security Beyond Probability.* Durham, NC: Duke University Press, 2013.

Andersson, Jenny, and Eglė Rindzevičiūtė. "Introduction." In *The Struggle for the Long-Term in Transnational Science and Politics: Forging the Future*, edited by J. Andersson and E. Rindzevičiūtė. New York: Routledge, 2015.

Autio-Sarasmo, Sari, and Katalin Miklóssy, eds. *Reassessing Cold War Europe.* New York: Routledge, 2011.

Beissinger, Mark. *Scientific Management, Socialist Discipline and Soviet Power.* London: I. B. Tauris & Co, 1988.

Bessner, Daniel. "Organizing Complexity: The Hopeful Dreams and Harsh Realities of Interdisciplinary Collaboration at the RAND Corporation in the Early Cold War." *Journal of the History of the Behavioral Sciences* 51, no.1 (2015): 31–53.

Biggart, John, Peter Dudley, and Francis King, eds. *Alexander Bogdanov and the Origins of Systems Thinking in Russia.* Aldershot, UK: Ashgate, 1998.

Bockman, Johanna, and Michael Bernstein. "Scientific Community in a Divided World: Economists, Planning and Research Priority during the Cold War." *Comparative Studies in the Society and History* 50, no.3 (2008): 581–613.

Boldyrev, Ivan. "The Strategy of Getting Together, or How Mathematics Found its Way into Soviet Economic Discourse." Unpublished paper presented at the workshop *From Technocratic Socialism to Neoliberal Rule: Expert Cultures, Technocracy and Governance in East Central Europe 1960s–1990s.* Prague, 3–5 November 2016.

Castells, Manuel, and Emma Kiselyova. *The Collapse of Soviet Communism: A View from the Information Society.* Berkeley: University of California Press, 1995.

Collier, Stephen. *Post-Soviet Social: Neoliberalism, Social Modernity, Biopolitics.* Princeton, NJ: Princeton University Press, 2011.

Collier, Stephen, and Andrew Lakoff. "Vital Systems Security: Reflexive Biopolitics and the Government of Emergency." *Theory, Culture and Society* 32, no. 2 (2015): 19–51.

Conyngham, William. *The Modernization of Soviet Industrial Management: Socioeconomic Development and the Search for Viability.* Cambridge, UK: Cambridge University Press, 1982.

Davies, Will. *The Limits of Neoliberalism: Authority, Sovereignty and the Logic of Competition.* London: Sage, 2014.

Dean, Mitchell. *Governmentality: Power and Rule in Modern Society.* London: Sage, 1999.

Efremenko, Dmitrii. *Ekologo-politicheskie diskursy: vozniknovenie i evoliutsiia* [*Ecological and Political Discourses: Emergence and Evolution*]. Moscow: INION, 2006.

Ellman, Michael. *Socialist Planning*. Cambridge, UK: Cambridge University Press, 2014.
Engerman, David C. *Know Your Enemy: The Rise and Fall of America's Soviet Experts*. Oxford: Oxford University Press, 2009.
Erickson, Paul. "Mathematical Models, Rational Choice and the Search for Cold War Culture." *Isis* 101, no. 2 (2010): 386–92.
Erickson, Paul, Judy L. Klein, Lorraine Daston, Rebecca Lemov, Thomas Sturm, and Michael D. Gordin. *How Reason Almost Lost Its Mind: The Strange Career of Cold War Rationality*. Chicago, IL: The University of Chicago Press, 2013.
Firsov, B. M. *Istoriia sovetskoi sotsiologii 1950–1980 gg.: Kurs lektsii* [The History of Soviet Sociology in the 1950s–1980s]. St. Petersburg: The European University Press, 2001.
Fortescue, Stephen, ed. *Russian Politics from Lenin to Putin*. Basingstoke: Palgrave, 2010.
Foucault, Michel. *Security, Territory, Population: Lectures at the Collège de France, 1977–1978*. Translated by Graham Burchell. Edited by Michael Senallart. Basingstoke: Palgrave, 2009.
Galison, Peter. "The Ontology of the Enemy: Norbert Wiener and the Cybernetic Vision." *Critical Inquiry* 21, no.1 (1994): 228–66.
Gerovitch, Slava. *From Newspeak to Cyberspeak: The History of Soviet Cybernetics*. Cambridge, MA: MIT Press, 2002.
Godin, Benoît. "National Innovation System: The System Approach in Historical Perspective." *Sciences, Technology and Human Values* 34, no.4 (2009): 476–501.
Gorlizki, Yoram. "Scandal in Riazan: Networks of Trust and the Social Dynamics of Deception." *Kritika* 14, no.2 (2013): 243–78.
Gorokhov, V. G. *Istoriia razvitiia avtomatizirovannykh sistem upravleniia v Sovetskom Soiuze, v 60-ee-70-ee gody* [The History of the Development of Automated Management Systems in the Soviet Union in the 1960s–70s]. Paper presented at the twelfth All-Russian Meeting on the Problems of Control. Moscow, 16–19 July 2014.
Graham, Loren. *The Ghost of the Executed Engineer: Technology and the Fall of the Soviet Union*. Cambridge, MA: Harvard University Press, 1993.
Gregory, Paul. *The Political Economy of Stalinism: Evidence from the Soviet Secret Archives*. Cambridge, UK: Cambridge University Press, 2003.
Guilhot, Nicolas. "Cybernetic Pantocrator: International Relations Theory from Decisionism to Rational Choice." *Journal of the History of the Behavioral Sciences* 47, no. 3 (2011): 279–301.
Halpern, Orit. *The Beautiful Data: A History of Vision and Reason Since 1945*. Cambridge, MA: MIT Press, 2015.
Hanson, Philip. *The Rise and Fall of the Soviet Economy*. Harlow, UK: Longman, 2003.
Hayles, Katherine. *How We Became Posthuman: Virtual Bodies in Cybernetics, Literature and Informatics*. Chicago, IL: The University of Chicago Press, 1999.
Hoffmann, Erik, and Robbin F. Laird. *Technocratic Socialism: The Soviet Union in the Advanced Industrial Era*. Durham, NC: Duke University Press, 1985.

Holloway, David. "The Political Uses of Scientific Models: The Cybernetic Model of Government in Soviet Social Science." In *The Use of Models in the Social Science*, edited by L. Collins, 110–29. Tavistock: Westview Press, 1976.

———. *Stalin and the Bomb: The Soviet Union and Atomic Energy, 1939–1956*. New Haven, CT: Yale University Press, 1996.

Hunter, Heyck. *Age of System: Understanding Development of Modern Social Science*. Baltimore, MD: John Hopkins University Press, 2015.

Ilic, Melanie, and Jeremy Smith, eds. *Soviet State and Society Under Nikita Khrushchev*. New York: Routledge, 2009.

Iudin, B. G. "Iz istorii sistemnykh issledovanii: mezhdu metodologiei i ideologiei" ["From the History of Systems Research: Between Methodology and Ideology"]. *Vestnik TGPU* 1, no. 75 (2008): 28–33.

Jardini, David R. "Out of the Blue Yonder: The Transfer of Systems Thinking from the Pentagon to the Great Society, 1961–1965." In *Systems, Experts, and Computers: The Systems Approach in Management and Engineering, World War II and After*, edited by A. C. Hughes and T. P. Hughes, 385–412. Cambridge, MA: MIT Press, 2000.

Josephson, Paul, Nicolai Dronin, Aleh Cherp, Dmitry Efremenko, and Ruben Mnatsakanian. *An Environmental History of Russia*. Cambridge, UK: Cambridge University Press, 2013.

Kaplan, Fred M. *The Wizards of Armageddon*. Stanford, CA: Stanford University Press, 1991.

Khlevniuk, Oleg, and Nora Seligman. *Master of the House: Stalin and His Inner Circle*. New Haven, CT: Yale University Press, 2014.

Kirby, Maurice W. *Operations Research in War and Peace: The British Experience from the 1930s to 1970*. London: Imperial College Press, 2003.

Kline, Ronald. *The Cybernetics Moment: Or Why We Call Our Age the Information Age*. Baltimore, MD: Johns Hopkins University Press, 2015.

Kopeček, Michal, and Piotr Wciślik, eds. *Thinking Through Transition: Liberal Democracy, Authoritarian Pasts, and Intellectual History in East Central Europe After 1989*. Budapest: Central European University Press, 2015.

Krementsov, Nikolai. *A Martian Stranded on Earth: Alexander Bogdanov, Blood Transfusions, and Proletarian Science*. Chicago, IL: The University of Chicago Press, 2011.

Larichev, Oleg. "Nekotorye problemy metodologii priniatiia unikal'nykh reshenii." In *Filosofskie aspekty sistemnykh issledovanii: VNII Sistemnykh issledovanii*, edited by Dzhermen Gvishiani, 24–32. Moscow: VNIISI, 1980.

Ledeneva, Alena. *Russia's Economy of Favours: Blat, Networking and Informal Exchange*. Cambridge, UK: Cambridge University Press, 1998.

Leeds, Adam. "Dreams in Cybernetic Fugue: Cold War Technoscience, the Intelligentsia, and the Birth of Soviet Mathematical Economics." *Historical Studies in the Natural Sciences* 46, no. 5 (2016): 633–68.

Löwenhardt, John. *Decision Making in Soviet Politics*. Basingstoke: Palgrave, 1981.

Medina, Eden. *Cybernetic Revolutionaries: Technology and Politics in Allende's Chile*. Cambridge, MA: MIT Press, 2011.

Milner, Boris. "Application of Scientific Methods of Management in the Soviet Union." *Academy of Management Review* 2, no. 4 (1977): 560.
Mirowski, Philip. *Machine Dreams: Economics Becomes a Cyborg Science*. Cambridge, UK: Cambridge University Press, 2002.
Moiseev, Nikita. *Matematika, upravlenie, ekonomika* [*Mathematics, Governance, Economics*]. Moscow: Znanie, 1970.
Moiseev, N. N., and A. G. Schmidt. "Some Problems of Centralized Economy." *Cowles Foundation Discussion Paper* No. 358 (5 April 1973).
Nowotny, Helga. *The Cunning of Uncertainty*. Cambridge, UK: Polity, 2015.
Oldfield, Jonathan, and Denis Shaw. "V. I. Vernadskii and the Development of Biogeochemical Understandings of the Biosphere, c. 1880s–1968." *British Journal for the History of Science* 46, no. 2 (2013): 287–310.
Ovchinnikova, N. V., ed. *Istoriia upravlencheskoi mysli* [*The History of the Management Thought*]. Moscow: RGGU, 2013.
Peters, Benjamin. *How Not to Network a Nation: The Uneasy History of the Soviet Internet*. Cambridge, MA: MIT Press, 2016.
Priestland, David. *The Red Flag: Communism and the Making of Modern World*. London: Grove Press, 2009.
Rindzevičiūtė, Eglė. *Constructing Soviet Cultural Policy: Cybernetics and Governance in Lithuania After World War II*. Linköping: Linköping University Press, 2008.
———. "The Future as an Intellectual Technology in the Soviet Union: From Centralised Planning to Reflexive Management." *Cahiers du monde Russe* 56, no. 1 (2015): 111–34.
———. *The Power of Systems: How Policy Sciences Opened Up the Cold War World*. Ithaca, NY: Cornell University Press, 2016.
———. "A Struggle for the Soviet Future: The Birth of Scientific Forecasting in the Soviet Union." *Slavic Review* 75, no.1 (2016): 52–76.
———. "Soviet Policy Sciences and Earth System Governmentality." *Modern Intellectual History* FirstView (2018): 1–30.
Rutland, Peter. *The Myth of the Plan*. London: Harper Collins, 1985.
Sanchez-Sibony, Oscar. *Red Globalization: The Political Economy of the Soviet Cold War from Stalin to Khrushchev*. Cambridge, UK: Cambridge University Press, 2014.
Sapagovas, Mifodijus, et al. *Matematikos ir informatikos institutas* [*The Institute of Mathematics and Informatics*]. Vilnius: Matematikos ir informatikos institutas, 2006.
Schrickel, Isabell. "On Butterflies and Nuclear Reactors: Media and Politics of Resilience at the IIASA." *Behemoth: A Journal on Civilisation* 7, no. 2 (2014): 5–25.
Skilling, H. Gordon, and Franklyn Griffiths, eds. *Interest Groups in Soviet Politics*. Princeton, NJ: Princeton University Press, 1971.
Smolian, Georgii. *Issledovanie operatsii: instrument efektivnogo upravlenie* [Operations research: an instrument of effective governance]. Moscow: Znanie, 1967.
Sutela, Pekka. *Economic Thought and Economic Reform in the Soviet Union*. Cambridge, UK: Cambridge University Press, 1991.

Thomas, William. *Rational Action: The Sciences of Policy in Britain and America, 1940–1960*. Cambridge, MA: MIT Press, 2015.
Turner, Fred. *From Counterculture to Cyberculture: Stuart Brand, the Whole Earth Network and the Rise of Digital Utopianism*. Cambridge, MA: MIT Press, 2006.
Vidmer, Richard. "Management Science in the USSR: The Role of Americanizers." *International Studies Quarterly* 24, no. 3 (1980): 392–414.
Vilkas, Eduardas. "On a General Approach to Optimality in Game Theory." *Cowles Foundation Discussion Paper* No. 419 (20 January 1976). Available at http://cowles.yale.edu/publications.
Young, George M. *The Russian Cosmists: The Esoteric Futurism of Nikolai Fedorov and His Followers*. Oxford: Oxford University Press, 2012.
Weick, Karl E. *The Social Psychology of Organizing*. 2nd ed. New York: McGraw-Hill, 1979.
Weinberg, Elizabeth A. *Sociology in the Soviet Union and Beyond: Social Enquiry and Social Change*. Aldershot: Ashgate, 2004.

8

PREDICTION AND SOCIAL CHOICE
Daniel Bell and Future Research
Jenny Andersson

In 1973, Daniel Bell published what would become his magnum opus: *The Coming of Post Industrial Society: A Venture in Social Forecasting*. Most scholarly attention on Bell has focused on his analysis of postindustrial society as a future social order dominated by information, science, and technology. Bell's thesis about "mass knowledge society" was a core contribution to a debate on postindustrialism that started in the late 1960s and continued for years.[1] Much less attention, however, has been devoted to Bell's interest in social forecasting and to his argument that a postindustrial society required new means of planning in a set of forward-looking political technologies. This lack of scholarly interest is striking, because, as this chapter will argue, Bell's belief that transformative social changes could be foreseen and perhaps modeled displays his fundamental ambivalence about postindustrialism and mass politics.

This chapter examines Daniel Bell's interest in future research and his notion that such research offered a set of planning technologies that could be used to solve what he saw as the key problem of democratic society: the relationship between elites and the masses. He referred to these technologies as "intellectual technologies" or "decision tools." For Bell, the phrase "intellectual technologies" referred to the application of computer technology to decision-making, and, ultimately, the replacement of human judgment with "algorithmic judgement"—i.e., analytical capacities underpinned by computer power.[2] As an intellectual technology, future research made it possible not only to foresee but also to control the countless different futures of a democratic mass society. Mass society, for Bell, required a mechanism that could establish a sense of priority for the myriad of decisions needed to satisfy the mass, and that mechanism did this by relating decisions to their anticipated consequences and effects on the social order. This corresponded to an idea of rationality that he considered crucial for the legitimacy of political interventions in a liberal society, since only by reference to "rational social choice" could ambitious political projects be made acceptable to a deeply individualist society. Convinced of the benefits of planning, but fundamentally anticommunist, Bell argued that forecasting could provide a liberal alternative to the five-year plans of communist societies by elucidating objectives of long-term desirability. Because it applied algorithmic judgement to the problem of decision, rationality was a way of replacing what Bell saw as the possibly undesirable (because unforeseen) effects of collective decision-making. As such, rational took the place, in his reasoning, of the collective, or indeed, the ideological. Rational decisions were decisions that had foreseeable consequences, consequences that could be subjected to expert judgement and evaluation of desirability, at the precise moment of decision-making. Ultimately, intellectual technology was therefore a rationalization of decision, or, as Bell himself would put it, an application of technological reasoning to the act of decision-making.

Similar to much of Bell's thinking, his ideas about future research were ambivalent, particularly in respect to its technocratic dimension. Bell's major focus—the relationship between decision-making and rationality in mass society—must be understood within the context of debates that since the interwar period had been warning about the dangers democratic decision-making posed to a liberal order. Bell's interest in future research reiterated a set of earlier discourses on technocracy as a necessary corrective to democracy that resurfaced in postwar notions of mass society. Nonetheless, Bell himself rejected the accusation, which was leveled against *The End of Ideology*, that he advocated technocracy (just as he would reject allegations of neoconservatism).[3] Indeed, Bell's arguments about intellectual technologies did not advocate for the replacement of political struggle by expert rule; instead, his interest in future research was motivated by his prevailing conception that mass society needed forms of elite guidance and steering. Bell was attracted to intellectual technologies because they seemed to structure a problematic relationship between technocratic expertise and mass politics by applying forms of systemic rationality to interest politics.[4]

This chapter also suggests that Bell's understanding of the purpose of future research contained two related yet distinct ideas. First, Bell thought that future research could function as a planning mechanism specific to a liberal society that would contribute to the process of making rational social choices. This was an essentially optimistic notion that drew on the idea that the tools of operations research and system analysis could contribute to decisions that improved the level of freedom and welfare in American society. This notion coexisted, however, with a more pessimistic idea held by Bell, according to which future research could, like other political technologies such as program budgeting, serve the specific purpose of protecting decision-making from the return of interest group politics. The latter idea carried an emergent critique of the effects of public action over the long-term that was directly related to Bell's observations of the Great Society programs and his idea that a new set of social claims had set in place a dangerous process of contestation in 1960s American politics.

The End of Ideology and the Future as Social Time

Future research was a set of highly heterogeneous approaches to the problem of social time. There were at least three reasons why future research surfaced in the post-1945 period. First, future research was a product of the Cold War and of the particular social science orientations that developed as reflections on the future of both the capitalist and communist world systems, especially modernization theory and convergence theory.[5] Second, future research was a set of artifacts and technologies designed to deal with problems of decision-making under uncertainty, which had emerged from wartime operations research (OR) and its offsprings—systems analysis, cybernetics, and technological forecasting—before migrating in the 1960s into systems of planning.[6] These approaches allowed for the modeling and precise imagining of the evolution of a system and the so-called branch points at which there might be systemic change. Bell, who served on the Automation Commission, which suggested the introduction of cost–benefit analysis into the American federal administration, was instrumental in transferring ideas derived from OR's application in a military or technological system to social and political systems.[7] In 1964, Bell assumed the presidency of the Commission for the Year 2000 (CY2000), which was appointed by the American Academy for the Arts and Sciences to examine how the new tools of future research could be used in a reflection on American society for the next thirty years.

Future research was also a product of ideological concerns that arose within specific constellations of liberal intellectuals in the 1950s and early 1960s. For these intellectuals, some of whom Bell had met within the Congress for Cultural Freedom, future research was a solution to both an ideological and strategic problem, namely, how could one develop theories of social development that could challenge Marxist teleology while also allowing for the rejuvenation of an ideological liberal project that many of these intellectuals considered to be exhausted.[8] The artifacts of future research—i.e., the planning technologies, modeling tools, and scenarios that it produced, which set out specific images of desirable and undesirable futures—were understood by these intellectuals as both planning tools suitable for a democratic and affluent mass society in which individual and market values were crucial and as mechanisms of coordination for enlightened mass politics.[9]

The main principles of Daniel Bell's social theory are often unclear. He was a borrower of ideas and concepts and sought to reconcile many apparently contradictory positions. Bell began his political trajectory in 1940s American social democracy and remained, according to his own account, a social democrat in economic matters—i.e., a believer in a planned market economy. Bell's intellectual trajectory, though, also typified what Howard Brick has described as the "decline of intellectual radicalism" in the postwar era.[10] Like many fellow travelers who emerged from New York's Lower East Side, Bell was profoundly marked by his rejection of Stalinism, which in the 1940s and 1950s transformed into Cold War liberalism *as* anticommunism. Though he moved away from Marxism politically, Bell nonetheless retained a deep interest in the logics of science and technology, and a theoretical interest in Marxism and planning. Indeed, both *The End of Ideology* and *The Coming of Post-Industrial Society* were dialogues with Marxism, and the latter even put Bell in direct contact with Marxist revisionist scholars of the Eastern bloc.[11]

The End of Ideology began with Bell's rejection of the fearful notion of the mass that had informed the writings of key intellectuals—especially Karl Mannheim, Hannah Arendt, and Karl Jaspers—who had been fundamentally marked by the destruction of the Weimar Republic by "interest group politics."[12] These experiences, Bell suggested, were no longer very useful for analyzing what he described in *The End of Ideology* as a new, developing mode of social organization: mass society. This emergent social formation stood in a complex relationship to the mass as such, as the mass was both the social force driving its development and the defining characteristic of mass society as a form of social order. Bell maintained that the future of the mass was, as such, undetermined. While the mass should not be considered a *hoi polloi* subject to irrational passions and destructive impulse, Bell, in a reflection similar to that of Edward Shils, declared that the "entry of the masses into society" was guided by rising expectations and by a set of increasing claims on the state.[13] Discontentment and frustration, Bell continued, could arise if expectations went unfulfilled, which posed the risk that a mass politics would develop radical energies that could lead to new forms of concentration of power. Therefore, for Bell, the future of mass society depended on the capacity of mass politics to channel expectations toward collective welfare choices, which Bell thought required a new mediation between the two poles of politics: group interest and expert rationality. Bell thus foresaw an important role for an educated elite in the form of intellectuals that might guide the energies of the mass toward desirable social objectives. In both *The End of Ideology* and *The Coming of Post-Industrial Society*, Bell affirmed that the tools of systems analysis, as well as the systems engineers that had emerged from OR as the controllers of the system, were the necessary mechanisms to help stabilize mass society.

Bell's interest in future research arose within the context of the Congress for cultural freedom. The Congress was the site for a fundamental shift in the postwar idea of the future, which transformed from an ideological to a pragmatic problem.[14] The first chairman of the Congress was John Dewey, the pragmatist philosopher who understood social science as part and parcel of an enlightened democratic process, the goal of which was the peaceful setting of overarching societal objectives.[15] Bell, who cited Dewey several times in both *The End of Ideology* and *The Coming of Post-Industrial Society*, similarly viewed future research and social forecasting as mechanisms that would deepen democracy by working through the rationality and hierarchy of social objectives.[16] As such, future research allowed one to "put change under conscious direction."[17] The purpose of social forecasting, he further explained, was to project "open futures," as opposed to the deterministic and closed ones of Marxism.[18] Future research could therefore help bring about a pragmatic revolution capable of replacing interest politics with forms of rational forecast that were premised upon empirical indicators, cost estimations, rankings of priorities, and scenarios of development.

The End of Ideology argument, which was the core concept to emerge from the Congress, emphasized a new and pluralistic economic order organized around affluence and democracy.[19] Planning and welfare statism had an important place in this order as ways of catering to the social expectations of the mass. Nonetheless, the end of ideology was a complex notion that also contained deeply conservative elements—including the rejection of interest politics that was central to Bell's interest in intellectual technologies—and progressive notions of the need to incorporate the masses within an idea of freedom organized around welfare. The reconceptualization of the future objective of liberalism as not just freedom but "freedom of choice," for an era of expanding state action was an important element in the Congress's search for ideas and plans that would challenge the ideological determinism of Marxism. For Bell and his colleagues in the Congress, the future would not be understood through the lens of prescribed social objectives related to a grand theory of history, but would rather be understood through piecemeal notions of change related to a process involving a multiplicity of social actors, especially states, individuals, and market relations. In his address to the 1955 seminar, for example, Michael Polanyi proposed that one could only ensure the free choice of future generations if one viewed the future as a question of finding rational solutions to the myriad issues endemic to mass society. As such, Polanyi asserted, social science must become implicated in the problem-solving process.[20]

Bell drew on Polanyi's linking of the future and free choice in a set of essays on future research he published in *Daedalus* and *The Public Interest* in 1964 and 1965. Studying the future, he argued, was a way to provide freedom of choice by increasing awareness of possible alternatives ahead. If these could be rationally analyzed, then politics would become future oriented and a "conscious approach" to the problem of social time would be found.[21] As Bell explained, "Conscious social planning is not to direct society, but to facilitate desired social changes."[22] Bell further clarified that future research and forms of prediction added to freedom by improving the rationality of decision-making, which therefore made planning acceptable within the framework of liberal values—by which he meant the safeguarding of a sphere of liberty and individual freedom of choice. As he said:

> Can we, with full awareness of the problem of choosing between conflicting values ... find some way of choosing the best planning process that is consonant with our belief in liberty? The function of planning is not just to set forth goals and alternatives and means of achieving these. Equally important and usually neglected are the specification of costs and benefits, the reallocation of burdens, and the possible consequences of different kinds of actions. The true function of the planning process is not to designate the most appropriate means for given ends, but to predict the possible consequences, to explicate the values of a society and make people aware of the cost of achieving these.[23]

Bell's essays in *Daedalus* and *Public Interest* built upon his earlier observations contained within *The End of Ideology* concerning the changing role of the future and its importance for social action. *The End of Ideology* concluded with the observation that the exhaustion of ideology deflated the utopian energies necessary to mobilize intellectual elites. As these elites were stripped of their religion, they needed something else to believe in, a new horizon of social change. The last chapter of *The End of Ideology* was a dialogue with Marx. Bell insisted that if ideology was class politics elevated to universal interest—concealing its dogmatic positions and functioning in reality as a conservative upholding of the status quo (Marx)—then utopia, as demonstrated by the exiled German scholar Karl Mannheim in his 1929 rejection of Marxism, was the spirit to change the social order. Whereas ideology was a product of the past, "a dead end" utopia—which had inspired a new turn to the sociology of knowledge, a reappraisal of science and technology, new forms of objectivist social science reasoning, and an emphasis on social scientists and intellectuals as the guardians of a pluralist order—was not.[24] Bell averred that it was through intellectuals imbued with a utopian spirit that ideology could be replaced with disinterested but passionate social science concerned with the future. Bell expressed this opinion well in the passage that concludes *The End of Ideology*'s final chapter:

> the end of ideology is not—should not be—the end of utopia as well. If anything, one can begin anew the discussion of utopia only by being aware of the trap of ideology. ... There is now, more than ever, the need for utopia in the sense that men need—as they have always needed—some vision of their potential, some manner of fusing passion with intelligence. Yet the ladder of the City of Heaven can no longer be a "faith ladder," but an empirical one: a utopia has to specify where one wants to go, how to get there, the costs of the enterprise, and some realization of, and justification for the determination of, who is to pay.[25]

In other words, a rationalist utopia, in which passionate decision-making was replaced by an engineering spirit and application of rationality to social problems, was Bell's solution to the problems faced by liberalism in a postwar mass society. In this sense, utopia stood against ideology, just as "rational" would repeatedly figure at the place of "collective" decision in Bell's writings.

Two years later, Bell contributed to this utopian project when he wrote a memorandum for the Automation Commission that presented cost–benefit analysis as a new tool capable of evaluating the best possible policy alternatives in an era of rising social expectations.[26] The notion of utopia Bell offered in *The End of Ideology* contained a plea for the conversion of Cold War intellectuals from ideologues into managers of social progress. Liberal intellectuals, Bell declared, needed a new and secular way of addressing the problems left by exhausted ideologies, especially the problem of social time. As social time was no longer moving toward a given ideological objective, time itself had to become the object of conscious and rationalist reasoning. For Bell, intellectual technologies such as forecasting, systems analysis, and cybernetics offered a means by which social time could be transformed into an operational exercise.[27]

A Transatlantic Detour: Prospective and the Spirit of Decision

French political theorist Betrand de Jouvenel profoundly influenced Bell's understanding of future research as a necessary coordination mechanism for the multitude of decisions and preferences in a mass society. Bertrand de Jouvenel, a close friend of Raymond Aron, was an enigmatic character. Despite his connections to French fascist circles during the interwar years, de Jouvenel reemerged after World War II as a deeply conservative political theorist whose thoughts on sovereignty and "pure politics" influenced early postwar neoliberal and conservative thought.[28] Like Aron, de Jouvenel had attended both the Colloque Walter Lippman and the first meetings of Friedrich Hayek's Mount Pelerin Society, and, more germane for our purposes, his work was adopted by Michael Polanyi and Michael Josselson during their search for an intellectual program for the Congress.[29] In 1962, de Jouvenel published the English translation of his book *L'art de la conjecture* (1958). *The Art of Conjecture* advocated for a future-oriented approach in political science and international relations that would be capable of providing informed and scientific speculation on the future. The book set out the idea that the future was the result of a number of open possibilities (*futuribles*) that had to be taken into account in decision-making. Conjecture was the act of wisely thinking through these possibilities in order to privilege the futures that were good and avoid the ones that were bad.[30] For de Jouvenel, making this judgment on desirability was an urgent task of political science, which could use *conjecture* as a form of forward-oriented explanation. As he developed his arguments, de Jouvenel engaged in correspondence with theorists of forecasts and conjuncture from Wassily Leontieff to Kenneth Arrow. *Futuribles* was also the name of a think tank set up by de Jouvenel in Paris with funds from the Ford Foundation. The *Futuribles* board included key intellectuals associated with modernization theory, such as Edward Shils, Eugene Rostow, and Bell himself.[31]

Conjecture was also a form of anti-planning, and, despite its emphasis on open futures, a deeply technocratic notion. De Jouvenel was a dispossessed member of the French nobility whose conception of political authority was, if anything, monarchist.[32] He abhorred Gaullism. For him, de Gaulle perverted the ideal of the Prince by concentrating power in the hands of a popularly elected politician who was now making concessions to organized interests. Planning, to de Jouvenel, was the prince's way of allowing organized interests to create strategies reaching far into time. Planning developed in France under the influence from the Soviet five-year plans. The French *Plan* was a corporate structure characterized by interest representation. De Jouvenel thought that planning epitomized the problem of exercising control over a growing state apparatus in which a nonelected bureaucracy, influenced by trade unions, could make an ever-growing number of decisions that impacted on an ever-larger temporal horizon. Planning, de Jouvenel concluded, was a threat to freedom.[33] As he stated, "Policies and programs imply a very serious threat to freedom. It is quite easy for a faction in power to regard some policies and programs as called for by the 'needs of our time' and extremely difficult for the remainder of the community to defend itself against this suggestion."[34]

De Jouvenel's own notion of freedom was distinctly authoritarian. The notion of conjecture, in fact, recycled ideas about order and the need for authority that de Jouvenel had published in the fascist pamphlet *L'économie dirigée* in 1928.[35] In this pamphlet, he argued that mass society needed a mechanism of future coordination to guarantee that chaos would not be the result of the multitude of individual decisions constantly taken in a society. The mass, de Jouvenel suggested, was akin to a school of fish in that it was susceptible of taking off in unexpected directions, frightened by sudden movement or play of light. Conjecture was the "art" of making informed judgments on what future decisions to pursue.[36] Unlike planning, it would enable one to think through the long-term and cumulative effects of decisions while at the same time preserving freedom. For de Jouvenel, freedom required a capacity of guidance that focused on the relationship between social objectives and ongoing social processes. Social objectives had to be separated from influence (interest), and the act of decision itself elevated beyond interests. *Conjecture* was a rational forecast and speculation concerning the desirability of ongoing trends in relation to the overarching objective of liberal society: freedom.

In fact, through a set of unlikely circumstances and a good dose of American interference, de Jouvenel became the heir to *prospective*, a particular French intellectual project with roots in interwar technocracy, social engineering, and eugenics. *Prospective*, a fusion between certain currents of practical philosophy and management theory, focused on the possibilities of rationalizing or "synthesizing" decision. The father of *prospective* was Gaston Berger, who, as the *inspecteur général de l'enseignement supérieur*, negotiated much of the American funding to French social science after 1945 and oversaw its postwar restructuring.[37] When Berger died in 1960, the Ford Foundation was on the cusp of funding the so-called *Centre de Prospective*, which was set up by Berger and a group of actors known as *conseillers de synthèse*.[38] The *Centre de Prospective* was apotheosis of interwar experiments conducted by the X Crise architect Jean Coutrot and the eugenicist Alexis Carrel with the *Fondation française pour l'étude des problèmes humains*. X crise were engineers and economists who promoted elitist and authoritarian conceptions of economic order and who understood themselves to be a counterbalance to France's Popular Front governments.[39] The *conseillers de synthèse* were also the heirs to the interwar idea of *synthèse*, which referred to a biological, all-encompassing knowledge of human action.[40] It was hoped that such a total human science, capable of synthesizing all available knowledge, laws, and mechanisms governing the behavior of the human universe, would put Man in charge of his destiny by ensuring that all his actions had a concerted purpose. According to the *conseillers de synthèse*, this notion corresponded to freedom.

After 1945, the *conseillers* began to provide advice to French industry and also became key players in transferring corporate management practices to French state companies. Berger's *Centre de Prospective* was a particularly influential platform that, in the mid 1950s, helped introduce and spread the tools of systems analysis, techniques of forecasting, cybernetics, and operations research in France.[41] The purpose of spreading these analytical tools was to increase the future rationality of decision-making while training a new action elite imbued with what Berger labeled the spirit of decision.[42] This elite, Berger hoped, would counteract what was described in the *Centre de Prospective* essays as a "general phenomenon of crowding," which referred to the problem of coordination in a society in which a myriad of individual decisions were taken at every point in time.[43] The absence of coordination between these multiplicities of actions, Berger feared, created risks of collision and feelings of acceleration and confusion that threatened freedom: "As human behavior becomes more and more complicated, we have to make plans very far in advance."[44]

A Calculus for Social Choice

What Daniel Bell knew of the intellectual context of *prospective* is not clear, but the *Futuribles* venture was understood on both sides of the Atlantic as the intellectual heir of the *Centre de Prospective*. In fact, there are striking similarities between *prospective* as a solution to crowding and Bell's idea that future research could act as a coordination mechanism for mass society. Bell would indeed propose that future research could help solve an inherent problem of liberal politics, namely that of organizing the relationship between collective preferences and individual utility functions. He understood this problem as especially acute in a society driven by the emergence of a new set of social expectations and marked by new forms of government action. In particular, as stated above, Bell argued that forms of prediction would provide a measure of freedom to a society experiencing a rapid rate of change by increasing the "room for maneuver" and the degree of consciousness pertaining to future choices. Within this interpretation, prediction was a form of welfare mechanism, a way of arriving at a social choice that would satisfy mass expectations. But as the Great Society took off in the mid 1960s and President Lyndon B. Johnson announced his plans to change American society for the next generation, Bell would tie the question of freedom to the problems of, first, establishing a desirable future order, and, second, the necessity of anticipating possible unintended consequences of government action over time.[45] Both of these problems now appeared as problems inherent to state action, not problems to be solved by state action.

In 1966, Bell published an essay in *The Public Interest* that was a vociferous critique of what he labeled "government by commission."[46] The phrase "government by commission" referred to the perceived concentration of power in the American presidency that began in the mid 1960s with the creation of a set of presidential offices and presidential commissions that centralized control over economic and social policy in the executive branch.[47] Commissions, such as the Automation Commission to which Bell belonged, were a way, he argued, to bypass Congress. Citing de Jouvenel's critique of Gaullism as a new Principate, Bell asserted that American politics were following a similar course to France. In something of a turnaround from his previous appraisal of decision tools, Bell proposed that the centralization of presidential power, which had mobilized the technical skills of planners and engineers, might engender a new kind of politics in which the role of the elected official was no longer to mediate between expertise and "special demands," but rather to serve special demands without regard for future consequence.⁴⁸ The essay contained a critique of the Great Society that mirrored those offered by other writers in *The Public Interest* in 1964 and 1965, including Irving Kristol and Daniel Moynihan, who warned that new social policies—in particular the War on Poverty and the community action program—might transform the American social contract. Bell, however, was not concerned, as Kristol and Moynihan were, with creating an American welfare state. Rather, he wanted to make certain that the social priorities behind programs like the Great Society were based on rational decisions that took into account the possible consequences such programs could have on American society over time.

This argument cannot be understood without taking into account Bell's changing understanding of the logics of mass society and his conclusion, which he reached by the end of the 1960s, that the end of ideology thesis had been mistaken.⁴⁹ Bell's 1973 *The Coming of Post-Industrial Society* presented a major reinterpretation of the logics of mass society. The core claim of the end of ideology thesis was that affluence and welfare had led to the pacification of class conflict through the meeting of rising social expectations. But by the time Bell started working on *The Coming of Post-Industrial Society*, he had determined that the developing welfare state had itself transformed the nature of mass society. In particular, Bell believed that the extension of public power had created a social situation in which an increasing number of decisions were no longer taken by individuals but were instead taken by communities. The individual, Bell proposed, was no longer the relevant social unit of the postindustrial society; rather, postindustrial society was marked by the rise of unprecedented governmental ambitions and forms of public action that evaded the market as the primary mechanisms of coordination.⁵⁰ According to Bell, the Great Society reflected the emergence of an American *national society* in which decisions were made along collectivist lines unfamiliar to American politics. Bell argued that the programs of the Great Society reflected a new kind of mass politics that consisted of a new set of social claims and group expectations that could not all be satisfied and which, in fact, changed the nature of the social contract.⁵¹ Furthermore, Bell insisted that the problem of "social choice" was that the mass itself did not see the sum of its social expectations, nor was it capable of making informed choices between different expectations that might clash.⁵² In this context, the role of intellectual technologies—and future research in particular—was no longer to provide a logistical tool that helped rationally prioritize different social programs but to solve what Bell understood as central value conflicts.

Bell's first address to the CY2000 in 1964 argued that future research must outline a theory of moral choice for decision-making by working on the problem of desirability. This problem could be dealt with, Bell thought, by predicting the consequence and effects of decisions on society. Bell modeled his idea of social forecasting on the experiments with technological forecasting contemporaneously conducted at the RAND Corporation and the decision tree developed at NASA. Transposing these activities onto an idea of social change, he set the purpose of *social* forecasting as to determine the moments of decision at which system change would take place and a set of imaginable consequences—leading to new necessary decisions—set out like branches from a tree. A decision thus led to a myriad of consequences that could all be imagined from the branch point. If these consequences could be made clear through forms of prediction and evaluated at the point of decision, a mechanism for rational social choice had been found. While Bell's thinking is, on these points, slippery, it is clear that he thought forms of forecasting might contribute to a kind of modeling of the social system.[53]

Nonetheless, Bell repeatedly argued that the social system was not a system in the technological sense and would not strive for equilibrium or move in a linear direction. There was therefore little purpose in embracing deterministic or static forms of extrapolation. Bell was also critical of gaming, which presumed forms of rationality that may not exist in the polity. For Bell, a social order was a "set of rules."[54] The purpose of the tools of conjecture, or of the scenario tool created by Herman Kahn, or the so-called Delphi method invented by Kahn's colleagues Olaf Helmer and Theodore Gordon, was that they did not depart from the assumption of rationality, but rather allowed for the active creation of rationality by envisioning the emergent social situations or orders that might arise as a matter of consequence and effect. These future societies could then be evaluated beforehand and their desirability judged.[55] Such methods could therefore contribute to the problem of "moral choice" and lay the basis for a "decision theory" for American politics.[56]

In *The Coming of Post-Industrial Society*, Bell proposed that future research could solve Kenneth Arrow's problem of social choice, also known as the impossibility theorem. The problem of social choice set out by Arrow in his 1951 *Social Choice and Individual Values* illustrated a problem endemic to liberal democracy, but solved in a system of planning: how to arrive at a rational ordering of collective preferences without violating individual utility functions. According to Arrow's game theoretical exposé, this was an impossible goal to accomplish, as collective preferences could be formulated only by violating optimal individual preferences. Democracy was, in consequence, a suboptimal system.⁵⁷ Bell, though, understood Arrow's problem somewhat differently. While the preferences of rational individuals could be ordered hierarchically, which to Bell was the great achievement of game theory, he nonetheless concluded that no such clear rational ordering could possibly exist for group purposes. "Individuals have their own scale of values, which allows them to assess relative satisfaction against costs, but there is no mechanism that allows us to consider in terms of costs and benefits the varying combinations of private consumption and public purchase of goods."⁵⁸ For Bell, then, the problem centered upon the question of how to order collective preferences in a way compatible with freedom. He proposed that the way to solve this conundrum was to commit to an idea of rationality and discover "how to set forth rational criteria consonant with the values of a free society."⁵⁹ Bell thought that this could be done and such rationality could be deduced by actively bringing notions of consequence to bear on social debate and the act of decision itself. His ideas of cost efficiency, desirability, and social efficiency were all ways of trying to find measures and concrete illustrations of future consequence.

The conception of social forecasting Bell expressed here is particularly interesting. To Bell, social indicators, by which he meant quantitative assessments of different aspects of social progress, were precisely the information that would allow for the quantification of social choice by making detailed assessments of the rationality of investment in a particular social program. A comprehensive system of social accounts, based on a myriad of social indicators, would thus allow for a process of forecasting similar to that of technological forecasts.⁶⁰ On one hand, Bell proposed that in this capacity future research was really a tool of public opinion, of putting the issue of social choice to the masses by clarifying costs and effects, anticipation and consequence. On the other hand, and in the context of the debates conducted in the pages of *The Public Interest* and in the proceedings of the CY2000, Bell also clearly understood the calculation of social choice as a task for the new kind of engineers that were entering public administration, the people who could "read trends" and who could therefore contribute to a "professionalization" of decision.⁶¹

Technocracy for an Era of Contestation: Final Remarks

Bell was sensitive to allegations of technocracy. He was hurt by the New Left critique of *The End of Ideology*; though at the same time, he was quite disturbed by the riots at Columbia and the apparent rejection of expertise and authority of the post 1968 era. *The Coming of Post-Industrial Society* concluded with a chapter entitled "Who Will Rule?" Here, Bell calmly stated, "The central question of post industrial society is the relation of the technocratic decision to politics."[62] Postindustrial society had the tools, Bell argued, to establish a new "social physics" that would realize Condorcet's dream of a *tableau entier* of decisions and choices with which to control social developments in time.[63] Nonetheless, Bell acknowledged that these tools highlighted the problems of technocracy. He understood why critics of US foreign policy would claim that the "McNamara revolution" could be thought of, in Saint Simonean terms, as the extension of technocratic power over all societal decisions. But Bell did not agree with such interpretations. Rather, he argued that the politics of postindustrial society were intrinsically value based and demanded a rationalization of decision that did not sideline, but rather directly addressed, the problem of values. Through the idea of rational weighing of consequence and desirability, Bell insisted that forms of prediction could solve the issue of values.

To Bell, the role of intellectual technologies was not to remove the question of values from politics, but rather to expose them to a process of rationalization by which the effect of pursuing certain interests or social desires would become clear. Bell considered both expertise and computer technology as critical means to achieve this end. Thus, for Bell himself, intellectual technologies did not represent a call for technocracy, but instead indicated a desire to strengthen a Deweyan future mechanism that would enlighten mass politics about costs and effects. Bell believed that this was essential to ensuring the future of liberal democracy. Still, Bell's project amounted to nothing less than the application of scientific or engineering skills derived from operations research to normative problems of welfare preferences, desirability, and social priority. Indeed, it was precisely through the application of expertise to the very problem of desirable forms of social change that future research gained its relevance in planning systems from the 1970s onward.

Nevertheless, if Bell originally understood the CY2000 as an arena for such future evaluation and a means by which to enlighten the American public about such consequences, by the end of the decade, his hopes were dashed. In the final report of the CY2000 in 1973, Bell wrote of the plebiscitary and violent politics of marches to Washington, and the need to take into account that the institutions created in American society would mark it for the next thirty years.[64] In 1972, Bell parted ways with emergent neoconservatives, particularly Irving Kristol. His conception of the need for forms of decisionist rationality in mass politics were nevertheless precursors of a debate, after 1968, on the complexity of postindustrial societies and on the (lack of) governability of democracies that would be the hallmark of the Trilateral Commission and of a larger backlash against the welfarist moment in American politics.[65]

Jenny Andersson is CNRS Research Professor at Sciences Po, Paris. She is the author of several books on social democracy, including *The Workshop and the Library: Social Democracy and Capitalism in an Age of Knowledge* (Stanford University Press, 2010) and several publications on the history of futures research and prediction. Her article "The Great Future Debate and the Struggle for the World" appeared in the *American Historical Review* in 2012 (117, 1411–30), and she edited, with Egle Rindzeviciute, *Transnational perspectives on the future in science and politics in the Cold War: Forging the future* (Routledge, 2015). Her most recent book is *The Future of the World: Futurists, Futurology, and the Struggle for the Cold War Imagination* (Oxford University Press, 2018).

Notes

The author acknowledges funding from the European Research Council through Futurepol ERC grant agreement 283786.

1. See, for instance, Howard Brick, "Optimism of the Mind: Imagining Post Industrialism in America in the 1960s and 1970s," *American Quarterly* 44, no. 3 (1992): 348–80.
2. Daniel Bell, *The Coming of Post Industrial Society: A Venture in Social Forecasting* (Cambridge, MA: MIT Press, 1973), 29.
3. Russell Jacoby, *Picture Imperfect: Utopian Thought for an Antiutopian Age* (New York: Columbia University Press, 2005), 57.
4. Howard Brick, the leading scholar on Bell, argues that Bell was not a technocrat but had an interest in the "system." Howard Brick, *The Age of Contradiction: American Thought and Culture in the 1960s* (Ithaca, NY: Cornell University Press, 2000), 124–26, 132; and Howard Brick, *Daniel Bell and the Decline of Radicalism: Social Theory and Political Reconciliation in the 1940s* (Madison: University of Wisconsin Press, 1986), 12, 72, 82, 94, 105.
5. This essay does not discuss the notion of Cold War science. Future research, as I understand it here, was a derivative of Operations Research and reflected a notion of rationality that was derived from gaming. See Paul Erickson, "Mathematical Models, Rational Choice, and the Search for Cold War Culture," *Isis* 101 (2010): 386–92; Paul Erickson, Judy L. Klein, Lorraine Daston, Rebecca Lemov, Thomas Sturm, and Michael D. Gordin, *How Reason Almost Lost Its Mind: The Strange Career of Cold War Rationality* (Chicago, IL: University of Chicago Press, 2013).

6. See works such as Philip Mirowski, *Machine Dreams: How Economics Became a Cyborg Science* (Cambridge, MA: Harvard University Press, 2002); Joy Rohde, *Armed with Expertise: The Militarization of American Social Research during the Cold War* (Ithaca, NY: Cornell University Press, 2013); David Jardini, *Out of Blue Yonder: The Transfer of Systems Thinking from the Pentagon to the Great Society* (Washington, DC: Carnegie Mellon University, 1996); Jennifer Light, *From Warfare to Welfare: Defense Intellectuals and Urban Problems in Cold War America* (Baltimore, MD: Johns Hopkins University Press, 2003).
7. Brick, *Age of Contradiction*, 124–26.
8. See works such as Nils Gilman, *Mandarins of the Future: Modernization Theory in Cold War America* (Baltimore, MD: Johns Hopkins University Press, 2003), 13; Michael Latham, *Modernisation as Ideology: Social Science and Nation Building in the Kennedy Era* (Madison: University of Wisconsin Press, 2000), 30, 34–35, 50, 67.
9. See Jenny Andersson, *The Future of the World: Futurology, Futurists and the Struggle for the Post Cold War Imagination* (Oxford: Oxford University Press, 2018).
10. Brick, *Daniel Bell and the Decline of Radicalism*.
11. These were concerned with the opposite problem to Bell: that of putting market mechanisms into socialist systems of planning.
12. Daniel Bell, *The End of Ideology: On the Exhaustion of Political Ideas in the 1950s* (Cambridge, MA: Harvard University Press, 1962), 25, also 15, 120, 224.
13. Bell, *The End of Ideology*, 35–38.
14. Francis Stonor Saunders, *Who Paid the Piper: The CIA and the Cultural Cold War* (London: Granta, 1999); Pierre Gremion, *L'intelligence de l'anticommunisme: Le congrès pour la liberté de la culture* (Paris: Seuil, 1995).
15. Dewey himself is the object of a conflicted American historiography, see Brett Gary, "Dueling Deweys: Moralism, Scientism, and American Social Science History," *Reviews in American History* 23, no. 4 (1995): 623–30; and John M. Jordan, *Machine-Age Ideology: Social Engineering and American Liberalism, 1911–1939* (Chapel Hill: University of North Carolina Press, 1994); Mark Smith, *Social Science in the Crucible: The American Debate Over Objectivity and Purpose, 1918–1941* (Durham, NC: Duke University Press, Publisher, 1994).
16. See Bell, *The End of Ideology*, 249.
17. Daniel Bell, "A Preliminary Statement," draft, *Commission for the Year 2000 Records*, box 1, folder 1 (American Academy of Arts and Science); and Daniel Bell, "The Year 2000: The Trajectory of an Idea," in *The Year 2000: Work in Progress*, ed. Daniel Bell and Stephen Graubard (Cambridge, MA: MIT Press, 1967), 1–17.
18. Daniel Bell, "Twelve Modes of Prediction," *Daedalus* 93, no. 3 (1964): 845–880.
19. Giles Scott Smith, "The Congress for Cultural Freedom, the End of Ideology and the Milan seminar of 1955," *Journal of Contemporary History* 37, no. 3 (2002): 437–455.

20. Michael Polanyi, introduction to the 1955 seminar, quoted in Gremion, *L'intelligence de l'anticommunisme: Le congres de la liberte de la culture* (Paris: Presses Universitaires de France, 1995), 154, 166.
21. Daniel Bell, "The Study of the Future," *The Public Interest* 1 (1966): 120–21.
22. Bell, *The Coming*, 313.
23. Bell, "Twelve Modes of Prediction," 870.
24. Both Mannheim and Polanyi were key to the development of the sociology of knowledge from the 1950s on, beginning with the Congress's reaction to the domestication of science and technology in Soviet communism. Elena Aronova, "The Congress for Cultural Freedom, Minerva, and the Quest for Instituting Science Studies in the Age of Cold War," *Minerva* 50 (2012): 307–37.
25. Bell, *The End of Ideology*, 405.
26. Brick, "Optimism of the Mind," 349.
27. Bell, *The End of Ideology*, 229f.
28. Zeev Sternhell sees de Jouvenel as one of the key intellectuals of French fascism. Zeev Sternhell, *Ni droite ni gauche: L'ideologie fasciste en France* (Paris: Fayard, 2013). Francois Denord, "French Neoliberalism and Its Divisions: From the Colloque Walter Lippman to the Fifth Republic," in *The Road from Mont Pelerin: The Making of the Neoliberal Thought Collective*, ed. Dieter Plehwe and Philip Mirowski (Cambridge, MA: Harvard University Presss, 2009), 45–68 has argued for de Jouvenel as a central character in French neoliberalism. See also Olivier Dard, *Bertrand de Jouvenel* (Paris: Perrin, 2008).
29. Jenny Andersson, "The Great Future Debate and the Struggle for the World," *The American Historical Review* 5, no. 117 (2002): 1411–30.
30. Bertrand de Jouvenel, *L'art de la conjecture* (Monaco: Editions du Rocher, 1962).
31. Correspondence between Shepard Stone and Daniel Bell, Ford Foundation Archives, Futuribles file 61, 22, letter from Bell to Stone 18 June 1962.
32. See Bertrand de Jouvenel, "Du principat," *Revue française de Science politique* 14, no. 6 (1964): 1053–86. Monarchism was a central element of French interwar fascism.
33. Bertrand de Jouvenel, "Sur L'évolution des formes de gouvernements," January 1961, Bertrand de Jouvenel's papers, Département des manuscrits, Bibliothèque nationale de France.
34. Ibid.
35. Bertrand de Jouvenel, *L'économie dirigée* (Paris: Editions de Valois, 1928).
36. De Jouvenel, *The Art of Conjecture*.
37. Gaston Berger, personal file, FF archives, 56, 21. See Vincent Guiader, "Sociohistoire de la prospective" (Paris: Dauphine, 2007).
38. FF log file on CdP L57 11, 28, letters to Shepard Stone 29 December 1955 and 30 November 1957.
39. Gabrielle Hecht, "Planning a Technological Nation," in *Systems Experts and Computers*, ed. Thomas Hughes and Agatha Hughes (Cambridge, MA: MIT Press, 2003), 133–60.

40. Olivier Dard, *Coutrot, de l'ingénieur au prophète* (Reims: Editions du Franche Comte, 1999); Andres Reggiani, *God's Eugenicist: Alexis Carrel and the Sociobiology of Decline* (London: Berghahn, 2007).
41. Gaston Berger and Lucien Febvre, *L'Encyclopédie française: Tome XX, Le monde en devenir (histoire; évolution, prospective)* (Paris: Societe de gestion de l'Encyclopedie, 1959).
42. Berger, "L'attitude prospective," *Prospective* (May 1958): 1–11.
43. Gaston Berger, *Phenoménologie du temps et de prospective* (Paris: Presses Universitaires de France, 1964).
44. Berger proposition for the Center for prospective anthropology, 29 December 1955, to Stone.
45. Bell, "The Study of the Future."
46. Daniel Bell, "Government by Commission," *The Public Interest* 5 (1966): 3–10.
47. Howard Brick, *Transcending Capitalism: Visions of a New Society in Modern American Thought* (Ithaca, NY: Cornell University Press, 2006).
48. Bell, *The Coming*, 309, 310. The Automation Commission was the site of a major controversy between American Labor and budding neoconservatives, and was, as Kristol wrote, a defining experience for the rejection of the Great society.
49. Daniel Bell, "Preliminary Memorandum for the Future of the Congress," International Association for Cultural Freedom Records, Box 85, Folder T. I am grateful to Daniel Steinmetz Jenkins for sharing this with me.
50. Daniel Bell, "1975–2000 AD: An intellectual reconnaissance." Draft. CY2000 records, AAAS, box 1, folder 3. Report of the commission for the Year 2000. American Academy of Arts and Science, Records, 1969–1970, 37–42, 41.
51. For a discussion of the Great society programs and the rise of the neoconservative critique, see Alice O'Connor, *Poverty Knowledge* (Cambridge, MA: Harvard University Press, 2002); Michael Katz, *From the War on Poverty to the War on Welfare* (Cambridge, MA: Harvard University Press, 1998); Andrew Hartman, *A War for the Soul of America: A History of the Culture Wars* (Chicago, IL: University of Chicago Press, 2015).
52. Daniel Bell, "The Year 2000," 1.
53. Daniel Bell, "A Preliminary Statement," draft; and "Bell Memorandum to the Working Parties, undated, 1965, part 1," *Records of the Commission for the Year 2000*, box 1, folder 1 (American Academy for the Arts and Sciences).
54. Bell, *The End of Ideology*, xviii.
55. Bell, "Twelve Modes of Prediction"; Bell, "The Study of the Future"; Herman Kahn, "Alternative World Futures," Hudson Institute discussion papers (April 1964); Sharon Ghamari Tabrizi, *The Worlds of Herman Kahn* (Cambridge, MA: Harvard University Press, 2005).
56. Bell, "Preliminary Memorandum," 22 October 1965, in *The Year 2000: Work in Progress*, ed. Daniel Bell and S. Graubard, 22.

57. Bell, *The Coming*, 313, 304; Kenneth Arrow, *A Theory of Social Choice* (New Haven, CT: Yale University Press, 1951); S. M. Amadae, *Rationalizing Liberal Capitalist Democracy* (Chicago, IL: University of Chicago Press, 2003), 83.
58. Bell, *The Coming*, 304.
59. Ibid., 304.
60. Ibid., 324.
61. Daniel Moynihan, "The Professionalisation of Reform," *The Public Interest* 1 (1965): 6–14.
62. Bell, *The Coming*, 337.
63. Ibid., 347.
64. Final report of the Commission for the Year 2000 (Cambridge MA: American Academy for the Arts and Sciences, 1973).
65. Trilateral Commission, *The Crisis of Democracy* (New York: New York University Press, 1973. Both Samuel Huntington and Michel Crozier were members of the *futuribles* project and Bell had invited both to the CY2000. See Ariane Leendertz, "Complexity Theory and the Crisis of Democracy," unpublished conference paper, June 2016, MPIfG Cologne.

Bibliography

Amadae, S. M. *Rationalizing Liberal Capitalist Democracy*. Chicago, IL: Chicago University Press, 2003.

American Academy for the Arts and Sciences. "Final report of the Commission for the Year 2000." *Records*, 1969–1970 (1973): 37–42.

Andersson, Jenny. "The Great Future Debate and the Struggle for the World." *The American Historical Review* 5, no. 117 (2002): 1411–30.

Aronova, Elena. "The Congress for Cultural Freedom, Minerva, and the Quest for Instituting Science Studies in the Age of Cold War." *Minerva* 50 (2012): 307–37.

Arrow, Kenneth. *Social Choice and Individual Values*. 2nd ed. New Haven, CT: Yale University Press, 1970.

Bell, Daniel. *The Coming of Post Industrial Society: A Venture in Social Forecasting*. New York: Basic Books, 1973.

———. *The End of Ideology: On the Exhaustion of Political Ideas in the 1950s*. 2nd ed. Cambridge MA: Publisher, 1962.

———. "Government by Commission." *The Public Interest* 5 (1966): 3–10.

———. "The Study of the Future." *The Public Interest* 1 (1966): 120–21.

———. "Twelve Modes of Prediction." *Daedalus* 93, no. 3 (1964): 862–78.

———. "The Year 2000: The Trajectory of an Idea." In *The Year 2000: Work in Progress*, edited by Daniel Bell and S. Graubard, 1–17. Cambridge, MA: MIT Press, 1967.

Bell, Daniel, and S. Graubard, eds. *Toward the Year 2000: Work in Progress*. Cambridge, MA: MIT Press, 1967.

Berger, Gaston. "L'attitude prospective." *Prospective* (May 1958): 1–11.

Berger, Gaston. *Phenoménologie du temps et de prospective*. Paris: Presses Universitaires de France, 1964.

Berger, Gaston, and Febvre Lucien. *L'Encyclopedie francaise. Tome XX, Le monde en devenir (histoire; évolution, prospective)*. Paris: Publisher, 1959.
Brick, Howard. *The Age of Contradiction: American Thought and Culture in the 1960s*. Ithaca, NY: Cornell University Press, 2000.
———. *Daniel Bell and the Decline of Radicalism: Social Theory and Political Reconciliation in the 1940s*. Madison: University of Wisconsin Press, 1986.
———. "Optimism of the Mind: Imagining Post Industrialism in America in the 1960s and 1970s." *American Quarterly* 44, no. 3 (1992): 348–80.
———. *Transcending Capitalism: Visions of a New Society in Modern American Thought*. Ithaca, NY: Cornell University Press, 2006.
Dard, Olivier. *Bertrand de Jouvenel*. Paris: Presses Universitaires de France, 2008.
———. *Coutrot, de l'ingenieur au prophete*. City: Presses Universitaires Franche comte, 1999.
De Jouvenel, Bertrand. "Du principat." *Revue française de Science politique, décembre 1964* (1964): 1053–86.
———. *L'art de la conjecture*. Monaco: Editions du Rocher, 1962.
———. *L'économie dirigée*. Paris: Editions de Valois, 1928.
Denord, Francois. "French Neoliberalism and Its Divisions. From the colloque Walter Lippman to the fifth republic." In *The Road from Mont Pelerin: The Making of the Neoliberal Thought Collective*, edited by Dieter Plehwe and Phillip Mirowski. Cambridge, MA: Harvard University Press, 2009.
Erickson, Paul. "Mathematical Models, Rational Choice, and the Search for Cold War Culture." *Isis* 101 (2010): 386–92.
Erickson, Paul, Judy L. Klein, Lorraine Daston, Rebecca Lemov, Thomas Sturm, and Michael D. Gordin, et al. *How Reason Almost Lost Its Mind: The Strange Career of Cold War Rationality*. Chicago, IL: University of Chicago Press, 2013.
Gary, Brett. "Dueling Deweys: Moralism, Scientism, and American Social Science History." *Reviews in American History* 23, no. 4 (1995): 623–30.
Ghamari Tabrizi, Sharon. *The Worlds of Herman Kahn*. Cambridge, MA: Harvard University Press, 2005.
Gilman, Nils. *Mandarins of the Future, Modernization Theory in Cold War America*. Baltimore, MD: Johns Hopkins University Press, 2003.
Gremion, Pierre. *L'intelligence de l'anticommunisme: Le congres de la liberte de la culture*. Paris: Presses Universitaires de France, 1995.
Guiader, Vincent. "Sociohistoire de la prospective." PhD diss., Universite Dauphine, 2007.
Hartman, Andrew. *A War for the Soul of America: A History of the Culture Wars*. Chicago, IL: University of Chicago Press, 2015.
Hecht, Gabrielle. "Planning a Technological Nation." In *Systems, Experts and Computers*, edited by Thomas Hughes and Agatha Hughes, 133–60. Cambridge, MA: MIT Press, 2003.
Jacoby, Russell. *Picture Imperfect: Utopian Thought for an Antiutopian Age*. New York: Columbia University Press, 2005.
Jardini, David. *Out of Blue Yonder: The Transfer of Systems Thinking from the Pentagon to the Great Society*. Washington, DC: Carnegie Mellon, 1996.

Jordan, John M. *Machine-Age Ideology: Social Engineering and American Liberalism, 1911–1939*. City: University of North Carolina Press, 1994.
Kahn, Herman. "Alternative World Futures." Hudson Institute discussion papers, April 1964.
Katz, Michael. *From the War on Poverty to the War on Welfare*. Cambridge, MA: Harvard University Press, 1998.
Latham, Michael. *Modernisation as Ideology: Social Science and Nation Building in the Kennedy Era*. Madison: University of Wisconsin Press, 2000.
Leendertz, Ariane. "Complexity Theory and the Crisis of Democracy." Unpublished conference paper, June 2016, Max Planck Institute for the Study of Society, Cologne.
Light, Jennifer. *From Warfare to Welfare: Defense Intellectuals and Urban Problems in Cold War America*. Baltimore, MD: Johns Hopkins University Press, 2003.
Mirowski, Phillip. *Machine Dreams: How Economics Became a Cyborg Science*. Cambridge, MA: Harvard University Press, 2002.
Moynihan, Daniel. "The Professionalisation of Reform." *The Public Interest*, 1 (1965): 6–14.
O'Connor, Alice. *Poverty Knowledge*. Cambridge, MA: Harvard University Press, 2002.
Reggiani, Andres. *God's Eugenicist: Alexis Carrel and the Sociobiology of Decline*. London: Berghahn, 2007.
Rohde, Joy. *Armed with Expertise: The Militarization of American Social Research during the Cold War*. Ithaca, NY: Cornell University Press, 2013.
Scott Smith, Giles. "The Congress for Cultural Freedom, the End of Ideology and the Milan seminar of 1955." *Journal of Contemporary History* 37, no. 3 (2002): 437–455.
Smith, Mark C. *Social Science in the Crucible: The American Debate Over Objectivity and Purpose, 1918–1941*. Durham, NC: Duke University Press, 1964.
Sternhell, Zeev. *Ni droite ni gauche: L'ideologie fasciste en France*. Paris: Presses Universitaires de France, 2013.
Stonor Saunders, Francis. *Who Paid the Piper: The CIA and the Cultural Cold War*. London: Granta, 1999.
Trilateral Commission. *The Crisis of Democracy*. City: Publisher, 1973.

 9

Predictive Algorithms and Criminal Sentencing

Angèle Christin

The legal and sociological study of judicial sentencing revolves around two broadly opposed conceptions of the relationship between existing laws and the decision-making process in courts. On the one hand, "internal" analyses describe judicial sentencing as the unproblematic application of a given set of legal rules. In this view, which encompasses the "legalist" ideology of the legal professions analyzed by Judith Shklar, judges, prosecutors, and attorneys are expected to implement a law that is always already "there," in ways that are objective, impartial, and consistent over time and across cases.[1] Most internal analyses thus focus on the formal characteristics of the laws themselves and pay scarce attention to the daily proceedings of the court system, which are considered to be unproblematic.

On the other hand, "external" approaches emphasize the indeterminacy of legal rules and highlight the role of nonlegal factors—political, social, and cultural—in shaping how laws are implemented in courts.[2] This is the case of "Legal Realist" perspective, an approach that emerged in the United States during the New Deal. Legal Realist scholars argued against the formalism of most legal analyses of judicial sentencing, noting instead that discretionary decision-making permeates the legal system. For instance, Jerome Frank, a prominent figure of Legal Realism, is often credited with the idea that judicial decisions mostly depend on what the judge had for breakfast. This "external" perspective in turn continues to influence most sociological analyses of judicial sentencing.[3]

Over the past ten years, the question of judicial discretion has taken a new turn with the development of "Big Data" analytics and algorithms. There are currently more than sixty predictive tools drawing on large amounts of quantitative data in the US criminal justice system.[4] Based on a small number of variables about defendants, either connected to their criminal histories (e.g., previous offenses, failure to appear in court, violent offenses, etc.) or socio-demographic characteristics (e.g., age, sex, employment status, drug history, etc.), the algorithms typically provide an estimate of an offender's risk of recidivism or failure to appear in court when on bail, often expressed in a range of "low" to "high" risk. These predictive algorithms (also called "risk-assessment instruments") are explicitly designed to "structure" the criminal decision-making process and curtail judicial discretion by providing a clear set of guidelines, scores, and recommendations to judges, prosecutors, and probation officers in charge of making decisions about cases.

Risk-assessment tools have attracted increasing attention, both positive and negative. On the positive side, journalists and advocates for predictive technologies emphasize the benefits of using "smart statistics" in order to reduce crime and improve a dysfunctional criminal justice system characterized by racial discrimination and mass incarceration.[5] In this view, risk-assessment tools might help empty overcrowded jails by constraining judicial discretion and reliably identifying low-risk offenders who could be released. Drawing a parallel with the case of baseball, where the use of data-intensive techniques transformed the game, advocates argue that we need to start "moneyballing justice" and replace "conjecture" with "formulas."[6] "Evidence-based sentencing," as it is often called, has already attracted significant bipartisan support among practitioners, nonprofit institutions studying criminal justice, and governmental bodies in the United States.[7]

On the negative side, critics emphasize the dystopian and problematic aspects of Big Data analytics. They point out that predictive algorithms imply convicting defendants based on crimes they have not committed yet, creating a situation not unlike the one described by the film *Minority Report*.[8] Critics argue that algorithms tend to reinforce social and racial inequalities instead of reducing them; they also note that risk-assessment tools draw on variables that are unfair and unconstitutional.[9] More broadly, risk-assessment tools are analyzed as being part of a new "culture of control" based on the surveillance, prediction, and control at a distance of "risky" groups through actuarial techniques and digital technologies.[10]

Yet in all of this, there has been little research so far about what predictive tools mean for the conceptualization of judicial sentencing.

Are predictive algorithms putting an end to judicial discretion, turning sentencing into the application of a set of predefined rules? Or are they simply changing the form and locus of sovereign decision-making in the criminal justice context? More broadly, what are the representations and imaginaries of judicial sentencing embedded in predictive technologies, and what is the response of legal professionals? Moving beyond the history of decisionism, this chapter examines a modern debate surrounding algorithmic sentencing, a technology hailed by its proponents as capable of rationalizing aspects of the criminal justice system by detaching them from political considerations. First, I analyze the discourses surrounding the emergence of Big Data analytics in the US criminal justice system using the concept of "mechanical objectivity" developed by Daston and Galison.[11] The chapter then turns to the actual practices associated with risk-assessment tools. After listing the different types of predictive algorithms and actuarial techniques currently in use in criminal justice—and noting that many of them are not new—I offer a critical assessment of the main issues associated with the construction and reception of predictive algorithms in criminal justice. Specifically, I identify five major issues: algorithmic bias, heterogeneity and disparity, black boxing, gaming strategies, and changing values of punishment. I conclude by discussing avenues for future research on algorithmic decision-making, within and beyond the criminal justice context.

Making Sense of Big Data Analytics: The Myth of Mechanical Objectivity

"Big Data" has become a ubiquitous concept over the past ten years. According to boyd and Crawford,[12] three criteria need to be taken into account in analyzing the concept. First, Big Data encompasses a variety of new technologies involving the use of complex computational methods to analyze large data sets, themselves characterized by the three Vs: "volume" (there are unprecedented amounts of data), "variety" (the data frequently has different formats and structures), and "velocity" (data is frequently added over time). Second, Big Data involves novel forms of analysis and authority: the examination of large data sets, especially those where the entire population is included ("N=all"), makes it possible to identify new patterns that can later be used to make economic, social, technical, and legal claims. Third, Big Data functions as a mythology: it comes with a "widespread belief that large data sets offer a higher form of intelligence and knowledge."[13] An illustration of this belief is the idea that, with Big Data, "the numbers speak for themselves," as Chris Anderson, then editor-in-chief of *Wired*, famously declared in his 2008 article on the "end of theory."[14]

Big Data and the Transformation of Decision-Making

Big Data analytics are currently transforming many areas of social life, from finance to communications, healthcare, education, journalism, policing, and, of course, criminal justice.[15] There are significant similarities in the arguments developed to justify and advocate for algorithms across these sectors: algorithms are usually described as a rationalizing force.[16] However, on a deeper level, two slightly different versions of this argument emerge. First, there is what can be called an "information" argument: in this view, algorithms are simply better than humans at gathering and analyzing large amounts of data. Therefore, algorithms make better decisions than individuals, simply because they have more information at their disposal, which they can compute and analyze in a faster and more reliable manner. For instance, in the case of credit and loans, the adoption of credit scores in the United States was described as an improvement compared to the traditional way in which banks made decisions about credit and mortgage.[17]

A second argument relates to the purportedly "objective" nature of algorithms: algorithms would be better than humans at making decisions because they are value-neutral. In this view—and in contrast to individuals, whose opinions are shaped by a variety of social factors including class, gender, race, age, politics, etc.—algorithms would have no politics: their goal would be to analyze data in the most accurate way and maximize the amount of variance explained by the model. Therefore, Big Data analytics are often described as the cure for systems shaped by long histories of discrimination. This argument can be found in the case of credit mentioned before: the different companies promoting credit scores described them as a less biased and discriminatory method for calculating financial risk than face-to-face interviews. This argument is also mobilized for public services such as education, policing, public administration, and, perhaps unsurprisingly, criminal justice.

Both the "information" and the "objectivity" arguments reflect a belief in the superior value of "mechanical objectivity"—which Daston and Galison define as "the insistent drive to repress the willful intervention of the artist-author, and to put in its stead a set of procedures that would, as it were move nature to the page through a strict protocol, if not automatically"—over human judgment.[18] Like the scientists of the late nineteenth century who began relying on daguerreotypes and cameras in order to better represent nature, modern-day technologists, practitioners, consultants, and policy-makers strongly believe that machines are better than humans at making decisions and that they can process more information in an efficient, rational, predictable, and value-neutral way.

Justifying the Use of Big Data Analytics in the Criminal Justice System

This belief in the superiority of mechanical over human judgment is ubiquitous in the case of criminal justice. Advocates emphasize several benefits of Big Data analytics. Take, for example, the arguments developed by Anne Milgram, the former Attorney General for the State of New Jersey and former Vice President of Criminal Justice at the John and Laura Arnold Foundation where she supervised the development of a pretrial risk-assessment instrument. Milgram explained her views about "smart statistics" in an article published in *The Atlantic* and in a TED talk.[19] Milgram points out that prisons are overcrowded and that this has become a significant problem, notably because of the costs incurred by taxpayers. According to her, courts currently do not have enough data about defendants and inmates: "Who is in our criminal justice system? What crimes have been charged? What risks do individual offenders pose? And which option would best protect the public and make the best use of our limited resources?"[20] Because judges and prosecutors do not have the answers to these questions, Milgram asserted, they rely on their problematic "instinct" when making decisions:

> Judges have the best intentions when they make these decisions about risk, but they're making them subjectively. They're like the baseball scouts twenty years ago who were using their instinct and their experience to try to decide what risk someone poses. They're being subjective, and we know what happens with subjective decision making, which is that we are often wrong. What we need in this space are strong data and analytics.[21]

Big Data analytics, in Milgram's view, can lead to more informed and objective decision-making on the side of judges and prosecutors: "Technology could help us leverage data to identify offenders who will pose unacceptable risks to society if they are not behind bars and distinguish them from those defendants who will have lower recidivism rates if they are supervised in the community or given alternatives to incarceration before trial."[22] This, in turn, would help "minimize injustice" in the criminal justice system:

Our research has shown that the current system—which relies much more on subjective judgment than objective, evidence-based tools—does not adequately protect the public or ensure fairness. Defendants that you would expect to be locked up while awaiting trial—the very highest-risk individuals and those accused of violent crimes—are often released. Meanwhile, low-risk, nonviolent defendants often spend extended periods of time behind bars. This is counterintuitive and unfair, and it is putting our communities at risk.[23]

Milgram's arguments are echoed by Adam Gelb, director of the public safety performance project at the Pew Charitable Trusts, who further emphasizes that risk-assessment tools make judges and prosecutors more accountable, therefore curbing prejudice and increasing the overall transparency of the system:

A supervisor can question, "Why are we recommending that this kid with a minor record get locked up?" Anything that's on paper is more transparent than the system we had in the past. In many cases, you had no idea from probation officer to probation officer, let alone from judge to judge, what was in people's heads. There was no transparency, and decisions could be based on just about any bias or prejudice.[24]

Hence, advocates tend to understand Big Data analytics as a cure for a broken criminal justice system. First, algorithms help judges and prosecutors make more informed decisions about bail, sentencing, and parole by providing them with reliable information. Second, risk-assessment tools increase accountability by making the decision-making process more objective and transparent: legal professionals cannot solely rely on their "instinct" and "subjectivity." Thus, Big Data advocates strongly believe in the benefits of "mechanical objectivity" and the idea that human judgment can be improved by relying on data-driven, value-neutral algorithms. In so doing, they hope to eradicate or at least limit the discretion involved in judicial sentencing.[25]

Risk-Assessment Tools in the United States: An Overview

Moving away from the discourses and arguments supporting Big Data analytics, I turn to the concrete technological artifacts that are being developed and used in the United States. Risk-assessment instruments are not new and indeed have existed for most of the twentieth century.[26] Yet the number of instruments, methods used, and diffusion across jurisdictions has expanded exponentially over the past twenty years. Whereas early instruments relied only on "static," unalterable factors (e.g., history of substance abuse, age at first offense, etc.), recent instruments also draw on large data sets, increasingly sophisticated methods, and "dynamic" risk factors (e.g., variables about employment, criminal friends, etc., also called "criminogenic needs") that can be adjusted over time. The main risk-assessments tools currently in use in the US criminal justice system operate at three different stages of the criminal procedure: pretrial, sentencing, and probation.

In pretrial justice, the Arnold Foundation launched in 2015 the "Public Safety Assessment-Court" (PSA), a risk-assessment tool that can be used in every jurisdiction in the United States in order to "accurately, quickly, and efficiently assess the risk that a defendant will engage in violence, commit a crime, or fail to come back to court." The instrument relies on variables such as the age of the defendant, his or her criminal record, and previous failures to appear in court. Contrary to other types of risk-assessment tools, it does not use variables about the individual's level of education, socioeconomic status, and place of residence. Before the PSA-Court, only about 10 percent of courts had developed their own risk-assessment tools. The Arnold Foundation's PSA pretrial instrument is currently used by twenty-nine jurisdictions, including three entire states (Arizona, Kentucky, and New Jersey) and three major cities (Charlotte, Chicago, and Phoenix). According to the Arnold Foundation, the PSA led to lower crime rates and a decrease in jail population in the jurisdictions where it was used.[27]

A second area where risk-assessment tools are important is judicial sentencing itself. Efforts to standardize and limit disparities in sentencing are not new in the United States.[28] In 1984, for example, bipartisan efforts led to the Sentencing Reform Act, which created the US Sentencing Commission and the Sentencing Tables.[29] Though technically not a predictive tool (its main goal was to promote sentencing consistency by providing an average estimate of the sentences across jurisdictions in the United States), the Sentencing Tables nonetheless bear similarities with risk-assessment instruments: the columns categorize the criminal history of the defendants, while the rows describe their offense level, and each box provides an estimate of the mandatory length of incarceration (for example, ten to sixteen months of imprisonment). The Sentencing Tables became advisory instead of mandatory in 2005. Many risk-assessment instruments have emerged since then to complement them. For instance, Pennsylvania's Sentencing Commission is developing a risk-assessment scale to determine what level of recidivism risk is associated with all adult defendants.[30]

Finally, the number of states using a risk-assessment tool for probation and parole increased from about one in 1979 to more than twenty-eight since 2004.[31] Among the most popular prediction instruments are the Level of Services Inventory-Revised (LSI-R), a proprietary product of the private company Multi-Health Systems; the Correctional Offender Management Profiling for Alternative Sanctions (COMPAS), a product of Northpointe, Inc.; and the Salient Factor Score, used by the US Parole Commission. The types of variables included in these programs vary but are generally encompassing. For instance, Starr notes that "the LSI-R include not just the defendant's current living situation but also history variables outside the defendant's control; for instance, a defendant will be considered higher risk if his parents had criminal backgrounds."[32] These tools are used for many purposes, including the security classification of prison inmates, inmates' eligibility for parole, and inmates' levels of probation and parole supervision.

Five Issues with Risk-Assessment Tools

This section identifies five sets of problems with the risk-assessment tools currently in use in the US criminal justice system: algorithmic bias, disparity and heterogeneity, black boxing, gaming and shifting discretion, and the changing goals of punishment. These issues point toward a disconnect between the optimistic beliefs regarding the benefits of Big Data analytics and the actual practices surrounding the construction, diffusion, and use of predictive algorithms.

Statistical Bias and Algorithmic Fairness

One of the main arguments used to justify the development and diffusion of risk-assessment tools is that algorithms would be more objective and value-neutral than people. In this view, algorithms would help "cure" administration marked by long histories of inefficiency and racial discrimination, two issues that well describe the US criminal justice system.[33] Yet it is not clear whether algorithms actually fulfill this goal. At a basic level, it is important to note that algorithms always draw on past data, which is itself biased in ways that mirror the discriminatory features of the existing system. Therefore, an uncritical use of algorithms at best reproduces the status quo; at worst, they may engage in "unintentional discrimination," have a disparate impact on different groups, and even increase inequalities between groups.[34]

This is because algorithms tend to have a performative quality: they contribute to create the situation they describe. The case of predictive policing is a clear instance of such a self-fulfilling mechanism.

When predictive algorithms identify "hot spot" crime zones (usually low-income African American neighborhoods), policemen are more likely to patrol in these neighborhoods and arrest people who will later be convicted. If they never patrol in neighborhoods not identified as "hot spots" by the algorithm (for instance affluent neighborhoods), policemen will not make arrests in those places. This data will later be entered into the algorithm, thus producing a feedback loop: inner-city neighborhoods will be more frequently identified as "hot spots," which will shape the allocation of police effort, the arrests, and the algorithm's identification of "risky" versus "safe" zones. Harcourt describes this mechanism as a "ratchet effect": "the profiled populations become an even larger portion of the carceral population."[35]

Understanding precisely how statistical bias operates in the case of risk-assessment tools requires us to get a sense of how they are constructed. In order to build a risk-assessment tool, one first needs a dataset made up of criminal cases that have already been sentenced. Based on this data set, statisticians or computer programmers run a model and select the variables that are the most significant in explaining the outcome variable of interest, such as recidivism or failure to appear in court. As in all other types of statistical analysis, dealing with a small sample size or a large amount of missing data (e.g., cases for which variables such as age, criminal record, etc., are lacking) is a challenge because it makes the model less accurate. Statisticians also need to decide which modeling strategy to adopt, from linear regression to machine learning techniques where the algorithm automatically adapts its equation to take into account new cases and follows specific procedure to analyze the data (decision tree, neural network, random forest, etc.).[36] Statisticians then reverse the model: instead of examining the causes of recidivism, the model is used to predict the risk of recidivism for any given individual. Last, the algorithm is tested: its predictions are compared to actual cases that have been sentenced by judges, either in the past ("retrospective sampling") or based on new referrals received during a given period of time after the development of the algorithm ("prospective sampling").[37]

Thus, the mere fact that an algorithm does not include race as a variable in the model does not preclude it from having a discriminatory effect. None of the sentencing instruments or datasets mentioned above includes race as a variable. Yet many variables included in the models target ethnic minorities disproportionately (albeit unintentionally): they play the role of "proxies" for race, that is, they strongly correlate with race in the data set. For example, variables about a defendant's place of residence (e.g., zip codes) can end up targeting neighborhoods where residents are predominantly low-income African Americans. These group-based features are then incorporated into the algorithms, which end up having a stronger impact on specific groups, most importantly protected classes. Following this statistical line of reasoning, defendants are then sentenced based on their belonging to a specific group with "risky" characteristics rather than because of their individual actions, which goes against the jurisprudential value of individualism.[38] This, in turn, goes further than race. For example, most risk-assessment tools take gender, age, educational attainment, and socioeconomic background into account in their algorithm. As former US Attorney General Eric Holder pointed out, "By basing sentencing decisions on static factors and immutable characteristics—like the defendant's education level, socioeconomic background, or neighborhood—they may exacerbate unwarranted and unjust disparities that are already far too common in our criminal justice system and in our society."[39]

It has even been argued that this type of statistical sentencing is unconstitutional, because people have the right to be treated—and sentenced—as individuals and not because they belong to a group with specific characteristics.[40] As Starr explains, "the Supreme Court has squarely rejected statistical discrimination—use of group tendencies as a proxy for individual characteristics—as permissible justification for otherwise constitutionally forbidden discrimination."[41] In 2003, the America Civil Liberties Union challenged the constitutionality of risk-assessment tools along similar lines and filed an amicus brief in the Virginia Court of Appeals, arguing that sentencing based on statistical generalizations "cuts to the core of the fundamental Constitutional principles of equality and fairness."[42]

Heterogeneity and Disparity

A second issue regards the heterogeneity and disparity of risk-assessment tools depending on the jurisdiction. A wide range of actors contributes to the construction and implementation of algorithmic sentencing in the United States. These include governmental organizations, nonprofit organizations, and private corporations, all of which have different resources and objectives. Technology developers also make different choices about the data sets, computing skills, and testing methods used to build the predictive instruments. Such choices in turn shape the variables taken into account in the models, which can vary widely, and affect the results provided by the risk-assessment tools.

Thus, depending on the financial means of the organization constructing the algorithm and the size of the jurisdiction concerned, the quality of the algorithm will vary, together with the size of the data set, the amount of missing data, and the modeling techniques used. For example, the Arnold Foundation's PSA pretrial instrument uses a database of over 1.5 million cases from three hundred jurisdictions. Other instruments only rely on a few thousand cases. In some cases, the algorithm is even built using what is called the "consensus method," that is, without a data set or statistical test. Rather, judges and criminal justice specialists agree on a set of variables that, in their opinion, are significant in estimating the risk of an offender.[43] These differences in resources and methods come with significant variation between the algorithms and the variables that they take into account. For instance, whereas the Arnold Foundation's PSA-Court pretrial instrument only considers variables having to do with the criminal history of the defendant and her age, the Virginia Pretrial Risk Assessment Tool includes additional variables such as employment situation, length at residence, whether the offender is a primary caregiver, and whether she has a history of drug abuse.[44] Other risk-assessment tools even include a quick psychological survey and take into account so-called "subjective" variables, which are defined by psychologists, about the defendant's "emotional status" or "personal attitude."[45]

This piecemeal adoption of sentencing algorithms, developed using different methods and drawing on distinct variables, raises questions about the fairness of the judicial system as a whole. Will wealthier jurisdictions have more sophisticated predictive instruments than poorer jurisdictions? Will it make a difference for defendants to be sentenced in one jurisdiction rather than another because one or the other has a more punitive algorithm? Of course, judges also vary widely in their sentencing decisions, a fact that lawyers know well since they developed an online rating system for judges and jurisdictions.[46] Yet the crystallization of such disparities into the design of the algorithms is likely to harden inequalities between jurisdictions. Following former US Attorney General Eric H. Holder's reminder that the current system runs the risk of deviating from "the principle that offenders who commit similar offenses and have comparable criminal histories should be sentenced similarly," it is therefore important to consider whether or not the current proliferation of risk-assessment tools might contribute to increasing sentencing disparities between jurisdictions.[47]

Algorithmic Accountability and Black Boxing

Optimistic discourses surrounding the development of risk-assessment tools in the criminal justice system often rely on the rhetoric of accountability. In this view, the adoption of risk-assessment tools would make judges and prosecutors more accountable by forcing them to justify their decision when they differ from the "objective" and "value-neutral" predictions of the algorithms. Risk-assessment tools are therefore presented as adding a layer of transparency to the judicial decision-making process on top of existing safeguards such as written reports and appeal procedures.[48]

Yet many algorithms belie this hope for transparency and accountability.[49] In fact, most risk-assessments tools suffer from three different kinds of opacity.[50] The first form of opacity is intentional secrecy on the part of the organizations that construct, use, and sell the algorithms. Risk-assessment algorithms are usually proprietary products: most actors (nonprofit companies, for-profit companies, and jurisdictions) refuse to share either the algorithms or the training data sets that were used to create them, arguing that they do not want their products to be imitated. Second, opacity is connected to technical illiteracy: an overwhelming majority of actors using the algorithms do not have the technical skills to read or write code. This is particularly relevant in the case of criminal justice, since most legal professionals have no training in computer science. The third form of opacity is specific to machine-learning algorithms. Algorithms relying on machine-learning techniques are constantly evolving as new data is fed into the system. Consequently, even the computer programmers who built the algorithms are frequently in the dark regarding the specific procedures through which the algorithm achieves a given result.

Because of these different forms of opacity, there is a risk of what Pasquale calls "black boxing": important social, political, and ethical questions about sentencing decisions are not asked, because no one understands how the algorithm works.[51] The metaphor of the black box describes a complicated system that is opaque to its users. Thus, defendants and their lawyers do not have access to the algorithms, do not know which risk score they receive, do not understand the reasons why they receive a given score, and do not have the possibility to appeal when they disagree with the score included in their file.

Gaming Strategies and Shifting Discretion

The first three issues raised here about risk-assessment tools were related to the construction side. I now examine how risk-assessment tools are used in courts. One of the main arguments developed by advocates of data-driven sentencing is that algorithms reduce discretion: they argue that quantification helps hold judges and prosecutors accountable for their decisions. But little is known about the efficacy of such interventions. Historical examples can in fact be introduced as cautionary tales. Consider the dynamics surrounding Sentencing Guidelines, a process intended to address earlier concerns about discretion, bias, and disparity in sentencing. Beginning in the mid 1960s, a broad bipartisan movement emerged to promote sentencing reform. Left-wing advocates believed that existing disparities in sentencing revealed overt discrimination and a punitive mindset among judges. Right-wing groups, meanwhile, argued that judges were too lenient and saw them as the primary culprits for rising crime rates. Both groups thought that determinate sentencing—the use of predefined sentencing ranges—was the solution. They supported the Sentencing Reform Act and the creation of Sentencing Guidelines, which were sponsored by Senator Ted Kennedy and passed in 1984.

Yet it soon turned out that instead of eliminating discretion, the Sentencing Guidelines led to a *displacement* of discretion. Judges started complaining about the Guidelines, which they found constraining and complicated to use. The Sentencing Commission kept changing the Guidelines to take into account new categories of offenses; a more complex system of exceptions and reductions emerged over time, which judges struggled to follow and implement. Prosecutors, however, were not constrained by the Guidelines.[52] They saw instead a significant increase in their relative decision-making power: they were the ones who decided on the charges that would then constrain the decision of the judges, because the charges would in turn determine the "Offense Level" column in the Sentencing Tables. Over time, the increasing number of criminal cases and overload of the court system led to a dramatic increase in plea-bargaining, a mechanism in which prosecutorial rather than judicial discretion reigns. Today, 97 percent of cases do not go to trial: they end in a plea bargain with a prosecutor.[53]

In other words, discretion did not disappear with the Sentencing Guidelines. Instead, it shifted to the prosecutors, who learned to manipulate offense charges and then present the results to the defendants in order to gain additional leverage in plea-bargain negotiations. The Guidelines became advisory instead of mandatory in 2005, but their effects are here to stay: the exponential increase in plea bargaining is widely believed to have contributed to increasing rates and lengths of incarceration sentences for low-income minorities.[54] Learning from the case of the Sentencing Guidelines should encourage us to ask similar questions about algorithmic sentencing. Instead of assuming that risk-assessment tools will necessarily rationalize the decision-making process, make judges and prosecutors more accountable, and curb discrimination, we should pay more attention to the unintended shifts of discretion that these might entail.

In their work on legal rankings, Espeland and Sauder define "gaming" as "manipulating rules and numbers in ways that are unconnected to, or even undermine, the motivation behind them. Gaming is about managing appearances and involves efforts to improve ranking factors without improving the characteristics the factors are designed to measure."[55] Such "gaming strategies" have already emerged in the uses of risk-assessment tools. For instance, Hannah-Moffat and her colleagues find that legal professionals who use the LSI-R "adjust the assessment of criteria in order to control the final score, rather than relying on formal overrides."[56] In other words, probation officers tend to manipulate the variables entered in the instrument in order to obtain the score that they think is adequate for a given defendant, based on their instinct (or "clinical" expertise, as practitioners call it). According to Hannah-Moffat, this can:

> lead to "criteria tinkering" (adjusting the rating of individual items when filling out the forms), for which there is no recorded accountability. This result also clearly demonstrates that practitioners continue to rely on their own discretion, selectively using responses to interpret, target, and isolate facts about past experiences and to make claims about the probability of reoffending to affect the risk score.[57]

Gaming strategies complicate the accountability of algorithms. Thus, we should ask who will be responsible for filing the names and characteristics of the defendants into the software program. Who will be reading and interpreting the results? Which strategies will people use to change the settings of the risk-assessment tools when a result does not match their intuitions? Examining such questions is crucial in order to understand how evidence-based instruments affect the objectivity, transparency, and accountability of criminal sentencing.

The Changing Goals of Punishment

A last question regards the neutrality of risk-assessment tools, the values that are actually embedded in predictive algorithms, and the effects that such tools have on the goals and practices of punishment. In the criminal justice literature, punishment is traditionally analyzed as having four main justifications: retribution (punishment is justified because offenders have harmed society; their punishment should be commensurate with the crime committed); incapacitation (society has the right to be protected from offenders; punishment removes the possibility for offenders to commit further offenses); deterrence (the cost of punishment prevents previous and potential offenders from committing future offenses); and rehabilitation (punishment includes efforts to reform and rehabilitate offenders so that they will not commit the crime again).

Researchers have shown that the relative weight of these different goals of punishment is prone to change depending on the period, country, and political climate. In the lineage of Michel Foucault's work, scholars have mapped the development and consolidation of a "culture of control" in the United States and United Kingdom since the 1980s.[58] This new paradigm for punishment draws on a rather heterogeneous set of strategies and arguments, including an increasing reliance on mass incarceration, a punitive view of justice based on incapacitation and deterrence (*"prison works," "lock them out," "three strikes and you're out"*), the growing legitimacy of cost-benefit analyses of crime, and the rise of a system of surveillance and discipline through actuarial instruments and, more recently, digital technologies.[59]

Unsurprisingly, risk-assessment tools are frequently seen as part of the current "culture of control": the tools take advantage of digital technologies and rely on actuarial techniques in order to analyze defendants' likelihoods of recidivism. Risk-assessment tools, in this view, function as a technology of governmentality: they operate at a distance, through statistical analysis, defining classes of individuals who are more or less "risky" and should be controlled more or less forcefully.[60] In addition, most predictive instruments emphasize one major justification at the detriment of the others: incapacitation, that is, a view of justice based on estimating the risk to society posed by the offender when deciding on a sentence designed to incapacitate dangerous individuals. Recent initiatives in juvenile justice have tried to include rehabilitation ideals in risk-assessment instruments.[61] Yet, with the exception of the juvenile justice system, most predictive algorithms overwhelmingly focus on incapacitation rather than rehabilitation.

Do these broad penal changes also affect the concrete practices of sentencing? Practitioners and risk-assessment advocates say that algorithms merely provide "indicative" recommendations. Most judges and prosecutors argue that they do not blindly follow the results provided by algorithms when making a decision about an individual offender: they take into account all aspects of punishment when making sentencing decisions. In their view, risk-assessment tools merely provide information about the "incapacitation" aspect; legal professionals rely on their expertise and clinical experience to assess the defendant's personality and situation.

Yet it may be hard to "override the algorithm." In fact, judges and prosecutors are likely to "trust the numbers" and follow the recommendations provided by risk-assessment tools.[62] The quantitative assessment provided by a software program may seem more reliable, "objective," and scientific than other sources of information, including one's feelings about an offender, returning us to the complex of ideas about mechanical objectivity evoked above.[63] This is not only the case for laymen, but also for highly trained professionals: it is hard to challenge numbers and equations when one has not been trained in statistics. Thus, legal professionals may confuse correlation with causation, assigning strict causal influence to variables that merely affect the likelihood that a defendant will reoffend.[64]

Judges and prosecutors might also override the algorithmic information in biased ways. A recent report on juvenile justice shows that "detain overrides" (i.e., a judge's decision to incarcerate a defendant when the algorithm recommends release) are more frequent than "release overrides" (e.g., the decision to release a defendant when the algorithm recommends incarceration).[65] Eventually, judges and prosecutors might change their sentencing practices in order to match the predictions of the algorithms. As behavioral economists Amos Tversky and Daniel Kahneman have argued, "anchoring" plays an important role in decision-making: people draw on the very first piece of evidence at their disposal, however weak, when making subsequent decisions.[66] If the recommendations of the algorithms are higher than the ones that judges had in mind, they might increase their sentences without realizing that they are trying to match the algorithm. Hence, risk-assessment tools are not the value-neutral objects that advocates paint them to be: they crystallize specific political ideas about the role of punishment.

Conclusion

This chapter examined the recent development of predictive algorithms in the US criminal justice system. I first analyzed the discourses surrounding risk-assessment tools, which many advocates describe as a rationalizing force designed to "structure" judicial sentencing. In this view, algorithms can help cure "broken" systems by providing more information and increasing the transparency, accountability, and objectivity of the criminal justice system. After introducing the main risk-assessment tools currently in use in the United States, I offered a critical examination of the main issues associated with the construction, diffusion, and use of predictive algorithms. These include: algorithmic bias and the problem of fairness; heterogeneity and the question of disparity between jurisdictions; black boxing, accountability, and lack of transparency; gaming strategies and shifting discretion; and the political values embedded in predictive algorithms and how they contribute to changing the goals of punishment.

More broadly, this discussion of the debates surrounding the use of risk-assessment tools in criminal justice reveals how long-standing questions about the nature of decision continue to inform recent developments related to algorithmic technologies. Is judicial sentencing primarily the application of a set of rules? Or is it essentially an informed but discretionary act? In a way, risk-assessment instruments merge these two conceptions: algorithms do apply specific rules to compute quantitative outcomes; such outcomes are in turn designed to provide condensed information to the decision-maker—be it a judge, a prosecutor, or a probation officer—with the goal of making discretionary judgment more informed. In other words, not unlike the "Law & Economics" movement in the 1970s–1980s, Big Data advocates are hoping to transform both the technological infrastructure of courts and the cultural framing of judicial sentencing.[67] Yet a closer analysis of risk-assessment tools indicates that sovereign decision-making never vanishes from the picture. Not only do judges and prosecutors selectively ignore the outputs provided by the algorithms; the construction of the algorithms themselves is fraught with political decisions, including which model to choose, which variables to include, and which outputs to measure.

There is an interesting continuity between the arguments developed in the second half of the twentieth century to depoliticize decision-making—most importantly cybernetics and game theory, two perspectives at the center of several chapters of this volume—and the arguments used to justify Big Data algorithms. Similar claims about objectivity, neutrality, rationality, and technical efficiency can be found in all cases; similar criticisms also emerge. Future research might consider how different expert groups take on the mantle of rationalizing administration by considering the parallels between economists in the past decades and data scientists today. Are economists being trained in Big Data methods? Are "data scientists" —the "sexiest job" of the twenty-first century, according to the *Harvard Business*

Review—simply replacing economists as the main providers of rationality in the political arena, in the same way that economists replaced lawyers after World War II?[68] These are some of the larger questions raised by the reconfiguration of expertise and decision-making in the criminal justice system.

Angèle Christin is an Assistant Professor in the Department of Communication at Stanford University. Her research examines how algorithms and analytics transform professional values, expertise, and work practices. Her first book, *Comparutions Immédiates: Enquête sur une Pratique Judiciaire*, was an ethnographic analysis of a criminal court in the outskirts of Paris (La Découverte, 2008).

Notes

1. Judith Shklar, *Legalism* (Cambridge, MA: Harvard University Press, 1964).
2. Pierre Bourdieu, "The Force of Law: Toward a Sociology of the Juridical Field," *Hastings Law Journal* 38, no. 5 (1987): 805–53.
3. Angèle Christin, *Comparutions immédiates: Enquête sur une pratique judiciaire* (Paris: La Découverte, 2008), 10.
4. Anna M. Barry-Jester, Ben Casselman, and Dana Goldstein, "Should Prison Sentences Be Based On Crimes That Haven't Been Committed Yet?" *FiveThirtyEight*, 18 August 2015.
5. Anne Milgram, "Why Smart Statistics Are the Key to Fighting Crime," TED Talk, 28 January 2014.
6. Anne Milgram, "Moneyballing Criminal Justice," *The Atlantic*, 20 June 2012.
7. Kelly Hannah-Moffat, "Actuarial Sentencing: An 'Unsettled' Proposition," *Justice Quarterly* (2012): 2.
8. Barry-Jester et al., "Prison Sentences."
9. Bernard E. Harcourt, *Against Prediction: Profiling, Policing, and Punishing in an Actuarial Age* (Chicago, IL: University of Chicago Press, 2006); Hannah-Moffat, "Actuarial Sentencing"; S. B. Starr, "Evidence-Based Sentencing and the Scientific Rationalization of Discrimination," *Stanford Law Review* 66, no. 4 (2014): 803–87.
10. Donald Garland, *The Culture of Control: Crime and Social Order in Contemporary Society* (Chicago, IL: University of Chicago Press, 2002); Harcourt, *Against Prediction*; Malcolm M. Feeley and Jonathan Simon, "The New Penology: Notes on the Emerging Strategy of Corrections and Its Implications." *Criminology* 30, no. 4 (1992): 449–74.
11. Lorraine Daston and Peter Galison, *Objectivity* (New York: Zone Books, 2007).
12. danah boyd and Kate Crawford, "Critical Questions for Big Data: Provocations for a Cultural, Technological, and Scholarly Phenomenon," *Information, Communication, & Society* 15, no. 5 (2012): 662–79.

13. boyd et al., "Critical Questions."
14. Chris Anderson, "The End of Theory: The Data Deluge Makes the Scientific Method Obsolete," *Wired*, 23 June 2008.
15. Franck Pasquale, *The Black Box Society: The Secret Algorithms that Control Money and Information* (Cambridge, MA: Harvard University Press, 2015); Adam Reich, "Disciplined Doctors: The Electronic Medical Record and Physicians' Changing Relationship to Medical Knowledge," *Social Science & Medicine* 74, no. 7 (2012): 1021–28; Wendy N. Espeland and Berit Vannebo, "Accountability, Quantification, and Law," *Annual Review of Law and Social Science* 3, no. 1 (2007): 21–43; Chris W. Anderson, "Between Creative and Quantified Audiences: Web Metrics and Changing Patterns of Newswork in Local US Newsrooms," *Journalism* 12, no. 5 (2011): 550–66.
16. Max Weber, *Economy and Society: An Outline of Interpretative Sociology* (Berkeley: University of California Press, 1978).
17. Pasquale, *The Black Box Society*.
18. Daston and Galison, *Objectivity*, 121.
19. Milgram, "Moneyballing Criminal Justice"; Milgram, "Smart Statistics."
20. Milgram, "Moneyballing Criminal Justice."
21. Milgram, "Smart Statistics."
22. Milgram, "Moneyballing Criminal Justice."
23. Milgram, "Smart Statistics."
24. Barry-Jester et al., "Prison Sentences."
25. Starr, "Evidence-Based Sentencing"; David Steinhart, "Juvenile Detention Alternatives Initiative: 2013 Annual Results Report, Intersite Conference Summary," The Annie E. Casey Foundation (2013); Cynthia A. Mamalian, "State of the Science of Pretrial Risk Assessment," Pretrial Justice Institute, Bureau of Justice Assistance (March 2011).
26. Harcourt, *Against Prediction*; Hannah-Moffat, "Actuarial Sentencing."
27. Laura and John Arnold Foundation, "More than 20 Cities and States Adopt Risk Assessment Tool to Help Judges Decide Which Defendants to Detain Prior to Trial," (New York, 2015).
28. Espeland and Vannebo, "Accountability, Quantification, and Law"; Harcourt, *Against Prediction*.
29. Kate Stith and Steve Y. Koh, "The Politics of Sentencing Reform: The Legislative History of the Federal Sentencing Guidelines," *Wake Forest Law Review* 28 (1993): 223–90.
30. Barry-Jester et al., "Prison Sentences"; Pennsylvania Commission on Sentencing, "Risk Assessment Project: Special Report; The Impact of Juvenile Record on Recidivism Risk" (University Park, 2014).
31. Harcourt, *Against Prediction*, 78.
32. Starr, "Evidence-Based Sentencing," 813.
33. Michelle Alexander, *The New Jim Crow: Mass Incarceration in an Age of Colorblindness* (New York: The New Press, 2010); Loïc Wacquant, *Deadly Symbiosis: Race and the Rise of the Penal State* (Oxford: Polity Press, 2009).
34. Solon Barocas and Andrew D. Selbst, "Big Data's Disparate Impact," *California Law Review* 104 (2016): 671–732.
35. Harcourt, *Against Prediction*, 3.

36. Richard Berk, *Criminal Justice Forecasts of Risk: A Machine Learning Approach* (Berlin: Springer-Verlag, 2012).
37. David Steinhart, "Juvenile Detention Risk Assessment: A Practice Guide to Juvenile Detention Reform," The Annie E. Casey Foundation (2006).
38. Jonathan Simon, "The Ideological Effects of Actuarial Practices," *Law & Society Review* 22, no. 4 (1988): 771–800.
39. US Department of Justice, "Letter to the Honorable Patti B. Saris" (Washington, DC, 2014); US Department of Justice, "Attorney General Eric Holder Speaks at the National Association of Criminal Defense Lawyers 57th Annual Meeting and 13th State Criminal Justice Network Conference" (Washington, DC, 2014).
40. Starr, "Evidence-Based Sentencing."
41. Ibid., 827.
42. American Civil Liberties Union of Virginia, "ACLU Brief Challenges the Constitutionality of Virginia's Sex Offender Risk Assessment Guidelines" (Richmond, 2003).
43. Steinhart, "Juvenile Detention Alternatives Initiative," 12.
44. Pretrial Justice Institute, "Risk Assessment: Evidence-Based Pretrial Decision-Making" (Rockville, MD, 2013).
45. Starr, "Evidence-Based Sentencing," 812.
46. See http://www.courtroominsight.com.
47. US Department of Justice, "Letter to the Honorable Patti B. Saris"; US Department of Justice, "Attorney General Eric Holder Speaks."
48. Barry-Jester et al., "Prison Sentences."
49. Helen Nissenbaum, "Accountability in a Computerized Society," *Science and Engineering Ethics* 2 (1996): 25–42.
50. Jenna Burrell, "How the Machine 'Thinks': Understanding Opacity in Machine Learning Algorithms," *Big Data & Society* 216 (2016): 1–12.
51. Pasquale, *The Black Box Society*.
52. Espeland and Vannebo, "Accountability, Quantification, and Law."
53. Judith Resnick, "Whither and Whether Adjudication," *Boston University Law Review* 86 (2006): 1101–54.
54. Alexander, *The New Jim Crow*.
55. Wendy N. Espeland and Michael Sauder, "Rankings and Reactivity: How Public Measures Recreate Social Worlds," *American Journal of Sociology* 113, no. 1 (2007): 29.
56. Kelly Hannah-Moffat, Paula Maurutto, and Sandra Turnbull, "Negotiated Risk: Actuarial Illusions and Discretion in Probation," *Canadian Journal of Law and Society* 24, no. 3 (2009): 405.
57. Hannah-Moffat, "Actuarial Sentencing," 16.
58. Garland, *The Culture of Control*.
59. Garland, *The Culture of Control*; Harcourt, *Against Prediction*; Feeley et al., "The New Penology."
60. Nikolas Rose, Pat O'Malley, and Mariana Valverde, "Governmentality," *Annual Review of Law and Social Sciences* 2 (2006): 83–106.
61. Steinhart, "Juvenile Detention Alternatives Initiative."
62. Theodore M. Porter, *Trust in Numbers: The Pursuit of Objectivity in Science and Public Life* (Princeton, NJ: Princeton University Press, 1996).

63. Daston and Galison, *Objectivity*.
64. Hannah-Moffat, "Actuarial Sentencing."
65. Steinhart, "Juvenile Detention Risk Assessment," 44–46.
66. Amos Tversky and Daniel Kahneman, "Judgment Under Uncertainty: Heuristics and Biases," *Science* 185, no. 4157 (1974): 1124–31.
67. Thierry Kirat, *Economie du droit* (Paris: La Découverte, 1999).
68. Thomas H. Davenport and D. J. Patil, "Data Scientists: The Sexiest Job of the 21st Century," *Harvard Business Review* (2002). Yves Dezalay and Bryant Garth, *The Internationalization of Palace Wars: Lawyers, Economists, and the Contest to Transform Latin American States* (Chicago, IL: University of Chicago Press, 2002).

Bibliography

Alexander, Michelle. *The New Jim Crow: Mass Incarceration in an Age of Colorblindness*. New York: The New Press, 2010.

American Civil Liberties Union of Virginia. Richmond: ACLU Brief Challenges the Constitutionality of Virginia's Sex Offender Risk Assessment Guidelines, 2003. Retrieved 22 January 2016 from https://acluva.org/1671/aclu-brief-challenges-constitutionality-of-virginias-sexoffender-risk-assessment-guidelines/.

Anderson, Chris. "The End of Theory: The Data Deluge Makes the Scientific Method Obsolete." *Wired*, 23 June 2008. http://www.wired.com/2008/06/pb-theory/.

Anderson, Chris W. "Between Creative and Quantified Audiences: Web Metrics and Changing Patterns of Newswork in Local US Newsrooms." *Journalism* 12, no. 5 (2011): 550–66.

Barocas, Solon, and Andrew D. Selbst. "Big Data's Disparate Impact." *California Law Review* 104 (2016): 671–732.

Barry-Jester, Anna Maria, Ben Casselman, and Dana Goldstein. "Should Prison Sentences Be Based On Crimes That Haven't Been Committed Yet?" *FiveThirtyEight*, 18 August 2015. http://fivethirtyeight.com/features/prisonreform-risk-assessment/.

Berk, Richard. *Criminal Justice Forecasts of Risk: A Machine Learning Approach*. Berlin: Springer-Verlag, 2012.

Bourdieu, Pierre. "The Force of Law: Toward a Sociology of the Juridical Field." *Hastings Law Journal* 38, no. 5 (1987): 805–53.

boyd, danah, and Kate Crawford. "Critical Questions for Big Data: Provocations for a Cultural, Technological, and Scholarly Phenomenon." *Information, Communication, & Society* 15, no. 5 (2012): 662–79.

Burrell, Jenna. "How the Machine 'Thinks': Understanding Opacity in Machine Learning Algorithms." *Big Data & Society* 216 (2016): 1–12.

Christin, Angèle. *Comparutions immédiates: Enquête sur une pratique judiciaire*. Paris: La Découverte, 2008.

Daston, Lorraine, and Peter Galison. *Objectivity*. New York: Zone Books, 2007.

Davenport, Thomas H., and D. J. Patil. "Data Scientists: The Sexiest Job of the 21st Century." *Harvard Business Review* (2002). https://hbr.org/2012/10/data-scientist-the-sexiest-job-of-the-21st-century.

Dezalay, Yves, and Bryant Garth. *The Internationalization of Palace Wars: Lawyers, Economists, and the Contest to Transform Latin American States*. Chicago, IL: University of Chicago Press, 2002.

Espeland, Wendy N., and Michael Sauder. "Rankings and Reactivity: How Public Measures Recreate Social Worlds." *American Journal of Sociology* 113, no.1 (2007): 1–40.

Espeland, Wendy N., and Berit Vannebo. "Accountability, Quantification, and Law." *Annual Review of Law and Social Science* 3, no. 1 (2007): 21–43.

Feeley, Malcolm M., and Jonathan Simon. "The New Penology: Notes on the Emerging Strategy of Corrections and Its Implications." *Criminology* 30, no. 4 (1992): 449–74.

Garland, Donald. *The Culture of Control: Crime and Social Order in Contemporary Society*. Chicago, IL: University of Chicago Press, 2002.

Hannah-Moffat, Kelly. "Actuarial Sentencing: An 'Unsettled' Proposition." *Justice Quarterly* (2012): 1–27.

Hannah-Moffat, Kelly, Paula Maurutto, and Sarah Turnbull. "Negotiated Risk: Actuarial Illusions and Discretion in Probation." *Canadian Journal of Law and Society* 24, no. 3 (2009): 391–409.

Harcourt, Bernard E. *Against Prediction: Profiling, Policing, and Punishing in an Actuarial Age*. Chicago, IL: University of Chicago Press, 2006.

Kirat, Thierry. *Economie du droit*. Paris: La Découverte, 1999.

Laura and John Arnold Foundation. "More than 20 Cities and States Adopt Risk Assessment Tool to Help Judges Decide Which Defendants to Detain Prior to Trial." Arnold Foundation, 26 June 2015. http://www.arnoldfoundation.org/more-than-20-cities-and-states-adopt-risk-assessment-tool-to-help-judges-decide-which-defendants-to-detain-prior-to-trial/.

Mamalian, Cynthia A. "State of the Science of Pretrial Risk Assessment." Pretrial Justice Institute, Bureau of Justice Assistance, March 2011. Retrieved 22 January 2017 from https://www.bja.gov/publications/pji_pretrialriskassessment.pdf.

Milgram, Anne. "Why Smart Statistics Are the Key to Fighting Crime." TED Talk, 28 January 2014. https://www.ted.com/talks/anne_milgram_why_smart_statistics_are_the_key_to_fighting_crime?language=en.

———. "Money-balling Criminal Justice." *The Atlantic*, 20 June 2012. http://www.theatlantic.com/national/archive/2012/06/moneyballing-criminal-justice/258703/.

Nissenbaum, Helen. "Accountability in a Computerized Society." *Science and Engineering Ethics* 2 (1996): 25–42.

Pasquale, Franck. *The Black Box Society: The Secret Algorithms That Control Money and Information*. Cambridge, MA: Harvard University Press, 2015.

Pennsylvania Commission on Sentencing. "Risk Assessment Project: Special Report; The Impact of Juvenile Record on Recidivism Risk." University Park, 2014. Retrieved 22 January 2017 from https://sentencing.umn.edu/sites/sentencing.umn.edu/files/specialreportJCJC07012014.pdf.

Porter, Theodore M. *Trust in Numbers: The Pursuit of Objectivity in Science and Public Life*. Princeton, NJ: Princeton University Press, 1996.

Pretrial Justice Institute. "Risk Assessment: Evidence-Based Pretrial Decision-Making." 2013. Retrieved 22 January 2017 from http://www.pretrial.org/download/riskassessment/Risk%20Assessment.pdf.

Reich, Adam. "Disciplined Doctors: The Electronic Medical Record and Physicians' Changing Relationship to Medical Knowledge." *Social Science & Medicine* 74, no. 7 (2012): 1021–28.

Resnick, Judith. "Whither and Whether Adjudication." *Boston University Law Review* 86 (2006): 1101–54.

Rose, Nikolas, Pat O'Malley, and Mariana Valverde. "Governmentality." *Annual Review of Law and Social Sciences* 2 (2006): 83–106.

Shklar, Judith. *Legalism*. Cambridge, MA: Harvard University Press, 1964.

Simon, Jonathan. "The Ideological Effects of Actuarial Practices." *Law & Society Review* 22, no. 4 (1988): 771–800.

Starr, Sonja B. "Evidence-Based Sentencing and the Scientific Rationalization of Discrimination." *Stanford Law Review* 66, no. 4 (2014): 803–87.

Steinhart, David. "Juvenile Detention Alternatives Initiative: 2013 Annual Results Report, Intersite Conference Summary." The Annie E. Casey Foundation, 2013. Retrieved 22 January 2017 from http://www.aecf.org/m/resourcedoc/aecf-JDAI2013AnnualResultsReport-2014.pdf.

———. "Juvenile Detention Risk Assessment: A Practice Guide to Juvenile Detention Reform." The Annie E. Casey Foundation, 2006. Retrieved 22 January 2017 from http://www.aecf.org/m/resourceimg/aecf-juveniledetentionriskassessment1-2006.pdf.

Stith, Kate, and Steve Y. Koh. "The Politics of Sentencing Reform: The Legislative History of the Federal Sentencing Guidelines." *Wake Forest Law Review* 28 (1993): 223–90.

Tversky, Amos, and Daniel Kahneman. "Judgment Under Uncertainty: Heuristics and Biases." *Science* 185, no. 4157 (1974): 1124–31.

US Department of Justice. "Letter to the Honorable Patti B. Saris." 2014. Retrieved 22 January 2017 from http://www.justice.gov/sites/default/files/criminal/legacy/2014/08/01/2014annual-letter-final-072814.pdf.

———. "Attorney General Eric Holder Speaks at the National Association of Criminal Defense Lawyers 57th Annual Meeting and 13th State Criminal Justice Network Conference." 2014. Retrieved 22 January 2017 from http://www.justice.gov/opa/speech/attorney-general-eric-holder-speaks-national-association-criminal-defense-lawyers-57th.

Wacquant, Loïc. *Deadly Symbiosis: Race and the Rise of the Penal State*. Oxford: Polity Press, 2009.

Weber, Max. *Economy and Society: An Outline of Interpretative Sociology*. Berkeley: University of California Press, 1978.

Conclusion

THE MYTH OF THE DECISION
Daniel Bessner and Nicolas Guilhot

There is a long tradition in Western political thought that equates politics with the capacity for decision and condemns indetermination, uncertainty, and, in some sense, thoughtfulness as necessarily bad politics. For hundreds of years, Western thinkers have defined leadership in times of crisis as the ability to make difficult decisions. Due to the peculiar exigencies of modern history described in the introduction, this notion became deeply embedded in American political culture over the course of the twentieth century. For politicians and intellectuals navigating the "American Century," making decisions became the *sine qua non* of effective political leadership. While decisionism may have retreated into hibernation when the Cold War ended with an apparent US victory in 1989–91, the post 9/11 world has witnessed a resurgence of the decisionist mystique across the political spectrum. To take two prominent examples, President George W. Bush titled his autobiography *Decision Points*, while Hillary Clinton titled her account of her years in the State Department *Hard Choices*.[1] As this suggests, manifold elites consider strong leadership to be defined by the capacity of an individual to cut through the Gordian knot of reasons in the name of time and urgency.

This volume has argued that the decisionist imagination influenced diverse research programs across the postwar social sciences. Long believed to be confined to the legal and political debates that defined the Weimar Republic, decisionism was actually much more pervasive—and much more adaptable—than previously thought. Rational choice, decision theory, and other research technologies and programs have extended and transformed the decisionist mystique, giving it a smattering of scientific legitimacy and helping it undergird a number of intellectual trends and processes. One of the great intuitions of the political theorist Judith Shklar, confirmed by several contributors to this volume, was that in the postwar era, decisionism succeeded because it rebranded itself as *the* "rational" approach to politics. In this way, new decision technologies untainted by any association with fascist figures like Carl Schmitt smuggled the authoritarian edge of decisionism into the Western social sciences.

Decisionism is a versatile, protean doctrine capable of informing a wide range of intellectual movements. It can be exercised in the name of public opinion (Wertheim) or justified with reference to the defense of democracy (Accetti and Zuckerman); it can take the form of rational choice (Mirowski) or strategic doctrine (Amadae); and it can be vested in technologies and technology-focused research programs (Christin, Andersson, Rindzevičiūtė). But, as this volume demonstrates, the arguments of decisionism are anything but unassailable. In particular, its staging of time and existential threats as the critical variables of politics may not be as persuasive as it once seemed to be, and nondecisionist theories may be perfectly able to address the problems of politics and history (Palonen, Lazar). Indeed, perhaps the major question raised by this volume is whether the assumptions that support decisionism, especially the notion that democratic decision-making procedures are maladapted to situations of existential threat, are correct. The chapters collected here indicate that they are not, and that liberal democratic regimes have in fact developed a wide array of means to deal with time constraints and emergencies. Rules and accountability, rather than the absence thereof, are essential for wise decision-making, including in times of crisis.[2]

Simply put, this volume suggests that scholars must question the very notion of "the decision upon the exception" that sustains the decisionist imagination. While this idea conjures images of absolute authority, it is now clear that even the most dramatic and unprecedented sovereign decision possible—the decision to launch a nuclear strike—does not fit the neat pattern of top-down command valorized by decisionism. In theory, the decision to begin nuclear war is vested exclusively in the person of the US president; in reality, it is distributed widely and shared by dozens of individuals in the United States and abroad.[3] What this indicates is that in a number of cases, the notion of "decision" obfuscates the complexity of the technical and collective processes of will formation and execution that truly undergird whether or not an action is undertaken. As anyone who has participated in academic committee meetings knows all too well, reaching a decision is a very difficult thing to do and regularly requires the lengthy, painstaking labor of discussion, persuasion, and negotiation—quite the opposite of the divine *fiat* of decisionist political theologies embedded in the decisionist mystique.

In retrospect, it seems that decisionist arguments essentially aimed to preserve the autonomy of the political against any encroachment of social and economic interests; even in a liberal democracy, the argument goes, there are some decisions that are self-legitimating. At a time when the traditional subjects of modern politics—classes, social interest-based parties and institutions, and trade unions—seem to be in crisis, and private economic interests seem to reign unfettered, the appeal of decisionism may be precisely that it appears to be the last refuge of politics. It promises to recover a genuinely political capacity to prevail over economic interests and to make distinctions between friends and enemies. It is these promises that many of the contributions collected here show to be false.

Of course, this volume could not cover the entire range of decisionist theories, and there remain significant gaps in our understanding of decisionism. First, as highlighted in the introduction, "decisionism" as used here captures a specific vision of politics given voice by Carl Schmitt in the tumultuous context of the Weimar Republic. There are certainly other strands of Weimar decisionism worthy of our attention, and much work remains to be done on the decisionist ideas of those who did not share Schmitt's authoritarian politics, including those proffered by Herman Heller, Otto Kirchheimer, and Karl Mannheim. Second, it would be beneficial to learn more about the connections between decisionism and several currents of postwar philosophy, especially existentialism, as decisionist elements can be found in the thought of Hannah Arendt, Martin Heidegger, and Jean-Paul Sartre. Finally, the histories of early decisionist theories and themes must be better understood if we are to grasp the diversity of channels through which decisionism permeated the postwar social sciences.

Furthermore, this volume does not address several fields that must be encompassed within the history of decisionism. The most important of these is psychology, broadly conceived. From political psychology in the 1960s and 1970s to the cognitive neurosciences today, decision-making has been a central focus of psychological research. Psychology deserves special mention because while the field seems at times to have offered a corrective to decisionism, it has in effect a more complex and ambivalent relationship to it. Psychological experiments have often demonstrated that the rationality assumptions underpinning much of rational choice theory are flawed: people simply do not behave in the way the theory implies. Whether they are choosing soap or whether to go to nuclear war, people use heuristics that effectively deviate from the normative indications of rational choice cost-benefit analyses. Similar observations have been made in the field of international relations, where psychological research has been used to criticize deterrence theory. Deterrence presupposes that decisions are made on the basis of some rational cost-benefit calculus. Yet in reality, one's interpretation of an enemy's intentions is not self-evident and depends on broader perceptive frames that determine the ways in which single occurrences are understood.[4] The result is that miscalculations and misperceptions can be perfectly "rational" within a given interpretive frame. Despite the perspicacity of this critique, it is crucial to highlight that the psychology of deterrence is not a viable alternative to decisionism. This is because much of the cognitive psychology of perceptions and decisions in international politics has relied on the notion that these occur within fundamental frames. Often under the influence of Kurt Lewin or Thomas Kuhn, these frames are deemed incommensurable and nonrational in the sense that there are no overarching criteria for arbitrating between one and the other. As has been pointed out, this setup reproduces the basic structure of decisionism under the form of fundamental, nonrationalizable decisions that define subsequent reality.[5]

It would also be worthwhile to track decisionist themes in other intellectual programs, including historical and sociological institutionalism, behavioral economics, and the neurosciences. While this is a task that goes beyond the confines of this volume, a few points may be mentioned here. Crucially, it is important to stress that the critique of rationality or rational choice does not *per se* discount the need for a superior decision: on the contrary, by suggesting that people cannot be trusted to act rationally, even individually, such a critique opens space for decision-making mechanisms that derive their legitimacy from the fact that they are immediately superior forms of choice. As Herbert Simon once remarked, "it is impossible for the behavior of a single, isolated individual to reach any high degree of rationality."[6] For Simon, the purpose of institutions was precisely to supplement the impaired cognitive and calculative capacities of the individual by selecting and processing information for her. Institutions, in this sense, are essentially decision-making machines that are more rational, and hence more authoritative, than the individuals who comprise them. Similar claims can be made about culture, traditions, and customs: they help shape individual choice while ensuring that people are not overwhelmed by endless possibilities. As one can readily see, all sorts of historical or sociological institutionalisms can be mustered to disqualify the individual capacity for decision.

Relatedly, in the field of economics, theories of market efficiency often posit markets as superior information processors and decision-makers to whose wisdom society should yield.[7] Or, alternatively, the assumption that people are not rational can justify a paternalistic—Foucault would say "pastoral"—program of training. For example, in the last decade, thinkers like Richard H. Thaler and Cass R. Sunstein have argued that individuals must be "nudged" (by incentives established by a presumably cognitively superior elite) to make good choices.[8] Behavioral economics thus ends up justifying a higher, restricted form of decision-making not accessible to the *hoi polloi*. Finally, the reconstruction of social-scientific models of decision-making is of particular importance because they are today being naturalized by the cognitive neurosciences. To make sense of scans and brain imagery in situations of choice, neuroscientists use models inherited from psychology and economics.[9] In this way, scientists project back into the brain a long prehistory of cybernetic and economic metaphors of decision that allow models of hierarchy, or, conversely, of economic competition, to become central to current understandings of cognition and rationality.

This is all to say that even critical refinements of rational choice theory do not necessarily challenge decisionism. As the examples above reveal, the critique of rational models of decision-making may actually reify old antidemocratic claims about authority as a shortcut to rationality. It is for this reason that scholars must develop a familiarity with decisionist thought and train the eye to identify its contemporary—and often obscure—embodiments. If we do, we might be able to jettison decisionism and develop a more democratic understanding of political choice that considers it the outcome of the composition of new collectives, the expression of the multitude, or the lengthy labor of discussion and debate.

Daniel Bessner is the Anne H. H. and Kenneth B. Pyle Assistant Professor in American Foreign Policy in the Henry M. Jackson School of International Studies at the University of Washington. He is the author of *Democracy in Exile: Hans Speier and the Rise of the Defense Intellectual* (Cornell University Press, 2018).

Nicolas Guilhot is research professor at the CNRS (Centre National de la Recherche Scientifique). His work sits at the intersection of political theory, the history of political thought, and international relations. His publications include *After the Enlightenment: Political Realism and International Relations in the Mid-Twentieth Century* (Cambridge University Press, 2017); *The Democracy Makers: Human Rights and the Politics of Global Order* (Columbia University Press, 2005); and *The Invention of International Relations Theory: Realism, the Rockefeller Foundation, and the 1954 Conference on Theory* (Columbia University Press, 2011).

Notes

1. George W. Bush, *Decision Points* (New York: Crown, 2010); Hillary Rodham Clinton, *Hard Choices* (New York: Simon & Schuster, 2014).
2. Stephen Holmes, "In Case of Emergency: Misunderstanding Tradeoffs in the War on Terror," *California Law Review* 97, no. 2 (April 2009): 301–55.
3. For an overview, see Daniel Ellsberg, *The Doomsday Machine: Confessions of a Nuclear War Planner* (New York: Bloomsbury, 2017).
4. Robert Jervis, *Perception and Misperception in International Politics* (Princeton, NJ: Princeton University Press, 1976).
5. See in particular Nicolas Guilhot, "The Kuhning of Reason: Realism, Rationalism and Political Decision in IR Theory after Thomas Kuhn," *Review of International Studies* 41, no. 1 (January 2016): 3–24.
6. Herbert A. Simon, *Administrative Behavior: A Study of Decision-Making Processes in Administrative Organization* (New York: Free Press, 1976), 92.
7. Philip Mirowski, *Machine Dreams: Economics Becomes a Cyborg Science* (Cambridge, UK: Cambridge University Press, 2002).
8. Richard H. Thaler and Cass R. Sunstein, *Nudge: Improving Decisions About Health, Wealth, and Happiness* (New Haven, CT: Yale University Press, 2008).
9. See, for instance, Cleotilde Gonzalez, "Decision-Making: A Cognitive Science Perspective," in *The Oxford Handbook of Cognitive Science*, ed. Susan E. F. Chipman (Oxford: Oxford University Press, 2017); Lesley K. Fellows, "The Neuroscience of Human Decision-Making through the Lens of Learning and Memory," *Current Topics in Behavioral Neuroscience* 37 (2018): 231–51.

Bibliography

Bush, George W. *Decision Points*. New York: Crown, 2010.
Clinton, Hillary Rodham. *Hard Choices*. New York: Simon & Schuster, 2014.
Ellsberg, Daniel. *The Doomsday Machine: Confessions of a Nuclear War Planner*. New York: Bloomsbury, 2017.

Fellows, Lesley K. "The Neuroscience of Human Decision-Making through the Lens of Learning and Memory." *Current Topics in Behavioral Neuroscience* 37 (2018): 231–51.
Gonzalez, Cleotilde. "Decision-Making: A Cognitive Science Perspective." In *The Oxford Handbook of Cognitive Science*, edited by Susan E. F. Chipman. Oxford: Oxford University Press, 2017.
Guilhot, Nicolas. "The Kuhning of Reason: Realism, Rationalism and Political Decision in IR Theory after Thomas Kuhn." *Review of International Studies* 41, no. 1 (January 2016): 3–24.
Holmes, Stephen. "In Case of Emergency: Misunderstanding Tradeoffs in the War on Terror." *California Law Review* 97, no. 2 (April 2009): 301–55.
Jervis, Robert. *Perception and Misperception in International Politics*. Princeton, NJ: Princeton University Press, 1976.
Mirowski, Philip. *Machine Dreams: Economics Becomes a Cyborg Science*. Cambridge, UK: Cambridge University Press, 2002.
Simon, Herbert A. *Administrative Behavior: A Study of Decision-Making Processes in Administrative Organization*. New York: Free Press, 1976.
Thaler, Richard H., and Cass R. Sunstein. *Nudge: Improving Decisions About Health, Wealth, and Happiness*. New Haven, CT: Yale University Press, 2008.

Index

Adorno, Theodor, 9, 10
Agamben, Giorgio, 109, 112–15
agency, 177, 180, 190, 195–97
  collective, 193–94
  corporate, 175
  game theory and, 182, 189, 191–94
  purposive, 180, 182, 189
  strategic rationality and, 189
algorithmic rationality, 148, 159, 173, 177, 179, 180
Arrow, Kenneth, 15–16, 147, 193, 262–63
artificial intelligence, 176, 191, 197
  communication and, 195–96
  decision-making systems and, 178
authoritarian decisionism, 77, 87
authoritarian democracy, 73–74, 76
authoritarianism, 13, 77
authoritarian liberalism, 65–66, 74
authoritarian neoliberalism, 18

Bell, Daniel, 15
OR and, 252Arrow and, 262–63
  The Coming of Post Industrial Society: A Venture in Social Forecasting by, 250, 254
  CY2000 and, 252, 261, 263–64
  decision-making and, 251–52, 255–56, 261–62
  de Jouvenel and, 257–58
  The End of Ideology by, 253–57
  freedom and, 252, 255, 260
  future research for, 250–52, 254, 257, 260, 262–64, 265n5
  on government by commission, 260–61
  intellectual technologies and, 250–51, 264
  Marxism and, 253, 255–56
  mass society and, 250–51, 253–54, 257, 260–61
  prospective and, 260
  on rationality, 251, 255–56, 262–65
  on social choice, 251, 260, 262–63
  social forecasting and, 254, 261–63
  social theory of, 253
  technocracy and, 251, 263–64
Berger, Gaston, 259
Big Data analytics, 272–73, 288
  algorithms as rationalizing for, 275
  criteria for, 274–75
  information and objectivity arguments for, 275–76
  Milgram on, 276–77
black boxing, 283
Boards of Public Health, 124–25
Bonaparte, Napoleon, 30
bounded rationality, 138, 180
Bush, George W., 118–20

Campion, Gilbert, 86, 95–96
Carr, E. H., 27–28, 36
Christie, Chris, 115–16
citizenship, 75, 77
Cold War, 5, 67, 77, 147, 195
  Daston and, 148
  decisionism and, 163–64
  decision sciences and diplomacy in, 231–32
  future research and, 252
  militant democracy and, 64
  nuclear weapons and, 148–49, 193
  Prisoner's Dilemma and, 184–85
  rational choice theory and, 146
  rationality, 143, 180, 191
The Coming of Post Industrial Society: A Venture in Social Forecasting (Bell), 250, 254

command-and-control structure, 11, 176–78, 194–95
Commission for the Year 2000 (CY2000), 252, 261, 263–64
communication, 195–96
Communist Party of the Soviet Union (CPSU), 221
"Competition as a Discovery Procedure" (Hayek), 157
computational rationality, 190, 195
Congress of Vienna, 30
consciousness, 31, 156, 162, 260
constitutional democracy, 65, 67
  emotionalism and, 71–72, 80n32
  liberal, 68
  political constitutionalism and, 130n44
cost-benefit analysis
  judicial sentencing and, 286
  rational choice and, 192, 297–98
Covenant of the League of Nations
  drafters of, 37–38
  international organization and, 36–37, 47–48
  international public opinion and, 36–38, 44, 47
  legalists and, 46
  Smuts and, 37–38
  Wilson and, 36, 40, 47
  Zimmern and, 39–40, 45
Cowen, Joseph, 99–100
CPD. *See* Emergency Advisory Committee for Political Defense
CPSU. *See* Communist Party of the Soviet Union
criminal justice system. *See* judicial sentencing
critical decision, in liberal polyarchies, 113, 127
  Ebola outbreak (2013-2016) and, 115–16
  police power and, 18, 116
  power and, 110, 116
  prerogative and, 118
  rights and, 117
  temporal fallacy and, 126
CY2000. *See* Commission for the Year 2000
cybernetics, 16–17, 223–27

Daston, Lorraine, 145–49, 160
Davidson, Donald, 161
debate
  adjournment and, 96–98
  amendment and, 97–98
  Campion on, 86, 95–96
  in parliamentary politics, 86, 93, 95–98, 100–101
  Weber on, 94–95
decision, 85, 144. *See also* critical decision, in liberal polyarchies
  compulsion and, 114
  decisionism compared to, 113–14, 116, 127
  for Morgenstern, 151
  Schmitt and, 150
  theory, 159
decisionism
  antidemocratic, 77
  authoritarian, 77, 87
  Cold War and, 163–64
  decision compared to, 113–14, 116, 127
  democratic decisionism, 87, 100–101
  history of, 19
  intellectual movements and, 296
  law-based regimes and, 109
  liberal democracy and, 19
  liberalism and, 18
  neoclassical economics and, 163–64
  NTC and, 152
  as ontologically self-contained, 113
  philosophy and, 5
  political, 64
  prewar, 6–7
  psychology and, 297–98
  rational choice and, 13–14, 19, 299
  rationality and, 18
  Schmitt and, 3–4, 14, 72, 109–10, 112–13, 150
  as sovereign, 114
  in Weimar Republic, 295, 297
decisionist mystique, 295–97
decision-making, 182, 257, 259
  anchoring and, 287
  artificial intelligence and, 178
  Bell and, 251–52, 255–56, 261–62
  democratic, 296

economics and, 299
game theory and, 175, 181
Great Depression and, 7–8
judicial sentencing and, 272–77, 284–85, 287, 289
Moiseev on automated, 235–36
nuclear weapons and, 11–12
personalist, 224
in political science journals, 1–2
in post-war period, 14
probabilistic, 176
social science and, 3
system-based, 229
Weimar Republic and authoritarian, 13
decision sciences, in Soviet Union, 217
OR and, 221, 225, 227–29, 231–32, 237
autonomy and, 222–23
Cold War diplomacy and, 231–32
CPSU and, 221–22
cybernetics and, 223, 225–27
East-West exchange and, 227, 229, 231–32
economic planning and, 228–29, 234–37
global biosphere and, 219–20
governmentality and, 218
institutionalization of, 226–32
inter- and post-war systems thinking and, 230
international cooperation and, 225, 227
irrationality and, 218
Moiseev and, 221, 228, 232–37
personalized governance and, 236
planning problems and, 232
power and, 222
role of decision scientists and, 223
self-regulation and, 218–20
systems approach and, 229–30, 233, 238
decision sciences, in United States, 220, 226
East-West exchange and, 227, 229, 231–32
modern governmentality and, 224
decision theory, 9, 143, 163, 262, 297

Giocoli and, 141, 159–60
ideology discourse and, 15
Loewenstein and, 74–75
military and, 173–74
rational choice and, 6, 13
rationality and, 14
de Jouvenel, Bertrand
on conjecture, 257–58
on freedom, 258
prospective and, 259
democracy, 19, 146, 159. *See also* constitutional democracy; liberal democracy; militant democracy; prodemocratic dictatorship
authoritarian democracy, 73–74, 76
choice and, 160
decision-making and, 296
dictatorship and, 12
emotionalism and, 73
fragility of, 72–73
in Germany, 9–10
as ineffective, 19
legitimacy and, 72–74, 77
Lippmann on, 10, 16
Loewenstein on, 67, 72–74, 76–77
parliamentary politics compared to, 95
police power and, 18
radical, 65, 67
rationalist, 73
Schmitt on, 8
sovereign and liberal, 115
"Who decides?" and European, 7
democratic decisionism, 87, 100–101
Deudney, Daniel, 182–83, 194, 198
Deutsch, Karl, 6
Dewey, John, 8, 11, 254
Deweyan social science, 10
dictatorship, 5, 12–13, 146, 224. *See also* prodemocratic dictatorship

Ebola outbreak (2013-2016), 115–16
economics, 160, 163, 288–89. *See also neoclassical economics*
decision-making and, 299
decision sciences in Soviet Union and, 228–29, 234–37
inequality and market, 154
Neoliberalism and, 152–53

pure economics, 144–45
rational choice theory and, 181
rationality and, 139
Smith and, 136
electoral politics, 85
parliamentary government and, 99
regularization of, 90
Sartre on, 94
voting and, 90, 92–94
emergency, 110–11, 127
Emergency Advisory Committee for Political Defense (CPD), 75–77
emotionalism, 66
constitutional democracy and, 71–72, 80n32
democracy and, 73
fascism and, 67, 72
The End of Ideology (Bell), 253–57
enlightened men, 31, 34–36, 41
Enlightenment, 145, 147, 160, 179
Reason and, 136–37
exception, 110–13
executive power, 19, 110, 120
liberal polyarchies and, 109

fascism, 65, 71, 73–74
emotionalism and, 67, 72
"Who decides?" and, 10–11
freedom, 87, 259
Bell and, 252, 255, 260
de Jouvenel on, 258
Neoliberalism and, 154
Friedrich, Carl, 9–10, 12
future research, 288
Bell and, 250–52, 254, 257, 260, 262–64, 265n5
Cold War and, 252

game theory, 6, 198, 200n11, 263. *See also* Prisoner's Dilemma
agency and, 182, 191–94
choice and, 181
constitutional design and, 193
decision-making and, 175, 181
early, 14, 152
Hobbes and, 192
MAD and, 174
military planning and, 11–12
modeling, 191

nuclear deterrence and, 181, 183
nuclear strategy and, 174–75, 182
NUTS in, 174
orthodox, 191–94, 197
rationality and, 179–80
realism and, 194, 196
rules and, 190
Schelling on, 7
strategic rationality and, 174–76
surprise attack and, 185
zero-sum, 180–82
gaming strategies, 285
Giocoli, Nicola
decision theory and, 141, 159–60
Modeling Rational Agents by, 140–41
neoclassical economics and, 140–42
Great Depression, 7–9
Greven, Michael Th., 87, 100–101

Habermas, Jürgen, 91, 196
on arguments, 86
consensus for, 87–88
on criticism, 87
Hayek, Friedrich, 149–50, 153
"Competition as a Discovery Procedure" by, 157
consciousness and, 156
on information, 158
on knowledge, 155–58
on market economies, 154
psychology and, 155–56
Hegel, Georg Wilhelm Friedrich, 70, 89
self-development of reason of, 88
as ultrarationalist, 86
Hickox, Kaci, 115–16
Hitler, Adolf, 70–71
Hobbes, Thomas, 189, 192

idealism, 29
ideology discourse, 15
inequality, 154
intellectual technologies, 250–51
internationalists
Carr criticizing, 27
international public opinion and, 30, 38–39, 44
liberal, 28, 36, 44, 46
prewar, 28–29

World War I and, 46
international law
　international public opinion and, 30–34
　legalists and, 30–31
　Maine and, 33
　Oppenheim and, 33–34
　Westlake and, 33–34
international mind, 34–35, 40
international organization
　Covenant of League of Nations and, 36–37, 47–48
　popular demands of, 37–38
　UDC and, 44–45
international public opinion, 8
　beginning of, 29–30
　Congress of Vienna and, 30
　Covenant of League of Nations and, 36–38, 44, 47
　cultivated reason and, 28
　enlightened men and, 31, 35
　internationalists and, 30, 38–39, 44
　international law and, 30–34
　international mind and, 34–35
　international relations and, 30
　legalists and, 33, 39
　Lieber and, 32
　Morgenthau on, 48–49
　prewar internationalists and, 28–30
　Smuts on, 38–39
　Taft and, 35–36
　United Kingdom and, 32
　in US, 32
　Wilson and, 41–43
　Zimmern and, 40, 45

Jefferson, Thomas, 119–21
judgment theory, 162
judicial sentencing
　Big Data analytics and, 272–77, 288
　cost-benefit analysis and, 286
　decision-making and, 272–77, 284–85, 287, 289
　legalists and, 272
　Legal Realism and, 272
　predictive algorithms and, 272–74, 287–88
　PSA and, 278
　punishment justifications and, 285–86
　risk-assessment tools and, 273, 277

Kavka, Gregory, 186
Kierkegaard, Søren, 88–89, 91
knowledge
　Hayek on, 155–58
　of The Market, 158
Kuhn, Thomas, 135

Larichev, Oleg, 217, 238
law. See also international law
　customary law, 33
　decisionism and law-based regimes, 109
　sovereign and, 113
League of Nations. See Covenant of the League of Nations
League to Enforce Peace (LEP), 46
legalists, 273
　Covenant of the League of Nations and, 46
　international law and, 30–31
　international public opinion and, 33, 39
　judicial sentencing and, 272
　liberal, 28–29, 33
　prewar, 39
　Root as, 46
legal rationalism, 13, 64–65
legal–rational legitimacy, 73
Legal Realism, 272
legitimacy, 33, 66, 153, 179, 182, 226, 229, 298
　democracy and, 72–74, 77
　power and, 122
　rational choice and, 193, 195, 251
　Weber and typology of, 73
Level of Services Inventory-Revised (LSI-R), 279
liberal democracy, 7, 18, 48, 76–77, 120, 264, 296–97. See also police power; prerogative power
　critique of, 9, 19, 73, 112, 149–50, 262
　decisionism and, 19
　executive power and, 125
　Loewenstein on, 73

nuclear weapons and, 173
prelegal rights and, 117
Schmitt on, 9, 112, 149–50
sovereign and, 115, 121
liberalism
authoritarian liberalism, 65–66, 74
decisionism and, 18
liberal polyarchies, 109. *See also*
critical decision, in liberal
polyarchies
Lieber, Francis, 32
Lippmann, Walter, 8, 11, 15
Americans embracing, 9
on democracy, 10, 16
expert advice and, 17–18
public opinion and, 29
rational choice theory and, 149
Locke, John, 118, 120
Loewenstein, Karl, 13. *See also*
militant democracy
authoritarian decisionism and, 77
authoritarian democracy and,
73–74, 76
authoritarian liberalism and, 65
background of, 67
on citizenship, 75, 77
constitutional theory of, 70
CPD and, 75–76
decisionist theory and, 74–75
democracy for, 67, 72–74, 76–77
Hitler and, 70
internment and, 75–77
on liberal democracy, 73
Montesquieu and, 68
*People and Parliament in the Theory
of the State of the French National
Assembly of 1789* by, 67
*Political Power and the Governmental
Process* by, 65, 68–70, 76
rationality and, 72
on totalitarianism, 67–68
in World War II, 65–66, 74

MAD (Mutual Assured Destruction),
174, 180–83, 187, 198
Maine, Henry, 33
Mannheim, Karl, 4
The Market
knowledge of, 158

rationality and, 14, 158–59
Marx, Karl, 234–35
Marxism, 15, 234–35
Adorno and, 10
Bell and, 253, 255–56
Milgram, Anne, 276–77
militant democracy, 13
authoritarian liberalism and, 66
Cold War and, 64
decisionistic repression and, 77
as emergency powers, 71
Hitler and, 70–71
permanence of, 71–72, 74
in practice, 75–76
military, 159, 163, 231. *See also* nuclear
weapons
decision theory and, 173–74
game theory and, 11–12
rational choice and, 162
research in World War II, 159, 224
spending, 178
Mill, John Stuart, 88, 94
mindless rationality, 189, 198
Modeling Rational Agents (Giocoli),
140–41
Moiseev, Nikita N., 221, 228, 232
on automated decision-making,
235–36
conceptual consistency for, 237
on decision science and
government, 233
on Marx, 234–35
Montesquieu, Charles de Secondat,
68–69
Mont Pelerin Society (MPS), 152–53
Morgenstern, Oskar
decision for, 151
rational choice theory and, 150–52
rationality and, 150–51
Morgenthau, Hans, 48–49
Mutual Assured Destruction. *See*
MAD

Napoleon. *See* Bonaparte, Napoleon
Nazis
Hitler and, 70–71
parliamentary politics and, 110
Schmitt and, 112
neoclassical economics, 158

as backward-oriented, 142
decisionism and, 163–64
energy physics and, 141, 144–45, 148
Giocoli and, 140–42
Pareto and, 143
psychology and, 141–42
rational choice and, 13
rational choice theory and, 143, 145
utility function of, 144
neoclassical price theory, 142
neo-Hegelianism, 40–41
Neoliberalism, 146. *See also Hayek, Friedrich*
choice and, 158
economics and, 152–53
freedom and, 154
human labor and, 153
inequality of market economies in, 154
Lippmann and, 149
MPS and, 152–53
principles of, 152–53
Schmitt and, 149–50
Neumann, Franz, 4–5, 12
Neumann, John von, 151–52, 175, 180
norms, 110–11, 127
Nozick, Robert, 135
nuclear deterrence, 175
game theory and, 181, 183
NUTS and, 181
strategic rationality and, 176–78
Toxin puzzle and, 186
Nuclear Utilization Targeting Selection. *See* NUTS
nuclear weapons and strategy, 198, 296. *See also* nuclear deterrence
arsenals of, 11
Cold War and, 148–49, 193
command-and-control structure and, 11, 176–78, 194–95
decision-making and, 11–12
game theory and, 174–75, 182
liberal democracy and, 173
power and, 189
Prisoner's Dilemma and, 183–84
rational choice and, 177
rational deterrence theory and, 176, 178
rationality and, 173
in World War II, 10–11, 182
NUTS (Nuclear Utilization Targeting Selection), 174, 182–83, 194, 198
Deudney on, 188
nuclear deterrence and, 181
nuclear taboo and, 187

operations research (OR), 221, 225, 227–29, 231–32, 236–37, 252
Oppenheim, Lassa, 33–34

Pareto, Vilfredo, 143
parliamentary politics, 18, 85, 94
confidence in the government and, 98–99
Cowen and, 99–100
debate in, 86, 93, 95–98, 100–101
democracy compared to, 95
electoral politics and, 99
Nazis and, 110
principled neutrality and, 110
vote by ballot in, 92–93
vote in, 89
People and Parliament in the Theory of the State of the French National Assembly of 1789 (Loewenstein), 67
police power, 116
Boards of Public Health and, 124–25
court cases and, 124–26
democracy and, 18
rights and, 121, 125–26
smallpox outbreak and, 123–25, 130n58, 130nn55–56
sovereignty and, 124
US and, 121–22
political decisions, 101. *See also* debate; electoral politics; parliamentary politics; voting
consensus and, 89
estate representation and, 91–92
freedom of choice and, 87
irrational, 66
time and, 88
Political Power and the Governmental Process (Loewenstein), 65, 68–70, 76

310 • Index

power
  critical decision and, 110, 116
  legitimacy and, 122
  Loewenstein on, 66, 68–69, 76
  Montesquieu on, 69
  norms and, 110
  nuclear weapons and strategy and, 189
  rational distribution of, 69
  realism and, 195
  rights and, 117
prerogative power, 125
  after-the-fact accountability and, 120–21
  Bush and, 118–20
  critical decision in liberal polyarchies and, 118
  Jefferson and, 119–20
  in United Kingdom, 118, 120
  in US, 118–20
Prisoner's Dilemma
  Cold War and, 184–85
  MAD and, 180–81
  nuclear strategy and, 183–84
  Toxin puzzle and, 186–87
prodemocratic dictatorship, 12–13
prospective, 259–60
psychology
  decisionism and, 297–98
  folk, 161
  Hayek and, 155–56
  neoclassical economics and, 141–42
  rational choice and, 161–62
public opinion. *See also* international public opinion
  Carr and, 28, 36
  Great Depression and, 9
  international conflict and, 27
  Lippmann and, 29
  national context of, 34
  polls, 27
Public Safety Assessment-Court (PSA), 278, 282

rational choice, 155, 165n9, 174
  cost-benefit analysis and, 192, 297–98
  decisionism and, 13–14, 19, 299
  decision theory and, 6, 13
  legitimacy and, 193, 195, 251
  military and, 162
  neoclassical economics and, 13
  nuclear weapons and strategy and, 177
  postwar contributions to, 14–15, 161
  postwar social sciences and, 14–15
  psychology and, 161–62
  rationality and, 180
  realism and, 189
  science of, 159
rational choice theory, 1, 3, 6, 163, 177, 192
  applications of, 191
  Cold War and, 146
  components of, 137–38
  Davidson and, 161
  economics and, 181
  intellectual trends of, 145–46
  Lippmann and, 149
  Morgenstern and, 150–52
  neoclassical economics and, 143, 145
  Schmitt and, 149
  social cognition and, 138
  strategic rationality as, 188
  Veblen and, 138–39
rational decision theory, 183, 189–90
rational deterrence theory, 176, 178, 183
rationality, 13, 135
  algorithm and, 148, 159, 173, 177, 179–80
  American reconstruction of, 160
  Bell on, 251, 255–56, 262–65
  Big Data analytics and, 275
  bounded rationality, 138, 180
  Cold War, 143, 180, 191
  computational rationality, 190
  decisionism and, 18
  decision theory and, 14
  in disciplines, 136
  economics and, 139
  game theory and, 179–80
  Giocoli on, 140–41
  Loewenstein and, 72
  The Market and, 14, 158–59
  mindless, 189, 198

Morgenstern and, 150–51
nuclear weapons and, 173
rational choice and, 180
reason and, 147, 160, 179
Simon on, 298
technical, 15
realism, 49
   game theory and, 194, 196
   International Relations realism, 29
   power and, 195
   rational choice and, 189
reason, 151
   Daston on, 147–48
   rationality and, 147, 160, 179
rights, 117, 121, 125–26
risk-assessment tools, in judicial sentencing, 273, 277
   algorithmic accountability and black boxing and, 283
   gaming strategies and discretion for, 283–85
   goals of punishment and, 285–87
   heterogeneity and disparity and, 281–82
   issues with, 279–87
   LSI-R as, 279
   neutrality of, 279, 285, 287
   PSA and, 278, 282
   Sentencing Commission and the Sentencing Tables and, 278
   statistical bias and algorithmic fairness and, 279–81
Rolin-Jaequemyns, Gustave, 31
romanticism, 88–89
Root, Elihu, 46
rule-following, 179–80

Sartre, Jean-Paul, 94, 101
Schelling, Thomas, 6, 199n10
   on game theory, 7
   MAD and, 180–81
   Strategy of Conflict by, 183
Schmitt, Carl, 5, 66, 85, 91, 152, 158, 296
   constitutional theory of, 72
   on decision, 150
   decisionism and, 3–4, 14, 72, 109–10, 112–13, 150
   on democracy, 8

   on dictatorship, 13
   emergency for, 110–11
   exception for, 110–13
   on liberal democracy, 9, 112, 149–50
   Nazis and, 112
   Neoliberalism and, 149–50
   norms for, 127
   rational choice theory and, 149
   romanticism for, 88
   on sovereign, 111–12, 150
   sovereign dictator and, 89
sciences of complex systems, 17
scientific autonomy, 222–23
Shklar, Judith, 1, 3, 296
Simon, Herbert, 1, 298
smallpox outbreak, 123–25, 130n58, 130nn55–56
Smith, Adam, 136
Smuts, Jan Christiaan, 37–39
social science. *See specific topics*
sovereign, 126–27
   decisionism as, 114
   enemy and, 112
   Hobbes theory of sovereignty, 192
   law and, 113
   liberal democracy and, 115, 121
   police power and, 124
   Schmitt on, 111–12, 150
Soviet Union. *See also* Cold War; decision sciences, in Soviet Union
   computer science in, 225
   CPSU, 221
   Moiseev and, 221, 228, 232
   neoliberalizing projects and, 16–17
strategic rationality, 181–82, 192–93, 195
   agency and, 189
   game theory and, 174–76
   nuclear deterrence and, 176–78
   as rational choice theory, 188
Strategy of Conflict (Schelling), 183
suffrage, 85, 90–91
systems approach, 229–30, 233, 238
systems theory, 17, 235

Taft, William H., 35–36, 46
technocracy, 251, 263–64
temporal fallacy, 126–27

totalitarianism, 65, 67–68
Toxin puzzle, 186–87

ultrarationalists, 86, 88
Union of Democratic Control (UDC), 44–45
United Kingdom, 90. *See also* parliamentary politics
　international public opinion and, 32
　prerogative power in, 118, 120
United States (US). *See specific topics*

Veblen, Thorstein, 138–39
voting
　ballot, 92–93
　debate and, 86, 93–98
　electoral politics and, 90, 92–94
　estate representation and, 91–92
　Mill on, 94
　in parliamentary politics, 89
　tripartite division of, 90–91
　Weber on, 89–90

"Wahlrecht und Demokratie in Deutschland" (Weber), 85
Walras, Leon, 144–45
Waltz, Kenneth, 1, 17
Weber, Max, 66, 72
　debate for, 94–95
　election and acclamation for, 89–90
　on equal suffrage, 90–91
　estate representation for, 91–92
　legitimacy typology of, 73
　on objectivity, 95
　on voting, 89–90
　"Wahlrecht und Demokratie in Deutschland" by, 85
Weimar Republic, 4–5, 7, 253. *See also* Loewenstein, Karl
　authoritarian decision-making and, 13
　decisionism in, 295, 297
Westlake, John, 33–34
Westminster Parliament. *See* parliamentary politics
Wilson, Woodrow, 37, 44, 49
　Covenant of the League of Nations and, 36, 40, 47
　international public opinion and, 41–43
World War I, 7, 28–29, 37, 39, 44, 46, 90
World War II, 5, 27, 48, 67, 141–42, 146, 179, 226
　CPD and, 75–76
　decisionism before, 19
　Loewenstein in, 65–66, 74
　military research in, 159, 224
　nuclear weapons in, 10–11, 182

Zimmern, Alfred, 39
　international public opinion and, 40, 45
　nationalism of, 45

www.ingramcontent.com/pod-product-compliance
Lightning Source LLC
Chambersburg PA
CBHW072045110526
44590CB00018B/3048